The China Clipper, Pan American Airways and Popular Culture

The China Clipper, Pan American Airways and Popular Culture

Larry Weirather

McFarland & Company, Inc., Publishers
Jefferson, North Carolina, and London

Unless otherwise noted, all photographs are from the Weirather Family Trust Collection.

LIBRARY OF CONGRESS CATALOGUING-IN-PUBLICATION DATA

Weirather, Larry, 1944–
The China Clipper, Pan American Airways and popular culture / Larry Weirather.
p. cm.
Includes bibliographical references and index.

ISBN-13 978-0-7864-2820-5
(softcover : 60 and 70# alkaline paper) ∞

1. China Clipper (Airplane)—History. 2. Pan American Airways Corporation—History. 3. Popular culture—United States. I. Title.
HE9803.P36W45 2007
303.48'32—dc22 2006031088

British Library cataloguing data are available

On the cover: A girl rides a toy China Clipper on this 1930's mechanical valentine

Manufactured in the United States of America

McFarland & Company, Inc., Publishers
Box 611, Jefferson, North Carolina 28640
www.mcfarlandpub.com

To Linda and
the Pan American Airways
transoceanic pioneers

Acknowledgments

Thanking all the people who contributed to the making of this book could form an entire chapter if all the reference librarians, archivists, historians, air mail specialists, collectors, Internet contacts, and airline and government agency representatives were to be given their just due. Like any book of this nature, it has been decades, or a lifetime, in the making; so many helpers have given encouragement along the way.

Some primary institutions and individuals do need to be singled out. Rocky Mountain College and Clark College provided much needed sabbaticals along the way to enable research, travel, and writing. Had it not been for the support of such people as Don Erskine, Ray Korpi, Richard Fulton, and Sylvia Thornburg of those colleges, work on this book would have been much more difficult. The Clark College Foundation provided additional financial assistance. The National Archives, Parmly Billings Library, Clark College Library, and Fort Vancouver Regional Library all responded to my many requests for loans and information services. When Pan Am existed as an airline company staff freely gave helpful information.

Randy Weirather, my globe-trotting, scavenging brother of Kaneohe, Hawaii, has kept me supplied with an amazing stream of Clipper memorabilia from around the world. The friendship of Colonel R. E. "Doc" Nichol of Doc's Local Post supplies me with all manner of modern Clipper-inspired creations, often with a good dose of pictorial humor. John Johnson, Jr., the preeminent Pan Am historian, has filled my files with all manner of photocopied manuscripts and artifacts, for which I will always be grateful.

Any factual and grammatical errors in the book are strictly the fault of this author, and probably occurred after material was added or changed by me after my two primary proofreaders and editors helped turn original drafts into readable English. The editors performed yeoman duties, always humbling for an author. I am forever in the debt of Shirley Sackman, friend and book review editor of *The Victorian Periodicals Review*, and Linda Weirather, my wife, favorite reference librarian, and editor. It was she who put me back on the track of the Clippers several years ago when she gave me a gift of some pictorial Clipper envelopes. She created a monster.

Contents

Preface

This book shows how Pan American Airways flying boats, called Clippers, so captured the public imagination during the 1930s and 1940s that these icons permeated all of popular culture. From music to motion pictures to the Motor City, Clippers symbolized the most deeply held, and often contradictory, changing beliefs and needs of the United States. To understand the Clippers is to understand Depression and post–Depression sensibility. Clippers helped prepare the populace to fight a war, and would lead the country out of war. That same war, World War II, caused the demise of what many people have termed "the most romantic ships ever built," whose routes took them to the most romantic places in the world. Though no Clippers survive today, they continue to fly on in contemporary popular culture.

The importance of the Clippers outweighs their meager numbers. Only a handful of early Sikorsky amphibions, or Clippers, were manufactured to transport mail and passengers to Central and South America. The Martin Company built just three of the "China Clipper" model for Pan American Airways for use in crossing the Pacific. Boeing built but twelve of its massive Clippers for spanning the Atlantic and the rest of the world. Yet, despite being few in number, these ships became known as the United States' "Merchant Marine of the Air," "the Chosen Instrument" of the U.S. government, and America's flag carrier at home and abroad. Consequently, many books have traced the history of Pan American Airways (later Pan American World Airways or Pan Am) and the development of its aircraft. This book goes beyond those studies to explore how Clippers influenced the daily life of everyday people—in clothing, toys, advertising, pulp fiction, rituals, education, heroes, celebrities—in short, all dimensions of popular culture, sometimes in surprising ways.

To grasp the importance of Pan American Airways and its Clippers, consider how, for comparison, when the Apollo 11 moon mission brought back pictures of the earth as a blue marble in space, many people's perceptions changed significantly. Earlier in the twentieth century another revised vision of the earth changed people's global view, particularly in the United States. That earlier revision came in the form of Pan American Airways' ubiquitous winged globe logo.

Just as Apollo "earthrise" photographs denoted different meanings—the beauty of creation amid the cold loneliness of space, the fragility of this illuminated droplet of life spinning in darkness, the Cold War technological power and prowess that could take such a photograph, the heroic realization of a dream spanning the millennia—the winged globe also delivered many messages, some contradictory. Pan American's winged globe was to signify the United States' "merchant marine of the air." Through flight, the airline would unite the countries of the world through trade, thus extending U.S. influence. Early PAA logos in the 1920s and 1930s depicted a globe with the northern and southern hemispheres of North, Central, and South America since PAA first extended its international routes there. Once the Pacific was bridged to Manila in 1935 and to Hong Kong in 1937, logos included the Pacific on a new globe. Later in 1939 the Atlantic was spanned and depicted.

The U.S. government aided Pan American in its route development by ensuring, through contracts and regulations, that the airline would be the only international U.S. flag carrier. This situation existed until the exigencies of World War II forced the government and military to use other airlines for crossing the oceans. During the isolationism of the 1920s and 1930s, this civilian enterprise provided a way for the U.S. to extend influence and compete with world powers. Setting the stage for World War II, Japan was beginning to flex its muscles in China, Southeast Asia, and the Pacific. Germany was becoming restless in Europe. The threat was not only military but also economic. Hence the Pan American flag preceded the U.S. flag into many areas. Sometimes the reverse occurred, as in the Pacific where the U.S. flag was hastily planted on some Pacific atolls so that Pan American could legally construct flying boat bases as stepping stones to Asia. In reality, the U.S. government needed these stepping stones to counter the perceived Japanese menace. The Pan Am bases west of Hawaii—Wake, Midway, Guam, Manila—and the Pan Am bases south of Hawaii extending to New Zealand—Canton Island, Samoa, New Caledonia—were considered bulwarks of democracy.

The Clippers that flew to these islands and linked continents became even more iconic than the company logo. Clippers were the only long-range aircraft capable of carrying transoceanic payloads. This made them instantly valuable in time of war. Neither the Germans, Russians, Italians, nor the French had anything more advanced or that could compete commercially or militarily. In their civilian guise Clippers would be known around the world as the ultimate in swift, sophisticated travel. In their military service, they would be called upon for secret mission after secret mission.

It all began during the summer of 1909. Frenchman Hubert Latham tried to be the first to cross the English Channel in an airplane. He failed, as his *Antoinette* plunged into the sea. Across the Atlantic Ocean, a ten-year-old boy built a model airplane of the *Antoinette.* He had to build his model from scratch since no model kits existed then. The hobby had not yet really entered into popular culture. Most people still did not believe the Wright brothers had actually flown a heavier-than-air contraption. The boy believed in the Wright brothers' success and did better than Latham. He successfully flew a rubber band-powered flying machine in New York City's Central Park. Shortly after, his father took him to see what was billed as the first air race in the United States between Wilbur Wright and Glenn Curtiss. Wright was able somehow to guide his plane composed of wood spars, bicycle parts, and ladies' undergarment fabric around the Statue of Liberty and back across the waters.

That ten-year-old, Juan Terry Trippe, became president of Pan American Airways in the 1930s and 1940s. His giant flying boats would cross all the oceans and circumnavigate the earth. As in the race he saw between the two aviation pioneers, Trippe's own Clipper, the Yankee Clipper, would circle the Statue of Liberty thirty years later and capture the imagination of the world. Rather than the Wright brothers' 600-pound fragile bird, Trippe's Clipper would weigh in at 80,000 pounds, or forty tons of thundering Art Deco riveted duralumin.

When Apollo 12's lunar module landed men on the moon, its command module, called the Yankee Clipper, orbited above. Sea going clippers existed before the Clipper flying boats. Space-going clippers existed afterwards. But the flying boat era of the 1930s and 1940s represented a cathartic time in national values as the nation searched for Depression positives while it teetered on the verge of either becoming a commercial colossus or being annihilated. The lure of the United States' building and sailing Clipper ships through water, air, and space remains a source of pride and values permeating all facets of U.S. culture.

Note to the reader: Place names, as they were used in the 1930s and 1940s, have been rendered as they were treated then. The word *amphibion* instead of *amphibian* is used throughout the text. Igor Sikorsky, whose company built the first Clipper ships, insisted on *amphibion.* He argued that his aircraft were not reptiles. Unlike animals that could live on land or water, airplanes were machines that also lived in the air. Sikorsky lobbied dictionary makers long and hard to include both distinctive terms, but ultimately lost the battle. During the Clipper era, aviation writers did, however, use *amphibion*.

1

Bedrock Beliefs: Pan American Airways Advertising

The popularity of an object depends on how well it meets people's needs and desires. If that object goes beyond conforming to transitory fashions and fads by addressing bedrock beliefs that change little over time, it can become immensely popular, attaining iconic status. The China Clipper of Pan American Airways did exactly that in the 1930s and 1940s. PAA represented the Clipper as a paragon of U.S. interests, values, and the American people themselves.

Every nation tries to characterize itself by claiming a foundation of historic values, or what can be called bedrock beliefs. The United States has laid claim to a unique set of bedrock beliefs and values through which it seeks definition, builds national pride, and measures its progress. Some, such as a belief in a modified form of democracy, are obvious, others less so. Though often contradictory, these bedrock beliefs have remained clear and relatively stable. The PAA magazine advertisements read like a catalogue of these beliefs. To use one of the most repeated words in the ads, the Clippers came to embrace what is truly "American." Because of that, Pan American received much free advertising by making the cover of scores of magazines, from fraternal magazines such as *The Elks Magazine* to science magazines to such mass circulations as *Life* and *The Saturday Evening Post*, where it received cover prominence more than once.

Pan American Airways quickly capitalized on U.S. nationalism and pride. For its advertisements and press releases, the airline appropriated existing U.S. icons: the Statue of Liberty, the Stars and Stripes, the bald eagle, and the Lone Eagle (Charles Lindbergh). Just a few months after Lindbergh soloed the Atlantic in May 1927, Pan American opened its first

Boeing B-314 Clipper on cover of *The Elks Magazine* for July 1939 (courtesy *Elks Magazine*).

The Sikorsky S-42 Clipper on the cover of *Aero Digest* for March 1934 .

The giant engines of the Sikorsky S-42 Clipper on the cover of *Western Flying* for October 1937.

route from Key West to Havana. In rapid succession, and sometimes with Lindbergh as pilot, Pan American extended its routes throughout South and Central America, either through acquisition of other airlines or pioneering efforts. Lindbergh's heroic effort as an American in beating other countries across the Atlantic mirrored PAA's message. It, too, displayed rugged

The Samoan Clipper on the cover of *Stamp Age*, a stamp collecting magazine dated May 10, 1938.

American initiative, individualism, and pioneering effort in leaping the waters and tying whole continents together. Consequently, Pan American chose as its logo a winged globe that depicted the Western Hemisphere, which it was bringing together, as its name, "Pan American," stated. Later, the winged globe depicted the Atlantic and Pacific oceans, as the airline extended routes across them, and that did not take long. Following the

The cover of the May 1944 edition of *Air Trails* featured a military Coronado flying boat crewed by Pan American Airways during World War II. Note the PAA winged globe logo on the fuselage by the military star and U.S. flag.

experimental survey flights of Charles and Anne Lindbergh, Pan American would bridge the Pacific just ten years after Lindbergh's epic flight. For many people in the world, the winged globe became more synonymous with the United States than the U.S. flag. They would see the PAA logo long before ever having seen Old Glory.

This was particularly true in PAA's early years, when the clippers were being developed and tested but were not yet flying commercially. Pan American used land planes at first. The trick was to persuade people that flying a land plane across water was safe. In fact, saying that *any* airplane was safe was a hard sell. Until Lindbergh's appearance, much of aviation's reputation focused on disasters and scary barnstorming tricks. Still fresh in the popular mind were the numerous reported deaths of aerial daredevils, attempted record setters, and air mail pilots who died just before the brief shutdown of air mail service in the U.S. in 1921, when flying the mail became the most hazardous occupation in the country. Good news and bad news occurred in 1934, when the U.S. government again closed down air mail routes in the U.S. and reopened them, with disastrous results. Army pilots took over from civilian airlines. Due to bad weather, inappropriate aircraft, and unfamiliarity with the terrain, several army pilots crashed and died. Fortunately they carried no passengers. A public outcry arose for the return of commercial airlines. Pan American and other airlines were perceived as being safer than some alternatives, but not as safe as other luxury travel of the day—railroads and ocean liners in their golden age. Pan American had to sell not only safety but also what advantage it had over luxurious Pullman cars and shipboard suites.

To address the safety issue, Pan American wanted its winged globe logo to be associated with experience. Its pilots were not barnstormers; all had to have a minimum of 2,000 hours flying experience. The airline used other statistics as well in its advertisements to put the public at ease. By 1930 Pan American was flying an average of 88,522 miles a week along its 12,000 miles of routes. Twenty-eight to thirty of its planes were in the air simultaneously. Its aircraft communicated by radio with two airports at three-minute intervals throughout a flight. The aircraft were multiengined, so that if one motor failed the plane would still fly. The Pan American public relations machine went statistics happy. The implication was that air travel was safe, that no accidents occurred. At least they remained unmentioned! One could trust this airline whose ads and airplanes so prominently displayed its logo.

What the early land planes and Clippers had to offer that could beat ships and trains was of course speed in an age that treasured speed. The era of the late 1920s and 1930s worshipped speed. Faster music. Faster dancing. Faster trains. Faster ships. Faster boats. Faster cars. Faster planes. Who could have the fastest? Races became a national mania. National boat races, car races, air races prospered. Pan American trumpeted its faster, easier, more colorful way to travel south. It faced a problem, though. Passengers first had to reach Florida. To solve this, PAA advertised through

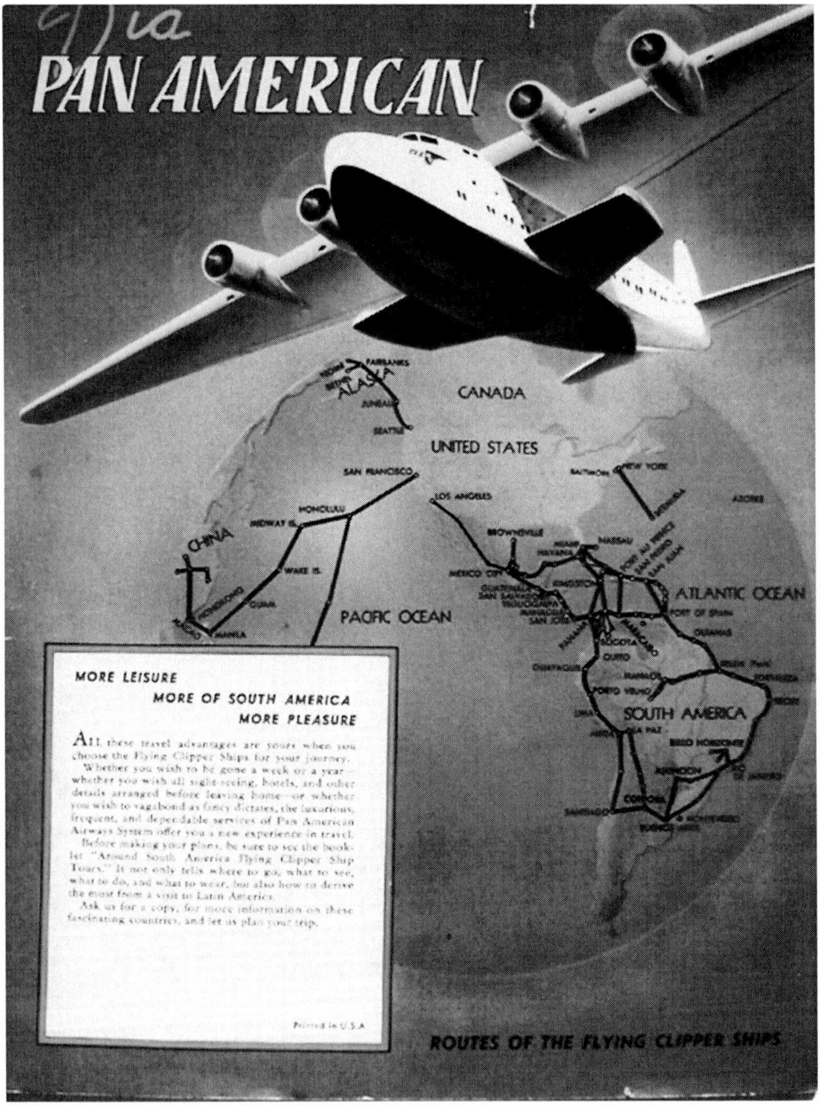

A Pan American Airways' publicity brochure for 1939 showing a Clipper over a globe with PAA routes indicated.

service by rail to its Florida base. Rather than fight the railroads, the airline, in part, joined them. It did the same with Grace shipping lines. The Havana Special, Palmetto Limited, and Florida Special trains all ran daily from New York City to coordinate with Pan American. So did the Flamingo from the Middle West, and the Dixie Limited and Floridian from

A PAA travel brochure for South America magnifying the size of a Sikorsky Clipper as it is moored under a globe showing the Southern Hemisphere.

St. Louis and Chicago. When passengers stepped from their trains into their Fokker trimotor aircraft, they would be treated to "luxury service." The plane carried modern toilet facilities. A cabin steward would wander the "wide aisle" attending to passengers' needs while they "lounged lazily back in cozy chairs with full-visioned windows" as they sped smoothly

Competing with luxurious Pullman cars and ocean liner suites for the rich, early Clippers carried fancy wood laminate interiors as shown in this postcard from the 1930s.

through the air and watched the "panorama of unparalleled beauty unfurl below." No mention was made of the severe gasoline fumes that permeated the cabin, the bumpy ride typical of warm tropical updrafts, the noise requiring cotton to be stuffed in ears, the near lack of temperature control. And no mention was made about how, if a passenger wanted to use the "modern toilet facilities," the chances were that whatever one put down that hole in the floor would most likely fly right back up due to the backdraft. A passenger could end up playing a kind of vertical tennis with himself.

One could also see sites differently from an airplane than from a boat or train. No boat or train could fly over recently discovered Mayan temples and pyramids buried in the jungle Charles Lindbergh had photographed. No boat or train could see the heart of mysterious Haiti, look down into an active volcano, or view both the Atlantic and Pacific oceans at once. The winged globe was literally opening up the globe to travel that had heretofore been accessible only to explorers and adventurers. Flying Pan American was the 1930s equivalent of the Apollo Mission crews looking back at earth from the moon. A new way of seeing was created. Best, the traveler could do this in a matter of hours. Tourism magazines such as *Travel* seized on the wonder of the Clippers.

Absent from the early Pan American ads was a key period icon, the whiskey or gin bottle. Many passengers were not as interested in quickly reaching exotic scenery as they were in reaching common booze. When you need a drink, you need a drink, and what better place to do your drinking than a place where drinking was legal and only an hour or so away? The wealthy in particular could take quick "vacations" or "business junkets." Pan American was born during the era of Prohibition (1922–1933). Some of its pilots, such as Ed Musick, had first worked as rum-running aviators bringing in illegal drink from offshore islands to Florida, often at night. When rum running was at its Prohibition peak, fifteen liquor planes each flew an average of three times per day between the Bahamas and Florida. Each carried between twenty and fifty cases of liquor, and could not linger more than four minutes to unload for fear of being caught by government agents. None of Musick's involvement could be mentioned in public ads, but it didn't hurt to have a bit of the "bad boy" or "outlaw" background to appeal to the American bedrock value of rebelling against authority. Americans have always prided themselves on chafing at the authoritarian bit, whether the British during the Revolutionary War or the Revenuers during Prohibition. Before Vegas boomed, there was Havana, which some derisively called "the brothel of America." Pan American knew that gambling, drinking, and fleshly sins could be virtues for travelers heading south for more than just to escape cold East Coast winters. The downside: occasionally crews had to restrain or knock unconscious unruly drunks on their way back to the States.

Once Prohibition was lifted, Pan American had no qualms about portraying its hotels and bases as places with all the amenities for the sophisticated traveler. Distillers of alcohol had no trouble piggybacking on the Pan American image, using the airline in their own ads to sell their products. These ads would typically show a stop in South America, where, no matter how far removed from the States, the traveler could still get a good drink. Usually the advertisement for alcohol showed a Pan American airplane or passenger terminal with the familiar winged globe logo. Drinking that brand of spirits would indicate you were partaking of life's rewards enjoyed by the rich, sophisticated set that could afford to travel during the Depression.

The coming of the larger Clipper flying boats brought the revival of an older icon of speed and Yankee ingenuity, the "clipper" ship. Pan American wanted to become "America's Merchant Marine of the Air" and to help the U.S. regain pride and dominance in the world of commerce. As Harry Luce, the founder of *Time*, *Fortune*, *Life*, and, later, *Sports Illustrated*, argued, the twentieth century was to be the American Century, and he

A December 29, 1941, Four Roses whiskey advertisement in *Life* magazine showed a businessman walking from the Dixie Clipper. He is reluctant to say where he has been, given wartime conditions, but not reluctant to sample Four Roses, which is as discriminating as the sophisticated traveler. The ad appeared just after the attack on Pearl Harbor. Artist John Falter would go on to produce 300 recruiting posters during the war, including the famous "Loose lips sink ships" (courtesy Four Roses Distillery LLC).

chose Lindbergh as his first *Time* Person of the Year to drive home the point. Ads reminded readers of how "leadership is being recaptured from that time one hundred years ago when the world envied the Yankee clippers of the sea." This campaign connected to America's bedrock belief in favoring the underdog. Ads implied that in a world increasingly eager for power, commercial and military, the United States had been out of touch and had fallen behind, but now it could regain its rightful place among nations, again to become the City on the Hill, the guiding light for other nations. Through the use of its own wits, technology, and reliance on the American values of free and fair trade, the underdog could not only win, but also be envied by all when it did. The rest of the world could learn from the U.S. model.

Pan American walked a tricky tightrope with the "recapturing leadership" idea. The idea works well in the popular mind as long as the underdog remains the underdog or briefly experiences the rags-to-riches American Dream; however, once the underdog achieves dominance or too much power, Americans tend to disapprove of the bully or the monopoly. When Pan American reached its peak during the flying boat period, it was temporarily saved from this bind by the outbreak of World War II.

Ironically, Pan American's linking of its Clippers with those masted sailing vessels of the past made for a self-fulfilling prophecy. Their two spectacular, though brief, histories paralleled each other. The great Yankee clippers with their masts sometimes as high as a twenty-story building enjoyed a brief heyday between 1845 and 1859—fifteen years. Similarly, PAA's flying boat clipper era, from 1931 to 1946, lasted fifteen years. Yankee sailing clippers were designed for a specific task: to haul small loads of specialized, profitable cargo long distances across water at high speeds. Designers sacrificed cargo space so that clipper bows could be narrow knives slicing through the water. These ships were the seagoing Concordes of their day. The flying Clippers shared the same design task: to carry small loads of mail, freight, and a few high-paying passengers across the oceans in record time, saving not only days but weeks. (The seagoing-clipper era matched that of the California Gold Rush. Forty-Niners and goods needed to reach California as quickly as possible.) On their way, clippers carried ice from the East Coast to Central and South America before it melted. On their way back, clippers could also reach China quickly and bring back tea, particularly to London, before the tea leaves lost taste. Likewise, the flying Clippers flew from California to Manila in 1935 and then on to China in 1937 with the support of the U.S. State and War departments, as the U.S worried about the growing threat from Japan in the Pacific and in China. PAA became the U.S. government's "chosen instrument," both in South America and in the Pacific. With the country in an isolationist mood, a civilian airline could create stepping-stone bases across the Pacific that the military could not. Later, these bases could become military bases, which happened. Both clipper ships and Clipper planes showed the American flag.

Both types of clippers met the same end. The great age of clipper ships ended with advancements in technology. The coming of the steamship lowered freight rates to the point that the clippers could not compete. Steam meant speed and huge cargo loads. World War II effectively did the same for the flying Clippers. With huge land bases created all over the world to service bombers and fighters, and land-based planes created that could fly the oceans, there was little need for flying boats with their reduced load capacity and expensive upkeep. Flying boats landed in salt water, and salt water meant corrosion and constant upkeep, and surplus military cargo and passenger carrying planes left over from the war were plentiful and relatively cheap.

But the word *clipper* and the clipper ship image remained a powerful icon. Flying Clippers were often named after sailing clippers. Just as there had been China sailing clippers plying the China trade, Pan American named its most famous clipper the China Clipper. Another PAA clipper, called the California Clipper, echoed the clippers to the gold fields. The most famous of the Atlantic flying clippers was the Yankee Clipper, named after the Yankee clipper sailing ships. Pan American used the clipper name on its aircraft into the jet age. When the flying boats were first introduced, Pan American began another clipper tradition. Pilots and officers wore uniforms patterned after maritime service uniforms. The main pilot was called captain, and he would have a first officer. A bell system would be used to signal the departure of the "ships." Early Clippers carried plaques on the wall depicting the old sailing clippers. Nautical terminology would be used onboard. Every chance it could, Pan Am would use the image of its greyhound of the air flying over a fully rigged greyhound of the sea.

The crew's paramilitary appearance became an interesting symbol in itself. On one hand, it again signaled flying safety by showing that crews were clean, well shaven, disciplined, trained, professional. The same could be said of gasoline station attendants of the time. Many oil companies required their station workers to wear pseudo-officers' caps and uniforms. You can trust the man who wears the star. On the other hand, this interlude between world wars showed citizen ambivalence over the growing unease in the world. Just as fascists, Nazis, and communists around the world pulled the masses toward uniformed proficiency, people in the U.S. flirted with more benign uniformed images. Should we be organizing too, or shouldn't we?

This was the great age of Boy Scout calendar art, the CCC, and the WPA. Acronyms and worker's art were everywhere. Masses of people organized and wore uniforms. Some wore sheets. Whereas a military uniform could symbolize authority, much like a police uniform, PAA recognized the antiauthoritarian streak that ran through America. The Depression had not helped. Revenuers, railroad bulls, and even the U.S. Army had broken heads by beating people, either individually or in groups, who marched or went on strike. So the airline made sure the public knew its crews were "merchantmen" of the air, not navy men. The Merchant Marine was a servant of the people, helping with commerce, as did the crews of the clipper sailing vessels. Nevertheless, the United States was, through its own images, already doing what it denied and did not want to do—transitioning to war. When World War II broke out, all that Pan Am crews had to do was exchange one uniform for another, or just switch uniforms, depending on whether their mission was considered civilian or military. Ads turned to war recruitment. Most products used the popular "every woman loves a man in uniform" motif that was used in earlier wars, so PAA ads were already on the bandwagon.

As war drew near, the airline drew more and more on patriotic icons. This was especially true in 1940 and 1941, when the Clipper was shown with a spate of eagles and flags. In the midst of all this patriotism, other bedrock beliefs emerged. Befitting the still young country, PAA promoted the bedrock belief in youth culture. A 1940 advertisement captioned "America's Pioneering goes on ... by flying clippers" connected PAA's pioneering spirit to that of earlier American pioneers. "The March of America" depicted in the ad showed Indians, scouts, pioneers, surveyors, pilgrims, and others. PAA went on to say that just twelve years before, *young* Americans had also set out on foot, by canoe, and by mule to carve out airbases from jungle and desert. The text claimed that, with the loyal support of Americans for the efforts and sacrifices of these young men, America would stay out in front. The appeal to pioneering spirit, loyalty, and youth was clear. Pan Am now reached back into history, beyond the sailing clippers, seeking pioneering roots, and even farther back than U.S. history. In the middle of the ad just below the rendering of one of the flying Clippers, a bronzed American eagle perched above the world route map sat like a gilded eagle on a Roman standard. Pan Am's world empire echoed the American empire running coast to coast (as seen in East Coast pioneers depicted on one side of the ad and West Coast pioneers depicted on the other side). Shades of the Roman Empire!

From East Coast to West Coast, from ocean rim to ocean rim, the expansionism captured in these ads satisfied America's belief in manifest destiny. Just as some early immigrants to what would become the United States were thought to have brought a light to the wilderness, and just as it was felt God ordained that western expansion occur in the United States, Clippers served the same purpose. They would bring enlightenment and catapult other nations into the twentieth century. They would bring the American way of life and American principles to others. Their role in manifest destiny would be tied closely to defending democracy. *Defense* would become a word just as central as *democracy* in the airline promotions.

For example, a prewar *Fortune* magazine advertisement titled "A Report to the American People" pointed out that America's Merchant Marine of the Air not only "typifies and spreads our traditions of freedom and good will" but also "is an important factor in our national defense." U.S. security was dependent on world transport, communications, and commerce as embodied in the Clippers. That the ad was presented as a "report" effectively said that the airline had a duty to Americans. It was a surrogate government or government service having to address the state of democracy to its citizens. In this way the airline could appeal to both young and old. While PAA's young men had been pioneering, they pioneered on behalf of tradition, something to appeal to older Americans, particularly conservative business readers of *Fortune* accustomed to reading corporate reports.

One of the more spectacular two-page ads to appear in *Life* reflected similar bedrock beliefs and traditions for a more general audience. "China saved a century ... when Pan American Clippers brought China modern air-transport service ten years ago" showed artistic renderings of the China Clipper in Hong Kong and the evacuation of Burma. The text compared China in 1933 with the United States in 1830, creating a link between the two countries, who were allies against the Axis powers. Much of the text explained how the Clippers saved more than just time or a whole century; they perhaps saved Chinese civilization. The ideas of "savior" and "the elect" contained within the bedrock belief of manifest destiny presented straightforward implications. Because the Chinese resembled Americans in their developmental status as a country, they were worthy of saving in the name of democracy. PAA identified itself in the ad as Pan American World Airways, the Wings of Democracy. The airline, now with the title change of "World" being added, was no longer an airline but a world defender of belief.

In another *Life* published just before the U.S. entry into World War II, "America's Outposts of Security and Defense" further linked the clippers with defense. PAA provided maps to educate the public about the locations of U.S. centers of defense outside the country. These maps revealed where Clipper bases were being converted into military bases. Meanwhile, the text talked of how PAA was Uncle Sam's "strong right arm." It reminded Americans that during a time when attention had to be focused on the military, the U.S., nevertheless, had to stay out front in commercial air supremacy too. Graphically, a sailor waved at one of PAA's Boeing clippers as it roared overhead. Even the military appreciated the airline's strength in keeping the U.S. protected. The war the Clippers fought commercially portended the war sailors would fight militarily.

What was more, these outposts served the rest of the world, as another *Life* advertisement proclaimed the clipper to be "The most watched-for ship in the world." Instead of a sailor waving at the clipper, a pith-helmeted soldier of the Empire holding a boy waved at the ship, probably in Hong Kong or Singapore. The clippers came in from PAA's and the U.S.'s strategic network of island outposts and bases to "carry the hopes of democracy everywhere." Clippers were described as being more than just emissaries of trade. They brought good will and hope, helping to shape history. If all seemed lost, and good will and hope were not enough, Clippers could evacuate youth and families (who could afford it) to safer parts of the world. For many, the Clippers were the only way out. They literally were saviors.

The defense or defender attitude of Pan American made public relations sense. Civilian airlines, particularly transoceanic airlines, would soon be conscripted into government service. Of this, Pan American was sure. Knowing that the U.S. would be forced into a war in the Pacific, the airline in 1941 began evacuating its own dependents from its island outposts, and prepared codes with secret instructions for its Clippers to follow whenever war erupted. Vacationers and businessmen would not be flying into war zones, so the war would end the commercial appeal of the airline, except to South America. How then could a commercial airline keep itself in the public mind, survive economically while making sure it contributed to the war effort, and lay the groundwork for increased revenues after the war—if the U.S. and the Allies could win it?

First, PAA had to portray itself as being absolutely important to the nation's survival, but beyond that, it piggybacked on President Franklin Roosevelt's concepts tied to bedrock values. The airline would ride Roosevelt's words throughout the war. One such concept in circulation even before the war was Roosevelt's Good Neighbor Policy, announced in his 1933 inaugural address. FDR pledged that a good neighbor policy would replace a big-stick or dollar diplomacy toward Latin America. Before this announcement, the United States had followed what many considered to be the dark side of manifest destiny; that is, since the U.S. was the most powerful country in the Western Hemisphere, it had a right to interfere in Latin American affairs. As far back as the Monroe Doctrine of 1823, the U.S. had professed a policy of nonintervention in the world of nations, but felt that South and Central America came within its sphere of influence. Hence, the U.S. government sought to support U.S. commercial interests in Latin America, often at the expense of local autonomy.

FDR carried out much of his pledge. A noninterventionist treaty was signed with Latin American countries in 1937, U.S. Marines were withdrawn from Haiti in 1934, the U.S. government did not intervene when U.S. property was expropriated in 1937 and 1938, payments for the Panama Canal were increased, Cuba was advanced from being not much more than a vassal colony of the U.S., and Roosevelt personally attended the Pan-American Conference in Buenos Aires. Friendship, cooperation, and noninterference would, it was hoped, replace gunboat diplomacy.

Pan American Airways provided another key tool to carry out much of this policy. Because it had to negotiate independently with every country along its route for landing rights, the airline could adroitly sell the concepts of opening up each country through freer trade with an airline that was truly "pan–American." Since most leaders of the time were as aviation happy as the populace, aviation was used to bridge some of the hard feelings of the past. PAA went out of its way to provide good-will flights and special flights for the leaders of the different countries. Showing itself a good neighbor, the airline provided much needed 1931 earthquake relief when Nicaragua was devastated. Charles Lindbergh, a people magnet wherever he went, and Juan Trippe, head of PAA, served as ambassadors. Another unofficial ambassador touring Latin America on PAA was Will Rogers. Like Lindbergh, the film star/humorist/cowboy played well in countries where his Indian blood made it easier for crowds south of the border to accept a gringo from the north. Even though it had suffered occupation by the U.S. military, Nicaragua honored Rogers and PAA by issuing a set of postage stamps (one pictured the humorist next to his Pan American Airways plane at Managua) just as other countries had honored Lindbergh and the Spirit of St. Louis on postage stamps. That the airline's leader, Juan Trippe, was named Juan could serve both the airline and the state department well in Latin America, and it did. That the Lone Eagle met his future wife, Anne Morrow, at the ambassador's residence in Mexico City wasn't bad either.

In hindsight, one can see how Pan American Airways clearly represented white male American values, even racist values, which worked against the desired good will between peoples. While espousing a Good Neighbor policy, the airline sometimes promoted itself by using racial stereotypes. Early Art Deco PAA luggage stickers and company pictorial

Two tourists receive their free cocktail at Puerto Rican Customs in the early 1930s PAA brochure, "Why Not Drop Off at Puerto Rico?"

envelopes showed big-lipped, somewhat bowlegged black porters in cartoon caricature as they carried suitcases and hat boxes for the airline's wealthy clients.

To cite another example, the PAA "Why Not Drop Off at Puerto Rico?" travel brochure began with a cartoon cover of a young lady parachuting from a Commodore flying boat into Puerto Rico's famous El Morro fortress. On this sexist cover, the young blonde's traveling companion did not drift to the ground while wearing a skirt; he apparently landed in the flying boat. She, however, never even lost her stylish hat. Inside, the brochure recounted an imaginary tour of Puerto Rico. The story led off with a pen-and-ink cartoon drawing of two Clipper travelers landing for the first time in "Puerto Reeker," according to the folksy lines of verse penned by Clipper Captain Marius "Lodi" Lodeseen, also known as the Flying Dutchman. Lodeseen, who was also the artist, showed a Prohibition-era young man and "his sugar" passing through customs, where they were greeted with a free cocktail served by an extreme, Black-Sambo caricature of a waiter. His huge, projecting mouth was outlined as in a black-face minstrel show. The stereotyping must have been seen as an acceptable way to lure tourist and business dollars from the mainland United States because Pan American Airways did not distribute the brochure on its own, but rather on behalf of the Department of Agriculture and Commerce in Puerto Rico, a good neighbor.

Beginning with its 1940s advertising, Clipper Cargo, the freight-hauling division of Pan American World Airlines, risked even more with its politically incorrect, promotional cartoon art. Not having to fear alienating passengers, it could distribute humorous, free calendars and ink blotters to its shipping customers, most, if not all, of whom were male, and either brown or white. Thus one blotter showed three black cannibals clustered around a boiling pot, sized to fit a human. These big-lipped caricatures resembled jungle versions of Coon Chicken logos from the same time period. Nailed to a palm tree, their menu sign stated, "Fresh Boiled Missionaries Daily," with "Missionaries" crossed out and replaced by "Maine Lobsters." The huge-bellied cook said, "Thanks to Clipper Cargo—I've Changed the Menu."

A carnival-atmosphere sexist or "weightist" blotter showed an equally large white woman in a polka dot dress. She was suspended in a seat slung under a tripod that served as a weighing scale. The Clipper Cargo advertising played on ambiguity. Was the obese woman simply a member of the general public, or was she the sideshow Fat Lady of a "Guess My Weight" game played at carnivals? A thin showman pointed his stick at her staggering recorded weight, and announced, "You'd never guess ... as weight goes up, rates come down." Clipper Cargo was needed to move her. Her polka dots did not fit any known airplane passenger seat. Apparently the Good Neighbor policy would not be hurt, providing that acceptable targets were chosen.

Pan American used the term "good neighbor" many times in different ads. An example: "The good neighbor who calls every day," which appeared in a 1941 *Life*, made the point that U.S. security depended not just on armaments but on friends as well. The advertisement pictured a gaucho waving his hat in greeting one of PAA's airplanes. Clippers were welcomed throughout the world. The text stated that the efficiency of the Clippers and their crews was something that U.S. neighbors could understand and admire (the City on the Hill or light-to-the-world belief again.) "Mere idealism. Not at all," the ad went on to state, for PAA had turned back competing airlines in Latin America and had "made thousands of miles of air routes safe for the democratic principles represented by the Stars and Stripes." Pan American Airways had become the chosen instrument in Latin America at the exclusion of other possible U.S. carriers by convincing the U.S. government that it was the only airline in position to ward off the threat to the Panama Canal. The U.S had been particularly worried about SCADTA, a German-controlled airline, operating in Latin America. In case of war, the commercial carrier could be converted to a military operation and bomb the canal. PAA made a concerted effort to defuse SCADTA by using its leverage in South American politics to legislate against it and to gain controlling interest.

When Clippers began flying the Atlantic, Pan Am again drew on the Roosevelt association. A 1941 *Saturday Evening Post* advertisement, "America's New Lifeline to Africa," depicted a Clipper in Africa flying over a scene where precious war materiel was being unloaded, in this case an airplane engine. Again PAA made reference to how it took over thousands of miles of Nazi air service in South America. More importantly perhaps, the ad stated how President Roosevelt had called upon Pan American Airways to open a route to Africa and to create a military ferry service that could deliver aircraft to North Africa and the Middle East. America's Merchant Marine of the Air was ready for this challenge and said it would be ready for the even bigger challenges. Basically, it was saying, "No sweat," for cooperating with neighboring nations was nothing new in meeting America's need for commerce and defense. The airline was simply dedicated to carrying out what the administration and nation required, and had been requiring for years.

The problem with the "America's New Lifeline to Africa" advertisement was that "Lifeline" was classified as secret. When Pan American workers built and ran the African bases during 1941 and 1942, military mail censors removed any mention of the workers' location. Operational plans had to be kept in a locked safe in Pan Am's New York office, with access granted on a need-to-know basis. The Army and Roosevelt administration also observed project secrecy. Yet, in the *Saturday Evening Post*, Pan Am's publicity department advertised and illustrated the route! International Harvester did the same with its own "Skyway to the Battle Fronts" magazine advertisement, which showed a route map and painting of one of its diesel generators supplying power for base construction as a Clipper flew overhead. Some secret. No wonder German U-Boats torpedoed several of the project's supply ships as they steamed across the Atlantic to Africa.

Roosevelt's "Four Freedoms" speech to Congress on January 6, 1941, addressed American bedrock beliefs and served as a cornerstone for sev-

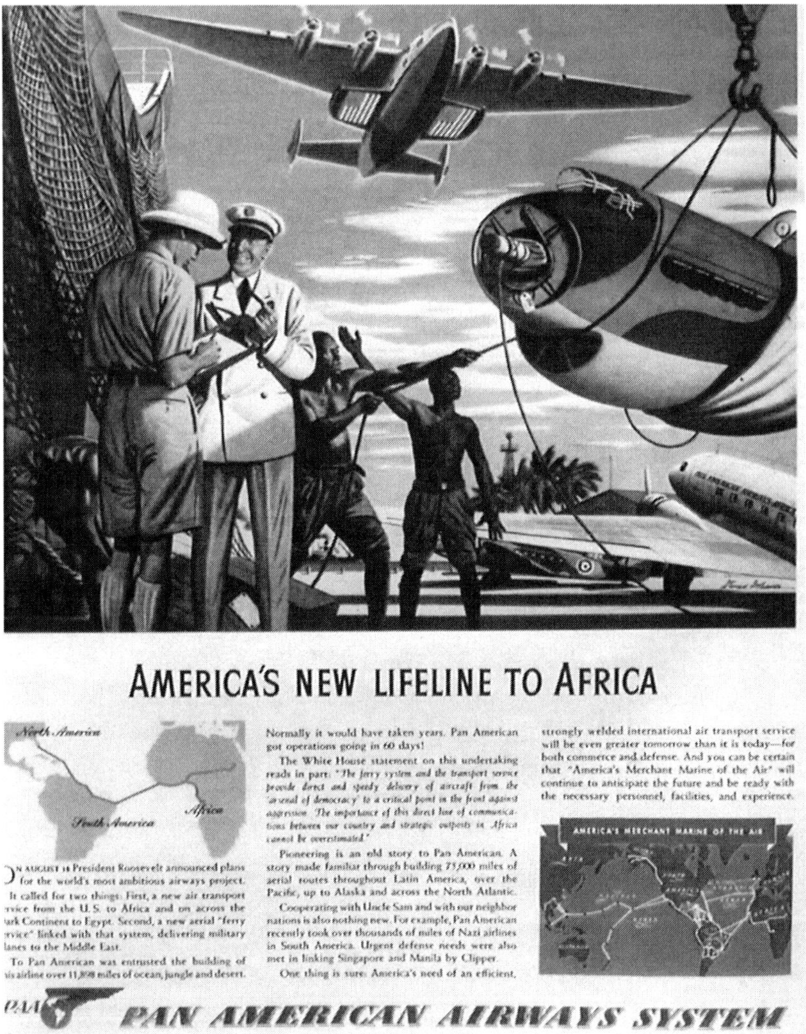

At the request of Prime Minister Churchill, President Roosevelt authorized PAA to open a Clipper supply route across the South Atlantic to Africa to stave off the German advance on Cairo.

eral PAA magazine advertisements. In this short speech, Roosevelt argued for the United States to enter the war. The speech's finale listed the four freedoms: freedom of speech and of religion, and freedom from want and from fear—leading to a call for the creation of a moral world order based on these freedoms that could serve as the antithesis of the dictators' "new order."

When Norman Rockwell's famous paintings of FDR's four freedoms became widely popular in print and poster formats to support the war effort, Pan American quickly copied their style and message. The airline ran a series of special two-page advertisements/commentary in *Life* and the *Post* entitled "Forum for the Future," which presented letters from "leaders of world thought" giving ideas from each about what kind of postwar world we were trying to create. Much like the earlier mentioned PAA ad that gave "A Report to the American People," the letter format broke the usual advertising tradition. An array of world leaders contributed, including Jan Masaryk of Czechoslovakia and Ezequiel Padilla of Mexico. Most, if not all, related in some way to Roosevelt's ideas of the four freedoms and a new moral world order.

Dr. Hu Shih, Chinese ambassador to the United States, in the forum entitled "Mankind must resolve to make this the last war," discussed how the world must demand a new world order and the four freedoms. The graphics revealed a Chinese woman holding a baby, to accentuate the suffering of innocents. These paintings carried Rockwell's nation-centered thematic treatment to the international stage. PAA used Shih's letter as a springboard to advertise how the airline stood by to assist in fighting the backwardness that Shih described. The world's woes could be mitigated through scientific and technological solutions. The Clipper would be one of those technological future solutions. Shih arrived in the United States by Clipper and returned the same way.

Noted philosopher and educator John Dewey, in "The future of the people will be up to the people," discussed how thinking beyond a single nation to a victory by a plurality of democratic nations could open the possibility of bringing health, education, and a higher standard of living to the four corners of the globe—again, a new moral world order based on the freedoms. The world would need a "widespread distribution of goods" for this to happen, and PAA stood ready to deliver. The graphics showed a man and a boy plowing, suggesting that weapons might be beaten into plowshares, ironically in an art style suggestive of socialist "worker realism."

Oswaldo Aranha, minister of foreign affairs of the Republic of Brazil, also made a pitch for democracies in his letter while decrying isolationists, as did Roosevelt in his Four Freedoms speech. Aranha spoke of respect for human personality and cooperation among nations as the basis for lasting peace. Like other ads in the forum series, the airline identified itself as "Wings over the World/Pan American Clippers." In keeping with Roosevelt's new moral world order, the airline's emphasis was clearly more on the world now rather than pan-America. Instead of the PAA winged globe, the graphics present a small globe with a peace dove.

Archbishop Samuel A. Stritch of Chicago put a slightly different twist on the Roosevelt idea in "We are fighting for ... the social emancipation of the family." This ad appealed to the American values of freedom, family, and religion. To Stritch the moral world order was one determined by God, and one the Axis powers were trying to destroy. Religion, and religion alone, could give binding force to international agreements. Therefore, the bedrock belief in freedom of religion became paramount. Just as the Allies fought to free individual families, they also had to fight for a free "family of nations," not the serf nations sought by the Axis powers. Stritch called for the world to be "delivered from the insupportable burden of large armaments," which meant that civil air transport (PAA) could come into its own to facilitate the family. Pan American Airways could not have written a better script. The airline had both the president and now God on its side. The (Angel) Wings of Democracy.

Media presentation of the Clippers used other icons and values created by the war itself to solve the problem of not being able to fly commercially around the world, yet needing to tell people the airline would be there for them whenever the war ended. For instance, some ads used places that had reached iconic status. One such place was Dutch Harbor, Alaska, where the Japanese had invaded North America. Instead of the familiar refrain that became a song, "Remember Pearl Harbor," a *Life* ad asked "Remember Dutch Harbor?" PAA tooted its horn in "Now you can fly to Alaska," citing how the airline had reopened its commercial route to Alaska after completing its two-year military contract with the navy. The navy had commended the airline for the work it had done. As in most wartime promotions, PAA could not reveal just what acts it had performed because they were still secret, but it could boast it had performed them well.

Selling war bonds in World War II became a momentous advertising effort also tied to the Clippers. The ubiquitous bond posters appeared in manufacturing plants, stores, and entertainment centers. Radio personalities and Hollywood stars pitched bond sales until the bonds became synonymous with winning the war and became icons as well known as gold stars, rationing coupons and nylon stockings. In a 1945 *Life* magazine, PAA's ad entitled "Today hundreds see Switzerland by television ... Tomorrow thousands will go to Europe by Clipper" told readers what they could do with all those war bonds they were saving until after the war: They could fly the Clipper to neutral Switzerland since its hotels had been undamaged by war.

With the war at an end and with defending democracy no longer crucial to Clipper promotion, the airline began again to emphasize other bedrock beliefs. The PAA war bond ad mentioned the new medium of television. Increasingly in the twentieth century America's destiny would be tied to technology, and the myth of technology as savior would become a major bedrock value. Technology and Yankee ingenuity, independence, and courage enabled the nation to overcome sometimes superior forces. In this way, the U.S. could still see itself as an underdog while assuming leadership as the emerging world power. Just as small squads or platoons of American troops were portrayed as fighting off the overwhelming banzai "yellow hordes" in the comic books of the time, so had the meager handful of Clippers conquered time, space, and the enemy in the Pacific. Just as isolated American forces used cleverness and "catch-up" technology in the form of Thunderbolt and Lightning aircraft to overcome the superior German scientific/war machine with its Tiger tanks, Stukas, buzz bombs, and secret weapons, so had Clippers, though few in number, become an important piece of U.S. technology to defeat the Wehrmacht. The atomic bomb would further reinforce U.S. faith in technology.

Pan American promised in its Clipper advertisements that the full story of its important involvement in winning the war would be known at the war's conclusion, and it had good reason to boast. Many of the secret missions flown by Clippers would not be revealed until decades after the war when documents were declassified. Clippers had secretly flown President Roosevelt to the Casablanca conference, had ferried Churchill across the Atlantic, had provided at the last moment the critical shell fuses needed to stop Rommel in North Africa, had brought in the uranium from Africa needed to build the Bomb, had supplied the Flying Tigers with replacement engines and ammunition in order to keep going, had flown critical rubber from the Amazon, and had flown both Allied and Axis spies around the world.

Clippers were the technological marvels of their time, the only aircraft capable of flying across oceans with large payloads and long range. They possessed the world's most extensive and advanced navigational and meteorological support systems. Consequently, attempts were made by Axis powers to obtain or steal the Clipper plans so they could build their own flying boats, which Japan ultimately did. Attempts were also made to sabotage Clippers and in prewar times to block Pan American's extension of routes across the oceans, particularly towards the Japanese mandated islands. Likewise, the U.S. military had its eye on the Clippers. At the beginning of the war, neither the navy nor the army had any plane capable of resupplying troops across the ocean. Thus the services quickly commandeered the Clippers as soon as Pearl Harbor was bombed. It would take some time for the military to catch up in aircraft development.

When the military did catch up, Clipper promotions reflected the transitional period from military to civilian use. "Can I fly to South America now?" in a 1944 *Life* announced that more commercial space was available to South America because of the magnificent job done by the Navy Air Transport Service and the Army Air Transport Command. The airline provided aircraft and had helped build the air bases for the armed services, so Clippers were part of that "magnificent" job. The airline took care not to create the image that people should be vacationing during wartime; instead, the graphics showed a businessman in an office overlooking a shipyard. He had just opened an RCA radiogram or cablegram. Obviously he needed to reach South America fast for business or defense purposes. Lucky civilians could fly if priority military passengers did not bump them. An unobtrusive line near the bottom of the ad read, "Buying War Bonds is a good way to insure that post-war pleasure trip by Clipper." At the end of the war, the military surplused the Clippers still in their service back to the airline. By that time, the great age of the flying boats was over, but not the values they represented.

Because of the advertising power inherent in the Clippers, just about any business one could think of picked up on Pan American Airways' advertising. If one needed a typewriter, then one should choose the Corona Zephyr "chosen for Transatlantic Clipper." If one needed a dependable wristwatch, then one should choose either the Gruen Pan American, the "world famous aviation watch now available to civilians" and official timepiece of the Clippers, or the Hamilton watch advertised as keeping "accurate time vital in Trans-Pacific Clipper flights." If one needed needles for sewing, then one should use the China Clipper Needle Book which pictured a Clipper on its fold-over flap. If one needed a pair of pants or a shirt, then one should choose union-made Lee color-matched shirts and pants worn by the PAA ground crews for the Clippers. Such

An aviation insurance underwriters firm made sure to use the Clipper as its logo in 1939.

Sylvania advertised how its fluorescent lights helped Clippers land at night from New York to Lisbon (courtesy OSRAM SYLVANIA Inc.).

clothes would show the wearers that they were "top notch men who are winning promotion, bigger pay" like the Clipper workers.

Everyone seemed to be using the image of the globe or the Clipper or both to sell. And, of course, any industry associated with any product remotely connected to Clippers did so. Associated Aviation Underwriters used the Clipper and globe for its logo. Jacob Aircraft Engines pictured the Yankee Clipper, saying that its engines were "training the Clipper pilots." Sylvania, maker of light bulbs and tubes, advertised a night scene showing how it had created special floating fluorescent lights to guide the giant Clippers into landing areas in Lisbon and Ireland. Electromet printed a metallic-ink page for *Fortune* to resemble the shiny metals it created to resist saltwater rust on the Yankee Clipper.

Near the end of World War II and close to the end of the Clipper flying boat era, Pan American World Airways returned the advertising favors given it by other companies. It encouraged the advertising wave of the future—television. In 1945, still dependent on magazine advertising, PAA ran a magazine ad declaring that "Last week hundreds saw Rio by Television ... Tomorrow thousands will go to Rio by Clipper." The airline was touting its new television show called *Wings of Democracy* on WNBT, New York, the nation's first commercial television channel (later called WNBC). The ad likely was accurate about the number of people who saw the program. The audience probably did number only in the hundreds. Because the wartime government forbade production of civilian television sets and creation of new television stations, the United States went into World War II with fewer than 7,000 sets and twenty stations. In 1945, the country was stuck at slightly less than that number, with somewhere under 4,000 of the surviving sets found in New York. By contrast, Los Angeles enjoyed a staggering forty sets!

Most stations went dark shortly after the attack on Pearl Harbor. The few stations that remained on the air during the war usually broadcasted only three times a week, and then for a mere one or two hours in the evening. WNBT was one of nine stations that had stayed on the air. Needless to say, advertising was difficult for stations to obtain because of such low viewer numbers. The Federal Communications Commission had approved television's moving from an experimental state to a commercial venture in 1941, but, even though television advertising was finally made legal, war quickly curtailed that opportunity. What little television programming there was, embarrassingly, had to be advertised via post cards sent to television set buyers. Similarly, magazines, not television, had to advertise television sets. With Allied victory assured, Pan American was one of a handful of companies to step forward to support the new medium and its belief in the future. Just as the airline showed faith in television as a democratic medium, Pan American believed its "Wings of Democracy" would allow America to move out to the rest of the world via Clippers. The projection was accurate. Both television and the airline used the airwaves as a democratizing force around the world.

2

Clipper Heroes and Celebs

"Age is something that doesn't matter unless you are a cheese," said Billie Burke, the Good Witch of the North in the 1939 *Wizard of Oz*. The same can be said of the concept of hero that transcends time, place, and culture. As Joseph Campbell in *The Power of Myth* and others have pointed out, we all share one monomyth: that of the hero. Heroes, whether real or fictional, give credit to our values and thus offer insight into our cultural mindset. Usually when an object such as the Clipper attains iconic status, associated heroes become part of the formula for its popularity. In this way the Clippers were no different from other icons of their day or of today. Behind the Coca-Cola bottles and ever-present cigarettes in 1930s and 1940s ads stood the military, sports, and entertainment heroes of the time. Behind the red slippers stood the fictional Glinda the Good Witch and heroine Dorothy decked out in nationalistic red/white/and blue. Behind Glinda stood the real good witch and celebrity, Billie Burke, married to theatrical producer Florenz Zeigfield. And behind Dorothy stood Judy Garland, a USO entertainer hero for U.S. troops abroad. Similarly, behind the Clippers stood Charles Lindbergh, PAA president Juan Trippe, Clipper pilot Ed Musick, and a host of heroes and celebrities who used the Clippers whenever possible for photo ops.

Photos of Lindbergh, Trippe, and Musick as representatives of the American hero all appeared on the front cover of *Time* as well as other magazines. Lindbergh became one of the main architects for the creation of the Clippers, for he served as chairman of the technical committee of the Pan American Airways system. He helped draw up the specifications for the proposed Clipper, and aircraft manufacturers sent their ideas and bids directly to him in 1931. Just as Lindbergh provided vision for the type of aircraft never before seen, Juan Terry Trippe provided the vision of spanning the oceans commercially. Ed Musick served as chief test pilot for the Clippers, and he would carry the major responsibility of conducting most of the early experimental and inaugural flights. All three men embodied the American Hero.

Although all people share the myth of the hero, the American cultural mind-set demands a particular version. Generally, American heroes need to come from common roots yet attain high achievement. Although they have special abilities, usually manifested at an early age, modesty becomes them. They make us feel we are all capable of achieving something as important as they did. They must avoid being "too far above us." To put it another way, they must not become so powerful that they threaten the very values they embody, for if they do, they quickly forfeit public good will. To keep the common touch, these heroes must engage in everyday activities and events. Heroes possess qualities we all value; furthermore, heroes must use these qualities to enrich and defend our culture. While freedom and independence are cherished, these values must serve the greater community. To use a common example, it's okay for the independent cowboy to ride off into the sunset at the end of a movie, but he does that only after saving the school marm and small town from uncivilized forces. While he will administer justice with his six-gun because of his own personal code of honor, that code of honor protects and promotes the greater good.

In the 1930s Charles Lindbergh was "the most well known man" in the world, a bona fide hero since his 1927 transatlantic solo flight. He fit the American hero mind-set, and the "Lone Eagle" was quickly connected to the eagle as American icon. Lindbergh's spirit seemed to cut across racial and ethnic lines. Few people could claim to have a dance named in their honor. And how many white people could claim to have a Harlem dance named in their honor? The Savoy Ballroom in Harlem opened the year of Lindbergh's famous flight. "Shorty George" Snowden, the top dancer at the Savoy, attended a charity dance marathon in New York City when, as the story goes, he improvised a few steps away from Big Bea, his partner. A reporter asked him what the steps were called. Since this was just after Lindy's hop across the Atlantic, Snowden replied, "The Lindy Hop."

Every nook and cranny of Lucky Lindy's life was scrutinized by journalists to explain and promote his heroism, so his biography has been well documented. A quick look at early highlights reveals how snugly he fit the American hero formula. Having grown up on a Minnesota farm, "Slim" Lindbergh came from the common roots of Middle America like his soon-to-be famous airplane, "The Spirit of St. Louis," representing St. Louis, the gateway to the West, and the heartland's pioneering spirit. Lindbergh had exceptional mechanical ability. Like many people migrating from farms during and after the Depression, Lindbergh could use his mechanical skills to serve society as it transitioned from agrarian to technological. Smart but no egghead, he quit college to enlist in the army so he could learn how to fly. First in his class of pilots, he quickly proved to be "the flying fool." After the army, he barnstormed and then flew the mail between St. Louis and Chicago, which proved his grit and dedication to the principle, "The mail must get through." Despite crashes and having to parachute out of aircraft, Lindy made sure the first priority was the mail, even if he had to walk out of a farmer's field and hitchhike to deliver it to the nearest railroad station. Whatever he was, he was an exceptional pilot and blue collar—happiest with grease on his hands.

He seemed the perfect modest hero, shunning publicity as much as possible and perhaps more amazed than anyone at his apotheosis after his 1927 flight. After receiving the Congressional Medal of Honor, he served his country by becoming a good will ambassador touring other countries. He continued to use his mechanical skills to help design the Clippers, to create an artificial heart, to promote the cause of aviation, and to help design the Boeing 747 jumbo jet. Working also behind the scenes, Lindbergh used his newly found influence to fund other important projects, such as Robert H. Goddard's rocket research in 1929. Lindbergh persuaded Harry Guggenheim to fund Goddard's research near Roswell, New Mexico. Goddard, in turn, fueled Lindbergh's imagination by saying that rocket flights to the moon were theoretically possible. This also fired the imagination of Juan Trippe and Pan American Airways. After the Clipper era, people wrote the company to reserve tickets on PAA's first flight to the moon.

Lindbergh achieved his major claim to fame as a young man but kept his youthful inventiveness throughout his life. This trait marks yet another part of the American hero formula. Heroes must be youthful, either in age or spirit. Lindbergh was still in his twenties when Pan American began sending him to all parts of the world to explore transoceanic routes. The cult of daring, talented, independent youth is ever with us—Luke Skywalker, Tiger Woods, Buffy the Vampire Slayer, James Dean, Lindbergh.

Lindbergh also conforms to the American hero formula by keeping in touch with everyday, or common, activities. Nothing can be more down-to-earth than marrying and having children. Lindbergh's marriage to Anne Spencer Morrow and the birth of their first child was closely followed in news and women's magazines. This further endeared the Lindberghs to the American public. Lindy was now a "dad." Lindbergh would later blame the excessive press coverage of this side of his life for causing the kidnapping and murder of his child in 1932. Subsequent threats to his family led to Lindbergh's taking his family to Europe for safety and seclusion.

Just as the withdrawal of Lindbergh from American public life after the Bruno Richard Hauptmann kidnapping case violated the American hero principle that a hero should actively protect and promote our values, so did his noninterventionist views, his perceived anti–Semitism, his claim that FDR would suspend elections, and his receiving honors from the Nazis in Germany. Suddenly the hero was tarnished and part of another value system not embraced by most of the American mind-set. Even though he would return to the U.S. and fly combat missions in the Pacific in World War II, other heroes would need to be promoted. Ed Musick would become Pilot Number One for the U.S., and Juan Terry Trippe would become the aviation leader.

Trippe's ascendancy as a public figure was remarkable considering the times. During the 1930s and 1940s the two major political parties fiercely argued, as they do today, over what was worse, big corporations or big government. In the public eye, Trippe managed to transcend both arguments. The airline was obviously the government's "Chosen Instrument," "an instrument of national policy." It was more than an airline; it was "an American institution," as Trippe himself called it, and was growing by leaps and bounds into a large corporation, so one might say it shared the worst of both worlds. But in the public eye, Trippe's public relations staff, headed by William Van Dusen, managed to transcend both by finding ways to conform Trippe and the airline to the American hero formula.

Like Lindbergh, he was portrayed as "pluck and luck." Though not of the heartland, the name *Juan* was played up by the Pan Am PR machine and given a folksy twist with a romantic cachet. It didn't hurt that the interest in Latin music and exotic South American settings were all the rage in Hollywood at the time. Instead of the usual corporate hyperbole and standard press releases, Van Dusen sent out informal, chatty "Dear Señor" letters appraising the press, politicians, and other influentials about the airline's noteworthy achievements. Without a drop of Latin blood in his system, Trippe exploited his name to play the "friendly good neighbor" to leaders and dictators south of the border in acquiring landing and fly-over rights. A gringo with the name Juan couldn't be all bad.

Trippe was intelligent and liked to write, just as Charles and Anne Lindbergh did, yet he was not perceived as elite or of the intelligentsia. Thus his image did not jar loose the anti-intellectualism so often found in American culture that caused many to be rejected as heroes. At Yale he founded a magazine but was so shy and retiring that classmates termed him the "mummy." Countering this seeming bashfulness was his prowess on the football team. Trippe also remained an excellent seventies-score golfer most of his life. Though he opposed Trippe during tough airline hearings, Tennessee senator McKellar called Trippe the smartest man in the United States. Trippe did not seem a brain at all. He stumbled on words and shied away from the spotlight. He was a man of few words. Even as head of Pan American, he still was portrayed as unassuming and humble, talking like an embarrassed college man on his first date, saying "Shucks" or "Oh, gee." In this regard, he comported himself as Lindbergh did in Paris when asked if he had anything to say to the folks back home. With understatement, Lindbergh replied "Hi, Mom," a safe catch-phrase that has become known to all non-media savvy professional athletes.

Similar to Lindbergh, Trippe left school to join the navy to learn how to fly. Like so many youths, he built model airplanes. In the navy he excelled with real ones to the point that when he returned to college to start a flying club he piloted himself to a first place finish in the first local air meet. This began a series of attempts to found an airline. Here, his blue-collar attributes held him in good stead with the hero formula. He showed he was a common man, unafraid of work, dirt, and failure. At first he played grease monkey and worked on his own planes, sometimes piloting them if necessary. If one airline failed, he would try another in his pursuit of the American Dream. Even at the pinnacle of his fame, when Pan American Airlines and the Clippers had been realized, magazines heralded his 80-hour work weeks, his refusal to accept a high salary, his driving his own car and flying his own plane, and his smoking only the cheapest of cigars (three for a quarter). Neither effete intellectual nor a rich captain of industry in a pinstripe, he was a hard-working married man with four kids. He commuted to work each day, avoided drink, and eschewed hobbies in order to better both his country's position in the world and the cause of aviation. He was also loyal and caring, hiring the widow of one of his former friends as his chief secretary. That was the public image.

His true skill lay in what he wasn't. Many ex-military pilots and ex-barnstormers wanted to start airlines during the 1920s and 1930s, but most were seen as reckless or lacking in business sense, so bankers shied away. While some of these early fliers were heroic in their own right, the public remained unconvinced about airline safety and reliability in the hands of stuntmen. Trippe, on the other hand, astutely used business and banking contacts, many from his Yale years, to plan an airline focused on the most highly skilled, highly trained professional staff and the most technologically advanced aircraft in the world. Nothing was to be left to chance. Safety, reliability, and, perhaps above all, imagination were the keys.

Like Thomas Edison and other inventors ushering in the new technological age, Trippe was a dreamer. The most widely dispersed photograph of Trippe showed him dreamily looking over the huge world globe that stood in his office. Presumably he was scanning the globe to plan in his mind the next route of the Clippers. Just as the Clipper was called "Trippe's Clipper" in a *Life* magazine cover story, the earth also seemed to be Trippe's globe. Writers proclaimed he possessed a more expansive, daring vision than anyone else. His mind never stopped thinking about where Clippers could go next. To capture more of this ruminating side of his personality, Trippe exchanged his cheap stogies for a pipe when greeting distinguished visitors and photographers, which gave him an air of a Norman Rockwell or a Walt Disney, other pipe smokers in the news. Like those artists, he, too, drew, but rather than down-home America or Mickey Mouse, Trippe drew lines on a globe, lines that would carry people and goods.

His globe became legendary in pointing out his "down-home" foibles. Press accounts reported how he asked his secretary to bring him a piece of parcel twine so that he could use it to measure possible routes on the globe's curved surface. Through one of the most common objects found in the American home—string—major decisions were made. Although his Clippers were the cutting edge of technology, the globe was "old-fashioned." It creaked, needed lubrication and repair, but it did the job. The globe echoed how heroes tended to ignore their own comforts to attend to the greater vision. Here was the supposed master of airline safety and reliability, yet his friends and family had to plead with Trippe to have his private airplane serviced.

In true hero fashion, Trippe used his vision to benefit all humankind, but particularly the U.S. press descriptions emphasized how he had beaten back the challenge of Axis airlines in South America, mainly the Italian Lati, and German SCADTA, thus ensuring the safety of the Panama Canal. He answered the nation's call in formulating a ferry service for bombers and pursuit fighters across the Atlantic to North Africa, the Middle East, India, and China when the U.S. joined the war. Pan American instructors trained military navigators, including eight of the Doolittle Raiders' navigators, who launched the first attack on the Japanese homeland. Trippe's pilots flying for China National Airways Corporation kept the American Volunteer Force, or Flying Tigers, in the air with emergency supplies. Whenever someone or something needed to cross an ocean fast, a star-spangled Clipper seemed to rush to America's defense. When war erupted, just how important the Pan American bases were as military stepping stones across the Pacific and around the Atlantic became all too clear. The private pioneer spirit had been working all the time to support public welfare during times of warfare.

That this was accomplished by a brilliantly tough negotiator, individualist, and visionary made the hero mantle that much easier for Trippe to wear. Though what he accomplished was for the public good and in the public eye for all to see, he was a deeply private person, which added mystery to his character. He kept hidden his true intentions, then sprang them on people and his own staff seemingly out of nowhere. His announcement that he was going to take one of the smallest airlines in the country and open an international route to Cuba in 1927 shocked other owners of the company. Likewise, he later announced that instead of crossing the Atlantic as originally planned the company would first fly the much more difficult Pacific. Technological and logistical breakthroughs in navigation, direction finding, radio communication, weather forecasting, and aircraft would have to scramble to keep up with his timetable and vision.

Trippe's legendary power and secretiveness led *The Saturday Evening Post* in its August 14, 1943, feature article, "The Columbus of the Airways," to call him the mystery man of the air, "the Sir Basil Zaharoff of air transport." Basilieios Zakharias (Zaharoff) was well known to readers during Trippe's time. As the world's most infamous arms merchant, he was also called the "Merchant of Death," accused of fomenting war and involvement with everything from assassinations to bribery at the highest levels. Yet he was knighted by King George V for running the Vickers-Armstrong munitions factory in World War I, and was awarded the French Legion of Honor. Never convicted of any crimes, he sold armaments to the Greeks to fight the Turks, to the Turks to fight the Greeks, to the Japanese to fight the Russians, to the Russians to fight the Japanese. He made arms for the British while owning substantial interest in arms maker Krupp. Zaharoff systematically stole or destroyed all evidence of his youthful past, shunned the press by not allowing himself to be photographed until well up in years, and used several doubles to avoid assassination. He kept diaries for fifty years, filling some fifty-three books, yet ordered them all burned upon his death. Like Trippe, he extended his ventures around the world. For example, he persuaded the British navy to stop using British coal in favor of Persian oil. Oil could make as much money as guns—or more.

In the spirit of showing that everything connects sooner or later, consider that the father of European comic books, Hergé (Georges Rémi), in his adventure comic TinTin series, included the evil arms dealer Bazarof, based on Zaharoff. He appears in Hergé's 1937 *L'Oreille Cassée* (*The Broken Ear*), which features flying boats and South American intrigue. The series featured a news correspondent hero, TinTin, who wore knickers, and traveled with his terrier, Snowy. The Tintin comics inspired Andy Warhol's art and a loose adaptation of *The Broken Ear* to be made into a 1963 movie by Philippe de Broca called *L'Homme de Rio* (*That Man from Rio*), an adventure/espionage spoof starring Jean-Paul Belmondo. Steven Spielberg wanted to buy the adaptation rights to the TinTin adventure series. Spielberg also reviewed *That Man from Rio* a dozen times to prepare for the filming of his own *Raiders of the Lost Ark. Raiders* featured similar scenes but replaced the flying boat of *The Broken Ear* with the Pan American Airways' Clipper.

The *Post* also exposed some of Trippe's Zaharoffesque warts, but said that his affable social manner disguised his "secretive, Ulysseslike craft." Author Matthew Josephson went on to put Trippe, a man of mystery, even more in the American hero tradition. Though forty-four, Trippe was "young and athletic." Again, he was posed at the "show desk," not his roll-top, and was shown with his pipe rather than his cigar.

Chief pilot Ed Musick became the flying hero who used Trippe's invention, and some of his own, to bring glory to the United States and Pan American. Musick completed the Lindbergh/Trippe/Musick Pan American triumvirate of heroes. Unwittingly, all three men first came together in 1927 when Musick happened to be at Roosevelt Field on the East Coast working for Tony Fokker of Fokker aircraft fame. A friend told Musick that Trippe needed a Fokker pilot to fly his new mail route from Key West to Cuba. At that moment a commotion interrupted activities at the field as a silver plane landed. Musick had never seen the airplane before nor the pilot. It was Lindbergh flying in from St. Louis to make his attempt to cross the Atlantic. And it was Musick who quickly took Trippe's job. Now the country was covered—with Lindbergh from Middle America, Trippe with the southern name from the East Coast, and Musick, born in St. Louis but raised as a West Coast L.A. boy.

Like the other two, the single-minded Musick showed great mechanical and piloting skills at an early age. Handsome, but not knowing how to dance or approach girls, he traded the usual high school and college social life for being a crack auto and motorcycle mechanic at California races. Sometimes Musick raced while keeping an eye on the flying machines appearing at the first California air exhibitions. When the price of an airplane was beyond their reach, he and a friend built their first airplane out of bedsheets and motorcycle wheel tire spokes. When that crashed, they built another. He worked a while at the Glenn Martin aircraft factory, not knowing that in a few years Martin would be the builder of the China Clipper that would insure Musick's fame. Soon Musick headlined West Coast aviation meets as an exhibition flyer, "Daredevil Musick" or "Monsieur Musick" (since French aviators were all the rage) doing stalls, tailspins, and rolls.

Musick's background offered classic hero material. The Musicks represented a long line of pioneers, soldiers, and Indian fighters. All were quiet men but driven to seek adventure and new frontiers. Colonel David Musick fought under George Washington. Ed also sought to serve his country by trying to enlist for service in World War I; however, his skills as a flight instructor were too good. The military kept him as a civilian pilot instructor so they would not run the risk of having him called up for battle and losing his services. The frustrated Musick ran off to another state and enlisted to fly for the marines, who commissioned him as a lieutenant. After the war in the winter of 1919 during the Florida boom, he flew for Aeromarine and pioneered their first passenger flight from Florida to Havana using overhauled World War I military surplus seaplanes. During summer he flew their New York–Atlantic City route. When that airline failed, he briefly tried to fly as an independent on the East Coast and Florida during the rich tourist and rum-running days.

But it was when he joined Pan American Airways in 1927 that Musick began to grab press attention. First he opened PAA's route to Cuba, where he was met by the Cuban president. This was the first of many photographs of Musick with world leaders. Other Central and South American routes followed. His pioneering heroics in the air began to reach the press. He knocked out a drunk on board one of the new Sikorsky flying boats out of Havana when the man stripped and threatened to kill all the passengers with a knife. He volunteered to fly a mercy crew into Lake Okeechobee during the second worst hurricane in U.S. history. The hurricane killed more than two thousand people at the lake in 1928 when a storm surge destroyed the towns and farms surrounding the lake. When the storm was still in progress, Musick flew his S-38 from Miami at tree level beneath the clouds to Okeechobee. Here he was met with a landscape of white and black corpses on piles of debris. He landed wherever he could on the water amid the carnage, so relief workers could tell survivors medical help and food was on the way. Some 1,600 people had to be buried in a mass grave a few miles from the north side of the lake, as that was the only dry land in the area.

When Musick became Pan American's chief master pilot and pilot trainer, his skills were respected by even those most veteran pilots. Each pilot he checked had to have taken radio school, navigation school, seamanship, Spanish, and a course of flying "under the hood" so they could fly blind if need be. Like Musick, each pilot practiced maintaining and fixing everything mechanical on a Clipper, including cleaning out the bilges. He was known for his legendary preparation, caution, and adherence to safety routine. Even the seams of his trousers had to be perfectly smoothed and aligned before he was willing to taxi a flying boat away from its moorings. This meticulous behavior kept him alive in his younger years. Even during his days as a kid mechanic for exhibition flyers, he had earned the nickname "the jeweler" because everything had to be perfect on the aircraft, perfect to the point that he would polish the turnbuckles every day. Even when he was the "Daredevil Musick," he left nothing to chance. He practiced each aerial trick over and over to minimize any safety risk. Finally he became "Uncle Ed," since his studious, cautious nature and hard-won experience could instruct all those under his guidance.

His nicknames changed when the adulating press took more notice of him. He became known as "the Sphinx of Aviation" because he would not discuss his own achievements or exploits. This typified the tightlipped nature and modesty of American heroes. The public relations arm of Pan American had as much trouble teasing anything out of Musick as did the press. For example, after years of planning, Pan American was primed to fly the Pacific from Alameda to Honolulu in 1935. The day of the epochal flight, all the major news sources were ready to hang on every word broadcast from the Clipper. When nothing came from the plane, the Alameda base radioed Musick, pleading with him to tell them anything newsworthy about the flight. He terse reply: "Sunset six thirty-nine." The same thing occurred when the China Clipper extended the Pacific route to Manila in 1937, officially joining East and West. Confronted with flashbulbs and a bank of microphones, Musick gave his speech. "We are glad to be here." End of speech. He then delivered the letter he carried from President Roosevelt to the president of the Philippines. Politicians, press, and company officials would have to deliver the bombast and puffery.

Musick's physical characteristics helped his hero status, too. Firm jawed, round shouldered, permanent crow's feet around the eyes from squinting into the sun, he fit the Hollywood leading man role. No wonder Hollywood wanted Humphrey Bogart to play Musick in *The China Clipper*. Unlike Bogart, Musick swore off liquor for life after only one try as a youth. Virtuous yet bold. Thus the public found it incomprehensible when Musick died in 1938 pioneering a route from the U.S. to New Zealand by way of Samoa. While Musick was piloting the Samoan Clipper, the Clipper developed engine trouble and had to return to Pago Pago. As the crew dumped fuel to lighten the airplane in anticipation of landing in Pago Pago's dangerously tight harbor nearly surrounded by mountains, the Clipper exploded and all crew were lost. He died the hero's death, doing what he loved in trying to open an important route to New Zealand and Australia that was to serve the U.S. in World War II. Some said Pan American and the U.S. government pushed too hard and too fast. Some said Musick was not only a hero, but also a martyr.

To further accentuate Musick's heroism, a year after his death

Musick's widow, Cleo, asked William S. Grooch to write Musick's biography *From Crate to Clipper with Captain Music, Pioneer Pilot* (Longmans, 1939). Grooch, a veteran PAA pilot himself, had pioneered routes in South America and China. As a close friend of the Musicks, he had complete access to Musick's records and interviewed close family and friends to recreate in glowing terms Musick's life, from his admiration of his first hero, Barney Oldfield of the "horseless carriage," to the heroic end at Samoa. Along with the book's appearance in school and public libraries, a lighthouse on Canton Island was erected in honor of Musick and the crew of the Samoan Clipper. During World War II a Liberty ship would also be named for Musick.

After Musick's death and the fall from grace of Lindbergh due to his isolationist stance, commercial advertising projected other PAA employees to hero status during the 1940s in order to promote products, much to the delight of Pan American. This proved helpful to the airline at a time when advertising itself was difficult because much of its effort was tied up in military activities that could not be discussed. How do you advertise yourself when you can't tell anyone what you are doing? Camels cigarettes ran various ads in most of the major magazines to tout Pan Am heroism. Most often, Camels' ads appeared prominently as a full-page, full-color ad on the coveted back cover of such magazines as *Life* and *The Saturday Evening Post.*

In September 1943 these magazines presented Captain Joseph H. Hart, who set a record by crossing the Atlantic twelve times in thirteen days while carrying vital war cargo in his Clipper. More important than those numbers, of course, was the fact that he had been a Camels smoker for twenty years. A color photo showed the smoking, smiling captain standing in front of his Clipper as it rode in the bay with the U.S. flag clearly painted on its nose. In a small cartoon-like insert, Hart claimed that on his Clipper, "Camels are standard equipment." The ad also made sure that readers knew that Hart was a former army pilot, so it would not appear unseemly to promote a civilian over a military hero in time of war.

The Pan American Airways' public relations department could not have presented the airline any better. Camels promoted both the airline's civilian/humanitarian mission on behalf of the "world" and its military mission. Hart had just returned from flying United Nations officials across the Atlantic, while carrying both serum and war materiel to the generals. Not only was Hart "First in Service" as the ad stated, but so were Camels for servicemen everywhere. A banner at the top of this ad announced the title for this series of hero ads: "They've Got What It Takes."

In 1944 Camels featured Pan American's Captain Charles Sharkey in full-page, eight-frame cartoon format on the back page of major magazines. The ad reminded people that Clipper pilots also flew for China National Airways Corporation (CNAC), flying the famous Hump from India into China. Unlike military pilots, Sharkey heroically confronted the enemy unarmed. The cartoon strip showed Sharkey's plane attacked by Zeros over the Hump. He escaped by his Yankee ingenuity, flying ability, and raw courage. In a daring maneuver, Sharkey cleared the Himalayas and hurtled his transport through a blinding wall of fire and smoke from a forest fire to escape the enemy and deliver his load of explosive, badly needed high-octane gasoline to China. It doesn't make great sense that Sharkey smoked while high octane gas was loaded and unloaded, but this was a Camels ad, so he did. In the last frame, he was shown wearing the "chit" on the back of his jacket made famous by the Flying Tigers, showing the Chinese flag and telling the Chinese that he was a friend. Like Captain Hart, Sharkey was "First in the Service." One frame at the beginning of the cartoon strip included a photo of the youthful, smiling hero/hunk smoking his Camel.

The cartoon format lent an added sense of dramatic narrative to Sharkey's heroism, copying the style of art used in the war and action comics so popular in the 1930s and 1940s. This ad came at a time when America's comic book heroes, from Dick Tracy to Superman, had been enlisted to fight the enemy. This portrayal followed the formula of the time for such adventures. American war heroism in comics involved several American myths, but mainly focused on belief in the underdog and individual freedom. Thus the war comics portrayed an independent individual—working for the greater team—taking daring action to outwit superior forces. Hordes of kamikaze or banzaiing Japanese surrounded lonely American squads; columns of German Panzers advanced on the solitary infantryman, who would save the day through his wits. Sharkey fit the mold. As underdog, he was unarmed and hopelessly outnumbered by a squadron of faster, more maneuverable Japanese fighters that in folksy pilot lingo he casually referred to as "Aunt Nellies." He outwitted the superior forces, saved the day, and in typical American hero tradition downplayed his role. While he was being congratulated in the last frame for a "terrific" performance, Sharkey redefined "terrific," meaning the whole event simply reminded him that he wanted one of those terrific Camels. Of such stuff are heroes made.

Not all heroes were men. Beauty products pushed Clipper women. In 1944 DuBarry extolled the "Clipper Angel," a full-page color advertisement in major magazines. The Clipper Angel was Miss Yolanda Floripe, pictured standing in an office overlooking a docked Clipper. In tune with

DuBarry cosmetics proclaimed Clipper service representative Yolanda Floripe a "Clipper Angel" (courtesy DuBarry, www.dubarryusa.com).

the World War II spirit of everyone's having to pitch in as a team (the Rosie the Riveter theme), the DuBarry ad told how Floripe did, and did well, what was a man's job before the war. Floripe's heroism made possible the release of a talented man for military service. As a Passenger Service Representative, she had become the "guardian angel" for each Clipper that crossed the Atlantic. She acted as hostess, guide, problem solver, schedule maker, reservation maker, and interpreter. She could do such a good job during trying times because the exacting job was "done best when I look my best." Enter DuBarry beauty preparation products and the Dubarry Success School which Floripe had attended.

Unlike the bold, comic book primary colors of the Sharkey ad, pastels and more muted colors dominated Dubarry's presentation of Floripe. Pink spelled out "Clipper Angel" and "DuBarry." Pink small graphics showed how to apply facial makeup in one minute. Floripe also wore a pink carnation in her lapel to fit the heroine image of the time. Women could be heroes but had to maintain their pinkness or femininity as defined by American standards. The watercolor format also reduced or washed out the "color" difference between Yolanda Floripe and the Clipper officer and male passenger she helped in the ad—important for the racially conscious U.S. mind-set. Likewise, since Floripe was single, it was important, and in keeping with heroine formula of the time, that the male passenger who exchanged papers with her not wear a wedding band.

Woodbury Facial Soap featured Pan American Airways' Vera Dawes Covell, the only woman "Flight Watch" in the United States. Covell's voice over the radio guided the Clippers to land and take off from LaGuardia, New York, the northern port of the Atlantic Clippers. The black-and-white photo, full-page advertisement entitled "She Keeps 'Em Flying and Keeps Her Beauty 'On the Beam,'" looked so much like a feature story that the small letters "Advertisement" had to be added at the top of the page in *Life* (11 January 1943). In contrast, when the same ad ran in 1943 editions of *McCall's* and *Woman's Home Companion*, the Covell piece was not identified as an advertisement. Rather than being just a product hawker, the ad made her quasi-news. Unlike Floripe, who wore a Pan American uniform, Covell wore a floral print dress, since her contact was not with the public but with Clipper officers. As she said, "I admire no end the clean-cut chaps who skipper our Clippers." The largest photo showed her speaking on the phone, with a framed painting of the Yankee Clipper soaring over its sailing ship predecessor.

The text made it clear that she put in fatiguing and tension-filled hours. Since she was the "only" woman "Flight Watch," she, like Floripe, had filled in for a man who would normally insure the safety of the Clippers and instruct "the clean-cut chaps." She, too, had to be both feminine and specially talented at the same time. The advertisement established both of these qualities. Immediately the ad stated that Covell was herself a pilot, but "grounded for the duration" because of civilian flight restrictions. She wasn't afraid to move out of the radio office into the hanger area

Vera Dawes Covell, the only woman flight dispatcher in the U.S., kept Clippers "on the beam" at LaGuardia, just as Woodbury soap kept her beauty on the beam.

to take breaks and mingle with the hangar mechanics. In other words, during wartime this down-home worker had sacrificed for the good of the whole. Like the common folk, she put both her coveralls and her dainties on one leg at a time.

Though she did a man's job and had manly skills (i.e., flying airplanes, operating radio equipment), she enjoyed her feminine role in U.S. society. For example, as she sat on a sawhorse next to a Clipper in the hangar, she observed the perceived traditional woman's role of serving a man by pouring cream or milk into a mechanic's coffee cup. And to make doubly sure that beauty was enlisted to help the war effort and men while not threatening American belief in a woman's role in the nuclear family, the advertisement concluded with "Back Up Your Fighting Man ... Buy War Bonds and Stamps." In fact, the article began with a play on the war bond theme. The heading, "She Keeps 'Em Flying" reflected the ubiquitous "Keep 'Em Flying" slogan used for the bond drive. Posters, flyers, newspapers, magazines, pins, and stickers across the land used the slogan to encourage people to buy bonds to build aircraft to win the war. "You Buy 'Em, We'll Fly 'Em," sang another variation of the slogan. The Covell presentation implied that whatever she did served the "'Em," that is, the Clippers and their pilot "chaps," who in turn served the fighting men.

Through one of the most widely dispersed ads in magazines during the war, Kellogg's lionized one of the Clipper's ground crew. Joe Wuller, chief of the Clippers' beaching crew in Miami, appeared in such magazines as *Better Homes and Gardens* (June 1942) and inside the cover of *Life* (22 June 1942). Wuller was the archetypal ex–navy chief, who knew how to bark orders and be "chief" of the Miami crew. Although the number of photos each ad contained in the different magazines differed, the messages and approach remained the same. The ads depicted Wuller wearing a bowtie and immaculately white shirt, pants, and officer's hat, as he stood by the Clipper mooring basin. From there he directed a group of young men in swimsuits as they guided a Clipper on to its wheeled carriage so that the flying boat could be pulled from the water. He was not only nursemaid to these twenty-one young men, but also, as the caption for the ad read, he was "Nursemaid to a 20-ton Clipper!" and "He's a Self-Starter," just as Kellogg's Corn Flakes was the "Self-Starter Breakfast."

If the history of the Clippers—or perhaps the American version of the "story" of World War II—are seen in the context of the conventional mythic formula found throughout popular culture, Joe Wuller's appearance in mass magazines made sense. Whenever and wherever a young hero exists, or a young institution, or a young country, the hero must not only face trials, show talent, and be daring, but also must be counseled by a guiding elder—a John Wayne, an Obi-Wan Kenobi, a Yoda, a Good Witch of the North, a Merlin, an Old Ranger, a fairy godmother, a Joe Wuller. Like all guides, Wuller understood the dangers of the new technology and knew how to handle these dangers and the people who lived with them. As the ad pointed out, he not only had to coordinate twenty-one young men but also a tractor and boat. They all had to work together as a team. That the ad mentioned "twenty-one" is interesting in itself: twenty-one, the age at which U.S. youth acquired independence and adulthood. Literally, as the ad depicted, when eager, talented, raw youth were stripped and baptized into their rite of passage, they needed someone who knew the ropes. Kellogg's presented the Man in White, the baptism and trial by water, and even the "ropes." As the ad said, he had to "baby" the Clipper. In the same way, he had to nurse his beaching crew, just as he nursed his corn flakes on milk. Yet he was your average "Joe." He ate the same cereal his crew preferred at the airline cafeteria. And there wasn't anything much more American than corn flakes, as that American airline, Pan American, nursed the country out of isolationism into expansionism. PAA was the nation's "self-starter."

Fred Noonan (1893–1937) was a different story, straddling the line between hero, antihero, and celebrity. Until his death as Amelia Earhart's navigator on their fateful 1937 flight, Noonan had received a great deal of publicity as the world's most talented nautical and aviation navigator. As chief navigator for Pan American, he accompanied pilot Musick on early transoceanic Clipper pioneering flights. He was there almost from the beginning of Pan American Airways, serving as navigator for South American and Pacific routes, as Port-au-Prince airport manager in Haiti, and as celestial navigation instructor. In the face of Musick's sparse utterances on the Clipper's first flight from California to Manila and back, Noonan became the color commentator the PAA public relations people wanted the press to hear on the heroic voyage. Whereas Musick stated baldly, "We're glad to be here," Noonan radioed from the China Clipper that "Never in my life have I seen so many stars or been so close to them. We are up ten thousand feet. A mile below us there's a mattress of blue white cloud half a mile thick.... It's a glorious night. Could see ocean and light of three ships at various times, and rolling bank of clouds mile below until moon went down. After that, flashed along at one hundred fifty to one hundred seventy miles hour over blueblack cushion air and under sparkling array billions stars in dark blue velvet sky."

If Musick was the calculating, precise "jeweler," Noonan was the wilder dark Irish, who remains controversial to this day. Noonan learned his navigation skills by working in the maritime shipping industry while learning to fly on the side. When the Depression crippled shipping, he took an airline job. His navigational skills came under question when Noonan and Earhart would be lost on their way from New Guinea to Howland Island in 1937. Was Noonan partially at fault since Earhart had some reservations about him?

While Clipper crews respected his talent, his laxness with procedures and his drinking bouts were bringing things to a head in 1937. Just before his attempted round-the-world flights with Earhart, he divorced his wife of ten years and remarried. Those who flew with him noticed his weekend disappearances for drinking bouts that brought him back to work hung over. He was involved in a car wreck for which he was ticketed for driving in the wrong lane. On one occasion the crew was unable to wake him so that he could perform his navigational duties on a transpacific Clipper flight. The last straw came when Musick put a "tail" on Noonan before a morning Clipper departure to prevent his drinking before the flight. Noonan slipped the tail that night and showed up under the weather. After that, Noonan no longer worked for Pan American, but took employment with Earhart.

If Musick was "The Sphinx," Noonan remains even more of a mystery enmeshed in the many theories about the disappearance of Amelia Earhart. Were his maps wrong? Had he made a navigational error? Were Noonan and Earhart flying with faulty instruments? Did both Noonan and Earhart lack of knowledge of radio use? Conspiracy? Were they actually spying on the Japanese and captured by the Japanese? Did they just use bad judgment? Are they alive and well with Elvis? Noonan lives on.

Entertainers, sports heroes, and politicos needing publicity dialed "C" for Clipper. Anyone wanting to be a celebrity—that is, his or her reputation depended on keeping a media image before the public—knew that the Clipper was a quick passport to free press coverage. Talent agents and political hacks took advantage of this. Press photographers made it a regular beat to snap photographs of those who disembarked at LaGuardia, Miami, Honolulu, Alameda. These Clipper comings and goings became regular features in newspapers and magazines. Because flying the Clippers cost more than flying today, passenger lists included the rich, the important, the famous, and the wannabees. And when Clippers crashed and people died, the world felt it.

Because Clipper pilots and staff were considered some of the most eligible bachelors in the world, inevitably trysts and marriages with Hollywood starlets occurred. Captain William M. Pryce, Jr., married silent screen actress Natalie Joyce (*A Girl in Every Port*, *The Circus Ace* with Tom Mix, and some thirteen other films). Colonel Clarence Marshall Young, who headed Pan Am's Pacific Division, was a former aviation pioneer, WWI aviation hero, and Chief of Air Regulation for the Department of Commerce. When he married star of screen and stage Lois Moran in 1935, she became Pan Am's first lady on the West Coast. The newlyweds met the first commercial flight of the Clipper in Hawaii that spring. Moran had acted in France before coming to Hollywood and successfully made the transition from silent movies (particularly *Stella Dallas*, considered one of the best silent movies) to the talkies and the New York stage.

When F. Scott Fitzgerald tried his hand at screenwriting in Hollywood, he became intrigued by Moran. She inspired him to create the performer in his short story "Jacob's Ladder," which appeared in *The Saturday Evening Post* (August 29, 1927). She also served as his model for the character of Rosemary Hoyt in his novel, *Tender Is the Night* (1933). While the marriage between Fitzgerald and Zelda was disintegrating, as was Zelda's mental health, Zelda became incensed at Fitzgerald's infatuation with Lois Moran. Consequently, Zelda gathered up jewelry from guests at a party and began boiling them to make a soup, then proceeded to burn her own clothes in the bathtub.

Lois Moran Young served Pan Am well as a gracious, glamorous hostess. She entered both popular and high culture through her stage and screen credits as well as appearing in Man Ray's and Edward Steichen's photographs of her. Young didn't do badly himself, appearing on the cover of the March 14, 1932, issue of *Time*.

The airline knew the value of using famous people, too. Since Pan American Airways regarded its Clippers as "ships," in keeping with maritime tradition, each ship had to be christened. Presidential wives made for excellent photo ops. The events made for free publicity and stroked government ego so that presidents might favor the airline. Mrs. Herbert Hoover christened the American Clipper. Eleanor Roosevelt christened the Yankee Clipper. The christenings appeared in printed sources as well as the news roundups and parades shown in movie theatres before the main feature. Other airlines and Pan American subsidiaries would follow the christening tradition for land planes that were not ships. Hollywood stars would inaugurate new routes and aircraft. For example, a tightly-sweatered, pre–Kennedy Marilyn Monroe helped commemorate a new route from Mexico into Tinseltown. Though Marilyn wielded a paintbrush rather than a traditional champagne bottle, who cared? Who was looking at the brush? Certainly not the public or male airline representatives.

A rivalry broke out over who was the "first woman of the air" and to some degree over who was the first "man of the air" among civilian passengers. Particularly in the 1930s, some affluent people tried to accumulate as

As the goldfish swallowing fad spread across college campuses and Ghandi began his hunger strike, Eleanor Roosevelt christened the Yankee Clipper on March 3, 1939.

many "first flights" as they could. In their attempts to be first around the world, or first to cross the Pacific, or first anything in aviation, several became celebrities.

Best known and most photographed at the time was Clara Adams. In 1918 Adams married a rich Easterner, an industrialist nearly forty years her senior. He died in 1929, leaving her with plenty of time and money to pursue her interest as a first flighter. Prior to his death, she had already pursued her own separate path from that of her husband. In 1924 she traveled to Germany to meet Dr. Hugo Eckner of Zeppelin fame. He allowed her to be a guest on one of his test flights for the ZR III, later turned over to the United States for reparations and renamed the USS *Los Angeles*. Because her grandmother was related to former German president von Hindenburg, and her cousin, Colonel Arthur C. Goebel, had won the Dole Prize in 1927 for being the first person to fly between the United States and Hawaii, Adams was able to use her German contacts in 1928 to buy the first ticket sold (for $3,000) for the Graf Zeppelin's first flight across the Atlantic. Part of her notoriety resided in her being the only woman on the flight. Likewise, in 1931 she was the only paying woman passenger on the German DO-X's flight from Rio to New York. The DO-X was a monstrous 12-engined flying boat or palatial yacht that gained maximum press attention while proving commercially impractical. When the super-dirigible *Hindenburg* made its 1936 maiden flight to the United States, Adams claimed her seat as one of the eleven women on board.

The Clippers proved a bonanza for Adams. In 1936 she was one of only seven passengers on the inaugural passenger flight of the China Clipper across the Pacific (Depression cost: $950 one way). Her competition, who also pestered crew members for autographs and mailed souvenirs from the flight, came from Mrs. Zetta Averill of Aberdeen, Washington. Both acted as on the-scene reporters who sent accounts of their flight back to area newspapers. Adams outdid Averill in this regard. She mailed six pounds of letters for just one leg of the flight—all good promotion for the Clippers and herself. When Clippers began service to Bermuda in 1937, Adams was one of twenty passengers on the inaugural commercial flight.

In 1939 she flew the first leg of her race around the world on the inaugural trip of the Dixie Clipper from New York to Marseilles. *The New York Times* printed a special rotogravure picture section in its 23 July 1939 edition to cover her record-breaking trip around the world in 16 days, 19 hours, and 4 minutes. For years prior to her record-setting attempt, the United States had been gripped by round-the-world mania. Newspapers offered prizes for those able to circumnavigate the globe fastest. The arrival of the fast Clippers and dirigibles crossing both Pacific and Atlantic changed the competition. Competitors no longer had to rely on steamships, trains, and interior airlines. Adams was able to fly the entire way on commercial airplanes. Gone were the days of *Around the World in Eighty Days*. Adams relished these photo ops and never shied away from being photographed with her aviation friends such as Amelia Earhart.

Knowing how President Roosevelt avidly collected stamps, Adams made sure to send him envelopes she had prepared and carried on her round-the-world record flight and other Clipper flights of note. Roosevelt thanked Adams through his personal secretary, M.A. "Missy" LeHand, that same July in 1939 when Adams made the flight. (Missy, the president's longtime confidant, was perhaps also FDR's longtime mistress, according to his son.) In any event, so closely had Adams connected herself to Pan American Airways' Clippers, that LeHand simply addressed White House thank-you letters to Clara Adams in care of Pan American Airways' main office in New York rather than Adams' home address.

Sometimes Clipper publicity backfired. Adams unwittingly became a part of Clipper humor when the *Burbank Post* mishandled pronoun reference in reporting the first passenger flight of the China Clipper:

> Among the first to enter was Mrs. Clara Adams of Erie, lone woman passenger. Slowly her nose was turned away from the hangar doors to face in a southwesterly direction. Then like some strange beast she crawled along the grass [255].

It is to be hoped that Adams also beat her wings hard enough to get off the water. The beast with the direction-finding big nose was almost good as the Chinese speaker who toasted the China Clipper's success by speaking of "frying on a creeper" instead of "flying on a clipper." Pan Am crews who suffered the Clipper's miserable ventilation laughingly agreed the Chinese speaker had it right on the money.

Cameras also clicked for Jack Dempsey, Charlie Chaplin, Babe Ruth, Ernest Hemingway, Clare Boothe Luce, Clark Gable, George Bernard Shaw, Prince Paul of Greece, Damon Runyan, Vivien Leigh, Errol Flynn, Will Rogers, a young Jack Kennedy, Admiral Richard E. Byrd, General Douglas MacArthur, to name a few. It was opening night, the Academy Awards, and a mysterious adventure each time a Clipper landed. The rich, the famous, and the adventurous were instantly recognized or were eager to tell reporters who they were. Those who shied away from publicity and weren't airline families or employees often were those who needed to keep their identities hidden—diplomats on special missions, spies, American Volunteer Group pilots for China, refugees not wishing to endanger those left behind.

Some of Pan American Airways' popular employees became notorious after their Clippering days were over. Charles "Bebe" Rebozo fell into this category. A self-made millionaire, Rebozo (1912–1998) became the classic rags-to-riches story. Who would have thought that this youthful chicken plucker and son of a Cuban cigar-maker would rise to be President Richard M. Nixon's official and only friend, drinking buddy, investment advisor, and real estate broker? During the Watergate investigations, Rebozo's contacts and business dealings came under close scrutiny. As president of the Key Land Company and chief officer for the Key Biscayne Bank, he was accused of being Nixon's bagman, his money launderer, his tie to the mob, his payoff go-between to Howard Hughes, and Nixon's tie to the Cuban intelligence community. Finally he became the subject for cinema, with Dan Hedaya playing the part of Rebozo in Oliver Stone's *Nixon*.

At the age of seventeen Rebozo went to work for Pan American Airways as a steward. He actually predated the Clippers by flying on PAA's first trimotor Fokkers from Florida to Havana. When the first of the flying boats came along, he became a steward on them and flew with pilots such as Ed Musick. Since Clippers were considered ships, Rebozo wore a uniform modeled after that worn by stewards on the great ocean liners of the time—black pants, white shirt, white waist jacket, black tie, white garrison hat. Duties included attending to the creature comforts of passengers, pointing out sights along the way, keeping drunks in their seats, helping passengers through customs, and helping those crossing the Equator for the first time to be initiated into the esteemed order of "Condors."

After a few years of flying out of Florida, Rebozo quit to open his own gas station and tire recapping business before going into real estate. As World War II closed in on the United States, Rebozo learned how to fly and bought a Piper Cub. In 1943 he returned to Pan American Airways, where he trained to be a navigator. PAA had organized a ferry service to transport warplanes across the Atlantic to where they were needed. Rebozo, who became part of this effort, ferried about one hundred warplanes from the United States to North Africa. After twice working for the airline, he returned to lucrative real estate.

He met newly elected Senator Nixon in 1950, when he was asked to take Nixon fishing on his 33-foot Chriscraft, *Cocolobo*. Nixon did not care for fishing, so he worked out of his briefcase during the outing. Rebozo reported that they probably did not exchange more than twenty words the entire day, yet out of this the friendship grew between these two children of the Depression born only two months apart. Though Rebozo thought Nixon very strange, he remained quietly loyal to him, and Nixon returned the friendship. What other private non-elected citizen had his own suite at the White House? Nixon trusted Rebozo to pick out the movies his family viewed. Rebozo funded the bowling alley for the White House. He bought a house, then rented it to Julie Nixon and her husband, David Eisenhower. Nixon and Rebozo swam together—and drank together, much to the consternation of Henry Kissinger, who commented on the president's slurred speech after Nixon's meetings with Rebozo.

Rebozo was the only outsider in the Ambassador Hotel in Los Angeles with Nixon the night he learned he had lost the election to John F. Kennedy in 1960. The election had been particularly ugly, with both parties trying to dig up maximum dirt on the opponent. Just when the Democrats were ready to report that Nixon had attended parties at Rebozo's mansion that included prostitutes, they found that Kennedy had done the same thing. The story was quickly dropped, but the infamous Watergate case and Nixon's subsequent resignation catapulted Rebozo into the limelight.

When *Newsday* began reporting how Nixon had reaped a small fortune from Rebozo's Fisher Island real estate deals in Florida, the infuriated Nixon barred *Newsday* reporters from accompanying him on any foreign trips. Despite all the accusations of shady dealings and crime contacts, Rebozo was never convicted of any crimes, yet he has remained a name forever linked to that landmark event in U.S. history. Before his death of a brain aneurysm in 1998, Rebozo reclaimed some of the romance of his old flying boat days by purchasing a twin engine Republic Seabee seaplane. When he substituted propellers of his own liking for safer, approved props, one of the blades sheared off and downed his plane near the Nixon compound at Key Biscayne. This crash put him in the hospital for eight months. When he died, the last surviving dolphin to play Flipper on the TV show of the same name also died. The dolphin's name: Bebe.

A colorful World War II flight engineer on the Clippers to Africa, Asia, and South America, Bill Haast appeared on such programs as *60 Minutes*, the PBS series *Nature* and the classic TV animal show, Marlin Perkins' *Zoo Parade*. Haast had two major goals in life: to work for Pan American Airways and to collect venomous snakes. He first took a job in the 1920s with a Floridian who owned a traveling roadside snake show for tourists. When the Depression killed that business, Haast worked as a moonshiner in the Everglades, where he collected his own snakes. He realized both goals at once during World War II when PAA finally did hire him. This gave him a chance to fly to regions of the world where the most poisonous snakes could be found. His smuggling of snakes past customs agents led other wary but bemused Clipper crew members to call him Dr. Hisst instead of Dr. Haast.

The money he made working for Pan American made it possible for him to open the Miami Serpentarium after the war. Here he milked sometimes as many as 100 poisonous snakes a day for their venom in order to produce anti-venom. Haast was bitten so many times, nearly 200, that his own blood came to be used as anti-venom. His serpentarium grew to be a celebrated tourist stop featured on Florida tourism postcards and brochures.

Another famous ex–Pan Am employee, Gene Roddenbury, left perhaps an unrivaled mark on American and world popular culture. The creator of *Star Trek* did not pilot flying boats during World War II, but he did fly B-17 bombers out of what was to become Henderson Field on Guadalcanal. For his service and valor, Roddenbury received the Distinguished Flying Cross and Air Medal. After completing eighty-nine missions, he returned to the States and took a job with Pan American Airlines when the war ended. As third officer on the Clipper Eclipse, he would demonstrate heroism again in June 1947.

The Eclipse was a Constellation, a land-based aircraft Pan Am used to replace the flying boats on international routes at the close of World War II. On June 18, 1947, the Clipper was on its way back to the U.S. from Karachi on its inaugural westward flight of round-the-world service when one of its four engines began to overheat and had to be shut down. This required the plane to divert to Baghdad, but since it was early morning, no one answered the Eclipse's radio calls at the Baghdad airport. With that airport shut down, the next closest alternate was Damascus. Before they could reach that new destination, another engine caught fire and fell off, and a fire started on the wing. When the plane crash-landed in the Syrian desert sand, the cabin split open back of the wings, and the cockpit and galley were completely engulfed in flames. No one survived in those forward areas. Passengers sitting where the cabin split died instantly or shortly thereafter. Both captain and co-pilot were killed. Out of the thirty-six on board, fourteen died.

Roddenbury, who had been deadheading on the flight, had left the cockpit to see to the passengers just before the crash. Suddenly finding himself as senior officer, he organized the evacuation of survivors, some of whom were too scared to leave the burning plane. He and other crew members pulled survivors and supplies from the wreckage. He sent two Englishmen to swim across the Euphrates to investigate a light in hopes of help. The remaining passengers and crew could survive at night in the desert, but water would run out quickly once the sun came up. When some

Bedouin showed up on camels and horses, purser Anthony Volpe was able to converse with them enough in French to ask them to go for help, too.

After spending the night in the desert, the next morning the group was able to shoot up a flare to attract the attention of a Syrian Air Force squadron out on a training mission. One of the planes landed, whereupon Roddenbury gave the pilot a note about their predicament and asked that it be taken to the nearest base. As the sun's rays became more intense, the injured were placed in the life raft they had saved from the Eclipse and covered with a nylon cover. Towards midday, a column of jeeps and trucks came to their rescue. In the true American hero tradition of modesty and professionalism, Roddenbury in his crash report asked that his remaining crew members, purser Volpe and flight attendant Jane Bray, both be cited for valor, courage, and merit just as would someone in the military. Roddenbury received a Civil Aeronautics commendation for risking his own life to save others.

Roddenbury's love affair with Pan American and the flying boat tradition shows up in the *Star Trek* movies and television series. Captain Kirk's starship *Enterprise* and other starships of the United Space Federation carried "NC," or civilian aircraft designation, like the Clipper flying boats, and Roddenbury's fictional craft were certainly referred to as "ships" and not airplanes. The original flying boat Clippers were named after sailing ships; so, too, were some of the starships, particularly the *Enterprise* itself. Nautical terminology was used for both the Pan Am Clippers and Roddenbury's creations—starboard, port, "you have the helm, Mr. Sulu," "arm photon torpedoes." Roddenbury's crews were uniformed and had a naval chain of command like that of Pan American Airways, if not more so. Captain Kirk reported to various admirals. At least Pan Am had a president in Juan Trippe instead of an admiral. The crew of the *Enterprise* and other starships that followed and cadets at the Federation Starship Academy came from across the galaxy. Pan American recruited across international lines. Echoing Pan Am's ambiguous wartime roles, Kirk, Uhuru, Sulu, Chekov, Bones, and Spock found themselves walking the fine line between being thrust into military roles and serving scientific and diplomatic functions. Both China Clipper and *Enterprise* carried celebrities, secretive passengers, strange creatures, and dangerous cargoes, and each was sometimes diverted on humanitarian missions or faced with having their own technology fall into the wrong hands.

Through name, some people became associated with the Clipper without having anything to do with the seaplane. Such was the case in sports, a human activity always requiring instant celebrities or heroes. Such was particularly the case in Canadian hockey. Larry "China Clipper" Kwong (born Eng Kai Geong) became the first person of Asian ancestry to break into the National Hockey League. Born in Canada on June 17, 1923, he came of age at the same time as the flying Clippers. In 1941 the talented teenager tried out for the Trail, BC, "Smoke Eaters" hockey team, who were given jobs at the "smoky" local smelter during the day so they could play hockey at night. All but Larry Kwong. Even though his father had lived in Canada for forty-three years and Larry had been born in Canada, prejudice banned him from working at the smelter and his family from voting. He could work as a bellboy at a local hotel, which he did. The next year during the war he played for the Nanaimo, BC, "Clippers" of the senior city league at night while he built minesweepers during the day. Then he played for a Vancouver team before enlisting in the army.

After the war, New York reporters dubbed Kwong with Hollywood movie epithets, "China Clipper" and "King Kwong." Undersized but skillful, he became the toast of Chinatown as he played for the New York Rangers' farm team. Since childhood, when he listened to hockey games on radio, his great dream had been to play in the NHL. This dream was realized when he was called up to play for the Rangers against the Montreal Canadians on the Canadians' home ice against the great Rocket Richard. Unfortunately, the China Clipper only played for a minute, but he had played in the NHL. Later he would go on to play hockey in Britain and Switzerland, and to become the subject of a documentary movie.

Another China Clipper would eclipse his notoriety. Normie Kwong, whose older family members also were Cantonese immigrants to Canada, starred in the Canadian Football League and was known as the China Clipper. Ironically, his name, not Larry Kwong's, is found etched on hockey's Stanley Cup, since Normie Kwong was co-owner of the Calgary Flames, 1989 Stanley Cup champions. The China Clipper name fit these athletes well, not just because of their speed or athletic prowess, but also because the name represented a meeting of East and West, a blending of the Chinese with the West's Clipper creation. At a time when race relations were strained during World War II, being able to connect oneself to Chinese rather than Japanese descent and being able to connect oneself to an American sport could cut through some of the prejudice. Having a name that echoed that other "Clipper," Joe DiMaggio, gave bonus points. The United States may have had Joe Dimaggio as its Yankee Clipper, but other countries had their Clippers as well.

The overriding sports figure connected to the Clipper remains DiMaggio since he was so publicly named after the Pan American Airways' Yankee Clipper. Cereal maker Wheaties hired Baseball Hall of Fame announcer Arch "The Old Pine Tree" McDonald to broadcast the first New York Yankees game on radio in 1939, the same year New York was all abuzz over the PAA's Yankee Clipper's flying from New York to open the Atlantic route to Europe. As the highest paid sportscaster of the time, making even more than Joltin' Joe, McDonald called DiMaggio the "Yankee Clipper." The nickname stuck forevermore.

Another sports Joe was also paired with the Clipper. The March 1940 issue of the boxing and wrestling magazine *The Ring* showed Heavyweight Champion of the World Joe "The Brown Bomber" Lewis in a crouch in front of a world globe with the Yankee Clipper soaring overhead. Lewis had just won *The Ring*'s Boxing Merit Award again. As the Yankee Clipper brought Atlantic rim nations closer together, with war already raging in Europe, Joe Louis had been the United States' protector by beating Hitler's Max Schmeling in 1938, thus damaging perceived Nazi superiority. While Louis was dispatching Schmeling in barely over two minutes of the first round, that same year the Jesse Clipper Post 430 of the American Legion was erecting a monument in Buffalo, New York, to honor African Americans who died in wars. Corporal Jesse Clipper, 33, was the first black soldier to die in World War I. Now many men of many colors would be going to bear arms again, including Lewis. Both Clipper flying boat and Lewis were the best in the world, at the height of their iconic powers.

The two most important personages to receive Clipper flight coverage were Franklin Delano Roosevelt and Winston Churchill, who used Clippers to meet each other in World War II. Though their Clipper missions had to be kept secret before departure, afterwards their trips received full news treatment. Clippers helped change history and helped transform the presidency into a global office.

Prior to FDR's Clipper flight to the Casablanca conference, no U.S. president had flown while in office. It was considered just too dangerous. Even in 1943, the Secret Service still felt air travel was too risky. But on January 9, 1943, a train carrying the president pulled out of Washington and headed north as if going to Hyde Park. When it reached Baltimore, with blacked out windows it doubled back south and headed for Miami and the Clipper base.

The Clipper crew did not know the names of its passengers, since the passenger manifest only identified them by number. When the Clipper reached Port of Spain, a man wearing leg braces hobbled on two canes into the Clipper's lounge. Only then did crew realize who passenger #1 was. FDR's advisor, Harry Hopkins, and Admirals Leahy and McIntire followed. This represented the first time a U.S. president had left the country during wartime. As soon as the Dixie Clipper took off across the southern Atlantic route for Africa, it in effect became the first Air Force One.

After FDR met Churchill, de Gaulle, and generals Eisenhower and Patton in Casablanca, the Clipper brought the president back. Fulfilling a special presidential request, Captain Cone brought the Clipper in low over Henri Christophe's mountainous castle, the Citadel, in Haiti, which Roosevelt recalled from his days as assistant navy secretary. The crew also broke out caviar and champagne so that Roosevelt could celebrate his sixty-first birthday in the clouds. To cap it off, the crew gave him a donation to his favorite charity, the Infantile Paralysis Fund, and Cone inducted FDR into the Short Snorters Club of Ocean Travelers by handing him a dollar bill signed by all the other passengers. As the country's most well known stamp collector, Roosevelt could now say he had flown on one of the Clippers whose first flight envelopes adorned his collection. The public around the world had sent him envelopes carried on each new route the Clippers had opened while FDR was in office.

Winston Churchill really enjoyed Clipper flying, so much so that he, too, went against the wishes of his protectors. They advised him to travel back and forth across the Atlantic using Britain's pride, the Royal Navy. The Prime Minister convinced himself that being torpedoed by a German submarine offered a greater menace than being shot down in the air. Once Churchill discovered the luxury in the air afforded by the three Clipper ships Pan Am had turned over to Britain, the Clipper's speed and accommodations trumped the battleships. On one of his several Clipper trips to meet with FDR, it also helped that he was given the thrill of sitting at the controls of one of the Clippers. Photos of him enjoyably sitting in the cockpit chewing on his cigar were published around the world.

His Clipper bravado almost proved his undoing. Upon flying back from the Arcadia Conference in January of 1942, when he met with U.S. and Canadian officials, his Clipper was blown off course when approaching the British Isles. Its course adjusted, it appeared to be coming in from Axis air space, causing the RAF to scramble Hurricane fighters to intercept and shoot down the intruder. Luckily, either the Clipper, which had been renamed the Berwick, landed at Plymouth before the fighters arrived or it had given proper identification, thus canceling the intercept. Churchill humorously reported afterwards that the RAF "had failed in their mission." Earlier, Churchill shocked the docking crew at Botwood, Newfoundland, when, with cigar fully lit he stepped from the fumes under the Clipper's wing tank, which was laden with aviation fuel. Onlookers did not dare say anything to the great man as they gritted their teeth for the explosion.

Some people have said that Churchill invented the seaplane. Actually, he took pride in having coined the word *seaplane* and popularizing it in the English language. Before Churchill invented the term, Clipper predecessors that could land on water were called water-planes or hydroplanes. When he was First Lord of the Admiralty before World War I, and Secretary of State for War and Air during World War I, he championed seaplanes for the Royal Navy, arguing for the expansion of seaplane forces, and flying at various military bases whenever he had the chance. It was unusual for a man over the age of forty to take lessons on the road to receive his pilot's license, but Churchill persevered. In 1913 he took his first seaplane ride with Tommy Sopwith, designer of the illustrious World War I Sopwith Camel, which was considered one of the best fighter aircraft. (Comic strip artist Charles Schultz brought popular culture fame to the Camel in the United States. His long-running syndicated comic strip featured Snoopy in his Sopwith being shot down again and again by the dreaded Red Baron: "Curse you, Red Baron!")

Churchill also cursed his own crash in 1919 at Croydon Aerodrome. After his close call with death when the plane he was piloting plunged to the ground, he avoided flying, despite his love for aviation. The safe, luxurious Clipper renewed the Prime Minister's love of flying after a long hiatus.

Finally, we come to a special case of heroes, the Shadow Heroes, or spooks, who worked for Pan American Airways during the Clipper era. Devoted to preserving democracy by working for Pan American Airways, the CIA, and its predecessors, these heroes lived their lives as they died—in anonymity. Perhaps their stories will never come close to being known due to their clandestine activities, but some information has been surfacing about two legendary figures, George Doole and Jimmy Walker.

Little was said about George Doole in the many books written about Pan American Airways and its pilots. He was certainly a Pan Am pioneer on the earliest Caribbean routes. Captain Horace Brock, in *Flying the Oceans*, recalled his first meeting with Doole in 1931, when Brock piloted a Commodore flying boat into Panama. Captain Doole flew the airplane shuttle ferrying passengers back and forth over the Panama Canal between Cristobal and Panama City, which he called the Critty-Pitty-Critty run (54). Doole also flew the Guatemala to Panama route, all of this after he had gained a commission in the army, where he learned to fly. After 1931 his activities become less clear.

We do know he rose in the ranks to operations manager in the Middle East for Pan Am and was active in airline development, so much so that, as Marylin Bender and Selig Altschul pointed out in *The Chosen Instrument: Pan Am, Juan Trippe, The Rise and Fall of an American Entrepreneur*, prominent Lebanese businessmen approached Doole for Pan Am's assistance in creating the regional carrier, Middle East Airlines (481). This occurred in 1945 just before Pan American lost its airline subsidiaries in China to the Nationalists and what would become CIA proprietaries. The state department cleared Pan American to create MEA in Lebanon as a way of extending U.S. influence into the Middle East. As he straddled roles between Pan Am and the CIA, the State Department also pressed him to persuade Pan Am to buy a half share of the Afghan airline, Ariana, in 1956. Soon Doole was working wholly for an employer other than Pan Am.

Though his non–Pan Am employer denied his payroll existence, Evergreen International Aviation of McMinnville, Oregon, made no secret about the revered member of their board. Inside an Evergreen hangar, a.k.a. the George A. Doole Aviation Center in Marana, Arizona, between Tucson and Phoenix, a plaque was placed after his death in 1985. The plaque honored Doole as the founder, CEO, and board director for Air America Inc. After retiring from the CIA in 1971, Doole kept his hand in by serving on the board of Evergreen, another airline involved in clandestine missions. Most of his former Pan American coworkers did not know he headed the CIA's covert operations for "Shy" Airlines, which shied from publicity but was known as "the most shot at airline in the world." From his Washington office, he ran all of the CIA's airlines around the world. At one point during the 1960s Air America was the largest airline in the world, outnumbering the rest of the CIA's stated number of employees. When his airlines became too successful at making money, CIA Director of Operations Richard Helms feared the airline would draw too much attention to itself in the press. Thus when Helms became head of the CIA, Doole was moved from his job of running the CIA's airlines and was promoted to assistant to the director of operations. Though he became well known to Washington insiders and foreign dignitaries along Embassy Row, few outside that elite group knew of Doole, and those who did, did not know what he did. That he kept vague to the grave.

Though he died somewhat anonymously, the efforts of the people under this ex–Pan American Airways pioneer live on in popular culture. One of the most striking pieces of film footage from the Vietnam War, still shown on most documentaries, captured the helicopter evacuation of people from the rooftop of the U.S. Embassy in Saigon during the fall of Saigon. While those lucky enough to escape on the choppers to waiting ships offshore seemed to have been rescued by the military helicopters, those aircraft belonged to Doole's Air America. Another of Doole's legacies resided in the cultural mix of people in the United States. Some U.S. cities contain populations of Hmong. The CIA recruited the Hmong to fight the communists in the secret war in Laos when the "domino theory" of communist aggression held sway in Washington. Air America evacuated many of these people in order to save them, and some Air America pilots fought on their own to bring Hmong to the United States.

Another unsung shadow hero, James W. Walker, Jr., rose through the Clipper ranks to end up working for Doole. Jimmy Walker became vice president of flying operations for Air Asia Company, Ltd., the Taipei subsidiary of Air America during the critical war years in Laos and Vietnam. Walker moved from being operations manager for Pan American Airway's Latin American Division to operations manager for the CIA's organization in Taiwan.

While Walker's CIA career events remain somewhat cloaked, his Clipper career contained illustrious achievements. He served as navigator on the first Clipper survey flight across the Atlantic from Baltimore to Marseilles in 1939 before regular service began. The Clipper nearly stalled once and just avoided crashing. Weather was so bad upon reaching France that the Clipper had to divert to a lake rather than risk landing at the harbor in Marseilles. Despite the difficulties, Walker still managed to sneak in a quick side trip to Cannes.

Walker achieved the rank of Pan Am Master Ocean Pilot, flying Clippers during the 1940s on both Pacific and Atlantic routes. Though lacking seniority, his skills led him to become the youngest elevated to chief pilot, serving at the Miami base in the 1940s. By 1944, he attained the position of head of the Latin American division. In this position he revolutionized world airline standards by instituting a written system of cockpit checklists. Prior to that, more informal oral checklists had been used, but the Walker system averted many tragedies. His system can still be seen played out in aviation movies and television programs today. After enforcing this written checklist, Pan American no longer had amphibion aircraft cracking up from landing on runways with gear up, or amphibians landing on water with gear down.

Walker also proved what he was made of when tragedy struck. On January 8, 1945, the China Clipper, remaining survivor of the three Martin Clippers, was destroyed at Port of Spain, Trinidad. On its way to Africa, the China Clipper slammed into the water, ripped apart, and sank in thirty feet of water while attempting a night landing. Having survived the war and having been returned from the navy and restored to her original colors, the China Clipper touched everyone's heart. This was a special flight, its first passenger flight after having been returned to Pan Am, and this was not the way the career was to have ended for the plane whose name become synonymous with all the Martin Clippers. Worse, people had died.

Along with some others from the Miami office, Walker jumped into a DC-3 to fly immediately to the crash site. Upon arriving and learning that bodies were still trapped inside the sunken plane, Walker stripped off his clothes and began diving through the gasoline covered water, bringing up two bodies for every one the locals retrieved. Many of the corpses were those of children, probably missionary children returning to Congo. Four of the eighteen passengers were rescued and did survive. Nine of twelve crew members somehow lived. When Walker visited them in the hospital, the survivors' lungs had taken in so much gasoline that no one dared ignite the fumes by lighting a cigarette or even turning a fan or light switch on or off.

Doole and Walker lacked the press or Hollywood exposure of most Clipper heroes and celebrities, but they considerably affected world events and culture. The same held true for others whose names, untold heroism, and celebrity status among those who knew them best do not appear here.

3
Hollywood: Clippers Go to the Movies

Even before motion pictures and flying boats were invented, the theatrical world in the United States claimed ties to the Clippers. Almost as soon as New England began building tall-masted Clipper sailing ships, *The New York Clipper* began publication, in 1853, to cover sporting and theatrical news. In the twentieth century, it billed itself as "The Oldest Theatrical Journal in America," merging with *Variety* in 1924. Many stars of stage and screen found their first jobs by reading *The Clipper.* Some made the jump from reading *The Clipper* to playing characters who flew the Clipper.

Broadway first embraced the shrinking world created by Clippers in Elmer Rice's *Flight to the West,* considered at the time to be one of the best dramas produced in 1940–1941. Brooks Atkinson, drama critic for *The New York Times,* declared Rice's original work "the most absorbing American drama of the season." Before writing *Flight to the West,* Rice had already distinguished himself by winning a Pulitzer Prize. As regional director of the New York Federal Theater Project, he, like many other playwrights and directors, became increasingly political and socially conscious with his themes. *Flight to the West* competed that season with such plays as Paul Green and Richard Wright's *Native Son,* Joseph Kesselring's *Arsenic and Old Lace,* and Lillian Hellman's *Watch on the Rhine.* Playbills for the Playwrights' Company production of Rice's play prominently displayed a Clipper.

This anti-fascist play took place aboard a Clipper on its way into New York from Europe. The Clipper carried people escaping from the Nazi menace as well as the menace itself. Europe's problems became America's problems whether isolationists liked it or not. The seven-scene melodrama followed one of the typical emerging plot formulas of the time: a white

American woman was involved with a man being chased by the Nazis, and the plot required an American willing to sacrifice himself to save the country from the European evil. Democracy was at stake. If the setting were changed to Rick's Bar in the movie *Casablanca* instead of the "plot-in-a-bottle" confines of the Clipper, Rice's play and the movie would not be very dissimilar. Both productions coaxed American involvement in European conflict by way of romantic involvement.

The stellar cast went on to Broadway, Hollywood, and television fame. Betty Field, who became Rice's wife, played the female lead. Rice later wrote vehicles just for her. Hugh Marlowe, who earlier had worked as a radio announcer with Ronald Reagan at WOC in Davenport, Iowa, went on to become known as television's Ellery Queen and Jim Matthews on the daytime serial *Another World*. A young Karl Malden also played his part aboard the Clipper. Malden became famous for a host of movie, television, and ad appearances, notably television's *Streets of San Francisco* and his "Don't Leave Home Without It" ads for American Express.

The *Flight to the West* actor whose popularity especially soared as a result of this Broadway appearance was Paul Henreid, who was making

Clothiers Rogers Peet Company used the Clipper idea in the programs for Elmer Rice's *Flight to the West*.

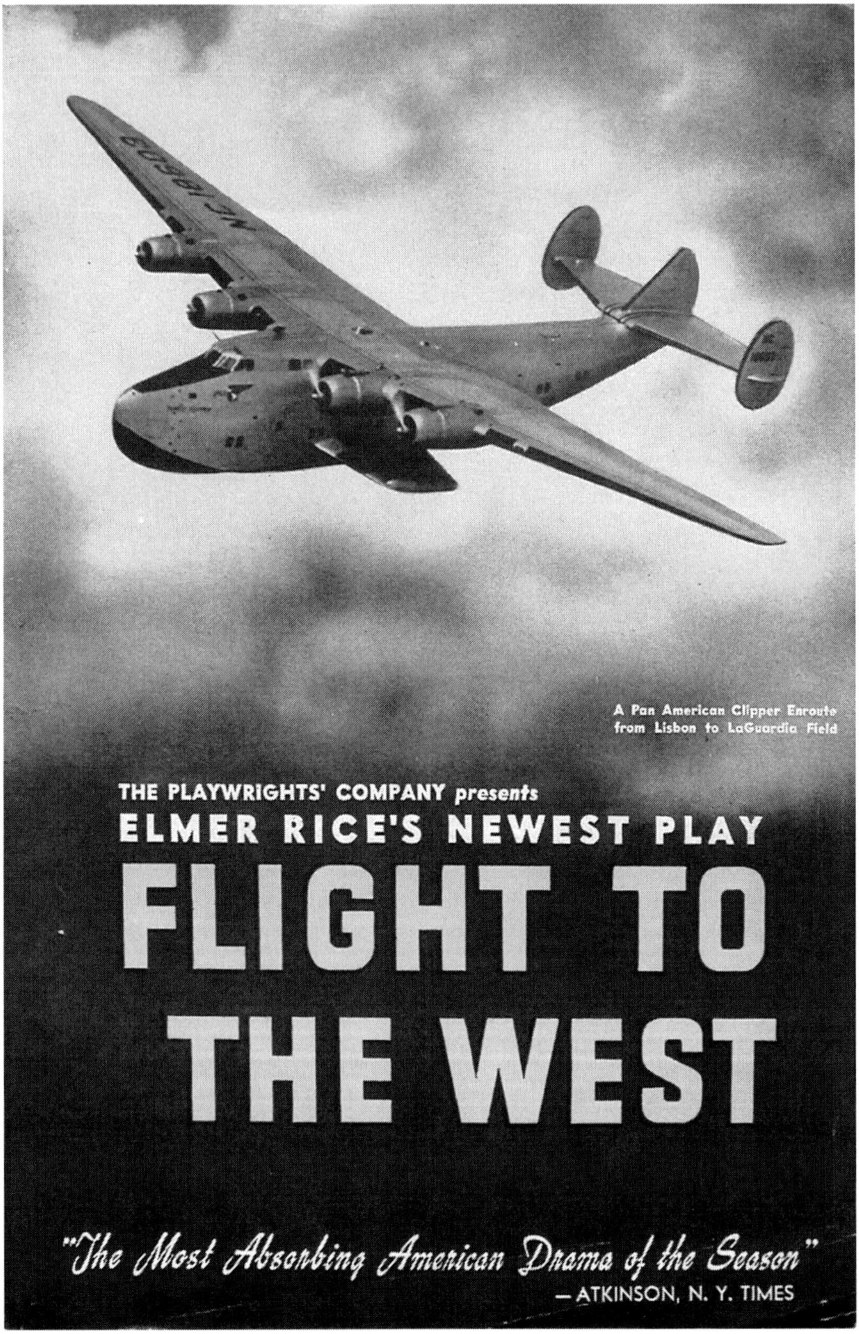

New York program cover for Elmer Rice's play *Flight to the West*.

his Broadway debut in the United States. As a result of his performance, RKO signed the Austrian refugee to a Hollywood contract. In short order, he found himself again with the Clippers in the motion picture *Casablanca*, again as a European refugee in the character of Victor Laszlo. Henreid's Laszlo would help establish one of the classic scenes in all filmdom when he led the customers of Rick's Café in singing the *Marseillaise*, and in doing so, drowned out German officers singing *Die Wacht am Rhein*.

The popularity of *Flight to the West* spread across the United States. Community and college theaters staged productions. In 1941 the theater department of the University of Arizona planned a production with a dress rehearsal for servicemen at the nearby Davis-Monthan Air Field in Tucson. As technicians arranged the lighting and scenery, the show was canceled. The base suddenly went on full alert. Real Clippers were being fired upon out in the Pacific while Pear Harbor burned. It was December 7. Time for mobilization and time for Hollywood.

Given the dynamism of their image, Clippers have enjoyed a long movie run. The actor most associated with the Clippers has been Humphrey Bogart. In that classic "Here's looking at you, kid" mist-shrouded

Lobby card showing Humphrey Bogart in the *China Clipper* (1936).

Lobby card showing Pat O'Brien and Beverly Roberts in the *China Clipper* (1936).

scene from *Casablanca*, Rick (Bogart) put Ilsa (Ingrid Bergman) on the plane to Lisbon, where she and freedom-fighter Victor Laszlo (Paul Henreid) would catch the Clipper for their flight to freedom to the United States. Earlier in the film, prefect of police Louis Renault (Claude Rains) stood with Rick as a Lisbon-bound plane roared over the bar:

> RENAULT: You would like to be on it?
> RICK: Why? What's in Lisbon?
> RENAULT: The Clipper to America.

The romance of the Clippers will forever be tied up in the world of international intrigue and passage to safety and freedom. Shadowy figures, spies, and diplomats who kept their identities hidden flew both ways across the ocean. Clippers served as a lifeline for European refugees during World War II. Like Laszlo and Ilsa, many fled with only what they could carry—often hidden, items such as jewelry that could be converted into currency or letters of transit, legal or illegal, as were those taken from murdered German couriers by Guillermo Ugarte (Peter Lorre) in *Casablanca*.

Talk about perfect timing. In a twist of fate, the *Casablanca* fictional Clippers became entwined with the historical Clippers. *Casablanca* was rushed into a quick release in New York on Thanksgiving Day 1942, a mere three weeks after the Allied landing in the North African city of Casablanca, and just a week before the first anniversary of the attack on Pearl Harbor. (*Casablanca* took place in early December 1941, just days before the attack, and the movie made oblique reference to how the U.S. "slept.") The public was primed for this motion picture. President Roosevelt watched a special screening on December 31 at the White House. Afterwards, in January, Roosevelt secretly flew on the Clipper to the Casablanca Conference to meet Churchill, DeGaulle, and Henri Giraud and to break off treaties with Vichy-France, just as Rick and Renault did at the end of *Casablanca* when a bottle of Vichy water was symbolically thrown in the garbage can at the airport as Rick and Renault began the start of a "wonderful friendship" working for the Free French.

Bogart's acting career tied even more closely to the Clippers when he played a character based on Pan American Airways' most famous Clipper pilot, Edwin Musick, in *China Clipper* (1936). Though not well known today, *China Clipper* played to packed houses in 1936. In another twist, Bogart and Musick looked much alike. And like Bogart's on-screen persona, particularly Richard "Rick" Blaine in *Casablanca*, Musick was an unassuming man of few words, who meant what he said, often with ironic humor. Also like Rick or Bogart, Musick the idealist masqueraded as a pragmatist, demanded perfection of himself, was known for occasional profanity, and had some shadows in his past such as working outside the law as a rum-runner. Rick made money running a bar; Musick had flown illegal booze from offshore to speak-easy bars.

In this early Bogart movie, Bogey did not play the main role, however. That fell to Pat O'Brien, who starred as the leader of the airline, a character loosely based on Pan American Airways' Juan Trippe. O'Brien played the part of Dave Logan, founder of Transoceanic Airline. According to the script, Logan would risk his marriage to his wife Jean (Beverly Roberts) and risk his old flying friendship with Hap Stewart (Bogart) in his drive to create an airline across the Pacific. In keeping with the time it was filmed, the movie was filled with the greased hair, cigarettes, and the use of the word *swell* in what seemed like every sentence. Pan American Airways cooperated with the filming so that the movie contains vintage shots of the China Clipper and other PAA aircraft, including early trimotors and rare views of Douglas Dolphin amphibions that PAA used in China. Crews were allowed to film at Pan American bases, particularly at Alameda, California, and PAA provided its stock promotional film footage to be spliced into the movie. The Dave Logan character may have run Transoceanic Airlines, but the aircraft in the movie all bore "Pan American Airways System" and the PAA winged globe. For the Clipper aficionado, this movie was just "swell" for shots of the China Clipper in flight. Clipper models were also used to create scenes where the Bogart character would have to fly at night through fog or typhoons.

Merchandising products tied to movie releases are nothing new, and *China Clipper* showed how far that could be taken in 1936. The same month that the motion picture opened across the country, Quaker Oats Company advertisements ran in newspapers nationwide. The company's ad for Quaker Puffed Wheat included what was called "A Minute Movie with Pat O'Brien and Beverly Roberts Appearing in *China Clipper.*" Six movie stills, complete with what appeared to be film sprocket holes on their borders, told a story entitled "Trial Flight." The Clipper captain was grumpy because he thought a woman newspaper reporter tagging along on a trial flight of the Clipper would bring bad luck. Instead, she brought good luck when she found Puffed Wheat in the galley and served it to the captain. This alleviated his grumpiness so well that he would have liked more of her company. Cereal love. Puffed rice rather than puffed wheat would have been more appropriate for the nuptials.

The other half of the page across from this romantic playlet "with the stars of *China Clipper*" showed O'Brien in his China Clipper aviator's garb offering children a chance to send in Quaker Puffed Wheat or Rice box tops with a few cents for gifts of a balsa-wood China Clipper, aviation goggles, a pilot's cap, a pseudo-gold plated bracelet with wings and the child's initials, or a gold-plated wing pin or ring showing the China Clipper spanning the Pacific. Few people could miss seeing this movie's publicity, an early version of *Star Wars*–type product placement.

Frank "Spig" Wead penned the screenplay for *China Clipper* and several other aviation films in the 1930s. As a navy patrol pilot into the 1930s, he began to write only after being crippled from a fall down some stairs. Since many Clipper pilots also were drawn from the navy and were people he already knew, he naturally could write the script. As Bogart might say, and plenty of modern audiences have said, the film was "sappy." It did do what Pan American Airways' own advertising did, though: show American ingenuity and pluck. Like PAA, Wead made his own contribution to the war effort. It was he who came up with the idea for "pocket carriers." A pocket carrier was a quickly built ship composed of a flat deck welded on to the hull of a mass-produced Liberty ship to serve as a small aircraft carrier. Wead, a close friend of John Ford, would pen his own autobiography, *The Wings of Eagles* (1957), directed by Ford and starring John

Wayne, who considered Wead one of his heroes. Also starring was Maureen O'Hara, who would herself marry a flying boat captain, Charlie Blair of PAA's rival, American Export Airlines. Later, Blair and O'Hara would create their own Antilles Airline, using one of the last of the old flying boats, still hooked on the romance of the Clippers long after the war. Recently, O'Hara has been instrumental in supporting the creation of the flying boat museum in Foynes, Ireland, the Irish Atlantic terminal for the Clippers.

The dramatic story of the making of the *The China Clipper* marked milestones in cinematic popular culture. Because O'Brien and Bogart became megastars, the supporting cast was frequently overlooked, particularly Henry B. Walthall. *The China Clipper* proved to be his final performance. What happened to his character in the script eerily paralleled what happened to him at the time of the filming.

Walthall was one of the most popular stars, if not the most popular star, of early pre–World War I and World War I Hollywood, largely due to his starring role in D.W. Griffith's *The Birth of a Nation*. He became known as the Little Colonel through his portrayal of the gentlemanly Confederate officer, the hero of the film. Contemporary cigarette cards proclaimed that he had appeared in more movies and places and had become more popular than any other actor of his time. As well as acting in several Clara Bow and Lon Chaney films, he appeared in *Wings* (1927), the first motion picture to win an Academy Award. He successfully transitioned from the silents to the talkies, working with such rising stars as John Wayne, Spencer Tracy, Clark Gable, and Will Rogers.

In *China Clipper* Walthall played Dad Brunn, an engineer who designed the China Clipper and who was being pressured by Dave Logan (O'Brien) to meet a deadline at any cost. The grandfatherly Brunn pleaded for time off, as the demands were too much, but Logan refused. Brunn's doctor told him that his heart would give out if he continued, but he sacrificed himself so that the Clipper could fly from San Francisco to Macao to meet mail contract demands. The melodramatic script called for Brunn to die as the Clipper took off across the Pacific.

Walthall himself became very ill, collapsing on the set. Nevertheless, he persevered. A nurse was brought onto the set to sustain him through the filming, but he could not finish. Just as the O'Brien character literally killed Brunn in the movie, the movie literally killed Walthall. He died before his movie death scene could be filmed. Consequently, the script required changes. Instead of showing his death, the movie showed pilot Hap Stuart (Bogart) of the China Clipper being informed of Dad Brunn's death by telegram as the Clipper landed in Manila and faced a typhoon for the last leg into Macao. Hap Stuart of course punched the plane through the storm for Dad Brunn's honor. Bogart went on to fame while the public forgot Walthall. In the cruelty that can be Hollywood, Warner Brothers ungratefully dropped Walthall to tenth billing on the movie credits after his death.

He did not fall alone. Another cruel blow struck aspiring star Ross Alexander, who was on nearly equal acting footing with Bogart at the time. Like Bogart, he played a pilot in *The China Clipper*, but he was also co-owner of the fictional airline. Five weeks after the release of the film, Alexander, age 29, committed suicide.

The China Clipper actually got ahead of Pan American's timetable. The real airline meant to complete its route from California to China in 1935. It made it as far as Manila, but negotiations over landing rights in China stalled completion of the final leg between Manila and Hong Kong or Macao. The full route bridging the Pacific was not completed until 1937, although the 1936 movie showing completion of the route obviously banked on its being completed earlier. In this way, the movie could serve as both a fictional adventure movie and pseudo-documentary following real events. Pan American was credited with an achievement not yet realized.

Bombay Clipper (Universal, 1942) starring William Gargan and Irene Hervey prominently featured the clippers too. Following the typical Clipper story found in many magazines of the time, the plot centered on an attempted hijacking of a Clipper. In this case the hero and heroine went up against Nazi agents trying to stop $4 million in Indian diamonds headed for Great Britain. Much of the movie was shot on a set made to simulate the Clipper's interior. Publicity for this movie in the way of posters and lobby cards featured the newer, larger Boeing clippers rather than the earlier Martin or "China" clippers featured in *China Clipper*.

Another 1942 movie, *Tales of Manhattan*, experimented with following the history of a tailcoat through five episodes and different sets of owners. In the very first episode, Charles Boyer tried to seduce Rita Hayworth (already married to Charles Laughton) into running away with him by jumping on the Clipper to Rio. Directed by Julien Duvivier, the movie appeared the same year as the suave Frenchman Boyer took out U.S. citizenship. Duvivier was himself exiled from Europe like many French who escaped on the Clipper to the U.S. and Canada.

John Wayne, in *The Flying Tigers* in 1942, had another Clipper connection. At the beginning of this movie, pilots were quitting CBAC, a Chinese airline, to join the Tigers because Japanese Zeroes were shooting at their commercial aircraft. These men wanted to shoot back. CBAC was a stand-in for the actual CNAC. China National Aviation Corporation, spelled literally in Chinese as the "Middle Kingdom Space Machine Family," was Pan American's subsidiary in China that flew an assortment of aircraft, including Douglas and Leoning amphibions. These planes flew the interior Chinese routes to link with the Clippers in Hong Kong. Some pilots flew both CNAC amphibions and PAA Clippers, which in Chinese pidgin English were called, "topside rickshaw, coolie no got." In other words, Clippers carried people like a rickshaw in the air, yet magically had no coolies to pull it. Japanese attack planes did shoot up CNAC's flying rickshaws, and former PAA/CNAC personnel did fly for the Flying Tigers. Some continued to fly for CNAC, opening up the famous lifeline for China during the war by flying "the Hump" to India.

In the movie, Wayne uses a twin-engine transport to bomb Japanese bridges with nitroglycerine after the Japanese attack on Pearl Harbor. Typical of many WWII "enemy movies," the story was not so much about the Japanese enemy as about how Americans must be "team" players. The renegade independent good flier, emblematic of the America hero found in westerns and detective and adventure films, had to think even more of others. This posed one of the main problems in being an American hero. Independence and rugged individualism were cherished, yet at the same time concessions had to be made for the good of the whole—the same publicity problem Pan American Airways faced in portraying itself concurrently as an independent underdog commercial airline needing airmail subsidies yet the chosen instrument of the U.S. government's team.

In MGM's *Honolulu* (1939), Robert Young was to catch a Clipper to Hawaii to stop his double from marrying his sweetheart. Eleanor Powell was featured in the unlikely combination of tap dancing hula style while George Burns and Gracie Allen provided jokes. If you think the dancing was a bit confused, so were the Clippers in the PAA promotional footage that has been spliced into the movie. One Clipper departed San Francisco as a Martin M-130 China Clipper but landed in Honolulu as an earlier Sikorsky S-42. What's more, the spliced footage showed the S-42 landing in Biscayne Bay, Miami, Florida! Passenger transfer in mid-flight? And this in a movie that already contained doubles. No wonder Eleanor Powell was confused.

In another romantic comedy, *Lucky Partners* (1940), Ronald Colman wanted to go on a pre-honeymoon trip with Ginger Rogers, who, as in *Honolulu*, was planning on marrying another man. The Coleman character brought Rogers luck through a sweepstake ticket. Tacked on the wall of his room, a poster of a B-314 Clipper, complete with palm trees and Aloha girls at the beach, proclaimed "Overnight San Francisco–Hawaii."

Both Sikorsky and Martin Clippers appeared in *Now, Voyager* (1942) with Bette Davis, Paul Henreid, and Claude Rains. The movie showed a shot out of a window at Rio of the M-130 China Clipper. It also captured an S-42 Clipper taking off. Given the prohibition of showing sex on the screen, the love affair between the Davis character and a married man played by Henreid had to be suggested. This led to *Now, Voyager*'s classic and often imitated scene of Henreid's lighting two cigarettes together and then passing one to Davis. It wasn't flames suddenly roaring up in a fireplace, but who needed logs in Rio?

Clipper posters have not been restricted to theatre house movies either. In the 1990s popular *Seinfeld* television show, George Costanza, played by Jason Alexander, stayed in a New York apartment whose wall prominently displayed a large poster of the Yankee Clipper flying past the Statue of Liberty. Any time one of the women in another of his disastrous romances would storm out of his apartment, she would fly by the Clipper. Not only did it remind the audience that *Seinfeld* was supposed to have New York City as its locale, where Costanza was a New Yorker through and through (even working for George Steinbrenner of the New York Yankees), but it also served as a sight gag for all the comings and goings.

Nor was television advertising in the 1990s immune from the Clippers. Lender's Big and Crunchy Bagels ad campaign featured a B-314 clipper pulling a sign across the sky promoting its bagels. This ad appeared regularly during several programs and specials, including *Ed Sullivan's All Star Comedy Special*, which in the nineties was nearly as retro as the Clippers from the 1930s and 1940s.

Hollywood also brought Clippers back from the dead in *Flight from Ashiya* (1964), with Richard Widmark, Yul Brynner, and George Chakiris. In a flashback, the pregnant news correspondent lover of Widmark flew from Manila to Hong Kong on the China Clipper. A brief glimpse of the Hong Kong Clipper terminal appeared when he chased after her. Later, in present time, a Pan American World Airways 707 had to relay a message of an air rescue plane to Hong Kong and Ashiya.

Over the years clippers have appeared in many PAA promotional, travel, and other historical television and motion picture documentaries. Just to give one example, PBS aired *Hollywood: The Golden Years.* One segment dealt with Orson Wells and how he was sent to Rio to make films with Brazil for the U.S. government in an effort to counteract Nazi influence in South America. In short, he was sent to Rio to do what the U.S. government wanted PAA and the Clippers to do in Rio also. A short clip showed an S-42 and PAA yacht disembarking Wells' film crew in Rio. Later, Wells arrived on a PAA land plane.

In a survey of Clipper films, it would be remiss not to point out the

Seinfeld's George Costanza's apartment poster copied from a 1940's Clipper postcard.

two films that so far serve as the clippersorial bookends in time: *Flying Down to Rio* (RKO 1933) and the Harrison Ford adventure-revivalist *Raiders* films, such as *Raiders of the Lost Ark.* Pan American Airways cooperated with RKO for the filming of *Flying Down to Rio*, one of the early musical extravaganzas. The plot introduced Dolores Del Rio as Belinda Rezende, who wanted to fly from Miami to Port-au-Prince, Haiti. She bummed a ride with a playboy who owned a flying boat equipped with a piano, but she ended up in Rio. Rockettes performed high kicks on top of the aircraft's wings and pontoons, while Fred Astaire and Ginger Rogers made their debut together dancing the "Carioca" to the sounds of the Yankee Clipper Band. This made-for-movie dance became so popular that Brazilian Cariocas learned it to the point that most people believed the dance was the genuine Brazilian article. Though they were not the leads in this movie, Astaire and Rogers delivered. Their performance initiated their string of memorable musicals, and, as is so often said, the rest is history. PAA would adopt the lyrics of "Flying Down to Rio" as its own theme song for its Miami base.

As Rosalie Schwartz pointed out in *Flying Down to Rio: Hollywood, Tourists, and Yankee Clippers* (2004), former pilot Merian Cooper of *King Kong* fame served not only as production chief for RKO-Radio Pictures but also as board member for Pan American Airways at the very time the airlines faced a political problem. Its Yale board and political connections made PAA favored by Republican administrations. When FDR took office, the film industry and the airline faced Democratic hostility for either eroding values or being monopolistic. They were Old Deal, not New Deal. As luck would have it, the film and airline fit into Roosevelt's Good Neighbor Policy and its accompanying problems.

FDR wanted to sidestep one of Latin America's main bones of contention with the United States. Tariffs had always been a sticking point, while the U.S. proclaimed free trade. To take the spotlight off the issue, FDR wanted to refocus countries on the idea of tourism and transportation. *Flying Down to Rio* sold the idea of tourism (albeit vicarious for most people), transportation, and a positive view of the U.S. neighbors to the south. The airlines and movie industry both began using FDR slogans to further the bond, particularly with such words as "good neighbor." Amelia Earhart, who had the president's ear through her good friend Eleanor Roosevelt, had opened Pan Am's terminal at Havana's airport. That also helped. Thus when the movie opened for New York's Radio City Music Hall's 1933 Christmas show, more was going on than the huge crowds lined up in freezing weather knew.

In the movie, two lovers were married in the air by the captain of one of the flying Clippers. Following up on Roosevelt's concerns over the growing German and Italian influence in Latin America, the movie's joining of Roger from North America and Belinda from Latin America symbolically joined the two continents together, while defeating villainous "foreign" European influences. Therefore this musical escapism successfully tied Pan American Airways and politics together.

In the Indiana Jones *Raiders* movies, Harrison Ford's character "Indy" tied in nicely with that other American "(L)Indy," Charles Lindbergh, who helped pioneer Pan American Airways routes across the Pacific and Atlantic. Jones also flew on Clippers whenever he needed to cross the Atlantic or Pacific in search of adventure, tombs, the Ark of the Covenant, temples, and damsels in distress. The Clippers initially appeared in the first of the Indiana Jones trilogy, *Raiders of the Lost Ark* (1981). Though the flying boat shown in the movie was not one of Pan American's flying Clippers, it was the next best thing and captured the romance and luxury of the "Orient Express of the Air."

Director George Lucas was able to find a decrepit Solent Mark III flying boat in Oakland close to where the movie was being shot. Though landlocked and not flyable, with the help of matte, a false dock built around it, interposed shots of the actual Clipper base at nearby Treasure Island, and pans of water reflecting wave patterns on the undersurfaces of the wings, the plane looked as if it were in operation in the 1930s.

This aircraft, built by the British for military purposes near the end of World War II, had a past worthy of any adventure movie. Larger than the PAA clippers, the plane was converted to civilian use after the war. British Overseas Airways Corporation (BOAC) dubbed it the "City of Cardiff" in 1949 and assigned it to its Southampton, England, to South Africa route. This "Clipper" would fly to the Mediterranean, then the length of Africa to Vaaldam, South Africa, on the Vaal River about 58 miles from Johannesburg. Exotic water stops were enjoyed along the way, such as Luxor, Nairobi, Victoria Falls, Cairo. Camera, safari rifles, and plenty of money required—the same fate awaited the City of Cardiff as the Pan American Clippers. Larger land planes and airports phased out the African flying boats, but there was a place in the world where another era of flying boats seemed to be just beginning—Australia.

BOAC sold the *Raiders* flying boat to Trans Oceanic Airways of Australia in 1951. That the airline was called Trans Oceanic presented another Clipper tie-in. During World War II and the prewar years, many companies bragged in magazine advertisements about how they supplied parts to the Clippers; however, though they did not always want to give free publicity to Pan American Airways, they did want to use the image of the clipper. To get around this problem and trademark infringement, some companies advertising in such magazines as *Fortune* created paintings or drawings of Clippers and their bases using a fictitious airline called "Trans Oceanic Airways." As mentioned earlier, Bogart's *China Clipper* also used this then-fictitious airline name.

Trans Oceanic dreamed a great future for the Solent flying boat. The airline wanted to open up routes from Australia through various Pacific islands, such as New Guinea to Asia, but first the plane was used on the Sydney-Hobart, Tasmania, route, and at times, also flying to Port Moresby, Grafton, and Lord Howe Island. Bad luck and a series of mishaps on the airline led to its demise before the big dreams could be fulfilled.

As one dream died, another was born. The *Raiders* plane was sold to South Pacific Airlines (SPAL) in 1955 to tap what was hoped would be a lucrative tourist route between Honolulu and Tahiti. Like the clippers of old, it now flew under a U.S. flag and was poised to span the Pacific. What happened to Pan American's Clippers now replayed itself in this plane called the *Isle of Tahiti*. Pan American Airways had trouble in the 1930s gaining landing rights from the British in Hong Kong and on British-held stepping stones to New Zealand and Australia. SPAL faced the same problem. It needed Christmas Island as a refueling point to Tahiti. The British did not want to grant permission. Pan American was able to force the British to open Hong Kong and Singapore in the 1930s and 1940s to the Clippers because it threatened to use Portuguese-held Macao as an alternative Asiatic terminal, but SPAL had neither political clout nor another island to use as leverage. No wonder the British dragged their feet over granting landing privileges, for they successfully detonated their first hydrogen bomb at Christmas Island in 1957 a few months before the USSR launched Sputnik I. Just as World War II had overtaken the Clippers in the 1940s and ultimately ended their heyday, the Cold War and the Bomb overtook the SPAL "clipper" in the 1950s. The testing near Christmas Island killed any plans for using the island as a flying boat base for tourists unless they wanted to glow in the dark.

After the airline died, the master of aviation and Pacific intrigue, Howard Hughes, bought *Isle of Tahiti* and brought it to California. Always fascinated with flying boats, Hughes designed and built the famous Spruce Goose, a behemoth which still survives as a museum piece at the Evergreen Air Venture Museum in McMinnville, Oregon. Like the Clippers working on behalf of the U.S. government, Evergreen Air was known for its ties with the CIA and clandestine operations. When Hughes died, the *Isle of Tahiti* was sold to its current owners, who fortunately bought it for restoration purposes so that this "Clipper" may live on, perhaps forever, in *Raiders of the Lost Ark*.

The phenomenal success of Lucas's first *Raiders* film changed television minds. In 1979 ABC rejected a script for a series created by Donald Bellisario called *Tales of the Brass Monkey*. Producers argued that, because the series was set in the 1930s, it would not attract modern young audiences with little interest in history. Bellisario was told to update the setting and characters, which he was reluctant to do. Then came *Raiders* in 1981 and a burgeoning interest in 1930s superheroes and adventure tale revivals. Between 1982 and 1983, twenty-one episodes of the series aired, now under the title of *Tales of the Gold Monkey* rather than the brass monkey. Gold had more allure than brass, and there were already too many crude jokes about brass monkeys on cold nights.

The *Monkey*'s plots depended heavily on new characters flying into a Pacific Island on "Pan Pacific's" China Clipper for many of the episodes. Jake Cutter (Stephen Collins), the hero, owned a small Grumman amphibion called the Goose, which he used, when it wasn't broken down, to engage in adventures in the South Pacific. Jake's landing was right across from a larger Clipper landing dock. He was headquartered at Boragora, where the Monkey Bar was located, giving the series its name. Jake lived in an upstairs room of the bar run by French magistrate and freelance doctor Bon Chance Louie (Roddy McDowall). Before becoming an independent, Jake had copiloted the Clippers in the early 1930s, then had joined the Flying Tigers in 1937. He flew for them until wounds disqualified him from military flying. Corky (Jeff MacKay), his mechanic, also had worked on the Clippers as chief mechanic for PAA until a Clipper went down with his sister and her baby aboard. The crash was blamed on mechanical difficulties, so Corky had to quit the airline, after which he began to drink heavily. This information in the plot somewhat paralleled the actual loss of Pan American's Hawaii Clipper in 1938, especially since the Bellisario series was set in 1938. No one knew positively what happened to the Hawaii Clipper, dubbed the "Yangtze Clipper" in this series. Navy ships from Guam did spot an oil slick, but that was all. Other pilots blamed a typhoon in the area.

In *Tales of the Gold Monkey* the China Clipper landed each Wednesday at Boragora, and the Monkey Bar filled with passengers. Since Boragora lay close to the Japanese Mandate, plenty of Japanese and German spies arrived to join the usual cast of characters, with split allegiances already populating the islands around Boragora. Keeping an eye on them was Sarah (Caitlin O'Heaney), the love interest in the series. Working undercover as a torch singer in the Monkey Bar, Sarah was an American intelligence agent, whom Jake tried to help and often rescue. Also keeping an eye on visitors was Corky's dog, Jack. He literally kept *an* eye on them because he only had one eye and wore an eye patch, like an old pirate. Jake lost Jack's glass eye—an opal with a sapphire center—in a poker game, and now it floated, and sometimes rolled, from person to person throughout the islands. The appearance and disappearance of the eye provided a thread through the twenty-one episodes. At one point it fell into the hands of the Dragon Lady, Princess Koji (Marta DuBois).

Jake's Grumman amphibion resembled Pan American's "Baby" Clippers, and had other close ties to the famous flying boats. The television series' Grumman, *Cutter's Goose*, was a sister ship to one of two used by Pan American Airways in Africa and purchased from test pilot Boris Sergievsky. Along with Charles Lindbergh, Sergievsky tested the Clippers that Sikorsky built for Pan American Airways. He became famous, setting load and altitude records in the Clippers, and sometimes accompanied PAA's first flights in the Caribbean. PAA–Africa used the two for shuttle service between its Clipper base at Fisherman's Lake in Liberia and Roberts Field, the land base at the Firestone Rubber Plantation, about eighty miles southeast of the lake. During wartime, these civilian planes distinguished themselves by successfully engaging in search-and-rescue operations of downed military pilots along the West African Coast.

Louis L'Amour, best known for his western novels, used a Goose in his World War II pulp fiction stories of heroes with such masculine names as Turk Madden and Buck Rodd. Madden, a soldier of fortune, foreshadowed Jake. Out of the six stories it contained, the L'Amour collection, *Night Over the Solomons*, included four Madden/Goose stories: "Pirates with Wings," The Goose Flies South," "Tailwind to Tibet," and "Wings over Khabarovsk." If the story of the Clippers could not be told during wartime, L'Amour made sure the Goose got around, carrying its tough hero, an army of one, who fought for democracy against the then Axis of Evil. If the reader enjoyed fist fights, Turk Madden was always in the right place. In this way Turk was more violent than Jake in the *Gold Monkey.*

Although Bellisario may have been influenced somewhat by L'Amour's stories, he certainly was inspired by 1930s aviation adventure movies. His idea for *Monkey* came from Howard Hawks' *Only Angels Have Wings* (1939), starring Cary Grant, Jean Arthur, Rita Hayworth, and Richard Barthelmess. This was the film that led Cary Grant to do his famous self-impersonation of "Ju-dy, Ju-dy, Ju-dy." The action took place mostly in a small airline's office, just as much of *Monkey* took place in the Monkey Bar, which looked out on the Clipper landing. The character types were much the same. Flying Pan American Airways–type aircraft over the Andes, Grant's airline was located in the Peruvian town of Barranca. Movie makers are prone to pay tribute to earlier movies with in-jokes, so George

Lucas used Barranca as one of the first characters we meet in *Raiders of the Lost Ark*. Barranca betrayed Indy and tried to steal the treasure map from him at gunpoint.

Another series using the Clipper idea was *Robinson Crusoe of Clipper Island* (1936). This fourteen-chapter movie cliff-hanger starred half-Jewish, half-Inuit actor Mala, who was called upon to investigate the sabotaging of an airline's tropical island base in the Pacific. The series played upon the real threat to Pan American Airways' Clipper bases. Mala had to figure out whether Axis agents were responsible or a local witch doctor had gone bad.

While Clippers served as entertainment and escapism by appearing in musicals, adventure films and series, and romantic comedies, they also became part of the serious war effort in rallying the citizens of the U.S. and galvanizing them to action. The war cry "Remember Pearl Harbor" resounding in 1941 was quickly followed by "Remember Wake Island." Hollywood came out with *Wake Island* (1942), starring Brian Donlevy, Robert Preston, and William Bendix, to make the futile, gallant stand on the island legendary. Stock footage of the M-130 clipper was used in this movie, since Wake had been a Clipper base. The Philippine Clipper had itself been strafed as the initial wave of Japanese bombers struck Wake. The Clipper had been only ten minutes outbound from Wake when the crew received news that Pearl Harbor had been attacked and that the Clipper was to return to Wake. While the flying boat was being refueled for its emergency flight back to Hawaii, the Japanese aerial attack on Wake commenced. After the attack, the overloaded Clipper, now with holes in it but the only way off the island, evacuated as many civilians and wounded as it could take the 2,500 miles to the still burning base at Pearl Harbor.

While this was occurring at Wake, the Hong Kong Clipper was destroyed at its moorings in Hong Kong. Although no movie cameras were present to capture the destruction, Pan American Airways later included a reenactment of the loss of the Clipper in its promotional movies through the use of models. As the 1930s age of glamour turned to 1940s war, almost lost in the midst of the war reportage was the fact Clipper personnel had been made prisoners by the Japanese at Guam and Manila, some to be confined or assigned to work camps in China, Manchuria, and Japan. Those who survived would be liberated only at the war's end. This was the sober side.

Hollywood again picked up on Pan American Airways and the Clippers in 2004 with Martin Scorsese's *The Aviator*. This biopic covered the life of Howard Hughes during the 1930s and 1940s when his TWA competed against Pan Am. Alec Baldwin played Pan American President Juan

Trippe, while Leonardo DiCaprio played Hughes. Kate Blanchett starred as Katharine Hepburn, Kate Beckinsale as Ava Gardner, and Jude Law as rogue hero Errol Flynn.

In early *Aviator* sequences, Hughes wooed Hepburn by teaching her the magic feeling of flight in his S-38 amphibion. The Sikorsky S-38 amphibion went by many popular names, including the gentleman's air yacht or the explorer's air yacht. Sergei Sikorsky, son of its builder, Igor Sikorsky, said it laid the foundation for all the Clipper ships to follow. Lindbergh would use an S-38 to open Pan American Airways's routes in the Caribbean.

Hughes did own a Sikorsky for his private use. Scorsese used a flying replica of the S-38 that gave people rides at the 1933 Chicago's World's Fair Century of Progress. Chicago tried to pull itself out of the Depression by risking putting on a world's fair with aviation as a theme. The fair was hugely successful, with an estimated thirty-nine million visitors in 1933 and 1934. Italo Balbo's flying boat flotilla thrilled crowds by flying in from Italy. The public could also ride in an S-38 to see Chicago for the first time from the air.

Herbert Fisk Johnson of the Johnson Wax Company bought the plane after the fair and renamed it the *Carnauba*, after the wax of the same name. Flying from Wisconsin, he used the plane to embark on a three-month expedition into the Brazilian interior to look for more stands of the carnauba palm, which Brazilians called "the tree of life." The trip covered more than 7,500 miles. Johnson and the botanist onboard did locate what they came for. Upon completing the expedition, Johnson wrote a book about it and inscribed a copy to his eight-year-old son. The inscription said he hoped his son could someday make the same trip.

In 1998 his sons did just that. First they looked for the original S-38, which the Johnson company had sold in the late 1930s. While doing aerial survey work, the craft had been destroyed off the Indonesian coast during World War II, when it was thought to have been attacked by Japanese fighter aircraft. Despite all their scuba-diving, the younger Johnsons were unable to locate the wreck. However, a Minnesota company was able to build a replica from scratch for the 1998 trip from Racine, Wisconsin, to Fortaleza, Brazil. They followed the same path as the original flight. Herbert Johnson had followed the Clipper routes in 1935 and used Clipper base facilities where he could. Seeing this *Aviator* replica fly at air shows is probably about as close as people today can come to experiencing the romance of a Clipper in action.

4
Clipper Music

Changes in music indicate changes in cultural mind-set. Since the 1930s and 1940s were decades of fast music and dance—the Lindy, swing, big band, jitterbug—it was inevitable that speedy Clippers and speedy music should meet. The Clippers served as a funhouse mirror for contemporary music, both reflecting its values and shaping or inspiring the music at the same time.

A film from 20th Century–Fox, *With a Song in My Heart* (1952), bridged the topics of Clippers in motion pictures and music. This film biography traced the comeback story of singer Jane Froman, who was crippled when the Yankee Clipper crashed in the Tagus River on February 22, 1943. Twenty-four of the thirty-nine people onboard were killed. Seven of the passengers, including Froman, represented Camp Shows, Inc., and were on their way to entertain the troops. Froman's singing mate, Tamara Drassin of "Smoke Gets in Your Eyes" fame was killed outright as the Clipper broke up and sank in under ten minutes. Froman was seriously injured, but was rescued by the Clipper's first officer, whom she later married—a Hollywood story to be sure. Paralyzed from her injuries, Froman on crutches heroically entertained the troops anyway. Lobby cards for the movie pictured Susan Hayward as Froman desperately clinging to Clipper debris after the crash. The movie tied the story of her dramatic comeback with pieces that she sang, such as the lead title song. Hayward lip-synched to Froman's voice as Froman dubbed over Hayward. *With a Song in My Heart*'s music director, Alfred Newman, won the Oscar that year by beating out *Singing in the Rain*. A Clipper had played its gruesome part in a long history of airplane disasters affecting the direction of popular music.

Glenn Miller and his orchestra recorded the fox trot, "Caribbean Clipper," for RCA Victor. A trombonist and the band leader, Miller played the composition for the last time on December 1, 1944, as he and his famous 418th Army Air Force Band recorded a radio show at Co-Partners Hall

A Clipper cargo label combining the fragility of shipping phonograph records with another kind of peek-a-boo fragility.

in Bedford, England, prior to their trip to France. On December 14, Miller was killed over the English Channel, an event quickly overshadowed by the beginning of the Battle of the Bulge on December 16. Miller's death in itself marked the range of Clipper music as bouncy escapist romanticism met the reality of war in martial music or marches. In 2001, Brisa U.K., Ltd. paid tribute to the Glenn Miller Orchestra by producing its compact disc entitled *Skylark*. Although "Caribbean Clipper" was not featured in this collection of the band's hits, both the metal protective case for the CD and the CD's label illustrated a Clipper soaring over the bay of Rio under a full moon.

Trumpeter Harry James and his orchestra recorded "The Clipper" in January of 1942. The Hudson-DeLange Orchestra recorded "The China Clipper" on the Burnswick label in 1938. Melody man Will Hudson and lyricist Eddie DeLange became best known for their collaboration on the classic hit *Moon Glow*. Once their group disbanded in 1941, Hudson became the arranger for Glenn Miller's Army Air Force Band. Before that they played in such arenas as the Hotel New Yorker where Clipper passengers often stayed. In London, England, a Clipper label featuring "Elephant True Tone Recording" turned out 78 rpm records for the Clipper Merchandising Company of Hong Kong. Likewise, an entire "Clipper" label was created as a division of Custom Recordings of Marion, North Carolina, featuring such country artists as Gene Smith, singing his own "Forgetful Avenue" and "The Teardrop That Fell." After World War II, another Clipper label recorded such groups as Johnny Corvo and the Moonbeams, complete with a land-based Clipper airplane pictured on the label. And Pan American Airways would adopt "Flying Down to Rio" from the movie of the same name as its unofficial theme song.

A musical score different from the one recorded by the Hudson-Delange Orchestra but also called "The China Clipper" was published by United China Relief, Inc., in 1941. With music by Norma Morton and lyrics by Ethel Powell, this sheet music featured the China Clipper on its cover. To raise money for China, United China Relief (UCR) published everything from music to Chinese cookbooks that featured ingredients available at any wartime grocery store from Los Angeles to New York. The "China Clipper" was one of its first endeavors, born in the same year as United China Relief itself.

In 1941 *Time* publisher Henry Luce persuaded the different major secular and religious organizations that were trying to provide charitable aid to China to unite under one umbrella organization. Thus United China Relief, Inc., (UCR) was born. The organization carried on many functions to raise money. It maintained its own radio show on the MBS, featuring music and such musical stars as Judy Garland. Eleanor Roosevelt was honorary chairman. Pearl S. Buck was actual chairman. With such celebrity backing, many public events voluntarily turned over earnings to UCR. For example, on November 6, 1941, 50 percent of the take for the first professional hockey game to be played in Texas between the St. Paul Saints and the Dallas Texans was turned over to UCR. Texans were a bit confused by the Chinese candy and Chinese-dressed ushers at a hockey game. Outside of selling war bonds, raising money for China Relief became the biggest money-raising preoccupation of World War II and would inspire and change the direction, scope, and methods of appeal of such well-known charitable activities as the Community Chest and what has become the "other" United—the United Way.

Just as Pan American Airways had a vested interest in China through its transpacific routes, so had Luce. Born of missionary parents in China, he cared about the plight of the Chinese people. After he and journalist and playwright Clare Boothe married, he sent her as a reporter to China more than once to cover the war and to wake up the U.S. public about what was happening in Asia. Clare Boothe Luce traveled both to Europe and China on Clippers, sometimes at the behest of the U.S. State Department, and she gave the Clippers good publicity through her magazine correspondence. Sam Pryor, vice president and one of the original founders of Pan American Airways, a good friend of Charles Lindbergh, and later Pan American's main conduit with the CIA, persuaded her to run successfully for Congress in 1942. Music, politics, war, and mass media became deeply entangled.

Pitching the China Clipper through music served one of the overall roles UCR played during 1941. In the face of fierce opposition by America First and other noninterventionist and pacifist groups, the organization kept China in the American conscience. UCR became a way of breaking down U.S. isolationism, with the goal of gaining U.S. participation in the war to help those considered to be friends and allies abroad. Just as the Clipper had symbolized U.S. values abroad, now it was the turn of U.S. citizens to come to the aid of those who embraced democratic and Christian values. To further twang the conscience, UCR published an image of a burned Chinese child that became one of the classic images of World War II. This image of P'ing Mei sitting orphaned, alone, burned, and crying between railroad tracks in a bombed industrial yard would stand as one of the classic icons of the ravages of war on innocents. It would last until replaced in the Vietnam War by the photograph of a naked, napalmed Vietnamese child running towards the camera. The photo of the Chinese child appeared on postcards, posters, in church magazines and news magazines throughout World War II.

The image of the Chinese child was often accompanied by text that read:

> This is P'ing Mei—a child of China. He is one of thirty *million* children who have been left motherless, fatherless, homeless by four years of merciless war. He is one of *50 million* refugees who desperately need food, clothing, shelter, medical aid. He is one of *450,000,000* friendly, democratic Chinese who loved and helped America in the past—who need our help now in order to survive and be a free, independent, friendly neighbor in the future.

Just as Pan American Airways in its ads claimed to have helped the democratic process and fight for freedom in China by allowing China, a worthy kindred spirit, to skip a hundred or more years and jump into the future, so did United China Relief create a picture of the Chinese as being "just like us," only at an earlier stage of development paralleling that of the U.S. They are "friendly" and "democratic" and, by implication, "Christian." In short, as T. Christopher Jespersen has pointed out in *American Images of China, 1931–1949*, the Chinese appear in this blurred image as aspiring Americans. Pan American Airways, UCR, *Time*, and other organizations and media projected U.S. values onto China. The later communist rise to power in China would seem inexplicable to many Americans because of these comforting projected values. In reality, Chinese were often not friendly, democratic, or Christian. Many fought for a different kind of freedom.

Nevertheless, American support for General Chiang Kai-shek's China in the face of the Japanese was much appreciated and used by the general. His propaganda machine turned out many posters. One musical poster pictured the general standing on the Chinese coastline in full regalia. Next to him an army trumpeter rallied the assembling troops. As troops lined the shore, Chinese gunboats and a submarine cut past a lighthouse while the sky filled with Chinese aircraft to defend the homeland. This c. 1936 poster carried the title "Navy, Army, and Air Force Fight the Enemy." On the horizon, a line of U.S. battleships steamed toward the harbor to join the Chinese ships. Presumably, Chiang was counting on U.S. battleships to help him out since the Chinese navy had nothing along those lines. More curiously, the artist portrayed the Pan American Clipper flying in amid all the swooping military airplanes to offer relief for the good general.

Coincidentally, General Chiang's hated enemy, the Japanese, used the Clipper image to recruit sailors. A 1930s Japanese navy propaganda postcard showed a friendly sailor waving at the viewer before a Rising Sun flag. His Katakana message on the card said, "Happy New Year. Banzai!"

as a navy flying boat came in low overhead. After Japanese agents tried to secure blueprints of the Pan American Clippers, Japanese engineers worked to build their own versions, code-named Emily and Mavis. Before those airplanes could be manufactured, for lack of operational flying boats, the card's Japanese illustrator settled for painting a China Clipper with a radical color scheme change. The converted China Clipper sported Rising Sun emblems on its fuselage and wings, and the bottom of its hull was painted a brilliant red-orange to match the Rising Sun. To fuel its war machine, the Japanese not only were importing scrap iron from the United States, but also images.

Music, Clippers, and the United China Relief share another common history, this one concerning contralto Marian Anderson and one of the more famous incidents in American music. In the spring of 1939, at the same time Pan American Airways' Yankee Clipper was cornering the news by flying its first survey flight from the United States to Europe, Anderson was scheduled by impresario Sol Hurok, classical music's P. T. Barnum, to perform at Constitution Hall in Washington, D.C. The hall was owned by the Daughters of the American Revolution, who had a clause stating that only whites could perform there. As public outrage mounted over the cancellation, Eleanor Roosevelt and Secretary of Interior Howard Ickes intervened. The following Sunday, Easter Sunday, Anderson sang to some 75,000 people from the steps of the Lincoln Memorial. She would become the first Afro-American to be asked to perform at the White House. In 1943 the DAR would invite her to sing at Constitution Hall to benefit United China Relief.

A 1930/1940s postcard of the time also connected music, China, and Clippers. Mayer Post Card Company of Roanoke, Virginia, printed their "Sing unto God, ye kingdoms of the earth" postcard. This message from Psalms 68:32 was written across the bottom of the card, while another pointed, perhaps guilt-inspiring message stretched across the center, reading "Where in the wide World were you last Sunday?" Graphically it showed a world map over which flew a C-47 airplane with "Sunday School Clipper" painted on its fuselage and a cross on its tail.

The Sunday School Clipper was patterned after an airplane that flew missionary missions in China during the 1930s and 1940s. Lutheran World Missions gave the plane to its crew in lieu of salary when the communists took control in China. Pilots of the plane, which was named *St. Paul* in missionary service, flew between commitments with Pan American's affiliate in China, China National Aviation Corporation, and the Flying Tigers. Pilot Felix Smith wrote of his experiences in *China Pilot: Flying For Chiang and Chennault*, and Dick Rossi recounted his experiences in *A Flying*

Tiger's Story. Rossi, who became a combat ace, had before the war tried to hire on with Pan American Airways to be a purser on one of the Clippers flying out of Treasure Island in California, but he chose the offer the navy made him instead. Some of the Sunday School Clipper's pilots would go on to fly for Civil Air Transport, the CIA-run airline. In fact, after its missionary service, the *St. Paul* would itself be leased to CAT to sing a different tune. Max Springweiler's *Pioneer Aviator in China* (English Edition 1998) gave a full account of the *St. Paul*'s exploits in evacuating hundreds of Christians while under fire from bandits and communists.

The Clipper image graced other sheet music of the time. Martha Hastings composed "Flying on the Clipper Ship" as part of the Bernard Wagness piano series (1941). Its whimsical cover shows the China Clipper flying in a starry sky over North America to Hawaii. A girl waves a scarf out the window at hula and outrigger figures below while happy fish jump in the sea. "Flying on the Clipper Ship" was published again in Theodore Presser's *The Etude, Music Magazine* in the February 1945 issue. *The Etude* was the most popular music magazine of its time (1883–1954) for teachers, musicians, students, and scholars of music. This particular issue stressed patriotism and the role of music. Cover art showed men of different U.S. military services singing as they gathered around a woman playing a piano. After articles by such popular music personalities of the time, including Fred Waring ("The Music America Wants"), Victor Young ("How Motion Picture Music Is Written"), and Richard Rodgers ("Our Future Musical Theater"), the musical score section of the magazine concluded with a section entitled "Delightful Pieces for Young Players." After the patriotic "Flag of My Country," the old American jig "Turkey in the Straw" and "The Spinning Top," the section culminated with "Flying on the Clipper." *The Etude* was used extensively throughout North America, so the Clipper music was played by many a would-be pianist. The Magnavox radio-phonograph advertisement on the back cover of the magazine also spoke of Richard Rogers, inviting consumers to enjoy "the true charm" of his recent composition, the musical *Oklahoma,* on a Magnovox. Rodgers later scored the music for television's long-running *Victory at Sea* patriotic series, which presented a history of the U.S. defeating Japanese forces in the Pacific, reclaiming such bases as Wake Island built for the Clippers and then for the military.

Junior high bands were also treated to selections from *Ascher's Clipper Bandbook*, which was "an all occasion collection of 36 best known favorites for young bands." The cover showed a land-based Clipper. Inside were the usual childhood musical punishments such as "Home on the Range," "I've Been Working on the Railroad," "Cielito Lindo," "Old Gray

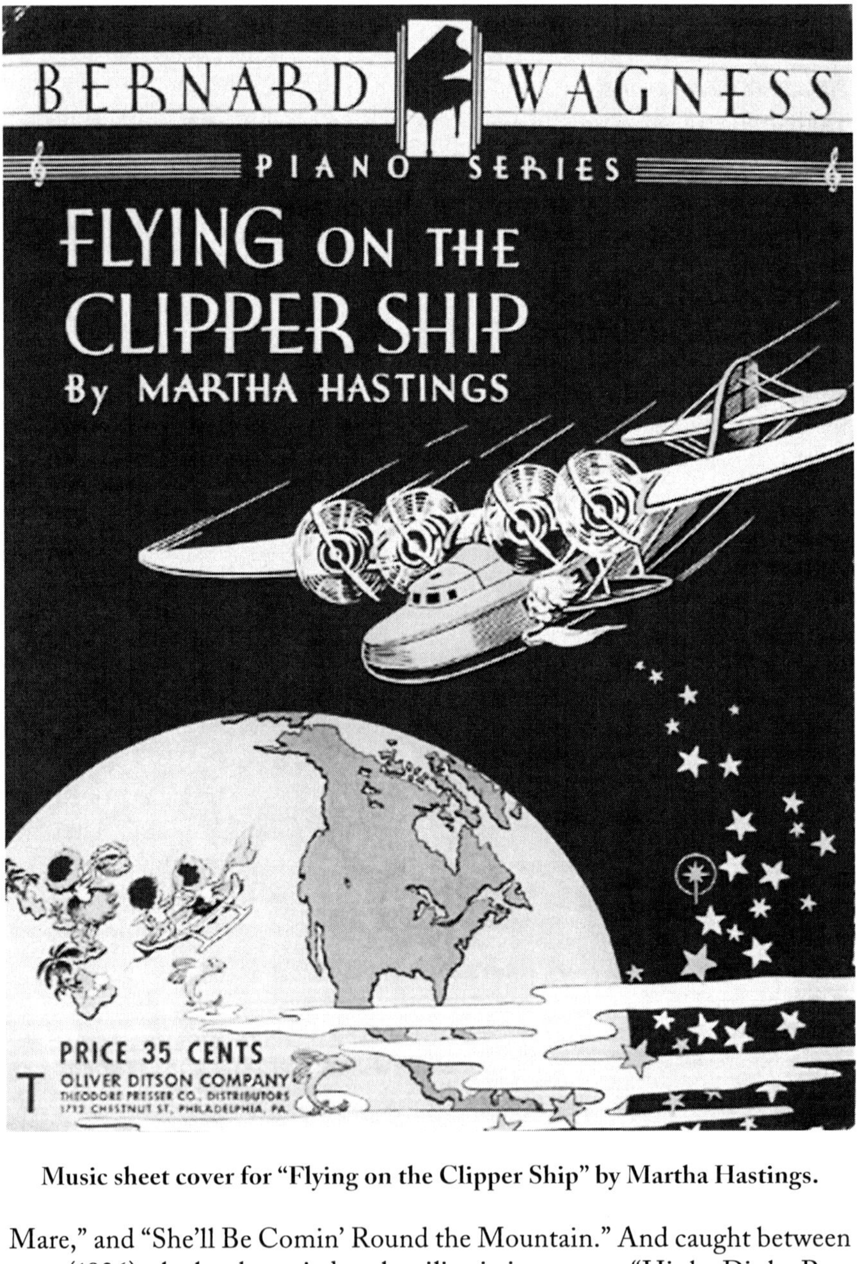

Music sheet cover for "Flying on the Clipper Ship" by Martha Hastings.

Mare," and "She'll Be Comin' Round the Mountain." And caught between wars (1936), the book carried such militaristic tunes as "Hinky Dinky Parley Voo," "Caisson Song," and "You're in the Army Now." Along with "Devil-Dog Marines" and "American Aerial Triumph" marches, the *Let's Go Victory March Album* (1942) contained "The Clipper March" by

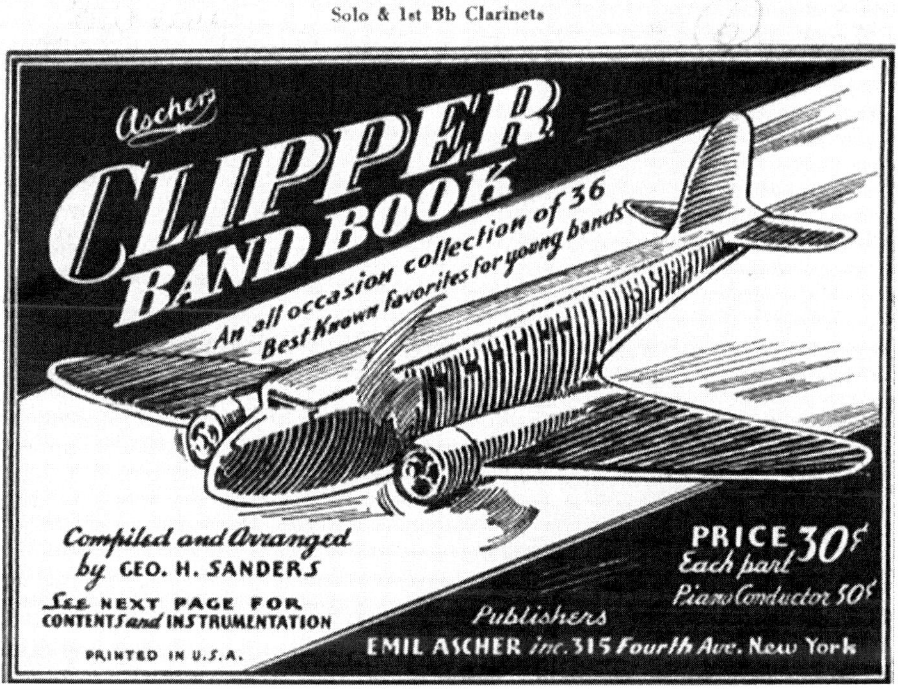

Thousands of copies of the *Clipper Bandbook* were used in schools across the United States.

D'Artega. Clipper history seemed to match that of the songs: a blue-collar, "frontier" airline extends itself south of the border and across the Atlantic to Europe to end up in the army.

After America went to war, a similar collection of music for young musicians, *First Steps in Band Playing: A Class Method for All Instruments* (Rubank, Inc., 1942), culminated on a military note with a march entitled "Clipper Ship, U.S.A.—March." The piece followed another march, "The Air Brigade March," as Clipper music shifted to the patriotic beat. Created by Harvey S. Whistler and Herman A. Hummel, the preface to "Clipper Ship, U.S.A." encouraged children to "practice the march slowly at first, counting four beats to each measure. Then play faster and faster until you can play in regular march tempo." Speed was important in music as it was in the air.

For the youngest musicians, toy stores offered the Clipper drum. This 11-inch diameter, 1930s toy drum came with cymbals attached and a colorful drumhead painting of a seadrome, an idea being popularized in the science magazines of the time. Since the Atlantic Ocean lacked many of the island stepping-stones found in the Pacific, architects proposed creating artificial island airports. The seadrome sported a landing dock, or floating apron, for the Clippers, plus an elevated runway similar to an extended oil drilling platform for land planes. The drum pictured a Sikorsky Clipper striped with red, white, and blue with "USA" scrawled on its side. It soared over the seadrome, whose directional signs pointed to London in one direction and New York in the other. A dirigible and another Clipper also circled while a sailboat and steamer passed by.

One of the more curious musical collisions of history, war, and religion involving Clippers occurred with a collection of gospel songs and choruses by evangelist Mervin "Merv" E. Rosell. This World War II collection entitled *Sing! Above the Clouds, Gospel Songs and Choruses for Radiocasts and Youth Rallies* (1942) was dedicated to Rosell's brother, who was serving in the Pacific theater of operations. The book presaged the youth rally movement that would catapult Billy Graham to fame with his Youth for Christ in 1945. Given the need for comfort at a time of great unease and discord, evangelism found the 1940s to be a hotbed. Rallies sprang up everywhere. *The Old Fashion Revival Hour* attracted a large radio following. From this era, most modern mass media evangelists sprang. Rosell was one.

In addition to his radio broadcasts and public appearances, Rosell had published other war books for troops and youth, including *For Men at War*, *Heart to Heart* ("A Personalized Book for Today's Youth"), and *Man to Man* ("Dynamic Book for the Serviceman"). *Sing! Above the Clouds* was the first songbook in his musical series. In addition to the musical scores, Rosell advertised on the cover that these pieces would be "Story-Styled by 'Merv' Rosell," meaning that each song would also carry with it a story, presumably the message of the gospel. The cover featured a Pan American Airways' photo of the Yankee Clipper, and the song "Above the Clouds," from which the book's title is derived, appeared after another of Rosell's own compositions, "Youth for Christ."

The story that introduced "Above the Clouds" related how this chorus was written in a Clipper at 11,000 feet over the Caribbean on Rosell's way back from South America. The Sikorsky Clipper (not the Boeing clipper pictured on the cover) encountered a storm from which the struggling flying boat could not free itself. Suddenly the pilot was able to break the Clipper into clear air at a higher altitude. They had been saved; hence, the song praised how God could lift listeners from a dark storm of mortal sin to heavenly sunshine. (4)

Rosell took out the air log that Pan American provided each passenger and wrote down what had come to him. Later, gospel singer Carlton Booth recorded the song and sang it at various rallies.

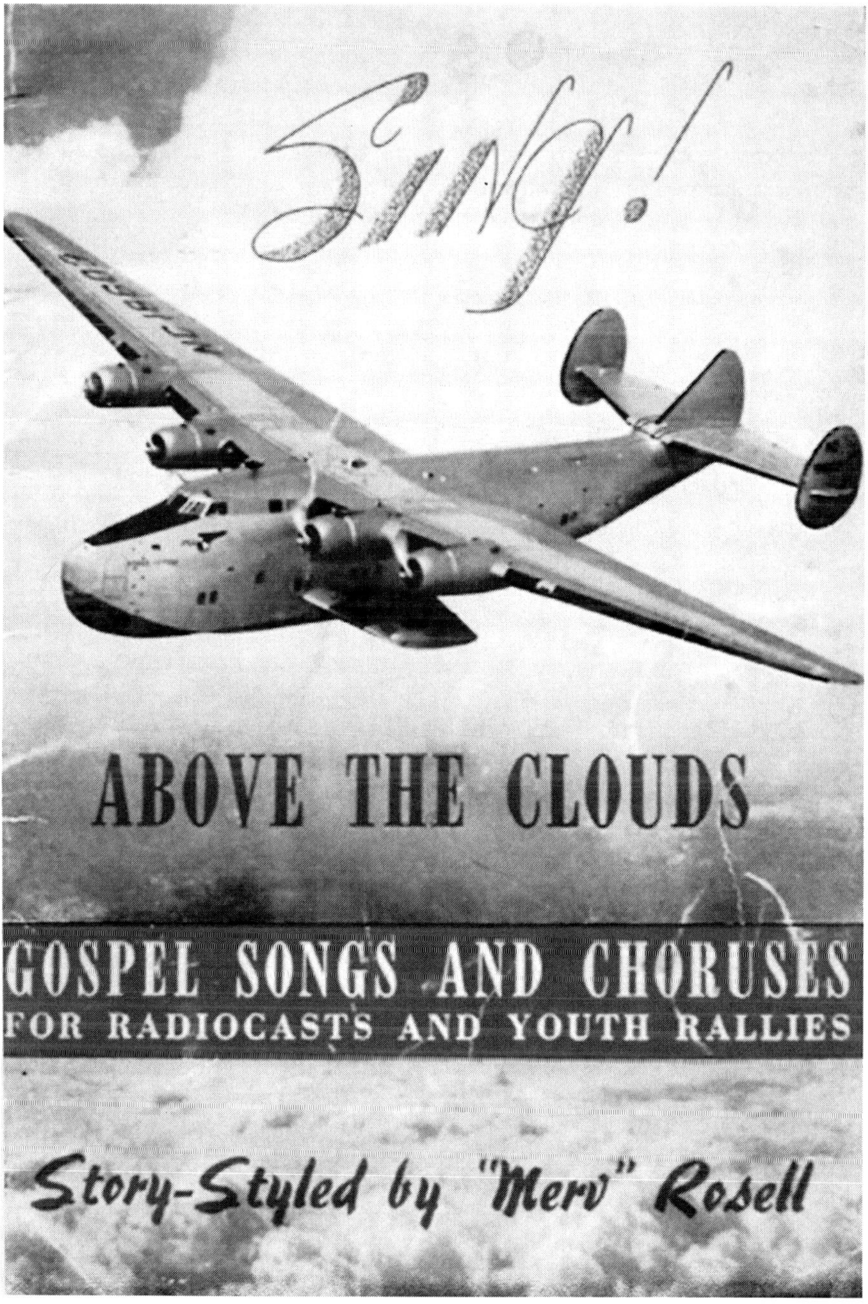

Evangelist Merv Rosell combined his Clipper experiences with music in this cover for his collected gospel songs.

Within the story of the Clipper, Rosell included a parable showing how even ground-bound city dwellers could have the Clipper experience. He related that in New York City above a certain level in the skyscrapers the windows suddenly had no screens. When a Midwestern newcomer asked why that was, he was told higher windows needed no screens because they were above the "fly line." Rosell explained the meaning of the Clipper and New York experience: "When you are living high in Christ Jesus you're not bothered by the buzzing. So live high above the petty buzzing of earth-born chatter; above the clouds of trouble and despair and by faith above the stars of God with your heart in the heavens, though your feet must walk the earth." (5) The Clippers were indeed inspirational. The song took its place among other wartime-inspired songs by Rosell and others, including "He's My Captain," "It Isn't Fair," "There's Victory," and "Prayer for Our Boys."

Rosell braved flying Clippers around the world and went on to become one of the more quoted evangelists, achieving perhaps his pinnacle of success on January 23, 1955, when he guest hosted Dr. Charles C. Fuller's *Old Fashioned Radio Hour* and delivered his hour-long famous "Heaven Sermon." Over 40,000 people responded the next week to his radio offering, the largest number in OFRH history. Airplanes also marked his death. He died in his home in Arizona on September 11, 2001, the day terrorists crashed airplanes into a Pennsylvania field, the twin towers of the World Trade Center in New York and the Pentagon.

Beyond musical scores, religious representations of the Clipper have continued in other mediums. Evangelicals could not have all the fun. In 1996 the Catholic publication *The Word Among Us: Daily Meditations for June 1996* used its cover to urge believers not to miss a single day of prayer and scripture reading while traveling. Travelers were invited to take *The Word Among Us* along when boarding an airplane. The front cover showed the colorful starry cosmos while the back showed the anvil head of a thundercloud. Against the cloud flew a small abstract image of a passenger jet. Superimposed on its route stood the black and white early photo of passengers lining up to board Pan American Airways' S-40 Clipper in Miami. Given the ominous presence of the cumulonimbus, passengers would have done well to do as the cover advised, to "Turn 15–20 minutes each day into a mini-retreat."

Even earlier, the March 5, 1938, edition of *Signs of the Times: The World's Prophet Weekly* used the Pan Am's travel bureau poster for its cover. An S-42 Clipper soared over a Clipper sailing ship and the rotting hulk of an even older one along a coast lined with palm trees. While the scene looked inviting, this Seventh Day Adventist organ took a completely different spin on technological advancement. It focused on progress and "a century of invention" as signs of the end of times, the imminent coming again of Christ. The crisis was at hand. While modern air transportation hastened war. destruction and the end of history or the world, on a more positive side, the Clipper aided in the work of world missionaries to prepare people for that end. The Clipper's flight paralleled the "flight of time." Everything had become speed, and speed meant there was barely time for people to put their spiritual houses in order.

Much Clipper music was ephemeral and has not survived. Inspired by Clipper accomplishments, many amateur lyricists were inspired to compose songs. If they sent their music to a magazine, it had a chance of being published and surviving. For every surviving piece, countless others were discarded. An example of this music that did survive was a piece that appeared in the January 1936 issue of *Paradise of the Pacific: Hawaii's Illustrated Monthly Magazine*. Los Angeles resident Walter Phillips Horner proclaimed on his letterhead that he was a writer of Hawaiian verse lyrics. He gave the magazine permission to publish his lines that soared "Into the Liquid Sunshine," the title for his lyrics. Although the lines may seem doggerel, they were meant to be sung to "Climbing Up the Golden Stairs to Glory." Again, the religious bent of the lyrics that so often connected the Clippers to heaven showed itself. Hymns were now to be sung to technology and the positive "paradise" it could bring:

> O my heart is filled with great anticipation,
> As Clipper Ship is winging to Hawaii;
> I'm day-dreaming about a happy landing,
> And beautiful mermaids of Waikiki.
>
> O we're sailing o'er the Pacific to Hawaii,
> We're flying o'er the brine into liquid sunshine,
> Into rhythm, song, and rhyme, that Paradise is mine,
> We're zooming o'er Pacific sea [5].

Orchestras and local bands, named after the Clippers, were as ephemeral as some of the music. These bands sprang up along the flying boats' coastal routes. For example, in British Guiana, the Yankee Clippers played wedding receptions in 1942. After the demise of the flying boats, musically Clippers flew on, often in unexpected places. Think psychedelic floral patterns and bell-bottoms. The Monkees' 1967 Headquarters album, their third, contained "Zilch," which has since become the name of band member David Jones's unofficial fan club. After the Monkees broke up, Jones opened a store called "Zilch." In the song "Zilch," Davey repeatedly mimics the radio transmission from the Clipper calling its home base in Alameda. Alameda was the original California Clipper base, and the line itself appeared in earlier movies and in the actual 1930s news reportage of Clipper first flights. This edgy song was quite different from their earlier pop hits such as "Daydream Believer," "A Little Bit Me, a Little Bit You," "Last Train to Clarksville," "Pleasant Valley Sunday," and "I'm a Believer."

Aside from the weird reference, this oddity song attained some cult status in that another repeated line mentioned Bob Dobalena, a reference to J. R. "Bob" Dobbs, also known as the King of Slack, icon of the SubGenius Foundation, and awning salesman turned savior for the Dallas-based SubGenius religion, who claimed to be the original investor and originator of the Monkeys concept. The Headquarters album was the Monkees' attempt to move beyond their manufactured TV personas and their bubblegum-set fans. For better or worse, this album represented the first time band members were given complete control over content, and the first time they were allowed to play their own instruments. Before auditioning and winning a part as one of the Monkees, Jones appeared on *The Ed Sullivan Show* playing the Artful Dodger in the traveling cast of *Oliver.* This was the same night the Beatles were introduced by Sullivan to the American public after stepping off a modern Pan American jet Clipper.

Following on the recording heels of The Monkees, Keith (James Barry Keefer) recorded "China Clipper" for his 1969 album, *The Adventures of Keith.* This teenybopper/pop/rock/white soul album capitalized on the success of his 1967 smash hit single, "98.6," which sang of a man's temperature being restored to normal after he reunited with his loved one. Army service during the Viet Nam War cut short Keith's stardom. At last report he was playing some gigs on the side, while working as a cameraman on television's *Judge Judy* courtroom show.

In 1958 Arthur Lyman's musical album *Taboo*, with its track, "China Clipper," climbed all the way up the Billboard Charts to number four, and stayed on the charts for an inspiring sixty-two weeks. Musically, this "China Clipper" was a far cry from those of Keith or The Monkees. Before making this album, Lyman played as a member of Martin Denny's band in Hawaii. Denny became famous for his first big hit, "Quiet Village," which employed bird and frog sounds. The Denny influence surfaced in *Taboo.* Hawaiian born, Arthur Lyman enriched the exotic music of "China Clipper" and the album's other selections by using jungle bird calls, conch shells, vibraphone, xylophone, marimba, and ukulele. The piece was again taken up in 1966, this time by an early Jamaican ska band. The Ska-talites did its own Jamaican rendition of Lyman's "China Clipper." The ska–Clipper first appeared in the band's *Ska-Boo-Da-Ba* album. Musically, the Clipper was really getting around.

After the demise of Pan Am as an airline, the Montreal-based art-punk-rock group called "fly pan am" formed, appearing on the anticonventional distribution Constellation label. The Constellation Website for "fly pan am" featured orbital lines around a globe, mimicking Pan American Airways' early use of the globe as a logo during the time of the Clippers. Such touring bands of the early twenty-first century have also appeared at such venues as the China Clipper Café in Olympia, Washington, which has recently hosted such groups as Dead Moon, The Giant Peach, Das Oath, Melt Banana, and Porn.

5

Air-Age Education: Youth and Clipper

As the United States placed more and more emphasis on its youth as the future of the country during and between the two world wars of the twentieth century, illustrators of calendars and prints linked youth and aviation as twin hopes. World War I and the first airmail in 1918 brought depictions of innocents looking heavenward at the new bird in the sky. At first, children appeared with a parent, but as time passed, the standard image became that of the flying machine, the child's pet dog, and the child without the adult presence. U.S. bedrock beliefs in rural simplicity and technology-as-savior became gospel. Boys and girls were illustrated as living an outdoor Shirley Temple, Becky Thatcher, or Huck Finn existence under panoramic skies. An airplane held their attention. On the eve of World War II, when youth were being encouraged to build model airplanes in preparation for the adult skills needed for the war effort, the image often added a model airplane held in the child's arms as he or she dreamed of piloting the real McCoy. Into this existing mix the Clipper came along at the popularity pinnacle of calendar illustrations used as pin-ups, scrapbook materials, and promotional material in the 1930s. Although the Clipper became THE romantic image in these illustrations, it also played a significant role in everything from children's education to games from adolescence to their young adulthood.

To understand the relationship of the Clipper and American youth, consider the unique position of youth during this time. During the 1940s, when the United States by necessity came of age as an industrial giant and world power, the nation's view of youth changed. As Robert Hines has pointed out in "Youth and the American Identity," the United States' vision of its youthful self depended on having a frontier, a westward expansion of the imagination. Once that American dream seemed close to realization and

The cover of the March 1936 *Youth's Companion* combined with *American Boy* illustrated the China Clipper against a huge red sun, in retrospect, an eerie historical reminder.

the U.S. had literally gone worldwide, the nation transferred its hope and ambition inward to its youth—to something it had already made or was making—rather than outward. The goal was to give youth more than their parents had in *their* Depression youth. Expectations of better things to come, defined as "progress" at the time, became expectations of youth, and youth as a new collection of individuals or subculture. In 1941, the term "teenager" was coined.

"Teenager" implied a large preexisting group, one that shared the common experience of high school and a popular culture. This group differed dramatically from the earlier concept of growing up in America. Heretofore, most young people were thought to move directly from childhood into adulthood. Prior to the twentieth century, children were needed to work on the farms or factories as soon as possible. They needed to grow up fast. Often there were no popular culture rituals involved in becoming an adult. One simply left home, married, got kicked out, or went to work.

Education changed that. In the first half of the twentieth century, most states extended compulsory education to the age of sixteen. Whereas in 1900 only 5 percent of students in public schools attended high school, by the time the Clippers came along in the 1930s high schools became a common experience shared by youth. The Depression's lack of jobs for youth made high schools even more attractive as a way of keeping high school age youth from getting into trouble. Likewise with the rise of modern mass media at this same time, youth were not regionally separated but joined by radio, movies, books, and magazines. The "teenager" likely began in the 1920s at the time of the first aviation calendar art, and the teen years became established as an essential part of American life rather than an interlude to adulthood in the 1940s. Teens had been given wings.

Into this changing freedom of youth and high expectancies flew the Clipper as a symbol of freedom, new-found national identity, and the future. If youngsters were not able to view news reports of the Clippers at the local movie house, they could become informed by reading *My Weekly Reader,* the children's newspaper distributed in elementary schools. In September of 1928, at the same time Pan American Airways opened its Miami base to provide regular passenger service to Havana, *My Weekly Reader* began publication. This current events paper for children has served as a bastion of American values to the present. It fostered reading and other life skills. Many of today's baby boomers, who avidly subscribe to periodicals and buy books, began their habit on Friday afternoons in the classroom, when they received their own personal subscription to *My Weekly Reader*. Inexpensive paperback books could also be ordered through the My Weekly Reader Book Club. For some children, the newspaper was the first possession they could truly call their own. Stressing the positive and downplaying the negative, *My Weekly Reader* found the Clipper an admirable blend of civic and scientific accomplishment. One 1937 issue devoted the entirety of its front page to the Clipper.

The Clipper pervaded all levels of the classroom. At the entry level of education, children began to learn how to read by associating pictures with words. Such books as *The Golden Dictionary* (1944), published by the Golden Press, featured the Clipper on the cover to illustrate the word "airplane," the key "A" word. This visual dictionary was "A Giant Golden Book," a counterpart to the ubiquitous Little Golden Books of the 1940s and 1950s that introduced children to many fairy tales and stories Walt Disney animated. Its 1,030 words testified to the importance of aviation. Airplanes illustrated such words as "above," "army," "away" (as in "Father went away in an airplane."), "do" (as in "Do you see the airplane?), "machines," "over," "vehicle," and "wing," Neither ships nor automobiles competed with the number of airplane appearances in the dictionary.

There was a difference between teaching children that two tanks plus two tanks equaled four tanks, or that three soldiers plus two soldiers equaled five soldiers, rather than two apples plus two apples equaled four apples. The child who grew up in a world of tanks and soldiers had a different mind-set from the student who grew up with apples and oranges. The same applied to words as well as arithmetic. The child who was taught to associate words with airplanes entered an altered state of time and space.

Once students mastered the basic words, they could move up to *The Newlon-Hanna Speller Grade Five* (1933), which featured a U.S. mail plane on the cover and a full-page rendition of the Sikorsky Clipper opposite the title page. Actually, the airplanes seemed to be used as "bait and switch" to entice the children's interest and to appear to be modern, only to give them older word lists. The best the speller could talk about in terms of transportation was how Indian trails had become roads. This Houghton Mifflin Company book strangely pictured the Clipper with its tail cut off. A similar image adorned the front and back covers of *Travel by Air* (1940), by Dorothy Judd Sickels. The painting by Gabrielle showed four children with luggage, dog, and doll awaiting the Clipper as its soared tailless overhead. How the seaplane would land on the runway and not destroy itself remained a mystery. Inside, this Whitman Publishing Company book gave the Clippers broad coverage, showing the early Sikorsky American Clipper, the later Martin China Clipper, plus a map of its Pacific route, and a rare picture of the Martin Russian Clipper, of which only one was made and sent to Russia. The book served as both a reader and activity book for children.

Another elementary book for the youngest of readers was The Little Wonder Book called simply *Airplanes*, by Maria Ellen Johnson (1939, reprinted 1946). It pictured the single-tail experimental version of the Boeing Clipper before it took on its triple-tail configuration. In "See Spot run" fashion, the child could read:

Tim sees this clipper ship.
It carries people across the ocean.
It carries bags of mail.
It flies fast.

The text reinforced the two announced themes of the book that teachers were to stress: humans' increasing control over nature, and the overcoming of distance through science. Published by Charles E. Merrill in affiliation with the American Education Press, *Airplanes* made sure it photographed both boys and girls riding airplanes as well as men and women enjoying aviation careers.

The American Education Press also produced *Current Events Yearbook and Defense Facts for the School Year 1941-1942: A Supplementary Text of Background Material for Classes in Current Events, History, Civics, and Economics.* The yearbook made students aware of the names of their government officials and national statistics. The war's influence was noticeable in the text's sections devoted to "Defense Facts" and "A Dictionary of Military Slang and War Terms." Beyond a few charts, the book presented no graphic displays, except for its cover, a painting of the China Clipper. The book reached a cross-section of students. For example, the Browning (Montana) School Library copy was available to residents of Browning, other local towns, Hutterite colonies, and the Blackfoot Reservation.

Echoing the same theme of *Airplanes*, the even earlier 1934 *How We Have Conquered Distance* trumpeted man's victory over nature with a Pan American Airways' photo of the Sikorsky S-40 Clipper over Miami. The photo appeared in the first unit, "Transportation Today and Very Long Ago," of this vocabulary-building text. This Clipper was set in contrast to a drawing of cavemen to show how far we had come. The text stated that perhaps some day airplanes would become so common that people would no longer even remark, "There goes an airplane" (2).

Other readers included Vol. 4, *Animal Friends and Adventures*, of the fifteen-volume set of Field Enterprises' *Childcraft*, which ran from 1931 to 1954. The very popular Whitman book entitled *Timmy Rides the China Clipper*, by Carol Nay, was adapted for *Childcraft*'s collection of stories for children. The *Childcraft* books used different paintings of the Clipper and gave only the first of the eight chapters from Nay's original 1939 book. Timmy flew from California to Hawaii, Midway, Wake, Guam, Manila, Macao, and Hong Kong in the original. Here, he flew only to Hawaii. The 1954 edition of *Childcraft* must already have been nostalgic for the original Martin China Clipper, since it pictured that aircraft for its story. In the original Nay books, which enjoyed successive printings from 1939 until years after World War II, the artwork shifted to showing the larger Boeing B-314 Clipper, which succeeded the Martin China Clipper. *Childcraft* looped back to a more distant past.

The third grade reader *Wide Wings* (Macmillan 1939), similar to the *Childcraft* books, served up an anthology of readings—all led off with a frontispiece of the China Clipper still bearing its experimental (X) number before being accepted into commercial service. Like most books affected by the Clipper's opening up an awareness of the larger world, this featured a "Friends in Other Lands" section to introduce students to geography and other cultures. Geography was now being defined as "wings." Since Pan American Airways became the United States' first international airline by pioneering routes to Central and South America, and, because the U.S. was part of the Americas, *Wide Wings* took the path of many geography books of the time, defining "other lands" largely as South America, and, more important to the war effort to come, emphasizing Brazil's history of rubber production. A section of this text considered "Where the Raincoat Grows." The stress on rubber became even greater in texts as rubber supplies from the East Indies and Malaya became threatened by war clouds in the Pacific.

The fourth grade *World About Us* (Bobbs-Merrill Company, 1948) showed one of the "baby" two-engined Clippers used at times to ferry critical rubber out of the Brazilian jungle. This cultural geography text focused on North and South America with both articles and stories. Its author, Sidman P. Poole, chaired the School of Geography for the Woodrow Wilson Institute of Foreign Affairs at the University of Virginia. Poole had just relinquished his position as a chief for the U.S. Army's Intelligence Services. Poole, together with the Military Geological Unit, had examined sand in sandbags attached to fire balloons designed to burn down Northwest forests during World War II. Since fossils and slag in the sand indicated it was neither U.S. beach nor Pacific island sand, Poole reported that the U.S. was under balloon attack from Japan, not from submarine launches off the U.S. coast, or from Japanese relocation camps, or from German POW camps, or from fifth columnists within the U.S., as some thought at the time. Of the 9,000 balloons launched from Japan, 300 were reported landing in the United States, ultimately killing six people and starting a few minor fires. One balloon descended on a power line running to the nuclear reactor at Hanford, Washington, that was producing plutonium for the Nagasaki bomb, causing the plant to temporarily shut down. In the circularity often found in history, one of the China Clipper's secret war missions was to deliver uranium from Africa to the U.S. for the atomic bombs dropped on Japan.

Poole's own biography also circles back to the Clipper in terms of topographical maps. With protection of the Panama Canal Zone of paramount importance and with large German populations in South America, not to mention German airlines, the U.S. military needed to expand its presence in the Caribbean island approaches to the Canal Zone through Lend Lease agreements with areas under British control. The military quickly had to build bases in these islands and Brazil to provide airfields for jumping-off places to ferry aircraft across the Atlantic Ocean to Africa during the war. The problem: no maps. Navy hydrologic maps of harbors and the oceans existed, which was fine for ships, but not flying ships. There was little in the way of maps to help pilots navigate. Before the war, Pan American Clipper pilots literally had to make their own maps. According to Clipper pilot Basil T. Rowe in *Under My Wings* (1956), pilots pillaged school geography books, tearing out maps to carry with them in their South American flights (127). As they flew, they would change what was misinformation, add what was not there, and name new features. They found that Spaniards had mapped much of the area, but that the maps used in schools based on earlier Spanish surveys had translated meters as feet. This meant that a 3,000-foot mountain was actually 9,810 feet, which made a lot of difference to a pilot and passengers. Pilots found mountains and rivers not indicated on any maps. The Pan Am maps would provide the basis for military mapping of the area. Just as children's school books owed much of their content to the Clipper, the Clipper crews owed much to children's geographies of the time.

Appearing in Poole's book was "Lost Cattle on the Flying C Ranch," a story about Clay Caldwell, who earns Clipper, the horse of his dreams, by finding lost cattle on a Western ranch. During the 1930s and 1940s, Clipper became a popular name for horses. So too in the 1980s. In 1988 toymaker Hasbro introduced another set of ponies into its already popular "My Little Pony" series of toy horses appearing both on television and in motion pictures as animated characters. Available by mail order only, the new set of seven Sparkler Ponies came with "one special baby pony—Clipper." It's interesting to speculate how close Poole may have been to Pan American Airways during his stint with intelligence. The boy hero of the story, Clay Caldwell, seems to echo the name of one the first pilots to open up the route to Cuba and points south, Cy Caldwell.

Similar to Poole's book and its focus on this hemisphere, the text of *Our Southern Neighbors* (Follett Publishing, 1942) linked Clippers, government war agencies, and geography. The frontispiece map of North and South America pictured sailing ships linking the two continents of old and a Clipper linking the two continents of recent times. While the book was written by two academics, the third listed author was Ralph Hancock of the Board of Economic Welfare. The goal of the book was "to develop fully the real meaning of the Good Neighbor Policy in the Western Hemisphere" at the junior high level (iii). The book described the journey of a group of boys and girls through the lands of Latin America by bus, train and Clipper. Students were taught, for example, that the West Indies were "Islands of Defense" and important Clipper bases for Pan American Airways—wartime geography and pointed political statement. Products vital to the U.S. economy and war effort were mapped out for each country.

Competing directly with *Our Southern Neighbors* was *Our South American Neighbors*, also debuting in 1942. Author Frances Carpenter took students on an imaginary airplane ride around all the countries of South America, using both land plane and flying boat Clippers. The book's cover showed an abstracted image of a four-motored Clipper over a map of South America. Other aviation photos were scattered throughout, with many supplied by Pan American Airways.

Typical of wartime texts, Carpenter's book stressed the importance of being neighbors for defense and critical trade. Thus the opening began with an anecdote about two people nearly shooting each other when they met in the dark jungle, only to find out they were really friends, not enemies. The strange, nearly violent beginning underscored the tension caused by the war. The text concluded with a unit on the Pan American Union and a unit on the importance of the Panama Canal for trade and connecting eastern South America with western South America, although photos showed U.S. warships. At a time when heroes were needed, South American heroes who fought for freedom were pictured at the end of most chapters as they appeared on postage stamps from their countries. Photos of postage stamps depicting Pan American Airways aircraft and a photo of a Clipper flying boat certificate that passengers were given in commemoration of their crossing the equator also appeared. South America was presented to students because the Clippers connected the United States to these countries and connected the South American countries to each other. Even the full-page geographic map of the Northern and Southern hemispheres inside the book showed a Pan American Airways airplane flying above with its route map below. Oddly, routes bypassed Guiana and Paraguay.

Though best known as a children's author for her children's "Little Friends" and "Grandmother" series—*Our Little Friends in China*, *Our Little Friends in Norway, Our Little Friends in Switzerland* or the recently reprinted *Tales of a Chinese Grandmother* or *Tales of a Korean Grandmother*—Carpenter kept up on technological developments. As a world traveler and Fellow of the Royal Geographical Society, she was well equipped to include

Clippers in her text. Her interest in transportation expressed itself in *The Ways We Travel: Carpenter's Journey Club Travels* (1929). Her newspaper columnist/photographer/lecturer father, Frank George Carpenter, had written many books about their travels around the world. After his death in China in 1924, she continued the travel tradition. *Our South American Neighbors* was somewhat of an updated version of his earlier sixth grade geography text, *South America* (1921). Frances Carpenter would also write another school geography text about the Pacific islands opened up by the coming of the Clippers, titled *The Pacific: Its Lands and People*.

One geography book featuring Clipper-route stops across the Pacific became schizophrenic once the United States entered the war. Helen Follett's *Ocean Outposts* (Scribners, 1942, 1943) first came out three months after the Japanese attack on Pearl Harbor and just before the fall of Corregidor. The text could not make up its mind whether it wanted to describe peacetime islands in the Pacific or admit to the Japanese conquest of many of the ocean islands it described; consequently, some entries are written in present tense as if nothing had happened in the Pacific, as if people were still jumping on Clippers to carry them to islands, where they could sip coconut drinks under swaying palm trees and watch natives weave floor mats when they weren't dancing and singing. Strangely, short passages usually tacked onto the end of each island entry that discussed Japanese incursions were written in past tense.

Like many of the books about the Pacific then, the book was mostly structured around the Clipper routes as if someone were flying the Clipper, although that was impossible at the time. Pacific islands that were now "outposts" for defense, hence the book's title, were discussed in sequence of how they appeared on the Clipper routes from the U.S. to New Zealand and from the U.S. to Manila and Singapore. The routes, of course, no longer existed, either having been broken by the Japanese or suspended. Even at this time of heightened patriotism and territoriality, Follett chose to refer to the islands where Clippers had their bases not so much as *U.S.* islands but as *Pan America's* islands, even though Pan American Airways no longer had a base there. Midway Island had been under attack, and no Clippers had flown there in months. The island was militarized. Also, Midway had served as a relay station for the Pacific Commercial Cable Company since the turn of the century, yet Midway was not referred to as the cable company's island. So persistent was the Clipper as icon that it overpowered other referents. Midway and other islands were portrayed as island "stepping-stones" for the Clippers across the Pacific, the same stepping-stones that could be used by our military.

Vernon Quinn's *Picture Map Geography of the Pacific Islands* (Lippincott, 1945) "for boys and girls" carried less of a geopolitical edge. While Quinn avoided mentioning Pan American Airways directly when discussing the importance of various islands as stepping-stones for the Clippers, Frank Beaudouin illustrated the Boeing Clipper to complement her text. Quinn also mentioned how air passenger service linked the islands and how World War II ushered in our new consciousness about these far-flung outreaches of the Pacific.

Houghton Mifflin hoped to aid teachers in attracting students to critical reading with *Happy Landings*, published in 1942 and 1943. The anthology wanted to "please teachers and delight students" because it "collects material in a field that interests them intensely: to them flying is a symbol of the world today and even more the world tomorrow" (vii). This compilation of fact and fiction reprinted the factual account of Clare Boothe's trip on a Clipper in "By Clipper to African Front." The wartime account by the correspondent (aka Mrs. Henry R. Luce) captured one of the few wartime reports of a civilian flying the Clippers in time of war.

The importance of the Clipper in opening the doors of the world to travel and trade made it an obvious choice for incorporation into social studies and geography classes. In some cases it led to the creation of such classes. To cite just a few textbook examples, for six to nine year olds the dust jacket of *My First Geography of the Americas* by Arensa Sondergaard pictured a Clipper leaving the U.S. Several more Clippers of differing models appeared chapter by chapter throughout this 1942 Little, Brown and Company book, as it took children on an aerial tour to South America to learn about the people and countries beyond the southern border of the U.S.

By 1954, the U.S. had become a bit more insular in its school texts, but the Clipper was still there. *Living Together in the Modern World, Transportation* (Vol. 1) by the Creative Educational Society did feature the section "A Journey by Plane," but this was just a coast-to-coast trip. Even though jets and stratocruisers existed in 1954 and the Clipper seaplanes were extinct, the text still chose to picture the S-42 Clipper for its section "Planes Go Farther," which described Pan American's Pacific and Atlantic routes, along with suggested student activities. Like so many other books during the Clipper era, the text focused on the progress made in overcoming distances through technological development.

In contrast to the fifties insularity, the 1941 prewar *Life in Modern America* addressed U.S. geopolitical concerns in terms of what to do about the Philippines and the problems America would have if cut off from America Samoa as a port for supplies of rubber and tin coming out of the East Indies. The book did not shy away from stating the Japanese threat.

To emphasize Samoa's importance, this Ginn and Company text by Mary G. Kelty provided a photo of "A Clipper Plane Arriving at American Samoa" (396). The chapter text described how the U.S. made a treaty with the native ruler to gain navy control of the Samoan harbor for use as a coaling station. Unfortunately for students, the photo of the Clipper was mis-captioned to suit the storyline. The photo actually showed the Clipper at its dock at Wake Island in the North Pacific, not Samoa in the South Pacific, so a bit of creative history was employed.

The blockbuster of all geography texts, however, was *Nations Beyond the Seas* (1938), a Ginn and Company book by Wallace W. Atwood and Helen Goss Thomas. A best-selling text, it was used extensively throughout the United States and the Philippines. Complete with maps, tests, and special credit work, it was a teacher's dream. There was no beating around the bush as to where U.S. increased contact with foreign lands came from, for the cover featured the China Clipper flying over a Pacific atoll. Inside, the revised edition carried a photograph of the Atlantic Clipper and described how its route completed an around-the-world route, linking the entire world. On the pages preceding the Clipper, a two-page map of the world appeared, and students were asked to plan their own flight on the map, making sure that the flight was made in seven hops: London-Moscow-Bombay-Tokyo-Sydney-Capetown-Cairo-Paris. This venerable text lasted long after World War II, even though its maps were outdated and the China Clipper would never see another atoll.

Such texts paralleled themes touted by Pan American Airways' promotional posters and ads of the time, particularly of the type that proclaimed "There Are No Distant Lands by Flying Clipper." Geography books were not just presenting maps of the world, but oftentimes maps of a world with colored lines indicating Clipper routes. The problem was that some nations were hostile. Some of the not-so-distant lands in the shrunken world of the Clipper saw those red and black route lines as a direct threat to their own ideas of empire. Because of this, agencies of the U.S. government worked hand-in-hand with authors, publishers, educators, and airline officials to invoke patriotism and preparedness in U.S. youth. They often employed the Clipper as a centerpiece, since it represented America's progress and extension into the rest of the world, at a time when the Clipper was not yet used for military purposes. Its civilian designation made it a safe sell in the face of prewar America's favoring noninvolvement in any war in Europe or the Pacific.

At first the government's interest in promoting aviation was largely commercial, but that soon changed to needing aviation talent for war. The Department of the Interior's Office of Education became the primary governmental agency in disseminating what was called "Air-Age Education." Its 1936 publication *Aviation in the Public Schools* was first suggested by the Department of Commerce's former director of aeronautic development. The bulletin was not a text but a primer teachers could use for ideas on how to incorporate more aviation emphasis in the classroom. Chapters encompassed aviation today, aviation in the public schools, model aircraft, aviation occupations, and vocational training in aviation. Clippers were in the limelight throughout. The opening of the text, for example, traced how far the U.S. had come. It first pictured the Wright Brothers' airplane at Kitty Hawk, but that accomplishment was overwhelmed by the next two pages of photos devoted to the China Clipper. Piloting as an aviation occupation received top billing. Clipper pilots were shown in their cockpit. Even when it came to aircraft fabrication, the China Clipper was the one pictured being constructed. And it's no wonder the Clipper showed the epitome of progress, for this text, like many of the time, listed many Pan American Airways personnel, past and present, as consultants. Hence, teachers were encouraged to teach their charges about the Pacific by incorporating studies centering on the newly opened Clipper route to China. PAA donated its romantic photo of the China Clipper on its maiden flight docked at Pearl Harbor beneath the palm trees.

As has long been the case with U.S. schools, the federal government's lead changed what local and state schools systems did. School districts and textbook publishers used what the government suggested. Macmillan Company's widely accepted *Air-Age Education Series* went through several printings in the 1940s. To illustrate just how intertwined education and government had become in bringing aviation into the schools, consider the title page of *Social Studies for the Air Age*, one of the books in the twenty-book series. Hall Bartlett, head of the social studies department, Garden City High School, New York, wrote the book, and described himself and the book as being a "Member of Aviation Education Research Group, Teachers' College, Columbia University" and "Prepared with the Cooperation of the Civil Aeronautics Administration." Also, it was "Sponsored by the Institute of the Aeronautical Sciences." The foreword proclaimed that the War Department, the Navy Department, the Civil Aeronautics Administration, and the U.S. Office of Education advocated this type of education.

The text meant to inform a citizenry about "the revolutionary world force" (vi) of aviation. Pan American routes and the B-314 Clipper were pictured in the unit on "International Unity." A chart showed how between 1939 and 1941 Pan American had helped reduce "foreign" ownership of airlines in South America from 60 percent to 32 percent, as the text explained how Clippers extended the U.S. good neighbor policy as "the good neighbor who calls every day" (71). The text politely ignored how Pan American was buying up and putting out of business non-foreign carriers in South America so that ironically it became the foreign carrier south of the U.S. border. The accolades were many: Chinese pandas for the Bronx Zoo came in by Clipper, and six U.S. tennis stars had flown a 25,000-mile exhibition tour of South America (74). The "Safety and Regularity" unit of the "Future of Flight" chapter showed the extensive flight deck of the Boeing Clipper, and a photo of a Boeing Clipper radioman in the unit on "Federal Government" illustrated how radio contact with the ground was one of the many requirements of the Civil Aeronautics Board. Rather than refer too blatantly to Pan American Airways as the United States' only international airline at the time, Bartlett sometimes referred to it as America's "flag carrier."

A collaboration between the Civil Aeronautics Board and the School of Education at Stanford University produced the monster 800+ page book of the era, *Aviation Education Source Book*, subtitled *Subject Matter Drawn from Aviation Suitable for Inclusion in Textbooks and Courses of Study for Elementary and Junior High Grades*. Although the book was published in 1946 after the war and the last flying boat clipper had retired, what did the book lead off with for its full-page frontispiece? A Pan American Airways photo of a flying Clipper over a sailing ship clipper with Tennyson's quote, "The old order changeth, yielding place to new...." Twenty other Pan American Airways photos or Clipper paintings illustrated different curriculum components. A child's painting of a Clipper was even included. Not bad, considering that all the Martin Clippers had been destroyed before or during the war, and what was left of the Boeing Clippers was being scrapped.

The curious relationship between the USSR and USA showed up in this book. The two countries, though allies during the war, were on shaky ground afterwards. For example, the Martin company had sold the last of its Clippers to the USSR when Pan American Airways had opted for the newer Boeing models before the war, and a ferry service for U.S. aircraft destined for Russia had been set up during World War II. After the war, that kind of mutual benefit ended, yet The *Aviation Education Source Book*, though ostensibly about U.S. education, used some photos of USSR classrooms where students were studying aeronautics. In one picture youths in swimming suits tried out their model flying boats on a lake. It's hard to know if the Russian photos were already heralding the Cold War race between the U.S. and USSR, celebrating the victory of the Allies, who incorporated aviation heavily into the classroom, prodding educators to strive for supremacy, or simply giving a gesture of goodwill in the name of aviation education, since the supplier of the photos, the American-Russian Institute, was located not far from Stanford.

Just as the Clipper had been used before World War II to transition youth into war, after the war it was used again to transition them back to peace. The foreword stated this change and illustrated how the government campaign to bring aviation into the schools had succeeded:

> Initial efforts ... focused on the science of aeronautics for the upper grades in the secondary schools. This emphasis was due largely to emergency war needs of the armed services in the early years of World War II. With the ending of hostilities, emphasis has shifted to the infusion of aviation subject matter into existing courses in elementary as well as in secondary schools. It is a tribute both to Civil Aeronautics Administration leadership and to our school leaders and teachers that few, if any, schools in our country have failed to respond to the new educational needs created by aviation and related developments [vii].

As the quotation stated, emphasis had indeed been upon emergency war needs. After the attack on Pearl Harbor, the U.S. Navy Bureau of Aeronautics distributed 1⁄72 scale model plane plans to schools so that shop students could turn out models to train personnel in aircraft identification. Students built wooden models of U.S., Japanese, Russian, Italian, and British aircraft. This freed factory workers and the military for other tasks, while educating students about aviation before they would enlist or be drafted. To make the building efficient, the 28-inch by 4-foot plans blueprinted full-size templates. One of the key airplanes chosen for this identification program was the Clipper. By 1942 some Clippers were flying for the navy, so it was not unusual in schools across the country to find a model of a civilian aircraft being built alongside military Messerschmidts, Heinkels, and Nakajimas.

If students were too young to enlist for military service, model building was one of the ways the nation could enlist them in winning the war. The cover of *Building Model War Planes for the Army and Navy* proclaimed, "Our armed forces need 800,000 model planes. Build them and help win the war." Published by Sloan and Pearce and written by Emanuel Stieri, this book further indoctrinated children into military thinking by describing the ten "ranks" of aircraftsman certificate awards they could receive based on the number of their models that passed inspection. Included in the sixty aircraft of the world described with photos and building plans, the unarmed Boeing Clipper was considered as a "War" airplane.

Adults invited youth to be involved in two American bedrock values that are often called upon to solve exterior threat: technology as savior (build something) and violence as justice (six-gun justice or get a rope). Here young people built smaller, imitative weapons used by adults facing off in the O.K. Corral, known as the theatres of World War II. Yet these small imitations, much like carving toy pistols out of soap or wood during the Depression and during World War II, were not going to be played with by children. They were destined for the adult world, where life or death could hinge on the accuracy of the models and the ability of spotters to tell the difference between an armed German or Japanese long-range flying boat and the Clipper.

School and public library books were devoted to training youth in aircraft identification. As the U.S drew closer to involvement in what would become World War II, more and more books were published to assist youth in plane spotting. Like young computer whizzes of recent times, teens and preteens could develop considerable skills outdoing adults in the 1930s and 1940s. Plane spotting was a natural for them, as many were already making scale models of the aircraft.

As an early example of a plane identification book, C.A. Weymouth, Jr.'s popular *What Plane Is That?* (Stokes Company, 1936) featured a drawing of one of the China Clippers for its title page. The plane still carried its experimental number. Captain Eddie Rickenbacker of World War I fame furnished the foreword, in which he expressed his hope that the book would aid not only boys and girls but men and women as well. The book considered only planes manufactured in the U.S.; however, later books included planes of other lands as the threat of invasion became real. Several types of Clippers were given. Specifications for what would become the famous B-17 bomber of World War II were kept secret, but specs were given for all the Clippers. The book even showed the rare single-engine Fairchild XA-92 "Jungle Clipper" amphibion used on the Amazon.

Aviation Science for Boys and Girls, a 1944 Macmillan text, used the Clipper to further link civilian and military education. The text's first photograph provided an aerial view of a New York seaplane/land plane airport. The second showed the China Clipper in its giant hangar at Port Washington, Long Island. So again, a text used the Clipper as the epitome of aeronautical development to ease young readers into the textbook dilemma of the time: how does one sell the public on the safety and promise of aviation when aircraft are capable of massive destruction and can threaten national security? In this elementary text's first sentences, author Charles Arey emphasized the New Air Age:

> This is a book for boys and girls of the Air Age.
>
> There are many reasons why boys and girls of the Air Age ought to know about airplanes. They live in a world where airplanes are used a great

> deal to transport mail, passengers, and goods. Almost every day boys and girls see airplanes in the sky.
>
> A second reason why boys and girls of today need to know about airplanes is because of their vital importance to the defense of our country [8–9].

No better example of an airplane that not only carried mail, passengers, goods, but also served the country's national defense could be found than the Clipper. Aside from the word *jenny* in the 150-word glossary, *Clipper* was the only other named airplane that students were expected to know.

Because of the war effort which took so many men into the military, young girls were being asked to consider preparing for jobs in aviation, too, both in and out of the military. *Aviation Science for Boys and Girls* was one text that gave a balanced portrayal of girls and boys performing experiments. It also provided young girls with adult models to emulate. A few examples included a woman flight attendant pointing out what a direction finder was. Navy "weather girls" charted wind currents with balloon and theodolite. A girl and a boy used a tape measure on a large world globe to demonstrate the great circle route used by Clippers between New York and England.

The Clippers' importance to U.S. education cannot be overestimated. This includes educational book format. During the age of the Clippers, then as now, most educational books for youth depended on pictures. Geography books in particular needed photos of the new lands of growing interest to the United States. Pan American Airways served as a ready and often only source of quality photos for world landmarks and the customs of people in other countries. As Clippers opened up routes through Latin America, the Pacific, the Atlantic, and finally the whole globe, PAA's public relations department generated promotional material to sell passengers on the wonders of these destinations. Thus positive images were produced appropriate to each country, not only idealized representations for flying tourists, but also nonthreatening images for school children. Since PAA catered to the business traveler and was the U.S. merchant marine of the air, its photo collection included views of various industries in foreign locations. Most social studies books of the 1930s and 1940s focused on the products each country produced, so the photos made possible by the Clippers were often the only game in town for textbook writers. And free was a very good price. Nearly all the photos, whether they pictured a Clipper or not, carried the caption "courtesy of Pan American Airways." Free advertising. Get them while they are young.

Such free advertising extended to Pan American Airways' subsidiaries as well. Pan Am's Compania Mexicana de Aviacion, S.A., was photo-credited in Mario Leal's physical and natural history textbook, *Ciencias Fiscicas y Naturales*, published in Cuba and Mexico City in 1945. The center of the book's cover exhibited a stylized wing with propellers over palm trees and a rising sun. Roughly in the center of the book, about where it would naturally fall open, was a single-page plate of Mexicana photographs devoted to dirigibles and Clippers that showed the gee-whiz factor of aviation for youth. This represented the only photographic plate in the entire text. The Clippers appeared in the physical science section between entries on barometers and the movement of gasses and fluids. The text was built around introductory scientific experiments students could conduct. How they could experiment with a Clipper was anyone's guess, but it did show practical application of something that moved through both gas and fluid. It also showed how the Clipper image was being replicated throughout the Americas.

Teachers fortunate to live in areas populated enough to have a travel bureau used PAA "Travel by Clipper" posters as display items in classrooms. Travel agents had little trouble disposing of old posters, as teachers quickly snatched them up. Colorful, large, dramatic, iconic, they were classroom-perfect. Except for news service images and a few other photographic services, Pan American Airways became one of the largest suppliers of photographs and art work for both adult and children's texts dealing with other lands.

These images left indelible impressions on the American psyche. For one thing, the images fed the U.S. bedrock belief of endless abundance by showing the rest of the world as a source of products that could supply the U.S. Images of "our friendly neighbors" also fed the U.S. preoccupation with the mobile society. These images advertised other lands as quaint, interesting, fun, colorful travel "destinations." Rather than seeing a country, people saw Grand Tour versions of country reduced to must-see landmarks, much like directive scenic turnouts in national parks where, as Edward Abbey said, tourists ask, "Where's the restroom, where's the Coke machine, and how long does it take to see this place?" With a focus on the simplified message of positive advertising and quick travel, Brazil became Christ's statue overlooking the harbor or the Copacabana without the poverty and revolution. Hawaii became a hula girl without the Japanese threat. Paris became the Eiffel Tower without Germans knocking on the door. Bolivia became a llama, Mexico a bullfight, Cuba a cigar. A worldview was being formed in a long tradition started earlier by the steamship and rail companies. Places existed for our benefit. Our going there would bring the world closer together. The risky downside to this worldview: the Ugly American and the negative aspects of U.S. hegemony.

To put this in context, Pan American Airways was not the only airline promoting such a view and looking for world domination. The Zeppelins challenged Pan Am until the *Hindenburg* disaster in 1937. The German Brazilian airline Sydicato Condor also competed in South America with Pan American Airways by appealing to sophisticated travelers. Typical Condor brochures, posters, and printed flight schedules showed what looked like well-heeled Europeans dockside waiting to depart on a seaplane. Sugar Loaf, Rio's standard landmark, appeared in the background across the bay with banana fronds in the foreground. Amid their hatboxes, travel chests, and stickered luggage, passengers waited in furs and trench coats, which seemed terribly hot for such a balmy atmosphere. The people dressed for the Alps rather than the Copa. On the other hand, they were making ready to cross the Atlantic to Germany and winter there; they just had a head start on appropriate attire.

The upside of this new worldview was a broader view of reality. Aerial photography was still somewhat novel in the United States, and even more so in many other countries. Looking down the throat of an active volcano in Central America fascinated readers, as did the golden evening necklace of lights around Rio's bays, the busy harbor of Hong Kong, France's former penal colony of Devil's Island, or the mighty Amazon. The immensity of objects could better be grasped in the air. The Temple of the Warriors in the Yucatan and the mysterious fog-shrouded Citadel of Haiti's King Henry Christophe fired the imaginations of children and adults, spurring interest in adventure and archeology as well as in aviation. No one minded that an occasional Clipper wing or engine also appeared in the photos to further prove photos had indeed been taken from the air.

The coming of the Clippers enabled whole realms of study and viewpoints to be redefined and to take wings, but beyond photography, social studies, science, and geography lay America's longer preoccupation with the hero. In the age of Clippers, American youth had not yet made the switch from hero to celebrity worship. Deeds in the service of humankind, rather than entertainment function, counted. Because of what the Clipper had accomplished, authors apotheosized the Clipper. This was clearly shown in *Heroes Take Wings* by C.L. Paddock (Pacific Press, 1942). Each chapter of this text discussed a hero. Alongside drawings or photos of Abe Lincoln, Florence Nightingale, or Johnny Appleseed came a photo of the Boeing Clipper leaving the Golden Gate in the chapter "When Men Took Wings." An earlier chapter had shown Orville Wright, but this Clipper photo portrayed the plane as hero, not a person.

Sometimes authors and illustrators mistakenly gave heroic accolades to Clippers. Such was the case with Katherine Shippen's venerable *A Bri-*

dle for Pegasus (Viking, 1943). Shippen, curator of the Social Studies Division of the Brooklyn Children's Museum, told the story of flight. For her World War II segment, instead of choosing a story about military fliers, she chose a story she first published in *Story Parade*. "High and Away: How Some Refugees Escaped the Japanese through the Air" recounted how a boy, Chen Chu Ling, barely escaped from Hong Kong on an overloaded Clipper. A Japanese Zero attacked the Clipper, both while it was on the ground and in the air. Luckily, the Clipper made it to Lashio and relative safety. The harrowing story began with an illustration by C.B. Falls of a Boeing Clipper being attacked by a fighter aircraft. Although aircraft of Pan American Airways' affiliate in China were shot up and did evacuate people from Hong Kong, these were DC-3 land planes, not Clipper flying boats. A Clipper flying boat would have had a difficult time landing on the very un-oceanic runway at Lashio. Nevertheless, the Clipper was credited with saving the grateful Chen Chu Ling.

The concept of the Clipper as hero continued into the jet age. To add spice to his *Famous Airports of the World* (Random House, 1953), Ansel Talbert included Wake Atoll, a Clipper base, as one of the featured airports. The book's largest painting by Clayton Knight was a dramatic, nearly full-page rendering of the Philippine Clipper under attack by Japanese warplanes in their initial assault on Wake Island, December 8, 1941. The painting exemplified artistic license. It depicted the Clipper taking evasive action in the sky over Wake as a horde of Japanese aircraft attacked it. Actually Japanese aircraft strafed the Clipper while it was moored at the dock. The text recounted how, though damaged, the flying boat escaped, evacuated base personnel, spotted Japanese warships, and brought the first news of war in the Pacific to Honolulu and San Francisco. Captain J.H. Hamilton did share some of the glory in this text, but it was the Clipper, rather than the base or the man, that Talbert held up to the light. All other chapters illustrated land plane successors to the Clipper or modern airports rather than this single heroic look at the past. It would be left to pulp or adult fiction and adult advertising to tell more of the story of heroic Clipper captains and passengers. For youth, heroism centered on the airplane itself.

Youths created their own books to show how their heroic view of the Clipper symbolized their own aspirations. High school and college yearbooks used the Clipper as a familiar image or organization motif from the mid–1930s on into World War II. This was particularly true in Hawaii, but also on the mainland. Various yearly issues of *The Crusader* of St. Louis College in Honolulu were organized around the Clipper. The 1936 *Crusader*, for example, featured a stylized flying boat on its cover. The inside of both front and back covers carried a map of the China Clipper's Pacific route and a drawing of the Clipper. The introduction to each division of the yearbook carried a Clipper photo and explanatory text that tied the pioneering skill of establishing a Clipper route with some aspect of student life. A picture of Clipper Captain Edwin Musick with Hawaii's Olympic star, Duke Kahanamoku, prefaced the sports section. The honored classes section was introduced with a picture of the crew of the inaugural Clipper flight to Hawaii being honored with leis as they lined up for their "class" picture. The "Graduates" section began with text addressing "one of man's greatest achievements in aviation," saying "what aviation is today is the result of a long period of experimentation and persistent labor that, like the ups and downs of high school life, has its bright and its dark moments." The accompanying photo showed a Clipper navigator plotting out a course just as graduates plotted their future course in life.

The yearbook's dedication provided a unique blending of "crusaders." First, the yearbook staff dedicated the book to a pictured former member of the teaching staff who gave up his position to become a missionary on the Chinese mission frontier. Next, the text was also dedicated to two other entities linking the Orient with the Occident: the China Clipper's Captain Musick and the China Clipper itself. Both are pictured. The dedication section ends with "Hail, modern Crusaders! Hail!"; thus was provided a unique blend of the religious with the new gospel of the air.

The 1939 *Crusader* was organized around sacred Catholic images, to remind students and graduates of the ideals of the school's intent. Nevertheless, when the Boeing California Clipper made its first foray to Hawaii that year, the staff included a kaleidoscopic montage of pictures of the new, giant Clipper wedged between the sports section and a painting of Joseph and Mary. How the Clipper related to anything in the yearbook was unclear, but its inclusion showed the extent to which the flying boat occupied youthful minds at the time.

The 1942 *Ka Mea Ohi* yearbook for Waipahu High and Intermediate School on Oahu carried a martial theme throughout, since students and staff were still recoiling from the Japanese attack on Hawaii. This book was dedicated to those students who had already left to serve in the defense of the American cause. The staff made no bones about linking American democracy with education in the face of war. Thus drawings of sailors and battleships were used throughout to introduce the different sections and to complement the simplified U.S. flag on the cover. One section combined aviation with the military nautical theme. In Art Deco style, two Clippers passed over two battleships.

On the mainland and on the college level, the 1938 *Quips and Cranks* yearbook of Davidson College, Davidson, North Carolina, presented a Clipper extravaganza. Full-page color photos adorned most of the introductions to each section. No expense was spared. The Clipper was the star and theme for the whole yearbook, as no college activities received color treatment. Additionally, small pen drawings of Clippers were superimposed over the identifications for each student's photo. Both embossed cover and first page carried Pan American Airways' global maps of Clipper routes. At first glance, the book could appear to be a bound promotion produced by Pan American Airways.

George Washington Junior High School of Long Beach, California, published a winter edition of its *Junior Patriot*, a combination running yearbook and newspaper. Patriotism ruled the day, beginning with the cover depiction of the Stature of Liberty. This was followed by a photo of students saluting the flag. Inside the *Patriot*, student writers proudly pointed out that former student Stanley Griffin had succeeded in becoming pilot of the China Clipper.

Students could delight in the fact that Griffin's career coincided with the Griffon's. Arch Whitehouse created the Griffon for the popular *Flying Aces* magazine, known for its colorful cover illustrations. This pulp magazine superhero-pilot starred from 1935 to 1942. Among his many heroics, the Griffon defeated evil forces in "Death Haunts the Clipper" in the May 1938 issue and in "Clipper Hi-Jack" in the July 1940 issue. George Washington Junior High enjoyed both its real and fictional hero, although Stanley may not have made a particularly riveting first name for a superhero. Stanley Hulk? Stanley Kent? Stanley Superman?

Fortunately, Stanley Griffin was known as just Stan when he worked for Pan American, and he certainly fit the hero mold. Like many U.S. superheroes, he came from someplace else, to suit a public's taste for heroes who were wholly American in values after their families had immigrated. He hadn't come from Planet Krypton, but he had spent his early years in Canada before his family moved to California. As Light Heavyweight Boxing Champ of the West Coast in 1937, he also served as Guard Guide when Clippers were displayed at the 1939 San Francisco World's Fair and Exposition. He could handle himself in tough company.

Another person who handled himself well in tough company was John Joseph Patrick Ryan, better known as Jack Lord. He became famous playing the part of Steve McGarrett (1968–1980) on the television series, *Hawaii Five-O*. Before his acting career and his famous refrain of "Book 'em, Dano," Lord aspired to be an artist. When he graduated from John Adams High School in Queens, he was artistic editor for its 1938 yearbook, *The Clipper*.

At the same time, Columbiana High School of Columbiana, Ohio, published its own *Clipper* yearbook. The use of the Clipper as mascot and team name has continued. In 2001, artist Christian Mrosko painted an enormous 55 by 17 foot mural on the cement block wall of the school's gymnasium to celebrate the Columbiana Clippers. This massive *trompe d'oeuil* mural made the Yankee Clipper appear to burst through the block wall and ceiling supports, as the flying boat flew in over the basketball court. Behind the airplane, blue sky showed in the newly created opening, as bricks exploded in all directions. The colors of the gleaming Clipper and white walls combined with red floors and wall mats to give viewers a dramatic, patriotic eyeful. The patriotism proved timely, since completion of the mural coincided with the terrorist attacks of 9/11.

Yet another example of Clipper mania can be seen in the *Gondolier*, the 1939 Venice, California, High School yearbook. Its aviation-themed cover looked like a Pan American Airways promotion with its airplane circling the globe. The yearbook culminated with end papers that consisted of a two-page spread illustrating the progress of flight. One side depicted an unmanned box glider, while the other showed the China Clipper as the culmination of achievement. Inside, a full page article and photo was devoted to John H. Tilton, chief pilot of the Clippers for the Pacific division of Pan American Airways.

Clippers were integrated into the education of America's youth through a range of classroom materials. The cover of the China Clipper Loose Leaf Note Book carried an embossed silver China Clipper flying on a navy blue background. Inside, students could keep track of their class schedules, autographs, activity schedules, football schedules, and basketball schedules on charts provided. Onward, a school supplier of pencil tablets, notebook paper and composition books, as well as nearly anything else that a student might need, featured a Clipper zooming low over a passenger liner ship, as a logo to sell its products. During the war, Onward depicted these seascapes in patriotic red, white, and blue. A Sky High pencil tablet advertised Pan American Airways with Deco image of an S-42 Clipper. Dennison, maker of gummed labels to decorate letters, scrapbooks, and notebooks, offered red/white/blue labels in the shape of a Boeing Clipper. Shaped, precut labels and self-adhesive labels would be invented in 1935, the very year the Clippers began to fly the Pacific. For youngsters just learning to spell and identify images, there was a miniature blackboard with a paper scrolling device at the top. Turning the handle would reveal drawings of common objects that the child could name. Among the dogs, automobiles, cats, and houses, was an airplane—the Clipper.

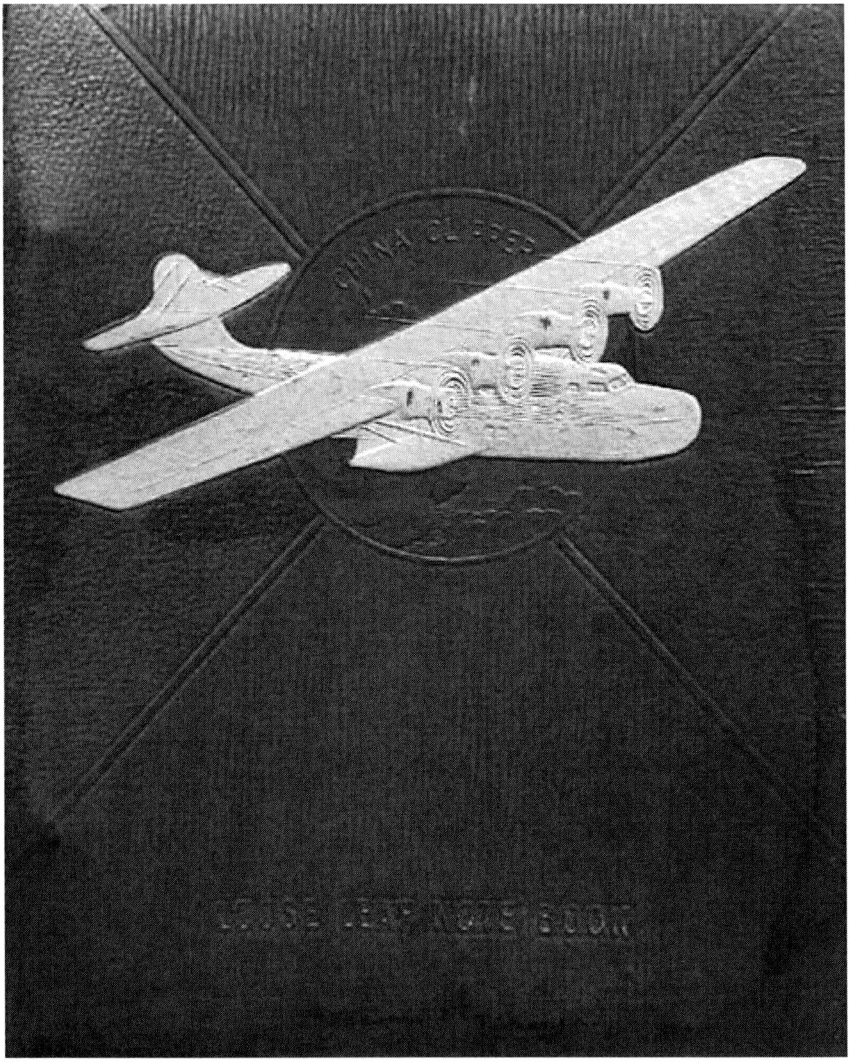

Embossed silver Clipper on a school notebook binder from the 1930s.

Teachers could avail themselves of promotional freebies from local merchants for classroom use. These brightly colored maps and displays were welcome additions to any educational system strapped for money and supplies. The Albert Richard Company, a division of the Fried, Ostermann Company, of Milwaukee, Wisconsin, distributed to its retail sportswear outlets for boys and men the 1944 poster display "Aviation Cavalcade: Wings Over the World ... Yesterday and Tomorrow," by artist F. E.

Onward Clipper tablet and pencil paper design, c. 1940.

Cheeseman. The display gave a map of the world encoded with insignia patches of the different U.S. air force commands, and renderings of all the different U.S. aircraft participating. The only civilian aircraft represented was the Boeing Clipper, "The World's Finest Long-Range Flying Boat," which flew nestled between a B-17 bomber and a P-38 Lightning fighter. In the lower right hand corner of the poster was the last aircraft the viewer saw, the Mars military flying boat described as "The Mars is today's promise of coming giant clippers which will carry 250 to 500 passengers from

A Sky High pencil tablet cover showing the Sikorsky S-42.

New York to London in 10 hrs. Fare: $100"—a promise for peacetime that was never realized. Though the poster fed the thirst for a perspective on the war, it began to prepare youth for peace, or what it called "The Skyway of Tomorrow." This skyway included automobiles with detachable wings, flying wings that towed powerless flying wings in tandem, helicopters, and seadromes in the middle of the oceans. Near the center of the poster, a small box contained a clock that showed it was 22:40 hours, which was how close the world was to "the coming Air Age." Presumably, it would begin at 24:00 with the help of the Clippers and the air force.

The Alcoa Aluminum Company made available its *Global Map for Global War and Global Peace*. The company did offer a few snapshots on the back of the map to educate students about how aluminum was made, but the main focus was what the map key called "Freedom of the Air," of essence during and after the war. In borders surrounding the map and printed on the back of the map, charts identified the rank insignia of the different military branches, Army divisional insignia, wing and tail insignia for the countries of the world, and a military airplane spotting guide to help differentiate friend from foe. In stark contrast to all the militarism displayed, the map itself carried paintings of but two aircraft, both civilian transports shown in civilian livery, not military. The featured aircraft pictured over the caption, "The Metal That Flies Best," was the Boeing Clipper, symbol of "Freedom of the Air" in both war and peace.

Local Coca-Cola bottlers and distributors engaged in the most concerted program to educate children during World War II. In the 1940s and 1950s Coca-Cola reached thirty million primary school children with Coke's *Our America* educational kits, "Developed by the Coca-Cola Company and approved by Leading Educators." These kits contained teaching materials for teachers and learning materials for students. Included were twenty-card sets of poster stamps, album-texts and colorful posters, designed to be used in eleven, four-week units for each industry covered. Units covered such major American industries as electricity, glass, steel, coal, oil, motion pictures, cotton, lumber, and transportation. To make it easy for each class, each four-week unit was further divided into weekly activities. Because the educational program began during wartime, the intent was to promote patriotism at home and to argue the merits of free enterprise. To underscore to students what was at stake, units showed how peacetime industrial uses for the products translated into wartime uses.

Naturally all the items bore logos of Coke bottles and carried statements saying that the Coca-Cola Bottling Company was responsible for all the wonderful, free materials. During a time of scarcity, free was a good price. The patriotic helpfulness at home dovetailed nicely into Coca-Cola's wartime advertising campaign showing scenes abroad. The company's magazine ads portrayed troops in Arctic and tropical settings enjoying a taste of home by drinking a Coke. Often the advertisements showed the men sharing Cokes with Allies, as Coke brought friends together. Coke boosted morale and helped gain friends. In ads, the company followed the lead of Pan American Airways by using images of the globe. Bottles in hand, Coke drinkers appeared in front of the Earth. It wasn't quite Pan Am's winged globe, but Coca-Cola employed wings in other ways.

Coke used the aviation theme and the Clipper for *Our America*. A Motion Picture unit poster entitled "Photographing an Air Adventure in Miniature" showed children the special effects used in a movie that appeared to depict an airplane "Flying the Hump" in the China-India-

Burma theater of war. Airplane images graced posters and poster stamps for the transportation unit. A 1943 poster in the *Our America*'s Steel unit, captioned "Iron and Steel Build the Future," depicted the history of steel in terms of U.S. strength. At its bottom margin, the poster showed farmers or slaves using steel plows. Both visually and historically, images progressed upward. Modern tractors replaced the plow. Streamlined mainliners replaced the Iron Horse. Swift automobiles and trucks on elevated highways replaced the Model T rumbling across rutted roads. Massive ocean liners replaced docked Clipper ships. Towering steel skyscrapers replaced earlier wood and brick structures, The Golden Gate Bridge replaced the wooden covered bridge. Against a sunburst sky, and soaring above the other technological wonders of steel, flew the Clipper. Winged steel was the ultimate expression.

Rituals connected with going to school included graduation and carrying lunches in the days when few schools had facilities, staff, or money for serving lunches. In the pre-cafeteria days of the 1930s, metal was used not only for toys but also for lunch boxes. A variety of colorful, illustrated boxes focused on modern transportation developments and featured the Clippers. Both China Clippers and Boeing Clippers adorned various boxes. PB&J sandwiches flew to school along with apples.

When graduation day rolled around, some students were presented with fountain pens for the next step in their educational life, as they moved

A metal lunchbox showing twin Boeing Clippers circling the globe.

either into high school or more likely into college. The Shaeffer Pen Company was right there with its Clipper Wasp and other Clipper model pens. Often these pens came in a box illustrating the China Clipper. Since Shaeffer profited from the school trade, its advertisements appeared in *Scholastic Magazine*, where it cosponsored writing contests for students. The company's support for schools, and particularly colleges, would continue into the next century.

Its product was advertised as being "streamlined," like so many other products of the time, and again this company took its cue from aviation. When Shaeffer produced the first Wasp in 1934, the name of a stinging insect perhaps seemed strange for a pen. But Wasp at that time connoted the most powerful airplane engine ever produced, soon to be used on the China Clipper, not just on speed-plane winners of air races. Shaeffer went so far as to advertise its pens as "radical writing *engines*." Prior to the China Clipper, earlier Clipper models were powered by Pratt & Whitney "Hornets." Stinging insects were in the air. When the China Clipper began flying, Shaeffer promptly came out with the Wasp Clipper model, which featured its patented Vac-Fill design, to replace the earlier Wasp. Aviation continued to permeate Shaeffer's approach throughout the war and after, as new models such as the Stratowriter mimicked the name of the new Stratocruiser aircraft that Boeing produced.

Just as Shaeffer capitalized on the Clipper in the 1930s and 1940s as a suitable symbol of American power, trade, and technological beauty, Shaeffer had long used patriotism. The company touted its pens in World War I as pens "For Uncle Sam's Fighting Boys." That fervor carried over into World War II as the company proclaimed the importance of troops overseas receiving mail. Clipper airplanes could deliver mail to the troops, while Clipper pens could write the mail. As a morale boost, Shaeffer introduced its Triumph model in 1942, when the population needed to hope that the U.S. would triumph after such a disastrous start to the war. Later, Shaeffer began to borrow design concepts from transportation technology itself, rather than just borrowing names. It came out with the idea of the "snorkel" pen, the snorkel being a concept and term first made famous when German submarines used snorkels as a way to bring fresh air into a submarine without risking surfacing. Shaeffer tied into aviation by not only advertising in general popular magazines such as *Life* but also by targeting aviation magazines such as *Flying*.

To produce its artistic advertising, pens, and pen boxes, including the one showing the China Clipper, Shaeffer employed industrial designers and artists. These artists were attuned to the icons and design fashions of their age. Take the case of William Bunn. As a WPA Depression artist he found work with the Federal Art Project (FAP), creating such works as post office murals. Here was a popular regionalist who had studied with that cornerstone of American art, Grant Wood. The China Clipper was the most recent manifestation of manifest destiny, as the United States moved westward across the Pacific. Such an image fit well into the outlook of the regionalist school that included Bunn, Wood, John Steuart Curry, and Thomas Hart Benton. Their narrative art often depicted U.S. expansionism through transportation. Bunn painted such scenes as "Fort Kearny Protectorate on the Overland Trail" and scenes of boats on the Mississippi. The Clipper was the extension of those great roads west. After the war, when Shaeffer shifted from making bomb components back to making pens, Bunn became design manager for the pen company. If, according to the adage, trade or the dollar follows the flag, then Pan American Airways certainly sold itself, using that idea in opening up world air trade routes with the Clipper. The Clipper pen must have helped Shaeffer's commercialism exploit its trade routes, too, because Walter Shaeffer's innovative son Craig became assistant secretary of commerce of the U.S.

Internationally, students were exposed to Clipper commerce. If a student happened to be schooled in the British Commonwealth, he or she might need some "clippers" or paper clips to hold school papers together. "Clipper" Paper Clips were manufactured in England to be used in schools, home, and offices. Boxes of the paper clips carried a drawing of the British version of a Clipper, one of their own Short flying boats. England had hoped its flying boats would prevent Pan American from obtaining a transoceanic route monopoly. An agreement had been reached for the Short flying boats and the U.S. Clippers to alternate flights across the North Atlantic in 1939, but limitations on the Short design and the war intervened to end competition for the British.

Clippers worked their way into many dimensions of a student's life, even in terms of how he or she reached school. Some who rode to school on horses rode on "Clipper." Those who skated could slip and slide to school on Clipper skates. Those who rode bicycles could ride on Clipper bikes. The few who rode buses or took a bus field trip could ride on Clipper buses. Those chauffeured to school could arrive in any of the various Clipper car models. For most kids, bikes were the prized conveyance. One of the Cadillac of bikes at the time was the 1941 26-inch Colson Clipper. Just as eagerly desired and much advertised was the 26-inch Columbia Superb, also called the "dashboard bike," because it came with a dashboard containing a clock, but better yet, a Stewart Warner speedometer picturing a Clipper flying boat. If one could pedal fast enough, one could fly.

Even the clothes students wore to school connected to Clippers.

Garment-maker Reliance Manufacturing Company based in Chicago advertised play clothes for boys in magazines across the U.S. To sugar the pot, it gave away pin premiums showing historical figures, such as Buffalo Bill, who might appeal to young boys. As early as its 1920s shirt and blouse ads, the company tied its products to aviation by picturing young boys casting rubber band-powered model airplanes into the air. When the Clippers came along, Reliance offered pins depicting "Caribbean Clipper S–42" and "Largest Airliner Clipper Ship," the latter showing the China Clipper. The Caribbean Clipper pin may have confused some astute youths, since the Clipper shown was not the reported S-42, but an earlier, outdated S-40. Nonetheless, the clothing line could appeal to boys in the same way that Lee pants used the Clipper image to appeal to adults during the 1940s.

Outside of the school system, special mention must be made of scouting and its contribution to air-educating children. William Heaslip's cover art for the April 1938 *Boys' Life, The Boys' Scouts' Magazine* showed the China Clipper flying over the ghostly presence of Lindbergh's *Spirit of St. Louis.* The feature article, "Following the Lindbergh Trail," by Captain Burr W. Leyson pictured the various Clipper types already existing and in development. Clippers appeared on other front and back covers of the magazine just before and after this issue. An April 1936 cover even presented a behemoth eight-motored futuristic Clipper with a feature article inside by Clipper designer Igor Sikorsky. This was the changing of the guard, as Clippers became the most featured aircraft in the magazine during the 1930s and early 1940s, replacing the earlier fascination with Charles Lindbergh's *Spirit of St. Louis.*

That Lindbergh now worked for Pan American Airways made the transition easier. Prior to this time, Scouts had claimed Lindy as their own as a hero exemplar. In 1928, The John C. Winston Co. published *The Lone Scout of the Sky* for the Boy Scouts of America. Written by chief Scout executive James E. West, the book presented Lindbergh's biographical journey and included chapters on "Lindbergh and the Boy Scouts" and "The Scout of Scouts." Eagle Scouts could emulate the Lone Eagle. Such heroism was important to the scouting movement. As motivational speaker Zig Ziglar wrote in the forward to *Eagle Scouts in Action*, Eagle Scouts personified the American Dream, and they would become tomorrow's leaders. Past Eagles who performed heroic deeds and accomplishments were for those who believed in heroes, whom the book documented.

The Scouting link between American patriotism and American destiny has been well established in popular culture. Norman Rockwell's famous painting of a Scout saluting next to an American flag serves as just

The April 1938 cover of *Boys' Life* with William Heaslip's rendition of the China Clipper flying over the ghostly presence of the *Spirit of St. Louis*. (©2005 *Boys' Life Magazine*, www.boyslife.org; used with permission; all rights reserved).

one example. More recently, Norman R. Augustine, past president, BSA and president of the Lockheed Martin Corporation, said that America's future reflected the future of Scouting. Scouting's involvement in aviation as part of the scouting experience and American destiny began at the founding of the BSA. Aviation and BSA developed nearly simultaneously. Scouting entered the USA in 1910, only a few years after the Wright Brothers' first flight. Immediately, in 1911, the BSA offered both an aviation merit badge and an aeronautics merit badge. As World War II began, even more emphasis on aviation directed young boys' interest to the field. The two aviation badges of the World War I era were now subdivided into four badges in 1942: Aerodynamics, Aeronautics, Plane Design, and Plane Structures. These merit badges would be carried into the Cold War until 1952. During World War II it became apparent that the country needed people to build and design aircraft as much as it needed people to fly them. Handbooks such as *Boy Scout Aeronautics*, designed to help Scouts attain the aviation merit badges, discussed and pictured the Clippers, carrying the American flag abroad.

Also during 1942 the Air Scout program was created for boys fifteen and over in cooperation with the United States Air Force. But it was also during the late 1930s and 1940s that questions about the military background of Scouting arose. Though many churches were proud to sponsor Scout troops, some people wondered about the military tie-ins of Scouting. What might be the difference between the BSA and Hitler's Youth Corps? The military-inspired regalia seemed to be about the same—emblems showing ranks or classes, proficiency badges, saluting, kerchiefs, pennants, uniforms, oaths, staffs, cords, "troops," to name a few. The origins of Scouting were there for all to see. One only needed to look at how Sir Robert Baden-Powell had transformed his military survival manual to something for boys. E.E. Reynolds' *Boy Scouts* (1944) responded to these concerns by writing that Scouting was a pre-citizenship, not pre-military, exercise. Considering that three and one-half million boys around the world were Scouts in 1939, these were not just idle concerns.

Other countries and other airlines shared the same concerns about the Clippers at this time. Was Clipper expansionism across the Pacific with the help of the U.S. government and military another form of American manifest destiny? The British believed so, and certainly the Japanese who saw Clipper routes extend to Asia through the Japanese Mandate. Here was an airline that was providing aviation leadership to the world through a monopoly given by the U.S. government to create civilian international routes that could be converted to military use. Clipper "Scouting" in the Pacific did not appear to be as innocent as airline publicity would have the world believe. The United States feared that German-owned airlines in South America would quickly threaten the Panama Canal by changing from civilian to military use; yet, when war broke out, the PAA Clippers made just that conversion. Suddenly these civilian planes were leased to the army and navy, and Pan Am island bases became military bases. Pan American had earned its merit badges. As U.S. flag carrier, it assumed the rank of Eagle Scout, and its pioneering spirit of entrepreneurship spread through the pages of *Boys' Life.*

Scouts built Clipper models out of balsa wood, learned aviation terminology, and nurtured the dream of flying, particularly in service to others—and that was how Pan American sold itself. It was drawing the world closer, making it a better place. The China Clipper was like a Lone Scout, alone but proficiently adventurous in the vast expanse of oceans. It could function as a heroic icon for the BSA as well as for its Lone Scout counterparts, those boys who became Lone Scouts when there were not enough other boys in the area to form a troop.

Scouting offered youth a positive identity in the hard-strapped Depression and post–Depression years. The Clipper gave the BSA one way to offer boys, young men, and their leaders a vision that the world was indeed advancing and that technological utopian visions were not out of reach for those who could and did dream. Youth not only lived in a great age of inventions, but Scouting encouraged them to become inventors of the future and skilled handlers of the new machines. Igor Sikorsky was one of several inventors patenting designs for monster Clippers in this new utopia of the air. Some physicists produced formulas proving that aircraft could not become any bigger. They believed such larger chunks of metal could not break free from water or fly. Sikorsky and others proved them wrong. What seemed like fanciful designs appeared in science and mechanics magazines as well as *Boy's Life*. Wind-tunnel specialist A.J. Harpstrite patented one of the more curious designs. His twin-tail flying boat carried seven engines, a triple-wing design, a fenced outdoor promenade on the upper wing, and a compartmentalized hull. The giant craft seemed a cross between the *Titanic* and the Red Baron's tri-winged plane. Even larger craft were proposed. For youth, energy was in the air, much of it produced by flying boats and flying the oceans. If it could be dreamed, it could be done.

A 1939 postcard for the Pan American–DeSoto Exposition in Tampa showing a tableau with the "winged" goddess of aviation standing on a globe and holding a Clipper.

A

Flying Aces not only showed Clippers on its covers as on this May 1939 issue, but also ran a potboiler in each issue starring the Griffon, a hero who often saved Clippers and crews from the forces of evil .

Left: Clipper Gasoline used this image on its glass pump heads as well as other promotional items. A collector's plate is shown. *Right:* An engineless S-40 Clipper was depicted on this tobacco trading card for the Philippine Clipper.

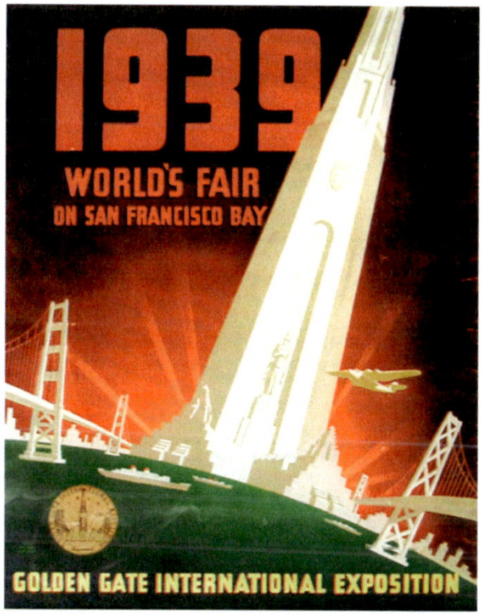

Left: To interest children in history and stamp collecting, the authors of *America's Stamps* depicted a Clipper on the Art Deco cover. *Right:* Poster for the Golden Gate International Exposition showing the China Clipper over the bridges on its way to the Art Deco extravaganza on Treasure Island.

The Top Flight orange crate label ranks among the most beautiful and rare of all the fruit box labels of the 1930s and 1940s.

Gordon Grant's painting, "Yankee Clippers Sail Again," appeared on the covers of many publications, including those of the Smithsonian and various commercial companies as shown here.

Left: The China Clipper on a 1930s Australian puzzle box cover. *Right:* An early 1930s needlebook showing the Sikorsky S-42 Clipper.

The Goudey Gum Company of Boston produced this card of the China Clipper available through its Air Service Gum.

A Clipper Cargo label from the late 1940s in Spanish reflected the close ties the Clippers made possible between North and South America.

E

Just as the Boeing Clippers were manufactured in the shadow of Mt. Rainier, so were the short-lived Aviator Ales as shown on this 1995 label.

Left: Bigger is better: the April 1936 cover of *Boys' Life* projected a futuristic vision of an eight-engine behemoth Clipper based on an interview with Igor Sikorsky (©2005 *Boys' Life Magazine*, www.boyslife.org; used with permission; all rights reserved). *Right:* Japanese Navy postcard using the China Clipper with Japanese markings. The card reads, "Happy New Year. Banzai!"

This sample from a bolt of cloth used for one of the Tori Richards Christmas issue Aloha shirt shows a jolly Santa, laden with toys, walking down the dock in his floppies from the North Pole Clipper, circa 2003 (©2001 Tori Richard, Ltd.).

Monte Dolak's painting of the China Clipper as it appeared on a Marley Hodgson Ghurka leather goods advertising postcard in the 1990s (courtesy Ghurka-Vergier Holdings).

H A 2002 Jimmy Buffett Parrot Heads Convention poster (courtesy Bob Masse Studios).

6

Clipper Toys, Games, Amusements

If you were a lucky child on Christmas Day 1937 or on your birthday or on some other gift-receiving occasion, you might have yearned for and been given a Wyandotte China Clipper toy metal airplane. Major magazines such as *Life* and catalogues featured it as one of the top toys of the year, along with Malibu dollhouse, the metal Cord automobile, and Skippy with his Skippy trailer. As a testament to its popularity and the number produced, many of these tough Clipper toys survive to this day. They may be missing a few props or a wheel or two, but they survived the rigors of the toy boxes across the country.

The Clipper toys' success is attributable to timing as well as an appeal to national myths. The China Clipper had just completed opening the final legs of the route from the United States to China that spring, so its image was splattered all over the newspapers and magazines, creating perfect production timing for Christmas. And even though toys were slow to catch on to the Wright Brothers earlier in the century, Charles Lindbergh and his *Spirit of St. Louis* gave the toy airplane industry a big boost in 1927. The Clippers flew in right on the popularity crest of air-minded-age toys.

While most Wyandotte toys were somewhat crude, the company's toy Clipper wasn't; yet it was clearly a toy, not a model. Though it carried realistic PAA nose decals and silver props that turned, realism ended there. Gaudy eye-catching colors enticed children. Usually the nine-inch fuselage of the Clipper was painted white to magnify the bright red that covered the length of the thirteen-inch wingspan. Sometimes the body was a bright red; sometimes the wings were blue. Wyandotte made sure the patriotic Red/White/and Blue was well represented. Unlike the real clipper which had no wheels, since it landed only on water, the Wyandotte did, so a child could taxi it across the floor.

The toy industry touted the brightly colored, pressed metal Wyandotte China Clipper in the late 1930s. Too heavy to float, it came with wheels so it could be taxied across the floor or sidewalk.

The Wyandotte China Clipper was also flying in on the crest of a fashion rage in the toy industry for "streamlined" toys that focused on transportation, mainly cars, trains, and airplanes. These toys moved away from earlier boxiness in design, as children followed adult design into the modern age. The toy industry fittingly focused on transportation, since it was transportation that made the mass production of toys possible in the United States. The still-young toy industry returned the favor. The earlier use of steam engines for trains and boats, the opening of canals, and the creation of roadways opened the way for mass distribution and made it possible for toy makers to move from cottage industries to factory production. Without advancements in transportation, major toy manufacturers could not have existed. New England or Midwestern toymakers would have remained what they had mostly always been—artisans using the scrap materials from their other pursuits—wood left over from furniture or frame making, cloth left over from upholstering, and the like. Now toy companies could concentrate on toys and ship them everywhere, particularly during the Depression and into World War II to the five-and-dimes. And now toy companies could celebrate the streamlined Clipper, the culmination of modern transportation.

The clouds of war also contributed to the Wyandotte China Clipper's popularity. Children grew keenly interested in airplanes, tanks, trucks, and military figures, as war weighed on the world. The China Clipper split the difference between civilian and military interests. The toy represented a flying boat involved in international affairs and intrigue, yet was still a civilian enterprise. Thus, it represented an intermediate toy that bridged the gap between the earlier *Spirit of St. Louis* racer planes and the bombers and fighters that were to come. Here was a civilian plane that became a war plane during the war, so children could play with it, using it to fit into their other military-oriented toys or domestic-oriented toys. A child could use the toy gas truck from his metal Marx filling station to gas up his Clipper and pretend toy taxis were taking passengers to their hotels, or the child could use it with toy army men on military missions. In short, the Clipper was the best of both worlds. It was an innocent "peaceful" present an adult could proudly give a child to foster play involving modern technological knowledge and possible future careers as aviators or flight attendants. For the child, it could satisfy those noisy, nasty, destructive, dive-bombing tastes.

The toy Clippers appeared at the time the United States boycotted silk hosiery and toys from Japan, which hurt small businessmen and cottage industries in Japan, but hardly punished the Japanese for their military actions in China. Meanwhile, the U.S. merrily sold Japan what it needed for its big toys of war. In 1939, Japan was purchasing 85 percent of its aviation gasoline from the United States. Materials for war materiel, and sometimes the bombs and airplanes themselves, came from the U.S. And when Japan lost most of its trade with European nations embroiled in their own war, the United States picked up the slack, providing up to 70 percent of the total war supplies Japan needed to conduct its campaign. In short, the U.S. became a major trading partner, paying only lip service to sanctions. The sanctions on toys did favor U.S. toy firms facing less competition.

During the late 1930s and early 1940s, children's interest in airplanes and military toys reached its height. As Richard O'Brien pointed out in *The Story of American Toys*, one toymaker alone was producing nearly a half million soldiers, vehicles, airplanes, and other toys every week by 1940 (122). Wyandotte, also known as the All Metal Products Company, had produced mostly weapons in the form of toy pistols, rifles, and automatics since the 1920s to feed the Depression tastes of children, "the last race of barbarians which show no signs of dying out." Streamlining Clippers and Tommy guns was a natural progression from the earlier products. As the Depression wore on, better and better materials became available for toy making. Toys no longer depended on scraps.

Therefore, the Wyandotte Clipper was a product of the Depression. Sheet metal became cheap. Rubber became cheap. Few people could afford high-ticket items, so their materials became available to the toy industry. The toy China Clipper could be built to last, unlike earlier, and even later, more breakable toys, while its price could stay low. After the Japanese attack on Pearl Harbor, the seemingly endless abundance of quality materials ended. Toymakers were prohibited from using materials critical for the war effort. That meant toys would have to be made out of cheaper, shorter-lived materials such as cardboard and composition materials made of sawdust and glue. Lead, sheet metal, rubber, and cast iron were all needed for the military. During the war, toymakers stopped most of their toymaking to turn to war production. Thus, the China Clipper remained the touchstone of flying boat toys. Later versions of the Clippers, such as the Boeing Clippers, which first began flying the oceans in 1939, came too late, missing out on the availability of materials to build toys based on them. Wyandotte issued a version of the Boeing Clipper just before the war by simply modifying the tail on its China Clipper toy. The Tootsie-Toy Company manufactured a tiny version of the Boeing Clipper, too, calling it the Atlantic Clipper, and the Auburn Rubber Company produced a small rubber version. But overall, the China Clipper ruled prewar aviation toys. In addition to the Wyandotte model, the popular Marks Company answered with its own very competitive China Clipper for the nickel-and-dime store market. J. Chien & Company manufactured its tin version as well. In England, Dinky Toys offered a miniature metal Sikorsky S-42, the predecessor of the China Clipper.

Long after the war, die-cast metal Clipper toys of the Boeing Clipper did become available in limited quantities. In the 1960s, the PlayArt Company of Hong Kong began manufacturing metal cars in competition with Hot Wheels. The company also experimented with producing a very few airplanes. One of these elite few that PlayArt created in its short, fifteen-year history, was the Boeing Dixie Clipper in a blue and white paint scheme.

Without the availability of metal for Wyandotte and other companies to continue building Clipper toys, wooden airplane model kit companies sensed the lack of competition and swung into action. The 1940s saw the rise of various companies producing wooden airplane model kits of the Clipper. These companies sprang from their roots of previously building wooden models for military use, after which it was discovered that the models could also be popular as toys. Their construction became a common pursuit for both youths and adults as long as no tendons were severed when an Exacto knife or razor blade slipped while cutting out the

The Guillow Martin Pan American Clipper Ship was one of the many Clipper wooden model kits produced in the 1930s and 1940s (courtesy Paul K. Guillow, Inc.).

pieces! Glue sniffing was not seen as a problem at the time. Comic books and other magazines for youth began to increase ads selling models. Cereals began offering promotions and cereal premiums featuring model kits. For instance, the Comet company offered its inexpensive, precut, balsa-wood China Clipper kit as a Quaker Oats cereal premium. The Megow Company first offered what it termed the Glenn Martin Clipper kit in 1935, renaming it the China Clipper in 1936 when the Martin Clipper was given that name officially. Strombecker produced a very popular solid pinewood version of the China Clipper. The Continental Model Airplane Company of New York used the Clipper image on boxes of all the different "Super Flyers" model kits it offered. It also used a winged globe nearly identical to Pan American Airways' winged globe as its own company logo on its plans. Virtually every model kit maker advertised Clipper kits.

The Cleveland Model and Supply Company best illustrated the dominance of balsa-wood Clippers over earlier metal toys. Cleveland produced a variety of Clipper models and sizes, some with wingspans big enough to fill a garage. The war proved a real boon for this company, the largest of all model kit makers in the Clipper age of the 1930s and 1940s. In the teeth of the war, in 1944 with money and goods in short supply and people using rationing books, the company set its own sales record in a single year of $7.5 million. Cleveland typified some of the other model companies where company founders came directly from the aviation industry. It was no wonder that the Clipper became one of Cleveland's featured kits, since its founder, Edward T. Pachasa (Packard), had previously worked for the Glenn L. Martin Company and Tony Fokker Atlantic Aviation in their upholstery, doping, and covering departments. Both companies produced aircraft for Pan American Airways. Martin, of course, built the three Clippers that together were known as China Clippers.

Though some balsa wood had been around for model building in pre–Clipper days as far back as 1911, Cleveland revolutionized airplane model building by producing the first glued, all-balsa construction kit in 1926 just as the Clippers were being born. Model building previously had been a trying affair. Modelers working with bamboo, pine, or basswood would have to nail or wrap thread around recalcitrant joints to hold the plane together.

Clippers and balsa enjoyed a close relationship in odd ways. Though the Clippers were not made of balsa, as World War II progressed many warplanes were. With the scarcity of metals, different countries experimented with sandwiching different layers of wood together in building airplanes. The British Mosquito was but one example of a famous warplane using balsa. Because of its lightness and strength, balsa was the perfect wood. High quality balsa went into war production, but this meant that much lower grade was available to the model aircraft industry. So important was this resource that Clippers were known to have flown emergency cargoes of rubber and balsa out of the jungles of South America. As will be seen, Clippers, rubber, and balsa were linked historically in other ways, too.

The importance of model airplanes in popular culture cannot be overstated. Alphonse Penaud flew the first rubber-powered airplane, the "Planophore," in Paris in 1871 after he had experimented with helicopter designs. When the Wright Brothers were children, their father gave them a present of a helicopter based on Penaud's concept, whetting their appetite for what was to come. Juan Trippe, the visionary who created Pan American Airways and the Clippers that spanned the oceans, began his aviation career as a child flying model airplanes in New York City's Central Park. He would transform his rubber band-powered, balsa-ribbed, tissue-covered, glued waifs into roaring aluminum monsters that could make villages shake when they took off. Though Trippe later could not land his China Clippers or Atlantic Clippers on the pond in Central Park, he came close to returning home again by landing them at the Clipper base at LaGuardia. Model airplanes fired youthful imagination on high octane.

Award-winning writer Barry Lopez wrote about this piquing of the imagination in his childhood reminiscence series, *A Scary Abundance of*

Water, which ran in *LA Weekly* (January 11–17, 2002). Lopez told how he looked forward to visits from Sidney Van Sheck, his mother's first husband, an artist/aeronautical engineer, and her best friend's husband. Van Sheck, a former World War I combat pilot, worked on the B-24 bomber's wing design in World War II for Bechtel-McCone, as well as the B-29, the B-36, Howard Hughes' Spruce Goose, and, later on, satellites. He held many patents and shared his love of aviation by bringing the young Lopez plans for models of the airplanes Sheck was developing. Lopez, however, loved putting the flying boat kits together. Rather than the Spruce Goose, Lopez's favorites were the Martin Company's China Clipper and the Boeing Company's California Clipper. Lopez remembered just wanting to fly off on the China Clipper to lands beyond the sea. As an adult he did just that. His book titles reveal how his travels and imagination connected in the National Book Award's *Arctic Dreams: Imagination and Desire in a Northern Landscape*; *Of Wolves and Men*; and *About This Life: Journeys on the Threshold of Memory*, which explored such places as Hokkaido, the Galapagos, and Bonaire, and *Light Action in the Caribbean*.

Pan American Airways fed the model airplane craze in the 1940s by sponsoring a special competition, which began at the Academy of Model Aeronautics "Nationals" competition held at the navy base in Olathe, Kansas. The PAA–Load Event for gasoline-powered free flight models in the ROG (Rise Off Ground) category required that smaller models carry a payload of eight ounces, while larger models had to fly with an extra pound. Payloads were made up of Pan American Airways envelopes specially printed for the event, then mailed to various PAA executives and other aviation notables—that is, unless the model flew too well and kept going over the horizon to be lost in some farmer's Kansas field. Trophies and certificates were given out at such events by Pan American and other major airlines, by flying heroes, and by the military.

Clippers entered the toy trade in many forms besides model airplanes. Tracking the mythos involved in these toys is difficult since toys perform so many functions. While adults may buy or create toys for children for certain reasons, children may use them quite differently. In addition, adults may keep or collect toys for themselves as revisionist or re-creative nostalgia for their own childhood. Thus, many American bedrock beliefs come together in toys. That "youth is best" and that, as part of the American Dream, Americans expect themselves to progress, not to stay in the same place, are but two central beliefs wrapped around toys. Adults hope toys will make children progress by helping them realize their full potential. Toys and games accomplish this by challenging children to figure out how things work, to use their imaginations in play, to practice cooperating with others in the socialization process, to engage in problem solving, to develop dexterity or muscle control, to encounter new ideas and new situations, to practice leadership skills, to gain knowledge about the world around them. Clipper-related toys and games fulfilled all these functions.

Often with toys and games, the adults use these mass-produced objects as a means to teach children what adults want them to realize as values of mainstream culture. Play becomes practice for adult roles. Therefore, a parent could give a child a jigsaw puzzle picturing a Clipper flying across an ocean to encourage interest in geography, applied science, transportation, or business. Children, to the contrary, could use toys to conquer their own fears, to make sense of their own experience, or to pursue their own unlimited fantasies. However toys function, they can attain iconic status. As Pamela B. Nelson pointed out in "Toys as History: Ethnic Images and Cultural Change," "Mass-produced toys are especially revealing because their designers, concerned with marketability, intentionally try to appeal to dominant attitudes and values." Clipper toys and games did reveal much about changing values and power.

Not all the Clipper toys and games were created by U.S. manufacturers. Germany exported a Clipper childhood diversion variously described as a hand puzzle, dexterity game, or BB puzzle. Shaped like a sealed, small circular Petri dish, the game consisted of an image of the "China Clipper" from "Amerika" pasted on the bottom of the dish. Two holes were drilled, one forward and one aft on the plane's fuselage. The object of the game was for the player to try to roll two red BBs into the holes by gently tilting the game back and forth. Because the holes were shallow, it was easy for one BB to roll out of its hole while the player tried to deal with the other BB. The metal backside of the toy was so shiny and smooth that it could be used as a personal or signal mirror. As an education toy, the puzzle had one problem: the flying boat it pictured was not the China Clipper but an earlier twin-tailed Sikorsky Clipper, which did fly some of the early survey routes across the Pacific before the China Clippers were assembled and tested. Close enough.

Clipper jigsaw puzzles promoted problem-solving skills, as did all interlocking puzzles, but the Clippers also taught the geography of a changing world. This was in keeping with the jigsaw tradition, for in 1767 mapmaker John Splisbury created the first jigsaw puzzle by applying one of his maps to a piece of wood and then cutting around the borders of the countries. Similarly, many Clipper jigsaw puzzles used Clippers superimposed over maps in showing how the rest of the world was entering into America's consciousness as Clippers opened up trade routes to the east, west, and south. A 1943 wartime example manufactured by the Platt & Munk

Company was designed to help children learn their states and state capitals. Typical of such map puzzles, states were contrasted in different colors. The title scroll to the map announced that this was a map of the United States die-cut on state lines. Two frontiersmen, one from the past and one from the present, stood on each side of the scroll. Representing the United States in history stood a Kentuckian in buckskin and coonskin cap. Facing him was a modern pilot in a flight suit. Above them, a Boeing Clipper departed California for the broad Pacific expanse.

An All-Fair "South America Map Puzzle" also depicted a Boeing Clipper winging its way towards Brazil in this geography lesson. The puzzle illustrated major products or natural resources for each country to further emphasize trade implications. Puzzles such as this became very popular during the war when metal toys became scarce. Toy and game makers turned to cardboard and paper instead.

Other puzzles focused on the technology and romance of modern aviation rather than geography. In 1941 the Saalfield Publishing Company of Akron, Ohio, marketed its box of three puzzles entitled "Picture Puzzles of Famous Planes." The plane chosen to grace the box's lid was the star of

Charles H. Hubbell's painting of the Boeing Atlantic Clipper on the box cover of a 1941 Saalfield Company puzzle set.

the lot, the Boeing Atlantic Clipper, pictured breaking out of dark clouds over a lighthouse. The works of Charles H. Hubbell (1898–1971), the painter of the Clipper, became quite popular. Not only did his Clipper appear in puzzles but also in books, in magazine ads, and on company promotional prints and calendars. Hubbell became the most famous artist-historian of the Air Age, getting his start by trading airplane drawings for flying time. Hubbell knew aircraft well, having joined the Naval Air Service in World War I. Stationed in Buffalo, New York, he redesigned experimental aircraft at the Curtiss factory.

Hubbell was hard to top, but Platt & Munk competed against the Saalfield puzzle by offering a six-airplane boxed set of puzzles that same year. They, too, offered a puzzle entitled "Boeing 314 (Yankee Clipper)" painted by Irvin Holcombe. In keeping with the streamlining and art style

The Yankee Clipper, painted by Irvin Holcombe on Saalfield Company puzzle.

of the time, Holcombe, like Hubbell, painted the Clipper trailing pale speed streaks from its tail and wing surfaces to suggest movement. His landscape of a dull sea was much more nondescript than Hubbell's. Nevertheless, Clippers were *the* popular aircraft for picture puzzles.

This held true in the British Commonwealth as well. From Down Under came one of the more spectacular and larger Clipper puzzles. It was included in a three-puzzle box called "The Modern Travel Puzzle" that included paintings of the *Queen Mary* and a modern locomotive. Neither artist nor company designations appeared, but the China Clipper stole the show because it covered most of the box cover as the Clipper soared over a tiny *Queen Mary* on the ocean below. The *Queen Mary*, the pride of the Cunard line, made its maiden voyage in 1936, when the China Clipper, pride of the U.S. aerial line, was completing its early trips between San Francisco and Manila. The puzzles likely date from that year or shortly after, when both ship and flying boat made news. One of the challenges for both young and old stamp collectors of the time was to plan an around-the-world mailing of letters transported by the *Queen Mary* and the Clipper, sometimes with help from a zeppelin and other aircraft or trains. Figuring out the timing and transfer points became educational experiences increasing knowledge of international datelines, postal rates, political entities, and geography. For a year, the *Queen Mary* and the Clipper shared the same stage.

The Clippers also appeared in board games. The granddaddy of all board game makers, the Parker Company, continued its Monopoly game success by churning out its South American Pictorial Travel and Trading Game. Just as Monopoly taught young and old would-be capitalists the importance of money and wise investment with property, houses, and hotels, the South American game allowed four players to engage in wise buying and selling of the major products produced in South American countries, while trying to fly Pan American Airways' routes. Players started in different locations and arrived by set, mapped routes in different ports. Once the player had both bought and sold two products, that player could return to the U.S. by any route to win the game.

Parker included a large cut-away artist's rendering of the Boeing Clipper, where tokens were stored. Most of the inside portion of the box to this game was devoted to giving specifications and other interesting facts about the flying boat. Players could learn what the Clipper's "hydrostabilizers" were or how the cargo bay actually extended into the wings of the giant plane. Pan American aircraft adorned nearly all features of the game. An earlier Sikorsky Clipper was pictured on the playing surface map. Other aircraft appeared on the spinner dial, travel tickets, box cover, and map cover. The connection between North America's trade with South America due to the Clipper connection was obvious. This was a money and speed game, quite different from Parker's other aviation games in the 1940s such as "Flying the Beam" or "Dogfight," which emphasized a combination of flying expertise and luck. Free enterprise and competition ruled.

Kellogg, the cereal maker, offered its Kellogg's Airways Game, which included twelve easy to assemble airplanes. This board game's cover showed various colorful airplanes flying over the Kellogg's Airport, the largest of the aircraft a bright red China Clipper. How this seaplane would land on the concrete runway was anyone's guess. Kellogg also created its own aviation corps to educate children for the new air age with its booklet *Kellogg's Cadet Aviation Corps Handbook*, which pictured the China Clipper on its cover and preconditioned young people to already think of themselves as "cadets."

For those who would rather shoot airplanes down than move tokens around, the Lindstrom Tool and Toy Company of Bridgeport, Connecticut, sold their 1940s Candid Camera Target Shot game. This piece of composition board served as a target for suction-cup darts fired from a toy gun. The player could also use actual darts to really wreak havoc on the photos of the aircraft pictured. The board showed a variety of aircraft and a dirigible. Different types of flying boats and amphibions included later model Clipper spin-off designs for the military that Clipper crews flew during the war. Strangely, except for one German aircraft represented, American youth were being asked to shoot down their own aircraft to score points. One four-engine artist's conception of what would become the Lockheed Constellation was even pictured upside down. That the game was manufactured in Bridgeport, the home of Sikorsky, who made the early Clippers, added to its rather bizarre, destructive nature. At a time when youth were being trained to be airplane spotters to detect friend from foe, this game awarded more points for shooting down an American flying boat than a German!

Clippers have become a part of the POGs fad that resurfaced several times in recent decades. The early evolution of the Clippers coincided with the creation of POGs, both as a game and the name of the cardboard disks used to seal milk bottles. The Boeing clipper was featured as POG #105 of a 200 airplane set of Jello Hostess Premium disks produced in the early 1960s. The disks were color-coded, with each color representing a subset of twenty-five related discs. The clipper was coded grey for the airliners category. Other categories included pioneers (white), fighters (red), bombers (black), bushplanes (green), trainers (yellow), and others (orange).

To understand how Clipper came to be depicted on a POG is to understand nearly 300 years of history, mostly Japanese history. In the twentieth century the fate of the clippers was tied up with U.S. and Japanese history in World War II. Japan fought the creation of Pan American's bases across the Pacific, and when war broke out, Japanese aircraft quickly destroyed the Sikorsky Hong Kong Clipper in Hong Kong, strafed and riddled the Philippine Clipper at Wake Island, and tried to intercept and destroy other Pan Am flying boats carrying important people. None of the hard-working Martin Clippers survived the conflict. Centuries before that, Japanese popular culture, influenced by militarism, already was preparing the way for the depiction of the Clipper on cardboard disks.

In the middle of the Edo Period in the early 1700s, long before the creation of milk bottle caps, young boys in Japan played with menkos. A menko ("small mask") was about the same size as modern day milk caps. The first clay menkos showed faces of people or animals. As in sumo wrestling, the object of playing with menkos was to "flip" the opponent's menko or knock it out of the ring, much like the Western idea of playing "ringsies" with marbles.

Cardboard or paper menkos came about at the time of the Sino-Japanese wars in 1894–1895 when Japan invaded Manchuria, and during the Russo-Japanese wars in the early 1900s. As Japan sought to extend its influence in Asia, menko topics turned even more to militarism. The faces of samurai and soldiers became popular. These menkos were printed on one side and round just as milk caps would later be. Like the munitions of the time, some menkos were made of lead rather than of paper, but lead menkos were quickly forbidden when child warriors suffered lead poisoning as a result of licking disks for luck and grip. Thus began the unbroken history to present times of the paper or cardboard disk.

Aviation first appeared on menkos during the 1920s and 1930s Japanese cultural renaissance when the country adopted Western motifs as a modern nation. In addition to Disney characters, theatrical stars, and baseball players, some die-cut airplanes could be launched through the air. It was at this time that the menko tradition merged with other traditions to become POGs. Japanese who had played menkos as youth settled in Hawaii. Some went to work in the many dairies that sprinkled the islands. Here, they would encounter milk bottle caps that would revive their old game.

That POGs originated in Hawaii is fitting because Clipper history is so closely tied to Hawaii. About the time Pan American Airways was developing the Martin and Boeing clippers as transoceanic transports in the 1930s so that commercial flying boats could reach Hawaii, workers during their breaks at the Haleakala Dairy in Maui began playing a game flipping cardboard milk lids. This game was passed down from generation to generation. Milk lids had been around for a long time; however, they had not been used as a type of currency or prize. In 1889, H.P. & S.I. Barnhart was issued U.S. Patent Number 8 for a milk cap that could seal the mouth of a milk bottle. But the craze for collecting the caps or lids would not take off until the Haleakala Dairy produced a Hawaiian Sun Juice called Passion, Orange, Guava in bottles. Children soon used "POGs," an acronym for Passion, Orange, Guava, to refer to any of the silver-dollar-sized bottle caps. Now we seldom refer to milk caps or milk lids; they are all called POGs, including other disks contained in other products such as chips, or disks sold separately as collector's items.

Pogmania really exploded in 1991 when Blossom Galbiso, "The Mother of POGs," started using POGs from the Haleakala Dairy for class activities with her sixth grade class at Waialua Elementary. The children went nuts for the disks. The craze quickly spread across Oahu and to the mainland where toy, cereal, and other companies such as Coca-Cola, American Airlines, and Taco Bell cashed in by creating their own promotional POGs. One can find nearly anything pictured on POGs today, from holograms to *Star Trek* and Disney movie characters. The craze died out as fast as it began, but revived again in 2002 when Waialua Elementary banned marble playing. Perhaps ironically, Vice Principal Tiffany Eason, a replacement for Galbiso who died in 1994, banned marbles, only to see history repeat itself with pogmania taking its place.

Playing the game of POGs or collecting POGs, attracted youth because many POGs cost but a few cents. Both boys and girls could play. Moreover, in a highly competitive world of sports, here was an activity for all participants irrespective of size and strength. Each player bet at least four POGs facedown in a stack on a sidewalk or other hard surface. A "slammer" or heavier object was thrown at the piles of POGs. If a POG landed face up and was not touching any other POG, the player kept it. Whoever claimed the most face-up POGs won the game.

POG collecting attracted adults as well, with scarcer or early POGs selling for many dollars, not cents. POGs also went by names such as Flippos (in Europe), Troves, or Tazos. No matter what the name, the Clipper's appearance on a POG illustrated popular culture's history of evolving and borrowing from past traditions. The Clipper on the 1960s POG showed the changes in menkos/POGS over time, reflecting our history. Clippers were caught between two worlds in the period surrounding World War II, when Clippers were used for both commercial and military purposes. Likewise, menkos transitioned from being "fighting pieces" to collectibles that were bought and sold in the consumer society formed after the war in Japan. General MacArthur banned the glorification of traditional Japanese heroes during the occupation; therefore, their faces disappeared from menkos. Without the military, Japanese boys no longer looked forward to military service, so menkos had to turn to topics more attuned to a nation's becoming an economic power. Likewise, the Clipper would be shown in the new world of the 1950s and 1960s in its commercial colors, not the military camouflage it wore during the war. It became a piece of nostalgia from a glorified past, the elite samurai of the international commercial air war.

Throughout the post–World War II years, children enjoyed playing with figurines of soldiers, cowboys, and others. The Clipper did make it as one of these through the character of Clipper King, the nephew of Sky King on the radio series of the same name (1946–1954), sponsored by Peter Pan Peanut Butter and the television series (1952–1959) sponsored by Nabisco. Ron Haggerthy played the part of Clipper in the early television versions. Gloria Winters played Sky King's niece, Penny. Kirby Grant played their uncle, Sky King. This World War II flying hero owned the Flying Crown Ranch in fictitious Grover, Arizona, from which he flew his Cessna *Song Bird* every Saturday morning to maintain law and order in the Southwest. All the characters were molded in semitransparent, colored plastic Marx figurines available in boxes of Nabisco Wheat Honeys.

The Clipper King figurine wore Western boots, cowboy hat, vest, kerchief, and jeans. In his hands he held a coiled rope and lasso. No guns—for Clipper was young, and this was modern 1950s Arizona. *Sky King*'s creators astutely combined the public's taste for Westerns, gangsters and war heroism, with aviation adventure. *Sky King* was the last of a long line of aviation hero series created by Robert Morris Burtt and Wilfred Gibbs Moore, both former World War I pilots. In 1933 they created *The Air Adventures of Jimmy Allen*, a radio serial sponsored by the Richfield Oil Company. In 1939 they created another flying radio drama, the famous *Captain Midnight*. After World War II, with the advent of TV, reviving past heroes became difficult. New heroes were needed. Sky King fulfilled that role until youth yearned more for celebrities than for heroes.

Sky King affected many young people for a lifetime. From commercial pilots to astronauts, person after person has related how they were moved to pursue aviation careers because of this program. Aviation wished to return the favor. Kirby Grant, the Flying Cowboy, was to be honored by shuttle astronauts in 1985. While on his way to be honored and to witness the October launch of the shuttle *Challenger* at Cape Canaveral, he died in an auto accident. Testimonials still honor him and the program.

As young people keyed on the aerial escapades of the *Song Bird*, older children kept their eyes on Clipper and Penny. They made great imaginary dates for many a lovesick preteen. The program that began with the magical words "Out of the clear blue of the western sky comes ... Sky King" appealed to many ages. There was even talk of a *Sky King* theme park. All of that was overridden by Walt Disney. Disney planned the grand opening of Disneyland in 1955, the same year that Ron Haggerthy as Clipper left *Sky King*. To further attract visitors, Disney created *The Mickey Mouse Club* television show. It did not take long for future *Bikini Beach* and *Beach Blanket Bingo* Mouseketeer Annette Funicello and the Club's "Adventures of Spin and Marty" to supplant Penny and Clipper in appealing to puberty-ridden viewers. Mouse ears replaced plastic Sky King and Clipper King figurines.

7
Detroit's Clippers

The automotive industry from the 1920s through the 1940s identified itself with the Clipper image to promote the speed, airstream-look, and efficiency of autos and trucks, but before automobile companies began piggybacking ads for their products onto those of the flying clippers, car builders had the same idea as Pan American Airways, which was to first name their designs after the speedy famous sea-going clipper ships. From the Roaring Twenties into the late 1940s, the Reo Motor Car Company manufactured its Reo Flying Clouds, named after the famous clipper ship. Each Flying Cloud carried a silver ship design on its instrument panel. Later on in 1941, parts from the Flying Cloud would be incorporated into the Graham Hollywood Clipper convertible. Bus drivers and riders were also familiar with the Reo Flying Cloud transit bus, which sold into the late 1940s. In the 1930s and 1940s, the Clipper flying boat would become the model for the auto industry rather than the clipper with sails.

The automotive and aviation industries enjoyed a close relationship during the time of Pan American Airways. Ford built its own aircraft, and in 1929 General Motors bought out much of Fokker Aircraft, changing its name to General Aviation Corporation. Fokker controlled interest in Dayton-Wright, Bendix Aviation, and Allison Engineering—companies that would produce parts for the flying Clippers. General Motors followed this up in 1933 by acquiring controlling interest in North American, which, in turn, controlled Eastern Air Transport (Eastern) and much of Transcontinental and Western Air (TWA). What GM learned from aviation engineers it applied to automobiles. Other companies did the same.

The 1930–1931 sales brochures for Fargo "Commercial Vehicles of the New Order" by Chrysler offered the three-quarter-ton Clipper truck. What's more, the Fargo logo of a world globe mimicked that of Pan American Airways. Fargo trucks were depicted as making deliveries to the homes of the wealthy or upper middle class. Usually a well-dressed woman answered the door to receive the household goods that had been ordered. These Clippers were not connected to the grunt work of hauling for heavy industry or the unloading of ships. Eschewing the effects of the Great Depression, delivery men shared in the society of the stylish "swells" by wearing what looked like tailored uniforms and military officer style hats.

In the late 1930s, Willys made a splash with its Clipper model that most often was pictured in promotional material with the China Clipper flying overhead. The ads served not only to promote the idea of a speedy vehicle but also to promote the idea of wealth and sophistication associated with expensive Clipper travel. Most people featured in the Willys ads wore suits, topcoats, hats, traveling dress.

Preeminent industrial designer Brooks Stevens consulted Willys on its Jeep designs after World War II. Stevens all but created the movement to aerodynamic, streamlined, industrial design. His achievements covered nearly the full spectrum of popular culture. He designed the first electric steam iron, the first clothes dryer with a window, the first colored kitchen appliances, Miller High Life bottles and labels, Briggs and Stratton garden tractors, the rotary lawn mower, styled farm machinery and trucks, and trains representing the peak of Art Deco and Modernism. He saved some of his most creative work for the automobile, inventing the preselect gear shift with gears indicated by letters, and emergency brakes that were built into the dash rather than occupying seat room. Whereas automobiles are categorized by being either two-doors or four-doors, Stevens designed the 1941 one-door Mercury Western Clipper. Its streamlined shape made it look like some kind of frontal escape Pod ejected from the Oscar Mayer Weinermobile.

The Cadillac Motor Car Company offered Clipper blue as one of its color choices for select automobiles, as the auto industry began to offer more freedom of choice instead of Henry Ford's declaration that car owners could have any color they wanted as long as it was black. In 1935, the year the China Clipper debuted, color chip guides for upcoming 1936 model Cadillacs and La Salle cars added a supplemental page of color choices. "Clipper Blue Metallic" was now available for those who wanted to make even more of a statement with their Caddy. This deluxe color augmented such other stylish choices as Harlequin Tan Metallic and Dartmouth Green, reflecting the 1930s interest in Art Deco's fondness for harlequin geometry and Ivy League wealth, elan, and sophistication. Across the pond in the 1950s and 1960s, Austin Morris Minis would come in "Clipper blue" as an auto body color choice, as would other Morris models. Into the 1980s, Clipper blue auto carpets and mats would continue to be offered for the Mini.

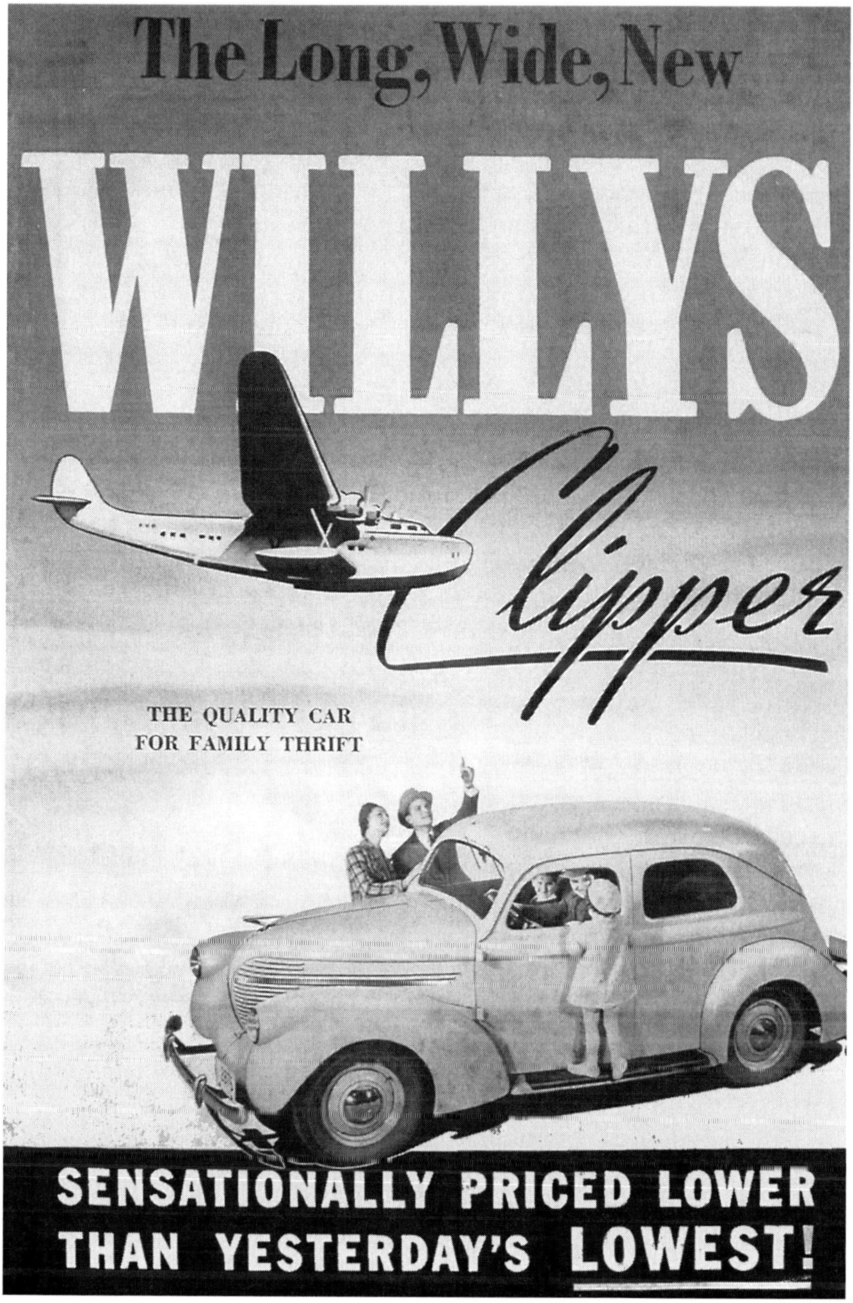

The Willys Clipper featured speed whiskers around its hood to mimic the speed and lines of the China Clipper (courtesy Daimler Chrysler Corporation).

Parts and accessory companies also became caught up in the thirties and forties clipper mania. The Yankee Accessories Company offered Yankee Clipper chrome fog lights for Chrysler Clippers. Ford owners in 1936 could order an art deco NORS Ford hood ornament called the Clipper.

Sophistication and engineering advancements were combined in 1940s sales brochures heralding Chevrolet's De Luxe and "business models." These models featured "Royal Clipper styling, vacuum power shift, valve-in-head engine, syncro-mesh transmission, and tiptoe-matic clutch." Now clippers were associated with royalty. And shiny, streamlined, Art Deco chrome already contained the automotive sex appeal found in later decades on Dolly Parton bump-out pointed fenders, erotically engineered curves and auto orifices.

Although World War II interrupted Detroit's development of Clipper automobile models, in 1941 Packard came out with its Clipper. The design was lower and wider than previous Packards and became so popular that its features were integrated into the rest of the Packard line. This affordable model was so successful that it took a bite out of Packard's image as transportation for the wealthy. In effect, the loss of identity helped lead to the demise of Packard. As World War II ended, Packard's new 1946 Clipper models also were promoted, alongside images of Clipper aircraft, this time with land based Clippers, since the flying boat era was over. The Packard Clipper line would extend into the 1950s. Again, ads suggested a certain degree of wealth and sophistication associated with Clipper travel, both car and airplane, even though the autos were for 1940s middle class buyers rather than 1930s elite. Advertising for models of this era stressed "aerodynamic" features, as if cars could fly. Graham, famous for its "shark-nosed" design, also had a Clipper model, which would have made Batman's Batmobile proud. The Clipper was part of Graham's Hollywood design series. It was a lower-priced Hollywood custom, available for $895 with an unsupercharged six-cylinder engine. Having been disrupted by economic crises and the beginning of the war, fewer than two thousand Hollywoods were built in the three months of their production, and only a portion of that total consisted of Clipper sedans or convertibles.

The cessation of auto production during World War II did not stop car makers from advertising and promising high performance after the war. The Hudson Motor Car Company directly tied the World War II performance of the Clipper flying boats with its own automobiles. In one Hudson magazine ad, a stewardess glanced at her watch while telling a Clipper captain, "Everything right on time, Captain." They stand in front of a Hudson car parked before a moored Boeing Clipper. The text related how Hudson cars maintained effective wartime transportation in emulating the

A wartime advertisement for Hudson tied Clipper flying boat precision and efficiency to Hudson automobiles (courtesy DaimlerChrysler Corporation).

"great commercial flying ships." The Hudson carried a horizontal winged speed strip on the sides of its hood so that its chrome mimicked the wings of the Clipper.

Wally Byam's 1936 classic Art Deco Airstream Clipper trailer borrowed heavily from the aircraft industry. This was his first trailer utilizing aerodynamic, rounded aluminum construction to replace earlier plywood models. The glistening surfaces of the trailers being towed down America's highways and across foreign deserts and mountains mirrored those of its China Clipper duralumin counterpart. World War II suspended Byam's production line due to the scarcity of aluminum. Byam went to work for Lockheed and Curtis Wright in the aircraft industry, completing the circle of aviation inspiration. After the war, in the late 1940s when Curtis Wright no longer needed to use its aluminum for airplane production, the company came out with its own Curtis Wright Clipper travel trailer based on Byam's 1936 design.

At the same time Byam was developing his streamlined trailers, the Flxible Bus Company came out with its Flxible Clipper, which became the standard for Trailways and Greyhound bus lines from the late 1930s into the 1950s. Its distinctively curved back resembled that of the Airstreams. Its windows slanted forward and its sides were horizontally lined with metal work to create the impression of speed. Often speed lines were further enhanced by paint design. They did not carry the "flames" seen on the cars of hot-rodders, but the paint often did make it appear as if air currents were flowing up and over the wheels. It is difficult to see any "road" movie of the 1940s or 1950s without seeing one of these buses. The Clipper bus became an icon in its own right, bringing together the restlessness and movement of a nation. In 1948 the bus was imported into Australia, where the Ainair-Flxible Clipper was born, and subsequently gave birth to the extensive cross-country motor coach business Down Under. Today many of the thousands of outdated Clipper buses are being restored as motor homes.

An even more famous bus appeared in the 1960s: the ubiquitous, hippie icon VW Clipper "bus." Appearing with the VW Beetle, or bug, the Clipper quickly attained symbolic status. For starting a band, a commune, or a family, this became the popular means of transportation for both counterculture and some mainstream people. In pre-van, pre–SUV days, the "bus" was the alternative to more expensive station wagons, campers, or even mobile homes. A person could live in a "bus," and some did. Many Clippers were individualized and decorated with peace symbols and flowers, sort of psychedelic mini-versions of Ken Kesey's larger bus, a 1939 International Harvester named *Further* by the Merry Pranksters. Many college students during the 1960s and 1970s teamed up in their VW Clippers and followed the Kesey example of pursuing a "road trip"—America's answer to the European Grand Tour.

And speaking of the Volkswagon, or "people's car," Clippers played an extended role in that concept. Just as Henry Ford had the capitalistic, democratic dream of producing cars affordable to average citizens, so did others. Adolph Hitler had been in power in Germany for only about a month in 1934 when he ordered his friend Ferdinand Porsche to design a people's car during the worldwide depression. Porsche visited the United States several times to glean what he could from U.S. production methods and design. At the time of Porsche's visits, Denver car designer Paul Lewis had a similar idea for an inexpensive people's car. Lewis called his 1937 aerodynamic teardrop prototype the Airomobile, which did seem to take its cues from the aircraft industry. Like airplanes of the day, it featured a tricycle landing gear, meaning it had three tires instead of four—two in front, and one in the back like the tailwheel of 1930s airplanes. Its low center of gravity and three-wheel design allowed it to turn sharper corners and go places that would ruin four-wheel designs. Just as in aircraft, luggage was loaded into the trunk by a side cargo bay door. Given the name Airomobile, the auto of course featured an air-cooled engine. The Airomobile even had a "tail" that looked more like Humpback flukes than aircraft stabilizers. It was Buck Rogers and Art Deco streamlining combined.

What intrigued Porsche most about what has been called "America's Almost VW" by *Special Interest Autos* magazine was the Airomobile's transmission/differential. This combination essentially became incorporated into the famous VW Beetle, from the first production model unveiled at the Berlin International Automobile and Motorcycle Show in 1939 to current editions. (In keeping with the aero-theme, VW's sporty Golf Convertible Clippers of the 1980s and 1990s also attained near cult status.) With the coming of world war in 1939, Porsche turned his attention to building Panzer tanks, while Lewis's dream ended. However, engine development for the Airomobile found its way into airplanes manufactured by Piper and Aeronca.

After World War II, the dream of a people's car was reborn in the United Kingdom with the Allard Clipper. Sydney Allard revived Lewis's three-wheel concept, except that he reversed the configuration by putting the single tire in the front of the Clipper and two in the back. Allard, a sports car designer and winner of the 1952 Monte Carlo Rally, intended to produce an economical micro car that was lightweight yet sturdy. To accomplish these ends and outdo the VW Beetle, the 1954 Allard Clipper made history, being the first automobile with what was termed an indestructible plastic body. Owners did not have to worry about paint scratches either, since color was impregnated throughout the plastic. About twenty Clippers rolled off the production line in 1954 and 1955 before manufacturing ceased.

Goodyear Tire Company produced this wartime advertisement explaining how its rubber boat bumpers protected the Clippers from harm when Navy crewmen had to tie up alongside the flying boats in rough seas (courtesy The Goodyear Tire & Rubber Co.).

Trident of England sold its very first car, the Clipper V8, in 1967. Designed by Trevor Fiore and built by Fissore in Italy, this prototype was produced until 1976. Few existed, since, according to company records, only 130 total of all five of their models were produced, including the Clippers.

At the turn of the millenium, popular Ford imports abroad included the Ford Scorpio Clipper, the Focus Clipper, and the Escort Clipper. The name continues. When flying boat clippers spanned the oceans, few if any individuals could afford a "Clipper." Few could afford the tickets even to become a passenger on one. Detroit quickly fixed that. Today people can still fly down the highway in their clippers.

Beyond Detroit, Clippers entered the trucking fleet. In Canada, Hayes produced its Clipper 100 and Clipper 200 series. These popular trucks appeared in the 1950s and extended into the 1970s. Brochures from the 1960s advertised the Hayes Clippers as trucks for logging, highway, construction, and oilfield. Today these trucks are the subject of restoration efforts and a modeler's delight for those who enjoy big rigs from the past.

Automobiles and trucks depended on oil, gasoline, tires and other parts produced by companies which appropriated the Clipper image. Various motor oils, some used by the Clippers and some not, displayed Clippers, either in the advertisements or on their products. Traymore Lubricants of New York offered Ocean Liner Motor Oil, promising "3000 miles of Lubrication," for sale in patriotic red/white/blue two-gallon cans illustrating the B-314 Clipper.

8

China Clipper Restaurants, Bars, Clubs, and Lounges

China Clipper eating and drinking establishments flourished in the 1930s and 1940s. They either promised elegant hotel-chic Art Deco/Art Moderne design for sophisticates, or promoted inexpensive Chinese American food and a place where servicemen could meet girls over a few drinks. Following in the tradition of eating and watering holes being linked to the history of locomotion, China Clipper businesses were conspicuous at the flying boat's ports of call. Places like San Francisco and Hong Kong, once ports for the sailing clipper ships, now became ports for the flying clippers. In place of stops for covered wagons, stagecoaches, and locomotives, cities became the way stations, the roadhouses, the boarding houses, the hotels on the new aviation frontier. Businesses at these air portals to the East and West adopted the China Clipper in name and logo.

In 1941 at the Aviation Terrace Restaurant at New York City's newly completed LaGuardia Airport, diners were handed menus with steel engraved cover art entitled "Wings of the Night Over Land & Sea at LaGuardia Airport." Moonbeams filtered through a cloudy sky onto a Clipper flying over the waters of Flushing Bay and Long Island Sound that bordered the airport. The skyways and waterways mirrored the tangle of taxiways and superhighways leading to the airport below. LaGuardia, "built for the aviation of tomorrow," was "a monument to the untiring efforts of Mayor Fiorello H. LaGuardia and his associates." The airport, Mayor LaGuardia, and the Clipper tied together as a vision of tomorrow existing in the present. The menu boasted that this ultramodern architectural showpiece had a Clipper hangar big enough to hold two football fields, an observation deck over a mile long, and the nation's most powerful signal beacon. The Aviation Terrace was not just another restaurant, but in New York style was operated by the Hotel New Yorker. Inside the menu, another Boeing Clipper was illustrated as it flew over the listing for the $2.50 lobster dinner with genuine Maine lobsters flown in fresh every day by air express from Boston. The 817-mile Clipper route to Bermuda was advertised as taking six hours and fifteen minutes. The Aviation Terrace would mail souvenir menus to the diners' friends postage-free.

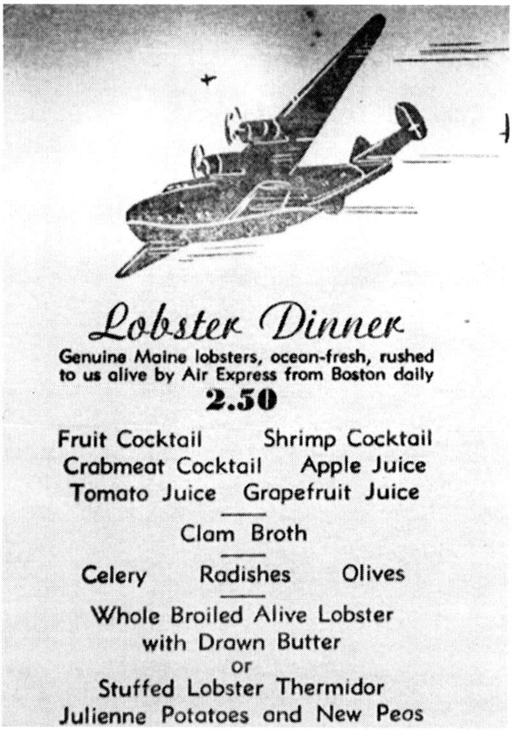

A 1941 menu page from the Aviation Terrace operated by the Hotel New Yorker at the just opened LaGuardia airport.

In making the connection to the flying boat's purported efficiency, speed, and streamlining, many establishments emphasized these attributes in their own businesses by choosing the China Clipper as logo and by using the most modern in industrial design to copy the Clipper. The flying boat image appeared on tableware, wall art, napkins, menus, matchbooks, and most noticeably on neon signs. The 1930s and 1940s represented the golden age of neon or "new gas." This liquid fire was still a novelty show-stopper. It had not yet earned a reputation as the scarlet whore of the advertising world associated with Vegas, sleazy motels, film-noir existential booze dives, or kitschy roadside attractions. Instead, it offered another-worldly dream blue and other magic colors that signaled modernity and a cure for Depression blues.

Neon did not enter the United States until 1923, when Earle Anthony's Packard dealership in Los Angeles ordered two of the blue and red signs for $24,000 from the French firm of Claude Neon. Georges Claude had displayed the first neon lamps to be seen by the public at the Grand Palais in Paris in 1910, just before World War I. Neon's introduction into the U.S. occurred at almost the same time Igor Sikorsky was building his first amphibion aircraft, which by the end of the 1920s would become the first amphibions flown by Pan American Airways. It was appropriate that a Packard dealer first used neon, since Packard would build a long-running series of Clipper automobile models. Soon Packard Clippers would be stopping under the neon signs that adorned restaurants and lounges featuring the flying Clipper from coast to coast, and in the heartland where no Clippers flew. Even Detroit's China Clipper restaurant at the corner of Grand River and Lasher displayed a large neon flying boat. The tradition is carried on today in modern neon, with a rendition of the B-314 clipper being used to sell Corona beer.

By the late 1930s China Clipper establishments had sprung up everywhere. One could take a trip across the United States stopping at nothing but China Clippers. Although they were, by and large, mom and pop operations, they appeared across the country like early renditions of McDonald's or Wendy's, exploding like corporate mushrooms. The name was quite popular with Chinese-American restaurant owners because it gave them an American cachet at a time when being of Asian descent could be dangerous to their health. Some China Clipper restaurant operators even wore "I am Chinese" buttons while they worked so that people would not mistake them for Japanese. "The China Clipper" had a different and perhaps safer, more far-reaching ring to it than did "Wong's."

One could start at the China Clipper in San Francisco's Chinatown or in the Clipper Ship Lounge of the Chancellor Hotel at Powell and Post Streets at Union Square. The Clipper Ship Lounge used the China Clipper as its logo. This swanky lounge featured a view of the bay, where Clippers landed and took off for the Orient, and an Art Deco stainless steel/chrome look that rivaled the duralumin of the flying China Clipper. Up the coast in Portland, Oregon, the China Clipper restaurant (Jim Lee, proprietor) on West Burnside advertised itself with the Boeing Clipper on beautifully silvered Deco menus. Lee's use of the B-314 Clipper made sense, since Boeing delivered the Seattle-made Boeing Clippers to Pan American Airways at Astoria, Oregon, just down the Columbia River from Portland, in order to avoid higher taxes on each plane in Washington State. The Aero Club of Portland also put the Boeing Clipper on its matchbook covers. In Junction City, Kansas, the "Air Conditioned" China Clipper depicted one of the early Clippers, the S-42, for its logo. In Houston, Texas, the China Clipper on Milam Street used the Boeing Clipper on its menu that carried instructions for how to use chopsticks, saying, "The Chinese use chopsticks because they consider the knife and fork barbaric. 'We sit at the table to eat, not to cut up carcasses,' they say." Just south of the Loop in Chicago, the China Clipper, also air-conditioned, offered its "beautiful Pacific Room" near Lake Michigan and used the Martin China Clipper as its logo. The Whitman by-the-Sea on Miami Beach used the Sikorsky S-42 Clipper on its menu cover.

China Clipper restaurants spread up and down the East Coast, since Miami had been Pan American Airways' first flying boat base, and New York City served as home for its main office as well as the main gateway to Europe for the Atlantic Clippers. New York's China Clipper restaurant on Seventh Avenue near Fifty-second Street was owned by Captain Frank Choy and Colonel Yen Ben Wee, who advertised themselves as "Air Veterans of the Chinese War." Guests needed only to write what they wanted on a postcard of the restaurant, and the China Clipper would mail it for them. Its menu logo showed a Boeing Clipper, which was based out of New York, flying over the globe. The Jersey City, New Jersey, air-conditioned China Clipper restaurant faced Journal Square Station. A sister China Clipper restaurant opened on Doyers Street in New York City. The Jersey version used an early Sikorsky version of the Clipper on its advertising. All of the restaurants offered both Chinese and American menus. Other China Clipper restaurants certainly existed, from mountainous mining towns in Idaho to desert areas where no Clipper could ever land. China Clipper eateries have continued into recent times, though the flying boats are no more. The China Clipper on Ventura Boulevard in Sherman Oaks, California, is but one example.

Top: A China Clipper napkin from the Clipper Ship Lounge at the Chancellor Hotel in San Francisco (courtesy Chancellor Hotel). *Bottom:* A 1930s napkin showing a Sikorsky S-42 Clipper.

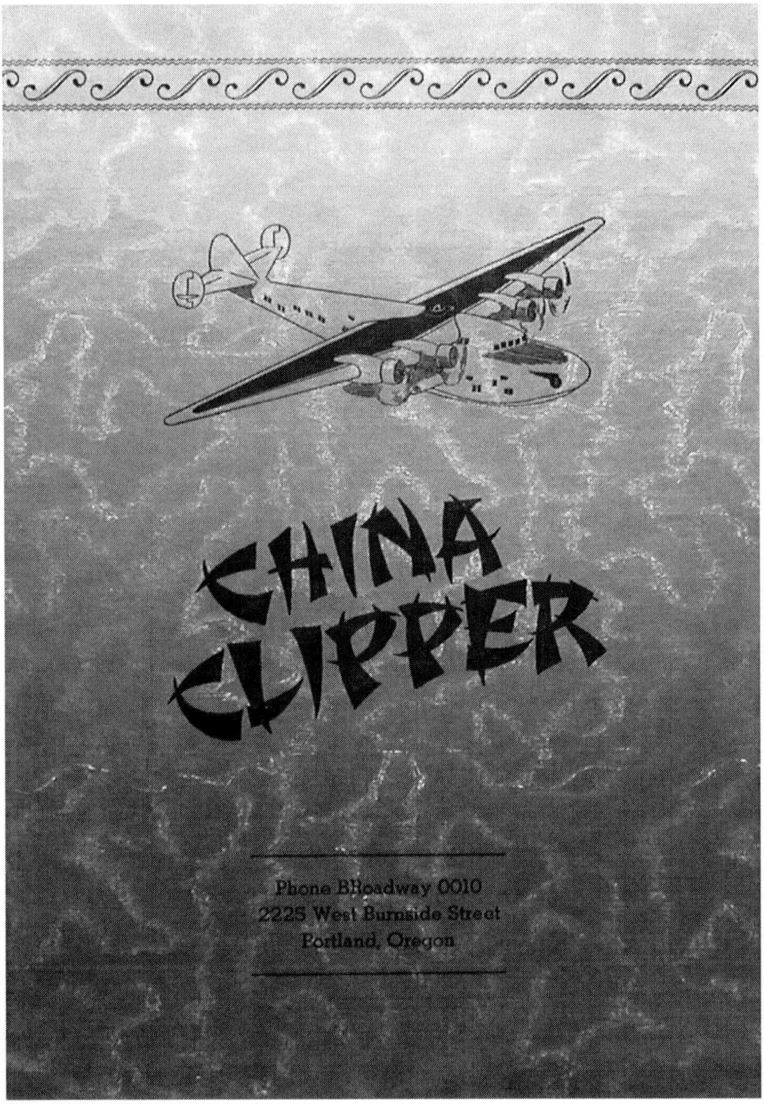

A fancy silver moiré-finished menu from the China Clipper in Portland, Oregon.

Some Clipper lounges served the same cocktails served on the flying boats. Clippers on the North Pacific route that flew from the U.S. to China served the Clipper Cocktail. This drink consisted of one pony White Label Puerto Rican rum, one pony dry French vermouth, plus a half teaspoon of grenadine. On the South Pacific route, staff served the Southseas Cocktail before dinner. The drink consisted of two-fifths gin, two-fifths orange juice, and one-fifth curacao served over ice with a cherry.

In boasting of the achievements of California, eating and drinking establishments that did not use the Clipper in name capitalized on it by image. San Francisco's Eddy's Ice Cream and "character candies" menu cover displayed the China Clipper. Other of its menus featured aerial photography of the Bay Area by photographer Clyde Sunderland, who created many of the Clipper photographs used for postcards on the West Coast. Bernstein's Fish Grotto in San Francisco also offered a 1945 menu depicting the Clipper and Clipper base in San Francisco. Drinking glasses from Denike's Tavern in San Francisco gave wrap-around images of the China Clipper over the San Francisco/Oakland Bay Bridge. Frisco's famous Cliff House and Seal Rocks published *193 Views of San Francisco Then and Now* showing the Clipper base at Treasure Island and the China Clipper over the San Francisco-Oakland Bay Bridge.

Bars, lounges, and restaurants additionally offered a host of Clipper branded hard and soft drinks. Beer companies jumped at the chance to host Clipper notoriety. The Renner Brewing Company of Youngstown, Ohio, used several Clipper images. It produced a stylized image of a multi-decked Clipper on an olive green label for its bottled Clipper Beer. Other Renner labels showed the China Clipper soaring above the Northern Hemisphere. These labels stressed additional sophistication by including a collar band cartoon illustration of two swanks who looked much like the iconic Monopoly Game Man, complete with eyeglasses, walking sticks, striped pants, vests, and moustaches. Another Renner product, Clipper Pilsner Beer, showed a Martin China Clipper painted on its cone-cap cans in red/white/black. After flat-top or punch-top beer cans came in during the late

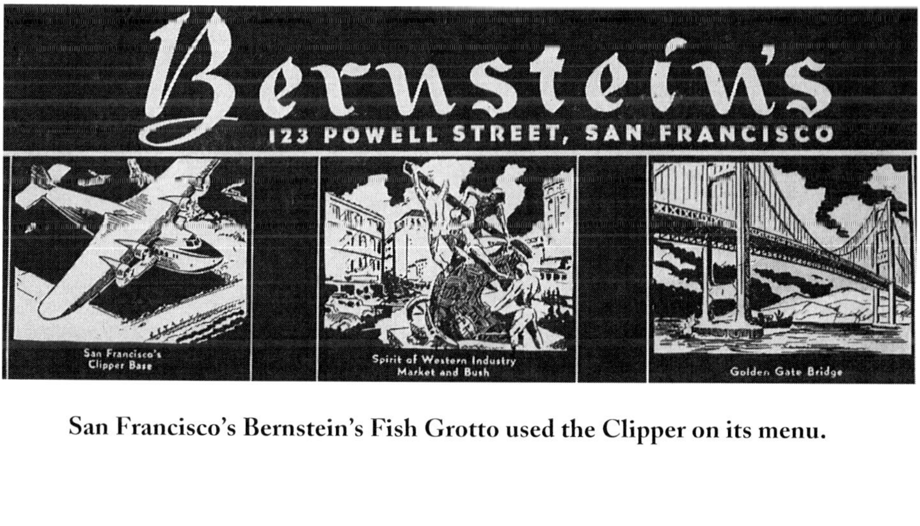

San Francisco's Bernstein's Fish Grotto used the Clipper on its menu.

1930s and 1940s, Renner was one of the few breweries that continued to use cone-cap cans until 1962, when it ceased operations. In 1938 Renner had switched from bottles to the new cone-cap Continental Can Company cans just for the release of its Clipper product. Since cone-cap cans sprouted a cap and had a neck, they could be filled with the same bottling equipment used earlier. Thus, the company could avoid installing costly canning machinery.

Clipper Pilsner reflected a short, distinctly transitional period in breweriana history. After Prohibition ended in 1933, the Clippers, Clipper beer, and the newly introduced cans grew up together. A new age of colorful shiny new cans triumphed over the gangster-era bottles. But in the 1950s, cone-cap cans and the Clippers had both been phased out. Just as the Clipper flying boats were replaced by technological advances in land aircraft and jets, the coneheads were replaced by flat-tops that echoed the popular 1950s style haircuts. Although the coneheads carried the romantic suggestion of still drinking non-metallic tasting beer from a bottle, beer sellers came to prefer the flat-tops because they were more easily stacked, took up less shipping space, and were accepted by imbibers once enough free promotional can openers had been distributed.

A 1941 flat-top can of Clipper Pale Beer also made recent history when it sold at eBay auction in November 2002 for $19,299.99. EBay wrote an article about the record sale on its Website, and other collectibles magazines and e-zines followed. The can was discovered in a crawl space underneath a house and was not considered to be worth very much by its finder. Grace Bros. Brewing Company of Santa Rosa, California, produced Clipper Pale Beer. This exquisite, multi-colored can depicts the Martin China Clipper.

Different bottled versions of Clipper beer also abounded. The Yankee Brewing Company (1942–1946) of Pittston, Pennsylvania, commemorated the Yankee Clipper flying boat with Yankee Premium Pilsner, "an All-American Beer." The B-314 Yankee Clipper was featured on its yellow-labeled green quart bottles. The Albion Brewing Company of San Francisco pictured the Martin China Clipper, "Ahead in Quality," set against a red setting or rising sun on its eleven-ounce amber bottles of Extra Pale Clipper Premium Beer. In 1942, the Atlantic Company of Charlotte, North Carolina, used the colorful image of the Boeing Atlantic Clipper to advertise Atlantic Ale and Beer. As the largest regional brewery in the South, Atlantic distributed advertising signs with cardboard cutouts of the Clipper up and down the Southeastern coast.

Not to be left out, hard liquor companies joined the fray. Johnnie Walker Black Label Blended Scotch Whiskey ran full-page advertisements in *Fortune* showing heavenly shafts of light pouring down over an amber whiskey bottle and Boeing Clipper, which were "Praised to the Stratosphere." The levitating bottle and flying boat appeared caught up in some kind of great apotheosis or rapturistic ascension into heaven of the deserving. By visual implication, both drink and plane were quite deserving, being "distinctive" and "smooth." Canada Dry Ginger Ale, Inc., of New York, importer of Johnnie Walker, revealed that heretofore Walker had been the finest scotch whiskey on earth, but now that the Clippers flew, the scotch also would have to be "praised to the skies" as the only scotch whiskey served aboard the Clippers. The red amber color of the bottle nearly matched the red coat with tails of the Johnnie Walker logo, an 1820s top-hatted gentleman in his riding attire complete with cravat and tasseled riding boots. Coupled with white shafts of light and clouds against a blue sky, this 1943 wartime ad spoke of USA red/white/blue patriotism.

The soda industry followed suit. The Three Star Bottling Works of Verona, Pennsylvania, sold Lift Beverage in seven-ounce green bottles with the Boeing Clipper logo. The flying boat could lift off the water, and the purchaser of these 7-Up–looking bottles could receive a lift, too, upon drinking. Perhaps the showiest of the soda pop Clipper images appeared on the larger one-pint eight-ounce Aircraft Sparkling Beverages. Produced by the Stratford Bottling Works of Stratford, Connecticut, these painted bottles depicted the early Clipper, the Sikorsky S-42. This was fitting since Stratford Bottling stood near the Sikorsky plant where the flying boats were born. The company not only "borrowed" the Clipper image but also showed local pride in the news focus placed on the area due to the Clippers.

The Clipper-as-icon beverage connection was revived for the micro-brew craze of the 1990s. Aviator Ales of Woodinville, Washington, labeled its India Pale Ale with a painting of the Boeing Clipper, which had been manufactured in nearby Seattle, as the flying boat took off from pristine blue waters rimmed by verdant green trees, with Mt. Rainier as a backdrop. The richly colored promotional flyers for the ale described for potential customers both this British-style golden ale and the Clipper. Like many of the micro-breweries of the time, Aviator Ales enjoyed a very short existence, opening in 1995 and closing in 1997.

9
The Clipper and Agriculture

One of the classic aviation tales involving the Clipper is the chicken story. Pan American Airways' Captain Basil L. Rowe was fond of relating the time he had Igor Sikorsky onboard in the early 1930s. Sikorsky had designed the S-40 American Clipper, and now he was keen to see how it functioned on one of its early flights. While the Clipper crossed Cuba on its way to Jamaica, Rowe paid a courtesy visit to the passenger cabin. There he found the designer on his hands and knees feeling the floor and sides of the flying boat. Sikorsky kept hearing a series of squeaks that he was afraid would unnerve the passengers and undermine confidence in his new creation (as if his weird behavior wouldn't do the same thing). Rowe told him not to worry; he would have a mechanic take care of it first thing in Kingston.

Once they were in the air again out of Jamaica, Rowe asked Sikorsky if he could still hear the sound, now that the "mechanics" had had time to fix it. Sikorsky was satisfied that the problem had been solved, but since he knew every bolt and nut in his creation, he was anxious to hear the cause. Rowe had put one over on the great man. Unable to restrain himself any longer, the captain explained that the Clipper had been carrying one thousand newly hatched chicks in the cargo space just under Sikorsky's feet. The squeaks and peep-peeps had been biological, not mechanical. As Rowe pointed out in his biography, *Under My Wings*, he had known the origin of the noise all the time, and was delighted to see that Sikorsky could laugh at himself and go down in Clipper, or chicken, lore.

The chickens point out just a small part of the influence the Clippers had on world agriculture. While most press attention centered on how Clippers carried passengers such as movie stars and Sikorsky, how they carried the mail, or how they opened the world up to fast, fashionable travel, their lasting effect in shaping world culture also resided in their service as freight haulers. Half or more of their cargo coming into Miami during the

1930s consisted of agricultural products. The chicks that Sikorsky heard under his feet changed the poultry and food industry in South America.

Although Central and South America enjoyed chicken-and-rice dishes as staples, chickens south of the border were poor producers until the advent of the Clipper routes. Earlier attempts to export chickens from the United States had failed, due to expense and the mortality rates of slow transportation. To improve the breeds to produce more eggs and tender meat, at first Pan Am began flying chicken eggs as far south as Panama, where they then could be hatched. In 1929, the first gross of eggs was shipped from Brownsville to Guatemala. Only two eggs were broken, so the venture had a future. Within ten months of this innovation, South American governments began importing their own chicks, publishing their own handbooks for poultry raising, and distributing them to their citizens.

Soon it became clear that chicks weighed less than eggs; thus, poultry raisers in Texas and Florida began shipping chicks south by the thousands in ventilated corrugated cardboard boxes. The problem with this improvement was that the chicks needed to be watered and fed en route. To get around this expense and additional labor, a Florida grower realized that newly hatched chicks did not feed in their first seventy-two hours. Engleman Farm of Avon Park, Florida, began shipping out of Miami day-old chicks in specially designed "pullman" boxes that traveled as far as Rio de Janeiro and Lima with less than a one percent mortality rate. Since feeding was unnecessary, these pullman boxes were smaller and less expensive to ship. Clippers carried 10,000 chicks per week in 1939. In 1941, according to *Country Gentleman* magazine, they carried 15,000 to 20,000 chicks per week. They could have carried more, but were limited by available plane space and the fact that chicks had to be loaded within twelve hours of hatching time.

A million dollar-plus business had been created almost overnight, thanks to the Clippers. The February 1938 edition of *Mechanics and Handicraft* pointed out the dramatic contrast. When the first Clipper passengers arrived in Maracaibo, Venezuela, they found chickens to be so tough as to be inedible, so inbred that hens had spurs and no neck feathers, so low quality that eggs were few and usually sterile. After the Clippers began their chick flights, a Maracaibo store sign proudly announced, "500 Fresh-Laid American Eggs Every Day." On the serious side, poultry raising was crucial to the population in some areas in Latin America because poultry was the only livestock that could be raised, given climate and terrain. On the less serious side, the story of the Easter-cute chicks and the Clippers appealed to women's magazines at the time. Articles about the chick airlift appeared in such publications as *Cosmopolitan*. The June 1939 issue even dubbed Juan T. Trippe of Pan American Airways "The Cosmopolite of the Month" for his efforts.

The Family Circle for September 22, 1939, gave readers a glimpse of how Clippers affected agriculture in the Pacific. Photographs of Ginger Rogers and childhood movie star Gloria Jean graced the front cover of this weekly, but the China Clipper was on the back. The magazine reported, "A 4,000-mile milk route!" Extending a Clipper route across the Pacific made it possible for the Honolulu Dairymen's Association to ship milk as far as Guam and have it arrive unspoiled, a feat difficult, if not impossible, to do by steamer.

Where livestock could be raised, quick delivery also meant improved production. As early as 1937 Hereford bull semen was air expressed in a vacuum bottle and successfully flown from Texas to Buenos Aires. Give this success, more experiments followed. In October 1939 the American Jersey Cattle Club offered a prize to see if semen from a prize bull at the San Francisco Exhibition could be packed in dry ice and flown across the country for artificial insemination into four registered cows being shown at the New York World's Fair. The first healthy calf was born in Arizona the following summer, the United States' first intercontinental mating. These early efforts changed the face of stock raising around the world. Soon Clippers flew cattle and horse semen along international routes. This alleviated the dangers of shipping large animals. Transported mules were known to kick out the sides of metal aircraft flying the Andes. Prize passengers would not mix well with prize bulls or stallions at several thousand feet over the ocean or jungle.

At the same time as the first flying boats were being christened Clippers, the name also caught on in naming livestock. Purebred animals in particular needed identifying names for the ritual of being shown in a ring. Livestock shows borrowed from England the idea of visually appraising named animals, and the granddaddy of all the shows was held each year in Chicago. In the 1930s, champion shorthorns owned and exhibited by F.W. Hubbell of Des Moines, Iowa, appeared at the International Livestock Exposition in Chicago under such names as Clipper's Favorite and Collynie Clipper Star. The name spread among other stock raisers, 4-H-ers, and FFA attendees in this city within a city that even had its own radio station broadcasting results. Soon ponies and other animals across the United States were named Clipper.

One of the highlights of the exposition was the entry of the hitch of ton-weight Clydesdales representing the Chicago Union Stockyard and Transport Company. August A. Busch, Jr., picked up on the idea by creating another show hitch in 1933, which became the corporate symbol of the producer of Budweiser beer to this day. Horse semen could be flown on the Clippers, but mature Clydesdales could not. Consequently, when Busch tried to buy adult Clydesdales from Scotland in 1940 to supplement his team, they had to travel by ship. A German submarine torpedoed the ship and the horses were lost.

Although the Clippers did not make it a habit of flying mature animals, cargo carriers did follow Pan American Airway's lead in international animal transport. One specialty airline filled the niche created by the demand for live big game or exotic animals. Much of this demand was driven by the establishment of hunting ranches, by animal collectors, or by the rage for animal fur clothing. To supply the clothing industry, silver foxes and chinchillas were especially desired. Originating on the arid slopes of the Andes, chinchillas did not travel well in the hot holds of ships or railway cars. Fast transport was a must. Soon, ads for raising these animals as get-rich-quick schemes for both youth and adults graced the pages of comic books and sporting magazines in the 1940s into the 1950s, as chinchilla "ranches" sprang up across the United States.

For youthful readers with big capitalistic dreams who did not choose to get rich quick selling *Grit* newspapers, the magazines promised fortunes to be made raising Golden and ringneck pheasants, quail, fox, African nightcrawlers, African bullfrogs, or chinchillas. Even the Carter ranch of Plains, Georgia, enticed young men to grow its worms. President Jimmy Carter wasn't just a peanut farmer; his family members were also worm farmers. As Americans moved from farm to city, many kept their desire to farm and ranch, albeit in miniature. An African nightcrawler wasn't quite an Anaconda, nor was a chinchilla quite an Ibex, but they were nevertheless exotic and air-expressed to fuel the imagination and, it was hoped, fuel the pocketbook. Such animal husbandry attempts also made for great 4-H projects in an era when the United States tried to hold onto its agricultural base. It did this by emphasizing an agricultural future for its youth by encouraging them to join such organizations as 4-H or Future Farmers of America.

The explosion of air delivery of stock to create animal farms or ranches coincided with changes in agricultural practices, particularly in the United States. Day old ringneck pheasant chicks could be air expressed the same way as chickens. The pheasant was perfectly suited to American agriculture in the 1930s through 1950s. Native species such as the prairie chicken that used to populate Midwest prairies had disappeared together with the prairies, but the pheasant was right at home with farmland, rotated crops, hedgerows, and some native grass or shrubbery areas. Pheasants could thrive where native species could not. Private and state agencies began stocking the pheasants for hunters in earnest during this time, as hunting attracted the tourist dollar and promoted the hunting and gun industry. Raising and releasing birds was also touted as part of the fledgling conservation movement, although the birds were not being conserved; rather, they, like carp and English sparrows, were foreign introductions. The perfect combination of environment and species created the classic age of bird hunting in the United States.

Pheasant populations peaked in the 1940s and 1950s before farming practices changed again. In the late 1940s, even Chicago businessmen could bag quotas of ringnecks over a long lunch. Today the pheasant heyday is over. Bird raisers struggle to ship their chicks by air, as airlines refuse either to accept the birds or to place temperature restrictions on their shipment. Though the Clippers have disappeared like the prairies, wild strain Oriental pheasants still need to be imported because natural selection of U.S.-raised birds favors those pheasants most docile and best acclimated to life in wire cages.

The Clippers did carry one adult animal, the honeybee, essential to crop and honey production. Without pollination, many crops would fare poorly or not at all. Clippers made it possible for the Mayhew Apiaries of Mayhew, Mississippi, and other apiaries to begin shipping bees around the world. Mayhew would pack one Italian queen bee, ten worker bees, and a ration of sugared water in a wooden box for air express shipment to the tropics. This not only made for better honey-producing strains of bees, but also made for the introduction of new crops in areas previously lacking efficient pollinators.

Clippers were literally crop and economy savers. Time and time again they played a role in staving off the devastating effects of plant diseases. As countries drew closer due to war and increased transportation in the 1930s and 1940s, plant diseases more easily spread. Farmers turning more and more to monoculture also increased the risks. Fortunately, Clippers could rush treatments to where they were needed. Charles Morrow Wilson's "Crops Take Wings" article in a 1941 *Country Gentleman* reported that California insectaries shipped between 40 million and 50 million insects by plane each year. In Seattle, Department of Agriculture entomologists air expressed two thousand parasitized coddling moths to Lima, Peru. South African wasps were flown to California to stem the red scale disease destroying the citrus crop. Clippers carried Puerto Rican lightning bugs throughout the Caribbean islands to attack sugarcane weevils. Likewise, out of the Amazon came a deep-water grass fly that could attack sugarcane borers. In the West Indies, burning fields and spraying thousands of gallons of pesticide had failed to stop the destructive borers. The desperate islands were about to lose their livelihood, but the fly arrived just in time to stem the tide, saving an estimated twenty percent of sugar cane production. A similar plague hit the sugar cane fields of Louisiana, but this time the borers were resistant to the fly. A more robust parasite from Peru was flown northward. Within weeks, the borers were under control.

The war against insect pests even produced night entertainment for Clipper tourists. In a November 1933 article, "Eagle Wings under the Southern Cross" in *Hearst's International Combined with Cosmopolitan*, writer/passenger Forrest Wilson described being put ashore at St. John's, Antigua, for overnight accommodations. Nightlife for the passengers was hard to come by. As Wilson put it, "Five-sixths of the entire industry of Antigua and six-sixths of its night life are represented in Gunthorpe's sugar mill" (65). Since the mill operated twenty-four hours a day and since the local Pan American Airways' manager was also a sugar planter, guests were treated to a tour of the borer-control laboratory at the plant.

The British entomologist in charge conducted the tour, which was like watching a modern episode of the television series *NCIS*, with pedantic Ducky as the forensic pathologist. In short, guests were treated to both long lecture and meticulous viewing of the bodies. Peering into a microscope revealed the whole fascinatingly grotesque process of how Malayan flies gave birth to live maggots, which instantly parasitized the white grubs of the cane borers. Fortunately, Clayton Knight, the famous aviation illustrator who accompanied Wilson on the flight, chose not to illustrate this for the readers of *Cosmo*. Before the Clippers, shipping these particular pest-control flies from their native Sumatra by land and by boat had been expensive and difficult. Given the flies' brief life spans, feeding and breeding stations had be set up across the oceans at one-day intervals, a nearly impossible task. It took a year or more just to transport flies from Sumatra as far as Hawaii. With the coming of Pan American Airways, Antigua could receive a shipment from a Cuban breeding lab in a day via African and the Brazilian Express Clippers. After this evening soiree in a clean, well-lighted place with all the charm of an autopsy, visitors retreated to the PAA manager's bungalow for some tall glasses, no sugar please.

Just as the Clipper could be a savior by carrying beneficial insects, it could also be a threat. When Clipper service first began across the Pacific, the Hawaiian Islands instantly became more vulnerable. The Hawaiian Sugar Growers Association (HSGA) recognized the threat of crop-damaging insects that could come into the islands, particularly from the East via Hong Kong, Guam, and the Philippines along the Clipper route from China, or from the southern Clipper route from New Zealand and New Caledonia. The HSGA dispatched entomologists to Midway Island to block pests coming in from the west, and to Canton Island to block pests coming in from the south. Insect screening commenced on Midway as soon as entomologist F. C. Hadden arrived on the Philippine Clipper November 24, 1936. Hadden also took over care of the gardens Pan American Airways was establishing on the island for its hotel. The HSGA also helped to beautify the Pan Am grounds by providing palm trees and other plants to make the coral islands more attractive.

Clipper passengers were "gunned down" with a flit gun before they could go ashore. A good spritz of insecticide in the face, sometimes eyes and mouth, quickly took the romance out of many a Clipper adventure for sophisticates. Hawaii also made sure that passengers coming from the mainland received the same treatment. On landing in Hawaii, a steward would fumigate the whole plane. Only after a health official declared the flying boat free of pests were passengers allowed off. Surveys and classification of the dead insects collected revealed a number of unwanted insect passengers did manage to stow away to the tune of fifteen to twenty insects per flight. One flight, however, carried over 1,000 insects. Rarely were no insects found. Around 200 species of bugs bummed a trip to Midway. The spraying prevented the spread of plant diseases, but it also yielded the unintended benefit of killing Anopheles mosquitoes, which kept malaria out of Hawaii and the mainland. If malarial mosquitoes did reach Hawaii and the mainland, health officials and the military feared that this scourge of the tropics could decide the outcome of the war. Similar health concerns were shown on the East Coast of the U.S. for flights coming in from Africa and South and Central America. For example, navy health representatives occasionally quarantined flights in Puerto Rico to prevent the spread of yellow fever and malaria. After passengers and crew debarked in Miami, the Clipper was periodically cordoned off so that deadly potassium cyanide gas could be pumped into the entire plane.

At times fumigators seemed overzealous to Clipper crews. This was especially true in Guam. The Clipper needed to be completely fumigated twenty minutes before landing. If the inspector did not think that each compartment stank strongly enough when he came aboard, he would order the entire plane sprayed again. Passengers and crew were forced to remain onboard in the heat, humidity, and fumes of their metal coffin for another twenty minutes while the Insect King sought coolness ashore. One crew member remedied the situation. He squirted bug spray into a glass of orange juice and offered it to the inspector when he entered the Clipper. As the inspector sipped his drink, he smelled the strong fragrance of aerosol in every compartment. No one was delayed onboard after that.

Just as important to the war effort was rubber. When the Japanese invaded the rubber plantations in the Far East, the United States lost ninety percent of its natural rubber supply. Without rubber gaskets, tires, and other critical parts, there would be no tanks, battleships, or aircraft to fight the war. Although the U.S. stockpiled supplies before the outbreak of hostilities, it was neither feasible to stockpile more than a year's supply at best, nor was it realistic to expect scientists and companies to be able to invent and produce enough synthetic rubber to fight a world war. As did Canada and Australia, the U.S. fought the rubber shortage by rationing, recycling, and searching for alternative plants that could produce latex. Alternatives would take precious time to develop as well, so plant hunters were dispatched into the far reaches of the Amazon, which had been the world's chief supplier of rubber before the industry collapsed early in the century.

The airlines depended on rubber as much as anyone else did. The public and companies learned of the critical dimensions of the rubber shortage when all production and sales of rubber tires were outlawed in the United States within days of the attack on Pearl Harbor. This effectively ended domestic automobile production in the country for the duration of the war. Ironically, the United States was still selling scrap rubber to Japan as late as 1940, and it would take the fall of France before the U.S. would even start to become serious about synthetic rubber production plants.

In the face of such an emergency, Pan American Airways took up the task of flying up the Amazon to the former rubber capital of the world, Manaus, located on the Rio Negro just ten miles north of where it flowed into the Amazon. Stripped of their passenger seating, Boeing Clippers flew several secret special missions to South America to fly out supplies of beryllium used in hardening metals, mica, and the much needed crude rubber. Twenty-seven tons of crude rubber were transported in these early missions. The maximum payload for an individual Boeing Clipper ranged from 835 pounds if the Clipper were flying 3,000 miles, to eight tons if the Clipper were to fly 1,000 or fewer miles, so several flights were required. But first the rubber had to be brought out of the jungle to the Clipper port near the mouth of the Amazon. As Clipper captain George Price recalled, under strict wartime secrecy he received orders to fly his S-42 up the Amazon to bring back bales of natural rubber. On behalf of the United States Rubber Reserve Company and Rubber Development Corporation, plant explorers scoured the jungles of the Amazon and its tributaries in Brazil and Colombia to locate any rubber trees left, after a devastating leaf blight wiped out the two massive rubber tree plantations at Fordlandia and Belterra, Brazil.

To avoid being held economically captive by the Dutch and British rubber cartels of the Far East, Henry Ford had tried to create his own rubber plantations. In 1928, he began converting two and half million acres of jungle into a rubber plantation, complete with its own U.S.–style town and power station. Houses, a school, a hospital, and a sawmill were shipped in. But as soon as the rubber trees were planted, South American leaf blight began to kill them. What he did not realize was that the native rubber trees usually grew at some distances from each other. This spacing protected them to some degree from the fast spread of disease.

Convinced that he had planted in the wrong place with inferior trees, Ford began again in 1934 at another site, dubbed Belterra. Here the young trees were again attacked by leaf blight, caterpillars, and dozens of other insects. The land refused to be cleared easily, and labor problems compounded Ford's problems. South American Indians and other job seekers were not used to punching time cards, as Ford expected workers to do in Dearborn, Michigan. Ford even expected them to learn one of his obsessions, folk dancing. After spending nearly ten million dollars to grow rubber in the Amazon, Ford finally admitted defeat in 1945 and sold out to the Brazilian government for a mere $500,000, not a good return. Nevertheless, some rubber was produced at Belterra, and plant explorers were able to find other producing wild trees in the Amazon Basin.

Captain Price was to bring back samples of this rubber. Flying the one thousand miles up the Amazon to Manaus was adventurous and somewhat dangerous. Price, like other travelers of the time, recalled how the jungle was reclaiming the once opulent city's opera house and other marbled buildings. He could hear the jungle just beyond the walls of the restaurant. When his dinner serving arrived, he realized he was eating monkey stew. Flying conditions from the mouth of the Amazon to Manaus resembled monkey business as well. With an almost constant overcast hanging one hundred to one hundred-fifty feet over the river, and with poor radio reception due to area static, aircraft flying up the Amazon had to fly low, using what landmarks there were for visual reference. This in itself was tricky for new pilots, because of the many confusing tributaries, islands, and look-alike channels of the Amazon. The intensity of sudden storms was such that a flying boat would immediately have to try to land in the river and ride it out.

Price realized how dangerous events could become on the Amazon when, on July 27, 1943, he flew to Manaus to bring parts to another disabled flying boat. Upon takeoff, someone opened a wrong valve, and the Clipper began dumping fuel. The gasoline pooled in an eddy and flashed, destroying the Bermuda Clipper. Price and crew were lucky not to burn to death. All escaped, although the radio officer who couldn't swim had to be resuscitated onshore. Such was the price of rubber and the wartime use of a civilian airline.

The Clippers were caught up in the murder and intrigue of the rubber business in the 1940s. As Clippers flew rubber out of the Amazon, they sometimes passed over ships whose registries, flags, and destinations changed overnight, and usually during the night as they tried to steam to Germany. Rommel's tanks and Goering's Luftwaffe needed rubber, and rubber trees did not grow prolifically in the German Alps or Black Forest. As a consequence, masquerading German freighters with their cargoes of black market or diverted rubber desperately ran the shipping blockade off the coast of Brazil. When intercepted by Allied warships, crews scuttled their ships rather than see precious rubber fall into U.S. hands.

As the U.S. government sought to create its own rubber tree plantations, the obvious place to collect seeds and grow grafts and clones lay near Pan American Airways' Clipper base in Miami. Here the Plant Introduction Station served as the main collection point and transfer station for the rubber trees and seeds. Specimens collected could be rechecked for any signs of blight before being reshipped to newly created wartime plantations. Wade Davis's *One River: Explorations and Discoveries in the Amazon Rain Forest* (Schuster, 1996) related how remotely separated rubber bases were established in Haiti, Mexico, Guatemala, Colombia, Ecuador, Peru, Bolivia, and Costa Rica. Seeds flowed into these sites from across the oceans. A year before the fall of the Philippines B-18 bombers delivered plant materials from the Philippines. Seeds also came from Africa's Firestone rubber plantation in Liberia. Thanks to the Clippers and the hard work of botanists, enough natural rubber was produced to keep the United States and its allies in the war going until enough synthetic rubber could be produced. After the war, ignoring the protests of manufacturers and scientists, bureaucrats refused to fund the disease-resistant plantations. Trees representing years of research and breeding were cut down, burned, or their acreage turned into parking lots. Now the United States and other countries are dependent again on the same non-blight resistant monoculture rubber plantations in Southeast Asia. But for a shining moment....

Flying plant discoveries out of war zones proved difficult, especially for wartime plant collectors in the Pacific, when Pan American flying boats and crews flew for the military. Roy Macleod's "Combat Science: OSRD's Postscript in the Pacific" and Richard A. Howard's "The Role of Botanists During World War II" in *Science and the Pacific War* (Kluver, 2000) both reported problems civilian scientists had with the military. Though plant samples were not supposed to be quarantined or shipments censored, area commanders still insisted. What good were specimens if they arrived only as rotted junk after the delays? Or what good were specimens if they were given precious cargo space, if military censors prevented the collectors from saying where the samples originated? General MacArthur interjected himself as an effective impediment. He feared that Vannevar Bush's Office of Scientific Research and Development's Field Service, which reported directly to President Roosevelt, was really just a sneaky way for his Pentagon enemies to spy on him. Consequently, his cooperation was not very forthcoming. By his decree, scientific mail in his southwest Pacific area of control could not be put into the diplomatic pouch for fast delivery, as it could in other theatres. Instead, it would have to move through channels and be cleared by his own adjutant general, thus slowing communications and shipments to the point where they would be months late and worthless.

On a more positive note, military needs influenced changes in floriculture. As soon as Clipper routes were established to Hawaii, husbands and boyfriends in the services saw the chance to wow the girls back on the mainland with exotic flowers. Overnight service by air meant that flowers could be shipped fresh and arrive fresh on the West Coast. The same thing happened in Central and South America. One Clipper pilot even began

This Clipper Cargo shipping label for flowers reflected the importance of these shipments to Pan American Airways and how Clipper service revolutionized the floral industry.

growing his own orchids in Rio. The vast numbers of troops passing through or stationed in Hawaii revolutionized its flower business, as they wished to share Hawaii's beauty with loved ones. Whereas, before, flowers were shipped with often disappointing results on Matson liners, now they could be shipped anywhere within the United States in one or two days. Mail-order flower business exploded. Leis, orchids, and anthuriums flowed across the Pacific on the Clippers, opening up new markets and making the anthurium the leading cut-flower export of Hawaii. Special packaging for floral shipment on the Clippers was quickly developed.

The Hawaiian Tourist Bureau and Pan American publicity machines revved up to promote the Clipper's floral delivery role. Celebrities touted the service. Swimming record holder Duke Kahanamoku was photographed crouched atop a Clipper, handing a bouquet to a Clipper officer for shipment. For publicity purposes, a giant tag on the flowers read "Pittsburgh." In winter 1936 the Hawaiian Tourist Bureau sent bouquets by Clipper to many winter-bound cities on the mainland. Pan American promised delivery to any of the cities within thirty hours.

The speedy access to exotic flowers in turn affected dating patterns and other rituals. Young men taking their best girls to proms or dances no longer had to settle for corsages of gardenias, roses, or whatever was available in season locally. They could splurge on something truly exotic and showy from across the sea. The expected ritualistic giving of exotic flowers with all its sexual implications now was within the financial reach of most middle-class American young men. Part of the ritual included the men awkwardly having to fish around to find out what color dress their dates would wear to the big dance so that the color of orchid would match that of the dress. They had to hope their flower competitively out-anthered and out-pistiled other flowers at the dance. Businesses also flew in flowers as giveaways to reward workers at special events, or as product promotions.

On the Atlantic route, Clippers played a role in the now well-known wartime story of saving the Peace Rose. In 1935 the young French rose grower Francis Meilland traveled 15,000 miles in the United States in a second-hand car to visit U.S. rose growers. While traveling, he met Robert Pyle, head of the Conrad Pyle Company, which ran a rose nursery outside of Philadelphia. On Meilland's return to France, war closed in on France and a new unnamed rose that the Meillands had developed. In 1939, before shipments were embargoed, Francis Meilland had managed to send one pack of budwood of the new rose to Italy and another to Germany.

Then, in November of 1939, Meilland received a call from a friend at the American Consulate in nearby Lyon. This rose-growing diplomat said he was leaving France immediately, but could take out a small parcel for Meilland, as long as it weighed no more than a pound. Within two hours, Meilland delivered to the consulate his small packet of unnamed rose material addressed to Pyle in the United States.

Germany had just invaded Poland, and Britain and France had declared war on Germany. This prompted the United States to invoke its Neutrality Act on November 4, which meant that Pan American Airways could no longer fly into Marseilles, but would instead use neutral Lisbon as its eastern terminus. In the diplomatic pouch on the last Clipper flight out of France rested the precious budwood of what would become the Peace Rose.

Meilland could not know whether the rose reached the United States, or whether Pyle had been successful in propagating it. Tragically, the Meillands did know they had to turn under their 200,000 rose bushes and replace them with wartime vegetable gardens. Pyle asked that the rose be christened the Peace Rose at the Pacific Rose Society show in Pasadena, home of the Rose Bowl Parade, in 1945. In perfect synchronicity with historical events, christening day fell on the very same day as the fall of Berlin. The next year, the rose was made the All-American Award Winner for 1946. Again, in perfect unplanned synchronicity, Peace Rose won the award on the day war ended with Japan.

It was indeed a Peace Rose. Shortly after its naming, the heads of the fifty delegations of the United Nations each received a Peace Rose when their teams met in San Francisco for the UN Conference on International Organization, where they signed the UN charter on April 29, 1945. Since then, each United Nations treaty signing has taken place at a table adorned with this refugee that flew out on the last Clipper. The Peace has become the world's favorite rose. In England, no stranger to the War of the Roses, red and white, the Duke of Windsor proclaimed the Peace as the most beautiful in the world. During recent conflicts, including the war in Iraq, rose growers have united in planting a Peace Rose to honor those fallen in battles and to hope for peace. Peace Roses adorned peace gardens across the world, a prominent example being the Expo-70 garden in Osaka, Japan. Unintentionally, Clippers united much of the world around the issue of peace through a plant as significant as the diplomatic mail carried in a pouch.

On the Clippers' route from Baltimore to Bermuda, lilies were the order of the day. In the 1930s the Bermuda Clipper was swamped with Easter lilies destined for the States. In the weeks leading up to Easter, it seemed that either onions or lilies for the Easter ritual covered every arable inch of Bermuda. If nearly every arable inch of Bermuda was filled, so was the Clipper. In the flights leading up to Easter, Clipper crews reported that every inch of space not occupied by passengers was filled with the flowers. As if in a more docile version of *Little Shop of Horrors*, flowers spilled over from the cargo bays into the seating area.

To a large degree, Clippers were also responsible for the acceptance of hydroponics, the science of growing plants without the use of soil. William F. Gericke of the University of California had experimented with the concept during the 1920s and 1930s, but not until the Clipper base at Wake Island introduced a hydroponicum was the first large-scale use of hydroponics successfully used in modern times outside the lab. With no soil on the island and ship and flying boat deliveries not always regular, barren Wake needed to supply as much of its own food as possible for its passengers and employees. But even shipping in soil proved to be of little help, since the topsoil would quickly leach down through the porous coral beyond the plant roots. Creating large redwood box-tanks proved the answer. As if on rafts, plants were suspended over these water gardens and fed weak solutions of fertilizer.

So successful became this first adventure into hydroponics that Pan Am quadrupled the size of its experiment in 1939. Prior to that, the water gardens produced twelve pounds of tomatoes, eight pounds of cucumbers, and some lima beans per week. Such production caught the eye of the military. Hydroponics farms, along with desalination units, sprang up during World War II at locations that were difficult to resupply with fresh vegetables, such places as Ascension Island in the Atlantic and Iwo Jima and Okinawa in the Pacific. British forces used similar techniques in desert areas such as Bahrein and Iraq. Today the economies of some islands and nations depend on hydroponics farming of vegetables or flowers, just as NASA and other space agencies plan to use it in outer space. Tomatoes can be grown in the Arctic, in the desert, or on a space station. Many of the corsages now used for social functions are still flown in by air, but their flowers are grown in a soilless medium.

While the Clippers were changing the world's agriculture in subtle and revolutionary ways, the agricultural product industry fed off the publicity to be gained from the Clipper image. Coffee imported from Central America became associated with the Clippers. The Consolidated Coffee Company of St. Louis, Missouri, packaged its Country Life Coffee in red/white/blue three-pound bags whose side panels featured artist renderings of an early Juan Valdez with guitar and burro on one side, and a cross between Carmen Miranda and Chita Rivera on the other. On the central panel, an S-42 Clipper soared over a map of Central America entitled "The Lindbergh Circle Route." The map marked all the Clipper stops around

An early 1930s paper bag for Country Life Coffee showing early Clipper routes in the Caribbean mapped out by Charles Lindbergh.

the Caribbean that Charles Lindbergh pioneered for Pan American Airways. The circumferential route as pictured on the coffee bag dates the coffee from 1931.

After 1939, the Centennial Flouring Mills packaged its all-purpose Clipper brand of hard wheat flour in ten-pound cloth bags. These bags carried the logo of the later model Clipper flying boat, the giant B-314, as it rose from the ocean surface. Again the color combination was patriotic red/white/blue. The Centennial flour mill stood as a prominent landmark on the Seattle waterfront. Since the Boeing Clipper was designed and manufactured in Seattle, the Clipper image was important. The flying boat was tested in the waters of Seattle's Elliot Bay just off property owned by Centennial. In addition to using the Clipper, the company often used such popular culture forms as cookbooks to sell its product. In the 1940s it also promoted its hometown icons with a four-set series of four-by-five-inch baseball trading cards, all showing Seattle Rainiers players of the vaunted Pacific Coast Baseball League. In this case the team's name of Rainiers trumped that of being called the Clippers because the team had been purchased by Emil Sick, the Rainier Beer baron.

A circa 1940 cloth sack of Centennial Clipper Flour showed the Boeing Clipper.

West Coast fruit growers produced some of the more colorful Clipper fruit box labels to draw attention to their products. The Exeter Fruit Association of Exeter, California, chose the Boeing Clipper to grace its Silver Clipper lug box. The Silver Clipper took its place as the culmination of a series of Exeter aviation labels. Others included homage to the

Spirit of St. Louis and Lindbergh, since the Ryan monoplane that Lindbergh used to fly the Atlantic was made in California. The Lone Eagle Blue Anchor label pictured Lindy's plane. Another label for East West Emperors showed a map of the United States with Lindy's plane flying eastward. On the eve of U.S. entry into World War II, the Pursuit Calex label featured a military fighter aircraft. Most colorful of all, the Silver Clipper featured bright yellow print on a red background.

One of the rarest and most dramatic orange crate labels was Top Flight, of the Goldenwest Citrus Growers of Tustin, Orange County. So rare was this label that most label collectors' reference books did not bother to list it or picture its vibrant image of the Martin China Clipper flying against towering and threatening purple cumulo-nimbus clouds. Originating in the heart of Sunkist orange country, this crate label demonstrated the best of the lithographic label art of the time. But the Clippers were killing themselves as images on this art form. The advances made in shipping air freight in strong cardboard containers, such as those used to air freight chicks, spread to truck and rail hauling in the 1940s. By the end of the 1940s, litho-labeled wooden crates went out with the Clippers. In a short while, the fruit grower cooperatives also became extinct. Goldenwest, the last of the cooperatives in Orange County, disappeared in 1968. The beautiful lithography that had captivated the public eye since the 1880s was replaced by cheaper, quicker printing methods lacking litho's multicolored artistry. Rather than being admired as popular art, the cardboard replacements usually ended up in incinerators, in the hands of grocery chain box boys, or in recycling bins.

Farmers or producers were treated to the Clipper image just as consumers were. Before the flying boats, the clipper concept had been used for such farm implements as plows, which, like clipper ships, could "sail" the plains. Farm work sounded so fast and easy! One of the largest plow makers in the world, the Parlin and Orendorff (P&O) Company of Canton, Illinois, started business just as the first clipper ships were being built before the Civil War. They advertised their plows as "Clipper Plows." After the great age of the sailing ships, P&O continued to tie the names of their over 200 types of plows to the clippers. For example, one of their trade cards, c. 1890, showed the Canton Clipper with full sails. The card made a pun on Canton, China, and Canton, Illinois. The card further captured the popular icons of the day by illustrating three beautiful women, dressed alternately in red, white and blue, on one of the main sails. They were Yum-Yum, Peep-Bo, and Pitti-Sing, who were "the three little maids from school are we," from Gilbert and Sullivan's *Mikado*—not typical Midwestern farm girls. After tremendous success in London, the *Mikado* played to equally appreciative audiences in New York just before the issuance of this trade card. No matter that the three little maids were Japanese in the opera and not Chinese as suggested by the trade card, still, they could sell Canton Clipper plows.

With the advent of the flying Clippers, implement dealers, large and small, really capitalized on the name. The A.T. Ferrell & Co. of Saginaw, Michigan, offered its Clipper Seed Cleaners for grain, seed and beans. Massey-Harris, one of the largest makers of farm implements during the 1930s and 1940s, advertised its line of Clipper combines. All a farmer

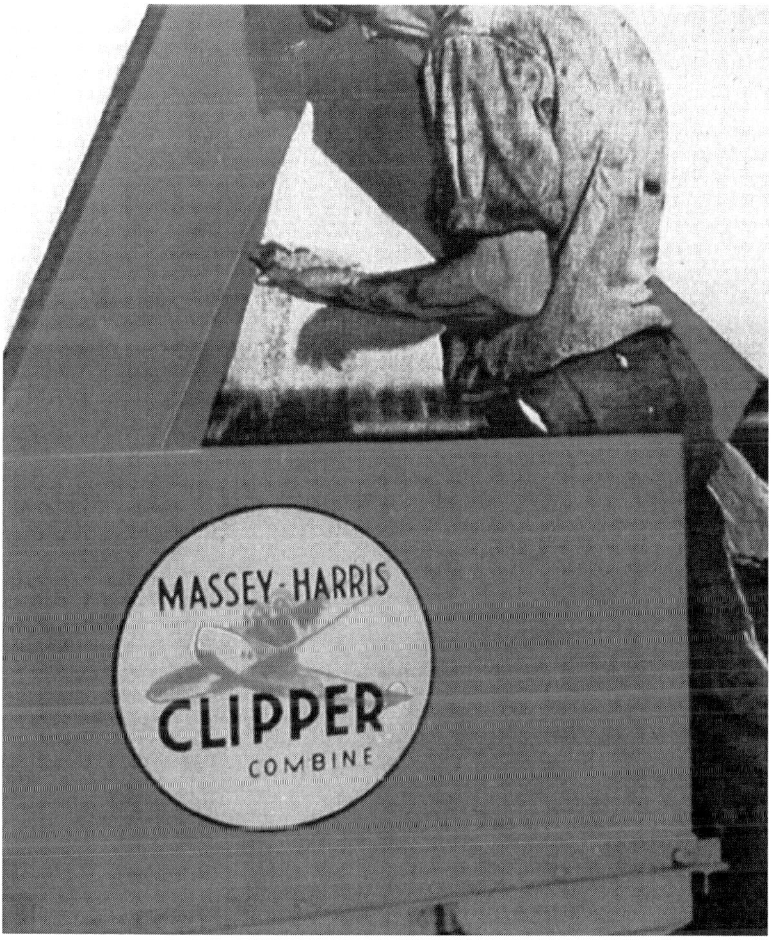

Similar to World War II bomber nose art, large yellow-and-red logos with the image of the Boeing Clipper adorned Massey-Harris Clipper Combines as they nosed their way through farm fields in the 1940s (courtesy AGCO Corporation).

needed to do at the time was to look out in the field and note the color of the other farmer's machinery to know what brand his neighbor used. Just as John Deere implements were green and Case's were orange, Massey's wore a showy bright red. Each of the various sizes of Massey combines carried a logo of a red Boeing Clipper in a large yellow circle, similar to and contemporaneous with the nose art on World War II bombers. Massey-Harris marketed the Clipper to farmers who wanted to avoid having to be dependent on threshing crews. These combines were touted as crop insurance, to avoid having a field of crops ready for harvesting when an expensive threshing crew was delayed by rain somewhere else. Why feed and pay a threshing crew, when you could harvest when you wanted with a Clipper combine that could fly through your fields? After all, straw was guaranteed to fly through your combine as "thin as pig's milk."

When it came to power for those combines, the Clippers appeared there, too. During wartime, when farmers were asked to save gasoline like everyone else, Champion Spark Plugs ran full-page advertisements about their economical gas-saving plugs in farm publications such as the *Farm Journal* and *Farmer's Wife.* These ads, entitled "Pan American Prestige Brings New Prestige to Champion Spark Plugs," showed a Boeing Clipper with a large U.S. flag painted on its nose, as the Clipper was being loaded with boxes of supplies at some tropical port of call. Even with farm engines, Clippers enhanced prestige and technical sophistication. Champion went so far as to include the Pan Am winged globe logo centered at the top of the ad, nearly as large as the illustration of its own spark plug. At first glance, the page could be mistaken for Pan American Airlines' publicity. Champion deliberately played second fiddle in the ad to make its connection with the giant Clipper that took up two-thirds of the page. The ad praised the work that the Clippers were doing during wartime for the army and navy, and guaranteed to farmers who had to power their Massey-Harris and other brands of machinery that the Champion Spark Plugs they bought for their cars, trucks, tractors, and stationary engines were "blood brothers to those used in Pan American's far-flying Clippers." These plugs would help save gasoline, save money, and win the war. Usually the ad appeared facing, or close to, ads for Caterpillar, Allis-Chalmers, International Harvester, or John Deere tractors, which could use the plugs.

Pan American Airways paid back the respect the tractor and other industries gave it by buying their goods, even tractors. After the United States entered World War II, the U.S. government suspended manufacturing of agricultural tractors to convert plants to wartime use. However, the Huber Manufacturing Company of Marion, Ohio, could manufacture its 1943 red Huber HK model for Pan American. These would be the last tractors to come off its production line until war's end. Most recently, as U.S. agriculture has shifted even further from the small family farm to larger corporate holdings, agricultural nostalgia has led to tractor restoration hobbyists and tractor museums. Among the rarer tractors stands Pan Am's Huber HK.

The connection between Huber tractors and the Clippers probably was not an accident. When the U.S. went on war footing, the company geared itself for making road-building equipment for the U.S. Army Engineers at the same time Pan American was cooperating with the Engineers in madly building a network of air bases in South American and Africa. Both needed the same equipment. It didn't hurt that the brother of the Huber company president happened to be John C. Schroeter, a former military pilot who joined Pan American Airways in 1931. After working as a part-time pilot and copilot, Schroeter worked his way up to becoming an Assistant Director of Operations for PAA. He even served as copilot with Kenneth Beer, who piloted early flights of the China Clipper across the Pacific, and with Harold Gray, who piloted some of the first survey flights of the Boeing Clippers and went on to become the president of Pan Am. The Huber family had direct ties to the Clippers.

After the tractors and farm machinery had planted, cultivated, and harvested crops, and after agricultural products were processed, the Clippers also showed up in food advertisements. Gerber's Baby Foods ran full-page ads formatted to look like news stories in major magazines. The headline was "Feeding Baby in the Skies: Like Everything They Tackle, the Four Major Airlines Make a Good Job of This, Too." The advertisement reported how Gerber supplied special baby kits, complete with bibs and dishes, to American, United, TWA, and Pan American Airways. In an obviously posed photo, dark-suited Pan Am flight officers rather than ground personnel in work-white coveralls loaded stacks of Gerber's boxes into the nose cargo hatch of one of the Boeing Clippers. The text proclaimed that "Pan American Airways thoughtfully supplies Gerber's Baby Foods to its employees with children, who are stationed at bases abroad." This claim made in 1944, deep into World War II, more reflected the prewar world. In 1944, Clippers had been leased for military missions, and women and children had been pulled out of most Pan Am bases in what would become war zones abroad, especially those served by Boeing Clipper routes. Like Pan American Airways, that faced the problem of trying to advertise itself during wartime when it could not divulge what it was actually doing for the country, Gerber's also had to image a hope for the future or look at the past to sell its strained foods. Gerber's had nothing to worry about. The baby boom that would occur with returning troops and postwar prosperity would far outpace the number of "Victory Garden" babies conceived during the war.

The public could connect babies, baby food, and Clippers in light of immediate events following the attack on Pearl Harbor. One of the first publicized jobs of the China Clipper after the attack was to evacuate expectant mothers from Hawaii to San Francisco. The Clipper had been equipped with delivery and life-support systems just for this purpose. For a time, the China displaced U.S. air mail with U.S. heir mail.

Young heirs must drink their milk. The SOLCOL Company of Plymouth, Michigan, climbed on the Clipper sales wagon by marketing its chocolate milk "health drink delivered right to your doorstep." The company claimed the visible cream separation ring caused by the use of whole milk proved the drink's glass-bottled benefits. Children received story booklets as company premiums from their local milkmen in the 1930s. In six cliff-hanger parts, the booklets carried the title of *The Thrilling Adventures of Jack and Jean, the SOLCO Twins in the Philippines*. The illustrated story followed the two youths as they crossed the Pacific on a Clipper. The China Clipper was illustrated on the cover soaring over a small bottle of SOLCO. Jack and Jean drank plenty of SOLCO, and they needed the extra energy upon visiting the cockpit of the Clipper at the very time armed men stormed the flight deck to hijack the Clipper. Recipes also were included on the booklet for Mom. The Borden Company, another milk company, reciprocated by providing a set of seventeen airplane trading cards as premiums, one featuring the Sikorsky S-42A Clipper. These were given away with Borden's promotion of Thompson's Malted Milk.

Heinz 57 Ketchup also ran full-page ads featuring the Clipper in *Life* and other major magazines. These photo displays showed a large Yankee Clipper in flight with photo inserts of the galley with food being served. Heinz promised that its "aristocrat" tomatoes rushed from the fields would give a "delightful lift" to food in the best restaurants, to meals on the Clipper, and to lowly leftovers at home. Heinz 57 Ketchup, found in every corner of the globe, was "as much at home on the Pan American Clipper ... as in any modest roadside stand." Just as the Clippers now served the war effort, Heinz made sure in the ad to apprise readers of the fact that the Naval Academy served Heinz, as did one of the most colorful restaurants in the South, Carvel Hall, "rendezvous of statesmen and top-ranking officers in all branches of the Service." This ad that ran early in the war combined Clipper sophistication and elegant dining with patriotism and working for the common person. A 1940s wartime exigency met 1930s Ritz.

Big tobacco sat atop the agricultural product chain, and many tobacco companies tied product promotion to the Clipper. Edgeworth Reed Tobacco Company advertised its Chelsea Cigarettes by picturing in the foreground a pack standing upright next to an ashtray containing a lit cigarette. In the background stood a barometer and a framed painting showing a romantic night scene of a Boeing Clipper flying over a tropical island. A U.S. flag was prominently displayed on the side of the flying boat. A theme of romantic patriotism evolved. Chelseas were included in some C-Rations Accessory Packets for troops during World War II.

Liggett & Myers Tobacco Company advertised Chesterfield Cigarettes with a 1937 advertisement picturing men on Wake Island running to meet the China Clipper as it zoomed in with ten thousand packs of Chesterfields desperately needed at the new Pan American Airways' Hotel on Wake where "nothing else will do." The company was proud of the fact that the huge order could be delivered to Wake in under four days. A map showed how far the cartons of cigarettes had to travel on the new route to China. The Chesterfield Clipper ad appeared in such places as the back cover of New York playbills at the Shubert Theatre to appeal to urbane, sophisticated travelers.

While Chesterfield appealed to the elites, Prince Albert tobacco used Clippers in comic book form. Prince Albert advertisements in major magazines often depicted authority figures recommending the tobacco. One ad showed a Clipper captain putting passengers at ease before a flight by telling them that the giant Boeing Clipper would roll as smoothly off the water as Prince Albert rolled up into "cool, good-tastin' 'makin's' smokes." While surrounded by a group of businessmen in the strip, he directed his down-home self-assurance to the worried young unmarried miss in the group.

The R. J. Reynolds Tobacco Company commandeered the back cover of several magazines for its colorful full-page ads touting the wartime exploits of various Clipper captains in either photographic or comic book formats. Meanwhile, the ubiquitous Philip Morris cigarette call boy graced many ads inside publications, as he cried the then familiar "Call for Philip Morraaaaisss" to passengers shown boarding a Boeing Clipper. The technological advancements made in Clipper design meant that people could actually smoke aloft in airplanes, something unheard of for most of the 1920s and 1930s when airplanes were flying gas cans and passengers breathed fumes from aviation fuel.

This call-boy advertisement again played on the desirable sophistication and exclusivity of Clipper flight. Only the finest people could afford to fly the Clippers, so only the finest would they smoke. Thus, the advertisement proclaimed, "Sky-passengers on Pan American Clippers are served with America's FINEST cigarette." If one was among the finest, one was also wiser than others; therefore, this much repeated ad pointed out that many more Americans were smoking more wisely by switching to Philip Morris. According to the ad, medical journals pointed out that all smoking irritation of the nose or throat cleared up immediately when smokers changed to Philip Morris. Cleverly, in the Clipper photo, a Clipper steward pointed and directed passengers onboard. The cigarette boy, superimposed alongside the Clipper steward, paralleled his pointing and directing. The difference was that the Philip Morris call boy looked out of the ad, inviting the viewer to not only vicariously board the Clipper but also to get on board with Philip Morris cigarettes.

The Philip Morris ad brought together two primary popular culture icons of the late 1930s and 1940s, the Clipper and the Philip Morris call boy. Call boy "Johnny," familiar to radio listeners and later TV viewers, was actually four-foot midget Johnny Roventina (1910–1998). Although in his thirties at the time of the Clipper ads, his size and high-pitched voice created a buoyant, youthful appearance. As bellboy at the Hotel New Yorker, he actually did wear a red monkey suit with brass buttons and a chinstrap pillbox hat. He was experienced with sophisticated travelers because Clipper passengers often did stay at the Hotel New Yorker. Johnny owned a lifetime contract with Philip Morris, so he continued to be salaried long after cigarette ads were pulled from radio and television.

Unlike regular packs, Clipper Cigarettes came in flat, nearly square, single-layer boxes, which illustrated the Boeing Clipper flying just above ocean whitecaps. The airlines could also cater to smokers' tastes by distributing other brands whose packs could be inserted into form-fitting boxes advertising Pan American Airways rather than the cigarette maker. Such cardboard boxes carried the PAA winged globe logo in red/white/blue.

Cigarette companies appealed to male smokers and youth by including aviation trading cards in their cigarette packs during the 1930s. Usually in sets of fifty, these thematic collections could be housed in albums also supplied by tobacco companies. This encouraged youth to hound adults to smoke more so that the trading cards would become more quickly available. John Players and Sons produced a set that included collectible cards of both China Clipper and a Clipper interior. The interior shot just happened to show people smoking in the Clipper's aerial lounge, while one man pieced together a puzzle and in a rear compartment a young girl occupied herself. Again, whereas most aircraft did not allow smoking due to gas fumes, smoking was permitted on the elite Clippers.

These cigarette pack stiffener cards served to educate as well as sell.

Planes were identified on each card's front with fuller descriptions on the back. The informational aspect of the Clipper cards might not seem that important today, but in the Depression when many people could not afford magazines, newspapers, or radio, and there were few television sets, product premiums became an informational resource. Such a direct appeal to youth by tobacco companies today would certainly be a no-no, but not then.

Other companies joined the advertising fray. Wings Cigarettes competed with its own "C" series of cards, picturing various Clipper types. Cards would be numbered so that collectors would always know whether their collection was complete. Some of the other Clipper cigarette cards have come down to us via unknown tobacco companies. Not only did these cards reflect the most recent developments in aviation at the time, but also they sometimes depicted the future. Such was the unknown maker of a crude card labeled "The Philippine Clipper." The back side read "No. 347. This card is one of a series of 48 cards. Philippine Clipper. They have great hopes of building a Trans-Pacific fleet of these planes, eliminating weeks of travel by boats." Whoever made the card had no idea of how the Philippine Clipper would look, so the artist drew a rough rendition of an early S-40, incapable of flying to the Philippines. Even odder, the artist drew the flying boat and left off all its engines.

The success of the cigarette makers prompted other companies to follow suit. Oil companies began their own promotions using youth to draw parents into their filling stations. Richfield and other gas/oil companies were not limited by the size of a pack of cigarettes, so they were able to produce larger labels or trading cards to fit into their albums. Richfield provided cards with a painting of the Clipper on one side and a three-way blueprint on the other. Rather than read word descriptions on the back of the card, collectors were to insert the cards over the descriptive passages printed in their albums.

Mobil Oil provided both a description on the back of its 1936 China Clipper trading card and in its album entitled, *Man Made Wonders*. This card showed a painting of the China Clipper over its route map across the Pacific. To encourage children to bring their parents back to the local Mobil service station, the album promised that an eight by ten print suitable for framing would be sent to them if they filled out the coupon in the back of the album. Their local petroleum dealer would countersign it and add the service station number. In an age when service was all important, this encouraged family contact between service manager and the public, while it connected the petroleum product with the speed and efficiency of the China Clipper.

In 1940, to match the forty-eight states, Tide Water Associated Oil Company offered forty-eight aviation poster stamps rather than trading cards. These could not be purchased or mail-ordered. They were available only upon "personal call" at any Tydol station in thirteen Northeastern states. Three different stamps were issued over a sixteen-week period beginning on May 16. This meant Dad or Mom had to gas up each week. These stamps were to be placed in the album provided. The Boeing Clipper was to be mounted in the "Wings Today and Tomorrow" album section, which explained that the Clipper was the largest airplane in the world, so big that engineers could walk through corridors inside the wings to service engines while in flight.

Some companies went beyond Clipper trading cards and poster stamps. Clipper Gasoline used the China Clipper as a logo on its illuminated glass pump heads. Wolf's Head used the Clipper as its petroleum products' logo as well. The Northland Oil Company of St. Paul, Minnesota, advertised Wolf's Head oil on its business envelopes. The entire reverse side of Northland envelopes carried a photo of an S-42 Clipper, pulled out of the water on a dolly, to be serviced. The photo's heading ballyhooed, "Clipper Ship Quality at No Extra Cost, Pan American Airways Uses Wolf's Head Oil Exclusively." Alongside the tractor that had pulled the Clipper out of the water stood a Wolf's Head oil truck. Two-gallon tins of motor oil advertising Traymore Lubricants of New York used a Boeing Clipper in red, white, and blue as their logo, with the promise of "3000 Miles of Lubrication." In scorching tropical temperatures and below freezing readings, if the Clipper could fly 3,000 miles across an ocean using this oil, then so could the consumer's automobile—or at least by land across the United States. Strata Oil tins also used the Boeing Clipper as a logo covering almost the entire container. Manufactured by Tiona Petroleum of Philadelphia, Strata Oil's Clipper soared into the heavens in yellow and maroon as the flying boat trailed whiskers to show its speed.

Chewing gum represented another product tied to the agriculture and food industry. If anything was quintessentially American during the 1930s, it had to be bubble gum. The Goudey Gum Company of Boston became best known to card collectors for its 1930s series of baseball cards featuring such notables as Babe Ruth and Lou Gehrig. Today ownership of these valuable cards has become the center of court battles, but back then the spirit of country loyalty or nationalism ruled for the youth. This spirit showed in series of cards devoted to baseball heroes, U.S. presidents, G-men, sailors, soldiers, anything connected with pride in the United States and in national defense.

Goudey's "Wings Over the Pacific China Clipper" was the No. 10

card in its 1936 History of Aviation Series, available only through its Air Service Gum. Goudey borrowed the image from *Boy's Life* magazine. Depicting the China Clipper flying over some tiny Pacific Islands, this lithographed card came with two punch holes so the entire set could be mounted in a loose-leaf binder, saving the company the expense of having to produce an album. The description on the card's back told of how the Clipper surpassed the earlier Clipper sailing ships in trim design, great speed, and "the prestige of foreign trade captured by America." With expansionistic Yankee pride and the jingoistic boasting of the era, the card paid tribute to the Martin Company for producing an airplane that made possible the *world's* longest transoceanic airway, just as Goudey was "the *world's* greatest penny value." The whole country seemed to be like a streetwise boy chewing his cud and cracking wise as it tried to find icons of optimism in digging out of the Depression. The Clipper became an icon of achievement rather than failure. Digging out would include education and entertainment through materialism or collecting, which meant being consumers even at the penny level.

World War II, with its scarcity of materials, effectively brought an end to the issuance of cigarette cards, thus hurting the hobby of cartophily. Yet some companies persevered, and as late as 1948 labels depicting the China Clipper were being produced. After the war, food companies continued their own brand of promotion. Clipper rings hid as premiums in various boxes of cereal. They also appeared as colorful cutouts on cereal box panels. Nabisco used the cigarette companies' idea of stiffeners to separate its rows of Shredded Wheat in the 1950s. These dividers carried all kinds of information to youth, everything from tricks for surviving in the wilderness to aircraft identification, including the Atlantic Clipper. This divider was published both in Canada and the United States. The Canadian version of the Clipper was entitled "How Canada Travels." It was meant to be colored, cut out, and its base bent so that the clipper could stand upright on a shelf or table. The card's final message was to "Ask Mother to get more Nabisco Shredded Wheat so that you can collect all 36 cards in the series." (That meant eating a lot of shredded wheat!)

Clippers were also tied to bread, a staple no matter how hard times might be. Bakeries tried to expand or maintain customer bases through a variety of techniques using the Clipper image. Some followed the cigarette/oil company model of issuing airplane trading cards and albums. The Cushman Bakery did this with its *Airplanes of America* card album. Youths were to paste in the album the brightly painted images of Fred Hoertz. Other bakeries took a different path. Neva's "Cakes for All Occasions" Bake Shop of Billings, Montana, gave out cardboard trivets of the Boeing

Clipper, over a Clipper sailing ship. These trivets were distributed around the country, accompanied by smaller coasters picturing travel scenes from around the world.

Bread makers also sponsored the radio serial *Speed Gibson of the International Secret Police*, whose 178 episodes began in 1937 and ended in 1940. Popular culture has known many Gibsons: baseball, its famous pitcher Bob Gibson; moviedom, its cowboy star (and pilot) "Hoot" Gibson and Mel Gibson; music, its Gibson guitars; space exploration, its astronaut Robert L. "Hoot" Gibson. In the 1930s, Speed Gibson became the Gibson of the day. Speed starred as the fifteen-year-old youngest member of the ISP. Each episode of this aviation series began with an ominous repeating radio message, "Ceiling zero, ceiling zero." Comic relief was provided by a cast member who popularized the phrase, "Suffering wangdoodles, Speed!" The phrase found its way onto the lips of many a radio fan. Howard McNear, who played the part of agent Clint Barlow, went on to become famous as Floyd Lawson on *The Andy Griffith Show*.

The Clipper was introduced in the very first scene when Speed used a heavy model of the China Clipper that he had been building to render

Bakeries and other businesses across the United States gave out cardboard trivets such as this one showing a clipper ship and Clipper flying boat.

unconscious an agent sent by the villainous Octopus. Having proven his worth in capturing Blackie, Speed is sworn in as an agent and then sent with other ISP agents to China by Clipper to thwart the Octopus's sinister plans. Throughout the series, Speed flies around the world in the "Flying China Clipper."

Bread companies distributed a variety of Speed Gibson premiums in the form of IPS agent badges, code books, and pins showing airplanes and advertising various breads. So that both boys and girls would be sure to eat the right brands of bread, Virginia Cooke, the serial's creator, added apprentice air-hostess Ann Burton to the cast. Often scripts fairly accurately traced the actual Clipper routes and locales across the oceans, such as when Speed must fly across the Atlantic to the Azores. Cooke must have read Pan American Airways Clipper accounts to fuel her scripts. Cooke's name fit in well with her baking sponsors as they served up one of the radio serials that became the bread and butter of young listeners in these pre-television days.

Blue Ribbon "Nature's Gift" bread offered Clipper trading cards. Originating from the Schmidt Baking Company, these premiums featured Clippers and were the size and thickness of playing cards, because that is precisely what they were. The company used playing cards that showed Clippers flying among the clouds or climbing above an ocean liner. Instead of face cards or the usual suited numbers on the back, Schmidt had the playing card company leave the backsides blank so that Blue Ribbon commercial messages could be printed there. These messages advertised Blue Ribbon bread or touted the company's delivery trucks, each of which could haul "enough bread in one day to feed 43,000 people."

These agricultural-related companies promoted the idea of clubs to promote their wares. Most aviation-related radio serials offered young listeners a chance to become members of a larger organization, such as the Young Birdmen of America, or, in the case of Speed Gibson, the International Secret Police. As the United States shifted from fighting gangsters to fighting other countries, these clubs made for an easy transition. Increasingly, villains became "international villains" rather than the usual "tough guys." Youths were encouraged to adapt to a wider worldview, and to do it for patriotic purposes. These teens and preteens would shortly be called on to join not only a club but also the club of clubs—the nation—as it marched off to fight the enemy. The full weight of U.S. agriculture, aviation, and youth would be brought to bear in 1941, but preparation for that effort began earlier.

10

The Comics: Of Dragon Ladies and Claws

Nineteen thirty-four marked the appearance of a comic strip about a young boy named Terry Lee, whose grandfather had left him a map of where gold could be located on property in China. Thus began the story of the boy who went to China. At first this youngster was depicted as an all–American boy still wearing knickers, but over the years he would become a manly pilot helping save China from the Japanese. Along the way, readers were introduced to memorable characters including Pat Ryan, April Kane, glamorous Burma, and that infamous pirate-of-all-pirates—the Dragon Lady. They would revolutionize this indigenous art form.

Had it not been for the Clippers, Milton Caniff's popular syndicated comic strip, *Terry and the Pirates*, would not have become one of the classics of the comics golden age. Most of Caniff's strip took place in China, where Pan American Airways had purchased a large interest in China National Aviation Corporation which competed against the Sino-German Eurasia Aviation Corporation for control of commercial aviation in China. Although the Chinese government held controlling interest in both airlines, CNAC was funded and equipped by Pan American. Most pilots were Pan American pilots who had flown the Clipper routes. Pan American wanted CNAC as a feeder system to join with its Clippers that landed in Hong Kong after crossing the Pacific.

Frank "Dude" Higgs, one of Caniff's fraternity brothers at Ohio State University, later served as an army pilot training pilots for the Chinese. Called Dude because of his snappy dress, he then joined CNAC as a pilot. Higgs began writing letters back to Caniff about his exploits in China. When the Japanese invaded that country in 1937, Pan American evacuated its personnel. Any who wanted to stay with CNAC in China would have to resign from Pan American. Higgs resigned both from Pan Am and from the army so that he could stay and do what needed to be done in facing the Japanese onslaught. He flew many important Clipper passengers around China, including Wendell Wilkie and Clare Booth Luce. As the Japanese closed in on Hong Kong, Higgs evacuated much of the CNAC/PAA staff, and flew out important Chinese officials. Before the Flying Tigers fought to keep China's supply lifeline to India open, Higgs and his fellow ex–Pan American pilots were dangerously "flying the hump" between China and India. These stories gave Caniff much fodder for his artistry. Dude Higgs became the comic strip pilot Dude Hennick in *Terry and the Pirates*. Both Dudes represented American rugged individualism, the romance of soldier-of-fortuning, and the dedicated desire to fight for the underdog, in this case the outclassed Chinese against the militarily superior Japanese war machine. Late in the war, when Higgs died as his plane carrying Chinese bankers and supplies of gold buried itself in a mountain, Caniff offered his accolades by having Dude Hennick die in the strip. From Higgs' stories Caniff derived knowledge for his strip in terms of the Clipper and CNAC actions in China.

He combined that knowledge of commercial aviation with knowledge of warbirds derived from another source. At the same time Higgs wrote to Caniff, another old college pilot friend, Lieutenant Philip Cochrane, led the 65th Fighter Squadron of P-40 Warhawks, the same aircraft the Flying Tigers flew in China. Tellingly, in the strip and on the first page of the *Terry and the Pirates Coloring Book*, Caniff portrayed a U.S. fighter aircraft with freshly painted nose art reading "Yankee Clipper (j.g.)." One of the strip's characters admiringly said to the painter of the "junior grade" Clipper, "That's perfect!" Cochrane wanted Caniff to design his "Fighting Cocks" squadron insignia, which he did. After Caniff saw the squadron perform maneuvers before they shipped off to North Africa, the development of *Terry and the Pirates* was clear. He would risk the innovation of patterning fictional characters after his known acquaintances. Cochrane gave him what he needed for the military side of the equation.

Cochrane became Flip Corkin in the comic strip and also a prototype for Caniff's postwar creation, *Steve Canyon*. For Caniff, real people carried more conviction than the usual comic strip adventure stereotypes. By using this method, Caniff took comic strips in the direction of realism, a somewhat dangerous direction for a comic strip artist at the time. He based his story line on serious, historical events—mainly the Japanese invasion of China—at a time when the United States was still quite isolationist. Ideologically, the strip clearly stated where the nation's sympathies should lie. His boss ordered him not to mention the Japanese in the strip, but Caniff's story line alluded to what was going on. Just as the Clippers themselves were breaking down U.S. isolationism, so was *Terry and the Pirates*, which first appeared just as Pan American Airways began planning its stepping stone bases to Asia.

Often referred to as "Rembrandt of the Comics," Caniff revolutionized comic strips in many ways. He described his work as a Hollywood movie put on paper, but filmmakers paid homage to him. Orson Welles reportedly wrote to Caniff upon the opening of *Citizen Kane*, and Fellini contacted Caniff several times. The influence reciprocity played can be seen in many ways in *Terry and the Pirates*. Caniff used his individual panels to pan as a motion picture camera could film a scene for the best emotional content. This camera action was accomplished by using long, medium, close, and extra-close-up shots. He experimented with using worm's eye view, chiaroscuro black solid ink blotches, changes in the size of the drawing panels to increase effect, sensuality, unusual characters (such as a lesbian, a gay, and the unforgettable iconic Dragon Lady), and no dialogue or dialogue balloons at times—just facial expression, such as would be used onstage.

In an era of comic book superheroes with superpowers, Caniff risked presenting non-isolationist, realistic people. Then, too, he risked going against the grain of post–stockmarket-crash escapism found in the jungle, science fiction, and *Prince Valiant*–type medievalism comic books of the time. At first, the risky method did not quite work. When the comic strip, which began at the same time *Flash Gordon* debuted, tried to find success as a radio serial in 1937, it failed to touch the mainly isolationist public. That changed as war grew nearer and nearer, and finally reluctance to accept stories of American involvement in faraway places ended with the Japanese attack on Pearl Harbor. *Terry and the Pirates* was then in the right place at the right time to enjoy enormous success. While superheroes had to struggle quickly to join the war effort, *Terry* was already there. The war needed heroes: common people who used their skills, courage, teamwork, and common sense to overcome obstacles. It was easy for military personnel and civilian readers alike to identify with characters in this strip. These were accessible heroes; thus, of the scores of comic strip and comic book aviation heroes of the 1930s, the *Terry* characters are among the few surviving. Of the hundreds of superheroes emerging in the 1930s and 1940s, most could fly through special powers often acquired by accident, capes, webs, rockets, and invisible aircraft, but Terry and his sidekicks flew the way we all could learn to fly. Technology as savior only worked if one worked hard enough to develop the talent to master the machine.

Terry and the Pirates became a favorite of U.S. troops, so much so that Caniff drew another strip just for military personnel, gratis. *Male Call* featured the comic strip pinup called Miss Lace, who could feed the dreams of lonesome, randy combatants. In addition to Whitman's Little Books version of *Terry*, and the radio version, the comic strip came to television in 1952. Pan American Airways' Clipper plans for China had indeed helped create one of the masterpieces from the golden age of comics and the comic strip.

Zack Mosley, however, created the longest-running aviation comic strip containing the Clippers in his *Smilin' Jack* series, which ran an incredible forty years from 1933 to 1973. Mosley began his drawing career with the *Buck Rogers* team before having his own comic strip. Clippers played a major role in his story sequences, as well as educational panels in enlightening the public on aviation concerns and terminology. Mosley knew something about flying boats, having qualified on PBYs during the war. (PBYs were World War II long-range flying boats used by the military.) As one of the founders of the Civil Air Patrol, "The Flying Minutemen," he flew some 300 antisubmarine missions out of Florida, mostly in civilian aircraft. Early in the war, after a German submarine ran aground on a sandbar off the coast of Florida and a CAP plane spotted it, no military planes were available to destroy the raider. Frustrated, the CAP asked to have bomb racks installed on its private planes. Since the military had sent most of its bombs and fighting planes to Africa and was mostly engaged in training in Florida at that time, they consented. After that, Mosley flew with bombs under his aircraft.

While *Smilin' Jack* may have set the record for the longest-running aviation comic strip, it also set the record for being the shortest-running radio series, lasting only three months in 1939, when it aired on Mutual Broadcasting and was sponsored by Tootsie Roll. *Smilin' Jack* proved a better bet for motion picture production during the war. Universal filmed a thirteen-episode movie version of *The Adventures of Smilin' Jack* in 1942, released the following year. Episodes followed at one-week intervals to keep the public coming back to the movie theatre each week.

In an episode titled "Escape by Clipper," the China Clipper lost a wing, caught on fire, and crash landed in the Pacific, after being shelled by a Japanese submarine just before the Clipper could reach Hawaii. The evil German spy mastermind, Von Teufel, masqueraded as an American newswoman onboard. She commanded a Japanese Black Samurai unit, whose job was to obtain the whereabouts of a road so secret that the mountain people had for centuries not even revealed its existence to the Chinese. Now Japan threatened all of China, and the Chinese hoped that the mountain people would reveal the road, so that it could serve as a secret supply pathway between China and India to save China from the Japanese invasion. Shades of the Burma Road! Emissaries from the remote province of Mandon traveled on the Clipper, as they had been persuaded to reveal their secret only if the Americans would oversee the signing of the treaty between the people of Mandon and the Chinese government. The closest U.S. ambassador at the time was in Hawaii, necessitating Smilin' Jack Martin and his associates to escort the dignitaries safely through a series of attacks by henchmen.

Events occurred just after word was received of the Japanese attack on Pearl Harbor. Jack was ready to resign his position flying for the Chinese to return to the U.S. to fight for his own country, but he postponed that to aid the cause that would help both China and the U.S. Jack, played by Tom Brown, was accompanied throughout by his girlfriend, played by Marjorie Lord, later of *Make Room for Daddy* television fame. The Chinese general who needed the secret and who had been in command of Jack was played by Sidney Toler. Keye Luke played his second-in-command. Toler and Luke were better known as Charlie Chan and Number One Son in the *Charlie Chan* film series. Basically they reprised their *Charlie Chan* roles in military uniforms.

Although the movie version of *Smilin' Jack* carried a lot of action and the jingoism of the time, it lacked the best attributes of the comic strip: humor, exaggerated character depiction, and the extreme sex appeal of Mosley's curvaceous, often mini-skirted "de-icers." Movie episodes lacked the caricatures found in the strip with The Claw, The Head, Tish the Dish, Fat Stuff, Stretch, and Limehouse. Instead, it offered the overly serious, clean-shaven, all–American Tom Brown, who did not fit the dashing, mustachioed, Smilin' Jack image of the comic strip.

But in *Smilin' Jack and the Daredevil Girl Pilot*, a 1942 Whitman book based on the comic strip, everyone was back in character, as was the Clipper. As a member of a Coast Guard squadron, Jack had been asked to report for duty in San Diego for special assignment. A criminal organization tried to hi-jack the navy's newest seaplane bomber, in order to turn it over to the Germans at one of their secret bases in South America. Jack was to stop them. Taken prisoner, Jack was sentenced to death by working in a sulfur mine with other prisoners on Death Rock off the west coast of South America. He quickly befriended Fat Stuff, a South Sea Islander who didn't seem to lose much weight on the poor food rations. Jack plotted his escape from the slave camp after seeing a Clipper flying on its route over the rock. Before escaping in a handmade glider fitted with the warden's daughter's silk gowns, Jack was manhandled by The Claw, a huge crude hulk with a hook for a hand. He also encountered The Head, a laconic Peter Lorre look-alike with a swollen bald head. Jack was able to wrestle the dastardly Limehouse off a cliff, where Limehouse plunged to his death, and then launch his glider so that he could be rescued by a friendly seaplane when it alighted on the ocean.

De-icer Betty Brown provided the love interest. This daredevil pilot appeared to be working as a German spy, but she turned out to be just the opposite. Her father was revealed to be president of South American Airlines, a fictional version of the real Panagra Airlines, a combination of Pan American Airways with its Clippers and the Grace Company, which commanded many of the cargo ships to and from South America. In the end, J.Q. Brown, Jack's friend Downwind (never shown because he was the handsomest man in the world), navy fighters and bombers, a navy cruiser, and the marines all descended on Dead Rock to free prisoners and take out the bad guys. Just as an international criminal gang conspired with the militaristic Nazis, it took U.S. commercial and civilian interests coordinating with the military to defeat the Axis plans. As usually happened with *Smilin' Jack* episodes, Jack avoided any marital entanglement with Betty by having to go on another special mission for his country.

While Mosley freely created his own imaginary aircraft to suit his story lines, when it came to the Clipper and many other aircraft he drew them realistically. Thus his comic strips and their comic book versions blended the real and the unreal. The same can be said for his characters. Though often caricatures, Mosley modeled Smilin' Jack's friends on his own acquaintances. Many of the people he flew with in the Civil Air Patrol or encountered at air races found themselves in *Smilin' Jack*. That was half the fun of the comic strip. One such character, Flannel Mouth Don, was based on Don Strimmel, one of Mosley's friends and a public relations man for National Airlines. Strimmel, who announced at air shows, also sought sponsors for the Miss Deicer Beauty Pageants that brought beauty contestants to Miami. Winners posed for photographs outside the Miami Pan American Airways' Clipper terminal.

So iconic were the Clippers that Mosley continued to use Clippers in other formats as well. He was frequently called upon to contribute his drawings to various publications and organizations—everything from airplane nose art to program cover design for air shows. Even when not drawing flying boat Clippers, he would draw other aircraft and label them Clippers. The 1937 Christmas newsletter of Roosevelt Field, for instance, showed a twin-engine land plane over the field. On its wings it carried the name Xmas Clipper.

Since Charlie Chan was mentioned earlier in regard to the movie episodes of *Smilin' Jack*, it should be pointed out that the comic strip *Charlie Chan* also appeared in syndication during World War II and used the

Clipper as icon. One particular storyline was translated into the motion picture *Charlie Chan at Treasure Island* (1939), with Toler as oriental detective Charlie Chan. Since the Chinese were considered friends of the U.S.A. against the Japanese in the late 1930s, American audiences could accept a Chinese detective as opposed to stereotyping him along with other Asians as a member of the Yellow Peril in earlier years. After all, the Clipper connected the U.S. to China, not Japan.

Many consider *Charlie Chan at Treasure Island* the best of the *Charlie Chan* movies. Chan expected a writer friend to fly in on the Honolulu Clipper to San Francisco to meet him. However, the friend apparently committed suicide on the flight, a fact which Chan disputed. More murders occurred as Chan tried to close in on the evil spiritualist called the Zodiac, whose name eerily presaged the name of the Zodiac serial killer who began terrorizing the Bay Area in the 1960s. The action took place in San Francisco, whose Clipper port was located at the World's Fair taking place on Treasure Island at the time (1939). In fact, Treasure Island, with its Clipper base, had been created expressly for the International Exposition. Chan was aided in his investigation by the charming stage magician Rhadini, played by Cesar Romero, who wished to expose the corrupt, blackmailing Zodiac. As Chan said, "Sometimes black magic close to black mail," an example of one of the many classic Charlie Chan aphorisms throughout the film. Following the classic detective formula where all the suspects are gathered in one location before the killer is announced, *Charlie Chan at Treasure Island* gathered all the suspects at Rhadini's performance for the fair at Treasure Island.

Before there was a Captain Kirk on the Starship *Enterprise* violating the Prime Directive and going where no man had gone before, there was the comic book navy flying ace Clipper Kirk. "Clipper" served as a popular name for comic book heroes. Although *Star Trek*'s James T. Kirk did not wear the Clipper moniker, the series did seem to draw on earlier aviation names. The brash starship Captain Kirk mirrored the comic book Kirk as an aviator, and Captain Picard of the *Star Trek* spin-off, *Star Trek—The Next Generation*, mirrored the name of August Pic(c)ard, who made the first stratospheric balloon ascensions in the 1930s, going into "space" where no man had gone before. Like the flying boat Clippers, *Trek*'s starships were named after nautical ships, and nautical terminology was used, such as "You have the *helm*, Mr. Chekhov, while I take the *Admiral's* message," and "This is the *bridge*, Scotty, how are things in engineering?"

In the pantheon of heroes of World War II vintage *Wings* comic books, Clipper Kirk appeared in regular episodes, where he defeated the Luftwaffe and saved scantily clad women from the enemy. In these pre–

Comic Code days, bondage scenes abounded. Clipper Kirk began as a daredevil Canadian pilot, but he went through several permutations during the run of Fiction House's *Wings* from 1940 to 1954. In the first sixty-eight issues, Clipper gunned down the enemy as a military pilot. As war clouds receded, he, like other heroes of the time, had to adjust. As the Clipper flying boats departed the historical stage, being transformed into giant land planes, Clipper Kirk transformed, too. Instead of appearing as a military pilot, in later issues he became the Phantom Falcon. This hooded, black-masked hero battled injustice rather than Axis powers. As a final manifestation, much like Superman's Clark Kent, he also assumed a civilian identity as a "too-timid clerk" assisting a big city police chief.

When Canada could not import U.S comic books during World War II, local publishers began producing their own comic books with black-and-white interior panels. To keep money at home, Canada forbade the importation of fiction periodicals, including comic books, because they were deemed nonessential goods during wartime. Ontario's Bell Features, the most prolific comic book producer in Canada, filled the void with *Action Hero*. Similar in concept to *Wings* and many other comic books, it gave readers several heroes and episodes in a single issue, with violent cover art showing destruction of the enemy. In addition to such heroes as Super Commando came one called Clipper. Clipper was short-lived however. The Canadian comic book industry was born with the war in 1941 and died with the war in 1946. As soon as U.S. comic books began shipping to Canada at the end of the war, Clipper and the infant Canadian comic book industry all but disappeared.

The Phantom was one comic strip and comic book hero that did not disappear. Lee Falk's *The Phantom* presented the first of the long line of skinsuited, masked comic strip crime-fighters, opening the doors for Superman and Batman and hundreds of others. Columbia released the serial in 1943 for movie theatres. The 1996 revival movie of *The Phantom* was based on the first two 1936 newspaper serials. In it, air pirates forced down the Pacific Clipper before the start of World War II. In the movie, the Phantom, "The Ghost Who Walks," a.k.a. Kit Walker, was played by Billy Zane, who appeared in the Phantom's trademark purple Spandex body suit, but this time without the striped trunks as seen in the comic strip. His white stallion Hero and his mountain wolf Devil accompanied him on his jungle island with its Skull Cave. The Phantom had to prevent the evil billionaire Xander Dax (Treat Williams) from gaining control of the Skulls of Touganda, which would give him the power to rule the world. Diana, his love interest, was played by Kristy "Buffy the Vampire Slayer" Swanson. Along the way, he encountered other characters, played by such

Hollywood stalwarts as Patrick McGoohan and Catherine Zeta Jones in the role of a pirate pilot.

The Phantom followed the other crime-fighting heroes mentioned in regard to story lines in which Clippers appeared. Their plots proclaimed the resident cultural values of the time, a peculiar blend of what might seem on the surface to be conflicting values. On the one hand, these heroes fought to protect the underdog—defenseless jungle pygmies, damsels in distress, innocent civilians, the free world—against the ruthless, seemingly unlimited power of egotistical tyrants, madmen, or women pirates with their international gangs. On the other hand, heroes supported capitalism, often coming down on the side of big money and the authority that supported and protected the rich.

As a consequence, pirates appeared in *The Phantom*, *Smilin' Jack*, and *Terry and the Pirates*, since pirates threatened free enterprise and parasitized capitalism. Likewise, blackmailing people to do the work of the evil ones accomplished the same purposes. Ill-gotten money and power made for bad capitalism. Good capitalism and the structure that supported it came in many forms. Often the male hero's lady love came from a very rich, powerful family. Usually her father was an esteemed businessman, important to the welfare of the country. Such was the case in *Smilin' Jack* with Betty Brown's father, who headed an international airline. He was outraged that some of his own employees were making fortunes out of slave labor on the sulfurous island. Similarly, in *The Phantom*, adventurer Diana's uncle ran a large New York newspaper and lived in a mansion. He was concerned that the billionaire Dax was accruing power and wealth through greed and nefarious means.

At the end of such comic strip, comic book, or movie episodes, the hero would need to perform two functions to satisfy both value myths: to free the underdogs and to restore the status quo for the money interests, so that trade routes, businesses, or the world could be safe again. Guardian symbols of the establishment aided the hero in the form of the FBI, Secret Service, various branches of the armed services, embassies, and police. If events took place outside of the prewar United States, as they so often did in the case of *The Phantom*, sometimes he or other heroes would have to operate with friends, rather than governmental representatives, to placate U.S. neutrality laws or to preserve Good Neighbor policies. In short, these heroes performed the same function as the Clippers themselves. They were symbols of freedom carrying out government policy abroad, with democracy defined largely as spreading capitalism.

Thus plot conflict reiterated the basic value conflict in all of American popular culture: the desire for individual freedom versus the need to give up some individual freedom, so that community could exist within humane laws. In the 1930s and 1940s Nazis, fascists, and Stalinists severely challenged the idea of the benevolent community and individual freedom as defined by American standards. Believing that people were not equal, these regimes sought to either eradicate the weak or have them turn over their freedom to a superman or strongman who would rule them for their own good. The Clipper, as a combination symbol of democracy representing both U.S. government (all of us, the flag-flying community) and private interests (the independent, daring, Horatio-Alger entrepreneur), evacuated refugees from these dictators as well as ferried war supplies to defeat these gangsters. As a consequence, the Clippers became the perfect targets for villains to intercept or destroy in the comic strips.

Although Clippers symbolized the United States, they also represented the world's first international aircraft tying all the oceans together. In this way, the flying boats could be seen as part of the world rather than just the United States. Like *The Phantom*, Clippers became acceptable comic strip icons marketed in countries other than the United States. Because *The Phantom* appeared in different colored suits, depending on the national colors of a particular country, the comic strip was received well worldwide. Its international appeal has continued into the present. Like the Clippers, the Phantom's base was on an ocean island, whose location shifted over the years, yet he traveled the world.

World War II brought home the importance of this comic strip internationalism, when Swedish and Norwegian readers encountered episodes of *The Phantom* in their newspapers. After the Nazi invasion of Norway, the Germans forced Norwegian newspapers to print propaganda news releases stating that the United States had been totally destroyed. Apparently thinking that comic strips were innocuous, the authorities paid little attention to censoring them. *The Phantom* continued to be smuggled across the border from Sweden. As long as *The Phantom* continued his exploits, Norwegians knew that the United States was alive and well, since the strip originated in the States. As related to Lee Falk after the war, Norwegians so enjoyed this joke on the Nazis that a favorite password for the Norwegian underground was "Phantom."

In Italy, after Mussolini forbade the importation of U.S. products, including comic strips and books, a young, subversive Federico Fellini kept the strip going by penning his own version of *The Phantom.* Instead of a purple suit, the Phantom now wore red. In many countries during the war, individual writers and artists kept this hero alive by creating their own episodes. It was no wonder that in later reincarnations Diana, now the Phantom's wife, worked for the United Nations. In the case of film director Fellini, he was so taken with Falk's comic strip style that he planned in the 1960s to take Falk's earlier creation, *Mandrake the Magician*, and turn it into a film, starring Marcello Mastroianni as Mandrake.

The Phantom's creator, Lee Falk, became involved in the World War II international intrigue and propaganda as well. He was engaged in secret intelligence operations with the Office of War Information, later becoming chief of the foreign language division. After the war, his life, like the comic strip, continued to be filled with drama. He took his interest in theater and directed one hundred plays, produced over three hundred, wrote plays and musicals, and directed the likes of Charlton Heston, Karl Malden, and Paul Robeson in the summer theaters Falk owned.

Besides the Clipper's appearance in *The Phantom,* Clippers also served the comic strip and book cause under many other titles. To mention a few, the February 1942 *Flight Comics* contained "The Case of the Chungking Clipper." The July 1956 *Suicide Squad* ran "The Case of the Pacific Clipper." Throughout their comic strip history, Clippers rode the changing currents of how *enemy* was defined. They helped move the reading public from seeing criminals as threatening the democratic status quo to seeing political/military international gangs as an even greater threat, and back again. Often those who had been enemies in prewar strips, such as the pirate Dragon Lady, would join forces with the righteous during war to defeat the greater enemy. Comic strip Clippers flew a clear media pathway. First they usually appeared in a comic strip, then in comic book or little book form, then radio serial, then movie serial, then feature movie, and finally television. Even Walt Disney's animated television series *TailSpin* (1990) owed much of the romance of its 1936 flying-boat bear-pilot Baloo to the earlier comic strip Clippers. *TailSpin* was *The Jungle Book* version of earlier Clipper tales, complete with air pirates, such as the villainous fox called Don Karnage and the wealthy magnate Shere Khan.

What of Superman, the ultimate hero, created at the same time as the Clippers? In "Menace to the Silver Clipper," the sixth Mutual Radio broadcast of the nearly 2000 *Superman* radio episodes, Superman flew to Colorado to save a train, *The Silver Clipper*. Railroads did use the Clipper name for passenger trains in the 1930s, just as new technology in the guise of faster airplanes competed with them. In fighting for "truth, justice, and the American Way," Superman *was* the Clipper. Like the Clipper, he flew, was all speed, and could circle the globe. The small figure of Superman circling Earth and trailing speed lines appeared in comic book after comic book. The other place readers saw nearly the same image was in the Pan American Airways logo and in all the PAA promotional materials showing a small figure of a Clipper trailing speed lines while it circled the globe.

Superman's creators, Jerry Siegel and Joe Shuster, came up the final version of the Man of Steel at the time the press was covering Pan American's vision of circumnavigating the world by air. Siegel and Shuster quickly converted their superhero from a man who could simply leap buildings at a single bound to one who could fly. Superman could even be mistaken for an airplane, evidenced by the famous words, "Look! Up in the sky! It's a bird! It's a plane! It's Superman!"

As the Man of Steel, Superman wore a streamlined, skin-tight, patriotic suit. Similarly, the Clipper's streamlined skin of stressed steel made it one of the first aircraft of its kind. Many other parallels can be drawn between Superman and the Clipper, particularly when considering the *Superman* radio broadcasts, began in 1940 and lasted through World War II. Like Superman, the Clipper possessed a double identity. The Clipper, in its Clark Kent civilian role, earned its living by carrying the news (mail). In its secret military role, it flew secret missions to help defeat evil powers. Resembling so many of the comic book superheroes of the 1930s and 1940s who as youngsters came to Earth or the U. S. from somewhere else, the first Sikorsky Clippers hailed from afar; but both machine and heroes clearly demonstrated American values. Whereas Superman came from the planet Krypton but was raised on a Midwestern farm, the Sikorsky family brought their aviation ideas from Russia but formulated Clipper design around suggestions from Midwestern hero Charles Lindbergh. The Clipper enjoyed Superman's superpowers as well. Superman used his X-ray vision, usually portrayed in the comic strip as a beam directed at an object. Airplanes could, too. Just before Superman's X-ray vision appeared, popular science magazines illustrated radio beams, which guided airplanes through darkness and storms. With its "eyes," a Clipper could not undress a person to see a hidden weapon, nor could it see through a building, but it could see through clouds to be guided to its base. The Superman-Clipper analogy could be continued. For instance, a lengthy discussion could ensue that considered how both served as bridges to reduce the shock of new technologies, or of how they served as bridges for immigrants moving from an old life to a new life in America. The point is that the heroes of comics' Golden Age were involved with Clippers, were born of the same needs represented by Clippers, and shared the same values.

11

Pulps and Trades: Murder and Romance Most Foul

Fictional accounts of the Clipper have proliferated in both the pulp and trade magazines and books from the 1930s to the present. While this investigation will focus on stories featuring the Clippers, many other writings paid lip service to them. More recent works have mentioned the Clipper to create nostalgic re-creation of the prewar and war periods. As an illustration of this, E.L. Doctorow's coming-of-age *World's Fair* (1985) climaxed as a young man, Edgar Altschuler, negotiated his way through childhood to finally end up visiting the New York World's Fair. In the novel, Edgar's brother Donald built a solid wood model of the China Clipper. The Clipper came back to fill Edgar's imagination after he had listened to a radio episode of *The Shadow*. In Edgar's mind, the Shadow lacked imagination as a hero. Like many boys with their thoughts on having superhero powers, Edgar dreamed of what it would be like to wear the cloak of invisibility. His first impulse, of course, was to spy on naked girls and their mystery. But he quickly turned his mind to more serious matters and dreamed of riding the Clipper to Germany, where unseen he would kill Hitler and his underlings. Then he would whisper in the ears of all Germans to be good. The Shadow was neither gawking at naked girls nor dealing with the problem of the Nazis, so he lacked imagination. As the novel and Edgar progressed, he finally arrived at the 1939 World's Fair, where the real Clipper was on display in the Hall of Aviation, and the world of the imagination for both adults and children had been converted into actual objects.

A Donald other than Edgar's brother also showed the influence of the Clippers on fiction. In the Walt Disney book, *Donald Duck Sees South America* (1945), where Donald was first introduced to José C. Carioca, the sociable talking Brazilian parrot, Donald flew around South and Central

America, following Pan American/Panagra Airways routes. Donald was at first his usual loud, complaining, Ugly American self, but later teamed up with José to fly into the Brazilian jungles to Manaos to find the learned Mr. D. Appley Whelpley, who had gone missing from a rubber plantation near the Amazon and Rio Negro Rivers. Manaos and the nearby rubber plantations had been the critical Clipper destination for crude rubber during World War II. In keeping with the need for a "Hands Across the Border" policy during World War II, the same policy Pan American Airlines had pursued before the war with the government's blessing, Disney arranged for the duck and parrot to echo the Roosevelt administration's Good Neighbor policy to prevent Axis inroads into South America. Thus, Donald and José became good buddies.

Pulp magazines seized on Clipper stories for their "Adventure, Romance, Mystery," to quote the subtitle of *Argosy*. The September 12, 1936, edition of this popular Munsey Company weekly led off with "Transpacific Plunder: A Novelette of the Reckless Skyways." Pan American Airways would hardly have enjoyed the skyways being portrayed as reckless when the company was doing all it could to sell safety and comfort. Nevertheless, author Frederick C. Painton, told the story of a Clipper hijacking as it left Manila for Guam. For legal protection and fictional purposes, Painton changed the name of the Pacific Clipper to "Pacific Cruiser," and Pan American Airways became "Pacific Airways."

The lurid cover art of this *Argosy* issue showed the dapper but evil Chinese thief Chang Tze storming the cockpit of the Clipper while in flight. He trained his gun on the tale's hero, captain and chief pilot Tony Blaine, while the lovely Nara Goddard gasped as she sat next to the good captain. Chang Tzu represented the transitional period during the "Yellow Peril" scare in the United States when Asians were vilified. Previously, stereotyped Asians had been seen as an economic threat in both the California gold fields and the Transcontinental Railroad, where they had begun to supplant such cheap labor as Irish immigrants. In the 1930s that began to change, with U.S. sympathies moving towards the Chinese as the Japanese began to exert their power in China. Consequently, Chang Tzu was half-good, half-bad. He was still a thief, but he aided in saving the Clipper from even more sinister forces—international gangsters. He had also prevented a fortune from being confiscated by a Japanese destroyer.

The October 1942 cover of *Argosy* continued the international intrigue by illustrating a Boeing Clipper used to fly to Europe. The flying boat was superimposed over a painting of a Nazi spy and winsome lass to advertise the lead World War II potboiler. By this time, gangsters had been nearly completed eliminated as villains in favor of the Axis powers. Skyways were indeed reckless. In pulp fiction, passengers and crew were more apt to be shot by other passengers, who were never what they seemed to be, rather than by belligerent submarines or aircraft attempting to shoot down a neutral civilian transport. The Perils of Pauline gained wings.

The December 1943 *Blue Book: Stories of Adventure for Men, by Men* contained "Remember December," with the Boeing Clipper amply illustrated by Hamilton Greene. The story, by Manuel Komroff, took place on the day Pearl Harbor was attacked. The Clipper crew overheard the bad news while flying between Guam and Manila. Since these ports were under attack as well, or soon would be, the Clipper put down at the hospitable small island of Little Jut. Japanese spies had already been on the island and had left a large chalk directional symbol inside the cone of the local volcano. The Clipper officers were in a quandary. A radio broadcast would invite capture, and they had no secret code. An ally came through. One of the passengers happened to be a Russian who could give the Clipper radio officer a coded message to be relayed to the Russian consulate in Washington and quickly decoded. The cooperation worked, and the girl war correspondent and the boy war photographer, who were also passengers on the Clipper and developed the hots for each other, were able to destroy the Japanese message in the volcano before they hastily departed. Given the short length of the story, events were truncated. It took Penny and Macdonald only fifteen minutes to walk from the bay, climb up the side of the volcano, and reach the top, where they saw the Clipper as a small shiny object in the bay—and the walk included time to come to an understanding with each other!

Love triangles blossomed in a *Good Housekeeping* serialized story by Ursula Parrott. The affairs-of-the-heart story involved a small group of New York socialites "kidnapped" at Christmas by a seventy-nine-year-old Madame Haverlock, who flies people in and out of her swanky Caribbean island digs on an S-39 amphibion. Although the aircraft played a minor role in the story, it played a major role in the illustration by Tom Lovell. Dressed in dinner jackets, high heels, or swim suits, the swells looked upward as the Sikorsky roared overhead in a lead-off, two-page illustration for the May installment. The plot depended on guessing who was really going to end up with whom and what the so-called kidnapping was all about. Adventure here was much more muted than it would be in wartime Clipper stories.

Like others of Parrott's novels and magazine short stories, the story might at first seem like romantic fluff for the housewife, but a closer look would reveal otherwise. The "Appointment with Tomorrow" title harkened to her novel *There's Always Tomorrow*, which was filmed in 1934 and 1956.

Her short story also contained daring features for which she became known, particularly looking at divorce from a woman's standpoint. Divorce and age differences between lovers entered into the *Good Housekeeping* story, as it had in her scandalous first novel, published anonymously, *The Ex-Wife* (1929), in which a wife matched her husband's infidelity score by score. After the book became an instant success, selling 100,000 copies the first year, Hollywood bought the film rights from her for $20,000, a huge sum at the time. Based on her book, the movie version, *The Divorcée*, became the first movie to challenge the new Production Code when Hollywood tried to police itself to avoid governmental censorship. The movie garnered the Academy Award for Best Actress when Norma Shearer beat out Greta Garbo. Parrott's monetary success allowed her to live as stylishly as the New York socialites she wrote about, a feat few writers, and women writers in particular, could accomplish in the 1930s. She was Clipper class.

Flying Aces ran a regular potboiler by Arch Whitehouse in each issue, starring the Griffon, a red-masked black-suited do-gooder, and his gang, out to thwart the Axis powers. This sometimes meant saving the Clipper or persons on the Clipper. Whitehouse often sold his stories by putting Clipper in the title such as in "Death Haunts the Clipper" or "Clipper Hi-Jack." In "Clipper Hi-Jack" (July 1940), a Jack McWilliams line drawing showed a giant Boeing Clipper under attack by seaplanes launched from a German pocket battleship, as the Griffon's *Black Bullet* dove between the Clipper and a German plane bent on ramming the Clipper.

The plot brought two of Whitehouse's pulp fiction heroes together, Crash Carrington and the Griffon. In the hijacking story, the Clipper was forced down on the last leg of its journey from Lisbon through the Azores to LaGuardia. The Griffon whisked Crash away in his own seaplane before Nazi seaplanes could attack the Clipper. The hero then shot down the enemy planes, saved the Clipper, and carted Crash off to the Griffon's secret base near Long Island, where his rock garden was really a hangar door. Carrington, an airplane salesman, actually was trying to deliver a secret message to Washington about German plans to invade Greenland. In the end, the Griffon captured a gang of fifth columnists, blew up a German submarine, and made sure Carrington was safely on his way.

In this Clipper story, the Griffon fit the usual formula for superheroes. Like Superman's Clark Kent, Batman's Bruce Wayne, and Wonder Woman's Diana Prince, the Griffon put on the double identity of also being Kerry Keen, to keep his superhero status secret. At his secret base, he surrounded himself with a stereotypical team. Pebbles (Miss Barbara Colony), his plucky girl Friday, liked to answer his door at night by herself, which predictably led to her being kidnapped so the plot would require her to be rescued. In contrast to Pebbles' feminine charms, Barney "the Mick" provided the muscle by convincingly threatening torture to villains and causing them to divulge information. In this way, Keen could bring together both white collar and blue collar to fight America's enemies, although, like any good rogue hero under suspicion by the authorities, he claimed he would offer his services to whoever paid. He might dress in black and fly a black plane, but readers knew his heart was red, white, and blue. He would risk his own life to save Clipper passengers and crew—without pay.

Whitehouse pitched Crash Carrington as a pre–Indiana Jones leather-jacketed American adventurer who was impatient to get off the Clipper, since it traveled a bit too slow for his lifestyle. To increase his rogue hero stature, he said flying in the Clipper was "like doing a cruise in a hotel lobby." The somewhat irreverent Carrington was more the rough-and-tumble type than New York high society. Clipper captain Meakins immediately admired the freedom Crash represented, even though Crash considered Meakins a "lug pilot," basically a truck driver. Few fictional stories during the Clipper age dared to refer to flying boat crews as unheroically manning tubs.

Whitehouse's Griffon stories, which ran from 1934 to 1942 in *Flying Aces*, covered the key years of the development of the transoceanic Clippers. Arthur George Joseph Whitehouse (1895–1979) wrote under the names of Arch Whitehouse and Jack Townsend. As a prolific aviation journalist, historian, fiction writer, and cartoonist, his work often appeared in *Blue Book*, *War Birds*, and *The Saturday Evening Post.* Like many period writers of pulp aviation fiction, he claimed to be a World War I ace who flew for the Royal Flying Corps. His claims of downing sixteen enemy aircraft and six kite balloons probably stretched the truth, but as an observer/gunner he was credited with some kills. Regardless of his actual history, his hyperbole and aviation knowledge created popular heroes intertwined with the Clippers.

Not all of Whitehouse's Clipper stories involved Crash or the Griffon. "Clipper Ship Curse" in *Flying Aces* (August 1937) told of a Clipper flight from Alameda to Singapore. The flight turned back after two mysterious murders took place on board and the assailant somehow escaped in midair. Later the crew learned that the evildoer had slain the wrong men. The target had been the head of British defenses in Singapore. A Dutch cartel was trying to keep the Clippers from having a route across the Pacific. It wanted to control the western Pacific, including Manila, and routes through New Zealand onward through Sumatra to Singapore. The Dutch criminal element felt that if they could first undermine defenses at Singapore, Pan American Airways would not fly into that port.

As the Clipper again tried to fly the route, a trap was set. Before the first incident, somehow the murderer had found a way to enter the Clipper from the outside while the flying boat was in the air, since the plane had been completely checked for stowaways before the first murders. On this trip, as the Clipper neared what was the probable first intercept point, an agent crawled out of the top hatch of the clipper. By pressing his body close to the aircraft's skin, he was able to slowly work his way back to the tail struts, where he hung on and waited. Soon another plane appeared, and a mysterious object began zooming and hovering around the Clipper. Improbably, the mad Dutch inventor had created a set of batlike wings that enabled him to fly like Rocketman, and this Batman tried to enter the Clipper hatch after landing on the back of the fuselage. He was manhandled inside the Clipper. Curses! Foiled again.

James Norman Hall's short novel, *Lost Island* (Atlantic Monthly Press/Little, Brown, 1944), presented a most unusual story of its time involving the Clippers. The story related how a fifty-year-old engineering colonel in the National Guard was tasked with transforming an isolated coral atoll into a military base. He donned civilian clothes to disguise the military nature of his mission. Because of the wartime emergency, no army or navy planes were available to fly George Dodd there; consequently, the military commandeered one of Pan American's Clippers. Flying from San Francisco, Dodd and seventeen other important passengers still could see the "appalling sight" of Pearl Harbor upon landing and departing. The next day, the Clipper zigzagged across the equator, secretly dropping off passengers on various uninhabited spits of land in the middle of the Pacific. The Clipper finally landed him at an island where the people had never seen an airplane, let alone a giant Clipper. Here, he caught a schooner which, after several days of sailing, took him to his island destination.

This early "green" book related how an engineer, who had been taught all of his life to care about machines and technology, found out that what he was asked to do would destroy people, environment and a way of life. As the title of the book stated, the island would indeed be "lost." Remember that this protest was registered in 1944 in the heat of war when winning came at all costs and when world environment caused little comment.

Hall's didacticism in protesting the industrial age's destruction of human values showed immediately in the book with the Clipper. The engineer became well acquainted with the Clipper crew. Though he realized their professionalism and maturity for people much younger than he, Dodd thought they had "lost the faculty for wonder" (20). They lacked "the free mind" and, given their responsibilities, probably rightfully so. This included an improbable competent, pretty stewardess, none of whom flew as actual flight attendants during wartime flying boat flights. Everything was being done in the name of expediency, the enemy of humanistic values. When he asked the pilot where the Clipper would be going next, the captain could only reply, "On." Dodd was already a part of that expediency. He realized that he was the advance man for doing what Pan American Airways had earlier done to construct its Pacific island bases. That meant blasting and bulldozing paradise.

The environmental message ran throughout the book. Dodd witnessed how nesting areas for giant sea turtles were destroyed, coral heads and reef fish dynamited, coconut palms toppled, and tropical bird eggs smashed. The Catholic priest's small church was demolished, so, too, his garden, whose soil had been brought by boat over decades. In seconds, the garden was bulldozed and reduced to fill dirt. Construction workers flattened the atoll's beautiful islets for unobstructed runways and Quonset huts to service the bombers and seaplanes. As Dodd's island guide Viggo pointed out, the only good thing about the war was that it stopped the Japanese and Norwegians from completing extermination of the whales.

The friendly Polynesians and other residents fared poorly, too. Almost overnight, they had to relocate to a smaller islet divorced from their traditional food supplies, to be fed canned government food instead. The three daughters of the island's agent would become pregnant, thanks to married and unmarried army, navy, and civilian workers flooding the island. Two European Jewish refugees on the atoll, who had only months before fled Hitler, now were forced by the military to leave the islands. Jobless, the refugees disappeared into a historical void. The civilian schooners that supplied the islands with supplies and mail no longer could visit this military base. Generators and motors drowned out and silenced island music and song. The island had been cut off and had even lost its name, now being designated as P-R-B 9 (Pacific Reserve Base Nine). No happy ending here.

Mission accomplished. As Dodd prepared to fly off the barren atoll, he noticed that the airplane that had come to pick him up was splattered with the carcasses and blood of birds mangled by the propellers. He flew back toward Honolulu along the old Pan American Airways' route to Australia and New Zealand. He asked himself if there could be found "any sanctuary for the living" (203). As for the gods and their trying to help humankind, he said, "The only one I was aware of in that ancient Polynesian homeland was the man-created, four-motored *deus ex machina* winging its way through falling night toward Honolulu" (203). Rarely in prewar and wartime fiction was aircraft cast in such "falling night" negativity.

A lesser known book by Hall, *Lost Island*, contained features present in his coauthored, best-selling *Mutiny Trilogy* (1932), parts of which became the movie *Mutiny on the Bounty* (1935) with Charles Laughton and Clark Gable. Hall dedicated *Mutiny* to one of his best friends, Viggo Rasmussen, a schooner captain. Viggo's name also appeared in *Lost Island* as the name of the compassionate island agent. This Dane married and raised his family there and showed the engineer the actual way people lived. Hall also married and raised his own family in Tahiti, spending most of his adult life there except for trips back to the States aboard steamers or the Clipper.

Hall had seen war, and his aviation ties were very strong. In World War I he joined Lord Kitchner's Volunteers before the British found out he wasn't Canadian after all. Discharged, he joined and flew for the famous Escadrille Lafayette. He was shot down, captured by the Germans, and allowed to escape. He became Eddie Rickenbacker's first commander, and Rickenbacker's first kill was shared with Hall. Hall, Rickenbacker, and Hall's wartime buddy Charles Nordhoff, coauthor of *The Mutiny Trilogy* and fellow resident of Tahiti, all wrote prolific stories and articles involving aviation. But it was James Norman Hall (1887–1951) who James A. Michener said was "the most beloved American who ever came to the tropics." *Lost Island* helped that reputation.

The murder mystery novel loved the Clipper. This popular culture genre thrived on exotic and, particularly, isolated settings. Clipper bases abroad lent themselves to this part of the mystery formula. Instead of the ritualistic gathering of suspects on the Orient Express or at the country manor cut off from civilization, Clipper bases and Clippers themselves provided the close setting where murder will out. The international nature of passengers on the Clipper and of those working for Pan American Airways matched the international conflicts of the times. Thus the roving finger of suspicion fell on nearly everyone. What was needed, of course, was the Great Detective.

The book jacket of *The Hong Kong Airbase Murders* (1937) pictured such a man, with knitted brow and receding hairline, as he sighted down the barrel of his shortened .32 automatic. Protecting the China Clipper, he stood under its looming, dark wing. Author Francis Van Wyck Mason (1901–1978) provided his famous great detective, Colonel Hugh North, U.S. Army Intelligence G-2 agent. Of Van Wyck Mason's some seventy books, North appeared in twenty-six. In *The Hong Kong Airbase Murders*, North served as chief investigator for the murders of the chief Hong Kong officers of Trans-Pacific Airlines (read Pan American Airways), whose Hong Kong Clipper was just about to make its maiden commercial flight to the States. Someone obviously wanted to undermine the effort of this U.S airline.

The plot realistically described how airline real estate was being negotiated in both Macao and Hong Kong. This actually did happen, since British authorities balked at first at letting Hong Kong serve as a Clipper base unless the U.S. would grant Imperial Airways reciprocal rights into the U.S. Pan American countered, threatening to move its base to the Portuguese colony of Macao if Hong Kong did not want its commerce. In the novel, a German airline called Air Oriental competed in Asia with Trans-Pacific. The Germans also wanted to reach North America by a Pacific route paralleling that of the Clippers. They were surveying a route that ran Macao-Formosa-Saipan-Marshall Islands-Clipperton Island-Acapulco instead of the Clipper route running Hong Kong-Manila-Guam-Wake-Midway-Honolulu-San Francisco. This too had a basis in reality, since Pan American Airways' China subsidiary, China National Aviation Corporation, competed directly with the Germans' Eurasia Aviation Corporation, whose route ran from Shanghai to Berlin. In both fact and this fictional account, U.S. officials considered it a bad idea to give German pilots in long-range aircraft access to the East and West Coasts.

In the novel, North was asked to take over the case of the murders because the airline was tied to the national interest of the United States, especially because a secret fuel formula that allowed Clippers to fly long distances without refueling had been stolen during the murders. The fuel formula allowed Clippers to land on the open ocean and convert saltwater into fuel. If the formula fell into the hands of the Dutch or French, they could take over the transpacific routes with their own airlines. If the formula fell into the hands of the Japanese or Germans, they could rule the world. If the formula fell into the hands of a so-called White Russian or other ne'er-do-well adventurers, who knew? The fate of the world depended on North's finding the formula, solving the murders, and making sure the Clipper proved itself in opening a route to China.

Lest the thought of making fuel or fire from water seem ludicrous, true believers continue to tout "free energy" cold fusion after it enjoyed its 1989–1990 media flap, when two scientists in Salt Lake City were reported to have produced a hydrogen fuel cell using cold water. In the popular mind, the wish for such a clean, cheap, readily available fuel has enjoyed a long history. In the detective's mind, his wish was to determine which of the possible four dragon ladies were not clean, not cheap, but readily available as they played him for a sap. They were the hydrogen that fueled the plot. This plot innovation complicated the otherwise expected conventions, including the use of invisible ink, red herrings, near-misses, and character differentiation, through stereotyped dialects of a Scot, a Southerner, a polite Chinese, a German, a Russian, some French, a Japanese, and one stutterer. North usually did an oral copy of Sam Spade.

As historian, world traveler and soldier, Van Wyck Mason was familiar with the Clippers and settings for his novels. He served in both the French and U.S. armies in World War I and he joined General Eisenhower's Supreme Headquarters, Allied Expeditionary Force, staff in World War II. Here the colonel continued his historical interests in wartime as a part of the history section for SHAEF, writing everything from training handbooks to discoveries at Buchenwald. Flying and sailing across oceans and crossing continents by camel and horseback gave him the cultural detail to bring history and his mysteries to life. This rich detail increased his popularity. Books such as *Winter at Valley Forge* became well known. When *The Hongkong Airbase Murders* came out in 1937, publisher Doubleday's Crime Club proclaimed Van Wyck Mason "unquestionably America's leading author of stories of international espionage and intrigue." In 1940 his *Stars on the Sea* vied for top ten honors for fictional bestsellers of the year, with Llewellyn's *How Green Was My Valley*, Hemingway's *For Whom the Bell Tolls*, and Steinbeck's *The Grapes of Wrath*. In 1948, he remained in the top ten, and continued into the 1960s to write about settings along the old Clipper routes.

Frederic Nelson Litten's *Airmen of the Amazon* (1942) fictionalized the story of Pan American Airways' flying boat routes up the Amazon. Instead of Pan Am, the book called the airline Trans Am. A young boy growing up on a Louisiana former plantation among racists found that his father had been lost in the Amazon. As he struggled to come of age so that he could find his father, his father was held prisoner by a headhunting tribe in the jungles after his plane crashed. He survived by being held hostage at a secret rubber plantation deep in the jungles. The former German scientist who created the plantation had died of jungle fever, but fortunately the American had quinine and was able to survive. The son, when he became old enough to fly for Trans Am, was able to fly the airline's survey route up the Amazon in competition with the German airline. The Germans were preparing to take over Brazil, and had been setting up secret radio stations in the jungles. In the end, the German airline competitor was defeated, the father was saved, and both father and son realized that the way to peace was to understand one another, even the tribe who imprisoned him.

The novel clearly promoted didactic democracy amid anacondas, caiman, piranha attacks, poison arrows, and witch doctors on the prowl. Bringing democracy to the indigenous people, and promise of bringing it to the whole world, became a major theme. Not only were the Germans defeated for control of air routes and rubber in the Amazon, but so was the power-seeking witch doctor who wanted complete control of the tribe.

A typical American hero was installed in his place, one who did not really seek power but cared for the future of his people. Litten concluded the novel by, saying that the busy sounds of the jungle people's axes "told of a changing order, of a fairer world, where the 'good life' was not for the *few*, but to be shared by every race and people of the earth" (280). Quite a thing to say considering the book was written just after the attack on Pearl Harbor, when Germany and Japan both became hated enemies of the U.S.

Airmen of the Amazon's book jacket, done in jungle-green and yellow colors, depicted a baby Clipper flying just over the heads of natives in their dugout on a tributary of the Amazon. Pan American did fly this kind of aircraft on its routes, as well as other types. As a pilot, author Litten also knew aircraft. He created series of aviation stories for youth, including those featuring heroes Jimmie Rhodes and Johnny Caruthers. *Airmen of the Amazon* was meant for older boys, but its adventure quality and quasi-history made for adult reading as well.

For verisimilitude, Litten used the names of real people, such as the head of the German airline in Colombia, and it was true as reported in the novel that Colombia and Brazil forcibly moved the Germans out and Pan American in. Even the geographical sources for the bark from which quinine could be extracted was accurate. Litten did acknowledge all those who gave him facts he needed to write the book. Most interesting was that he credited the facts about flying the Amazon not from Pan Am but from the United States Air Corps, Lieutenant Colonel George W. Hansen. Given the secrecy of rubber development going on in the jungles of Brazil involving special flights by the Clippers to fly out rubber, Pan Am probably was not permitted to give out information about its activities during wartime. Obviously Litten was not given all the facts. The novel reflected that he was unaware that, in Colombia, Pan American Airways already had bought out major interest in the German airlines, with the blessings of the U.S. State Department.

The allure of the Clipper has continued up to the present, including in modern best sellers. Ken Follett's widely successful *Night Over Water* was translated into several languages. This 1991 novel celebrated the romance and intrigue of the September 1939 flight of the Clipper from Southampton to New York. As if written as a fitting tribute, it appeared at the same time bankrupt Pan American World Airlines ceased operations, putting an end to the creators of the Clippers and the golden age of international flight.

The notoriety of Follett's novel served as the promotional basis for the 2002–2004 computer flight simulation produced by Pilot's GesmbH entitled, "Boeing B-314, The Clipper, Night Over Water, Fly the Book by Ken Follett." The flight simulation CD allowed players to get the feel of flying various Clipper routes in the Boeing Clipper from the safety of their own homes. Would-be pilots could literally fly the Clipper along the route followed in Follett's book to make plot events come alive even more. From a popular culture standpoint, this marked one of the first attempts to link an existing aviation novel to virtual reality. This simulation advanced to such a level that upon entering the cockpit of the Clipper the computer pilot would realize that the flying boat was bobbing up and down while tied up at the dock. Outside the window seagulls swirled.

Night Over Water was just one triumph for Follett. Another of his popular writings is *The Pillars of the Earth* (1989). Many of his bestsellers were made into movies. *Eye of the Needle* (1981) starred Donald Sutherland and Kate Nelligan; *The Key to Rebecca* (1985), Cliff Robertson and David Soul. *On Wings of Eagles* (1986) became a five-hour television miniseries with Burt Lancaster and Richard Crenna. *Lie Down with Lions* (1994) featured Timothy Dalton, Omar Sharif, and Marg Helgenberger. *The Third Twin* (1997) starred Kelly McGillis and Larry Hagman. Can *Night Over Water* be far behind?

The writing of *Night Over Water* in 1991 followed a familiar trend in American culture. When a country goes to war, as the United States did in 1991's First Gulf War, or Operation Desert Storm, consciously or unconsciously popular culture usually finds profitable escapism yet confrontation of war by retreating to past wars that offer safe distance and more clarity. Therefore, at the time of the Vietnam War, moviegoers and television watchers were treated to *M*A*S*H**, which took place during the Korean conflict, rather than Vietnam. Civil War soldiers and Spanish-American War soldiers read dime novels about the Indian Wars rather than their own conflict. For the *Night Over Water* audience, the World War II setting offered a clear demarcation of good and evil, from a safe, unambiguous distance. In doing so, the creative works of popular culture reassure people of their values by reinforcing national bedrock beliefs, through plot and theme in the case of novels.

A closer examination of *Night Over Water*'s plot can reveal that it functioned, and was representative of most fictional works about the Clippers, in promoting bedrock beliefs. After character stereotypes—a rogue hero who was a thief but rose to a better cause, villainous lugs, spoiled sophisticates, mistaken identities, a fascist ideologue, a plucky young woman coming of age, a starlet past her prime, a nervous older Jewish man, and the like—are peeled away, and after all the made-for-Hollywood hanky-panky that kept most of the cots aboard the Clipper heaving through the orgasmic night over the Atlantic are stripped away, solid democratic themes emerge.

The plot involved the chief engineer of the Clipper being blackmailed. A gang held his wife captive and threatened to rape and kill her if he did not arrange for the Clipper to land off the coast of Canada on its way in from England. On board was an FBI agent tending a mobster who was being extradited back to the U.S. The engineer believed this was the man to be freed, but that would make the plot too simple. The real person to be forced off the Clipper was a Jewish nuclear scientist fleeing from the Nazis. A German submarine was to intercept the Clipper upon its emergency landing and then take the scientist back to Germany to work on Germany's atomic bomb. The plot was foiled.

Evil came in the form of anyone who would cold-bloodedly impose his will on others by any means possible. The Nazis set out to rule the world. Gangsters killed anyone who got in the way of their racketeering money. A fascist Englishman dominated his wife and daughters. A jealous brother imprisoned his own sister in order to sell the family company out from under her. In other words, greedy control existed on many levels, involving world domination, capitalism, and family. Follett set these plot conflicts against the backdrop discussion of whether or not the United States would enter the war, with the United States most clearly represented by the iconic Clipper and its large U.S. flag painted on its side.

Good triumphed against all this evil by virtue of a clear democratic message. People had to be willing to risk themselves for the sake of others, willing to break through class barriers between the privileged and the poor, willing to find their "true" selves, willing to realize the importance of people over money, and willing to perform social integration through teamwork for a greater cause. Thus the book presented the democratic and typically American dilemma of trying to balance individual freedom with community responsibility. While some individuals on the Clipper saw it as a chariot to freedom and a chance to escape family or country, others experienced just the opposite. They had been expelled by their communities, as was the case of the captured gangster and the fascist businessman kicked out of Britain. Those who combined individualism with sacrifice for the greater good became the heroes and heroines. The American businesswoman about to lose her shoe company due to the machinations of her brother was willing to move in the opposite direction from the other Clipper passengers. She planned to leave the safety of the United States to run a business in Europe for the sake of following both the love of her life and the necessity of producing materials for the army. Likewise, the former selfish jewelry thief risked his life to save the Clipper and save his girl. He and his high society girlfriend would both defy their pasts and escape together to found their own legitimate business in Canada in order to contribute to society in time of war. And the Clipper crew embraced their blackmailed chief engineer, after thinking he had betrayed them. He was able to coordinate with navy friends to arrange for a cutter to scare off the German submarine. Like any good war tale, the heroic efforts of individual patriotic civilians coupled with the wider military community carried the day, and the Clipper carried the people who carried the day. It meant that the U.S. would have the bomb, love could flourish, honest business could win over capitalistic extremes, and freedom could ring for all but the bad guys.

To highlight the legendary status of the Clipper, Follett began the novel with a single sentence in its own paragraph: "It was the most romantic plane ever made." To increase realism, he included an actual Pan Am cabin diagram of the seating arrangements inside the Clipper, as well as the airline's route map tracing the short-lived northern Atlantic route of the Clippers from Southampton to Foynes, Ireland, to Botwood, Newfoundland, to Shediac, New Brunswick, to Port Washington, New York. He framed his fictional account with more realism after the final chapter. *Night Over Water* ended with an author's note describing how short the golden age of the flying boats was and what happened to the Boeing Clippers. Since three of the six Boeing Clippers were turned over to the British during the war, it was no wonder that this London-based writer would want to revive their contribution to the war effort.

George L. Flynn's *Escape of the Pacific Clipper* (1997) outdid Follett's book by including an appendix with nearly a dozen pages of Clipper photos, diagrams, maps, and photos of the original crew of Pacific Clipper. It also presented a list of actual crew members and other historical personages along with a list of fictional characters interlaced into this story based on real events. Though the cast was large—a full crew, passengers, ground crews, and all the people met on an around-the-world flight—the Clipper itself served as the overriding symbol and main force in the book, whose cover featured a painting of the Clipper, courtesy of Pan Am.

Here was an account that really tried to blur the boundary between fact and fiction. This was a tall order, since the actual events surrounding the Pacific Clipper were so dramatic that they needed no fictional embellishment. Flynn based his book on what became in the 1940s the most publicized story involving the Clippers in World War II. The story of Captain Robert Ford's around-the-world flight appeared in news stories, in comic book form, in magazines, just about everywhere in 1941 and 1942. Ford's flying boat was in the air between New Caledonia and New Zealand when it received word of the Japanese attack on Pearl Harbor. Deprived of its Pacific Ocean bases to return to Hawaii or San Francisco, the Pacific Clipper was ordered to fly westward around the world and back to the United States, while trying to avoid Japanese and German forces. This resulted in the first commercial aircraft flying round the world following a route near the equator, a feat proclaimed by journalists at the time as being second only to Lindbergh's accomplishment.

After hastily camouflaging the flying boat with an improvised concoction of buttermilk and lampblack, the crew faced their return trip without benefit of route charts, maps, tide tables, weather reports or resupply and maintenance facilities for flying boats. Worse, having to maintain radio silence, they could not always warn friendly countries of their approach. This resulted in Dutch fighter aircraft nearly shooting them down at Surabaya. Ford had to pick his own way home the best he could. The Clipper faced flying thousands of miles at a time across land masses, with no water to land on in case of emergency. Ports also lacked aviation fuel, so some legs of the flight had to be flown with the engines knocking on automobile gasoline as if they would come apart.

The Clipper's closest call came at Stanley Falls at Leopoldville, the Belgian Congo. Overloaded with fuel for its long flight across the Atlantic to Brazil, on takeoff the Clipper had difficulty, barely breaking from the waters of Stanley Pool. It just cleared the lip of the falls and actually dropped over the falls and began to descend into the canyon of the Congo River. The fuel overload created so much weight that the wings of the Clipper deformed, jamming the control surfaces so that the Clipper seemed doomed to plunge into the canyon wall as it descended further. Ford was eventually able to gain some control and gradually pull the giant flying boat out of the canyon. After over a month of flying, the Clipper's crew surprised the Pan Am base in New York by suddenly asking permission to land. The Pacific Clipper and Captain Ford were instantly lionized.

In *Escape of the Pacific Clipper*, the plot did in part track the actual route of the Pacific Clipper beginning at Noumea-Auckland-Darwin-Surabaya-Trincomalee-Karachi-Bahrain-Khartoum-Leopoldville-Natal-Port of Spain-New York. For romantic interest, a beautiful navy code breaker who could break Japanese code in a matter of minutes was onboard. She and Captain Ford followed the time-honored pattern of not liking each other at first but finding that they were fit to mate for life by the end of the book. As the most sophisticated aircraft in the world at the time and a flying laboratory for what would become long-range bombers needed by the major powers to rule the world, the Clipper made for a great war prize. Everyone seemed to want to skyjack the Clipper. The plot included attempts by the Japanese, the Germans, the British, revolutionaries in Brazil, and even the Shah of Iran. Did anyone mention the crocodiles? In a finale of comic book dimensions, the Clipper landed at New York, only to be torpedoed by a Japanese mini-sub smuggled into the harbor in a cargo ship with a false bottom. The Clipper had become the evil Commodore Tanaka's white whale, but his torpedoes missed and blew up shoreline warehouses instead. The Clipper rammed Tanaka's submarine, sank it, and docked without a scratch. The fragile hulls of the Clippers would not have survived bumping into a thickly hided sub, so the blurring of reality and fiction became a bit of a tough game to play. Fiction ultimately won out as the book even portrayed knowledgeable people in aviation as not knowing the difference between an amphibian and a flying boat. Still, Flynn's use of the Clipper gave an interesting variation in trying to merge history with fabrication by having historical characters play themselves.

Both Follett and Flynn may have been inspired by the earlier flying-boat fiction success of Richard Doyle, who published in England with Arlington Press. The 1977 novel *Imperial 109* by this descendant of Sir Arthur Conan Doyle became an international best seller and was followed in 1987 by his *Pacific Clipper*. *Imperial 109* recounted the adventures and misadventures of the crew and passengers aboard the British flying boat *Caterina* on the eve of World War II. The ship carried over two million dollars in gold bullion from South Africa to the U.S. Onboard passengers ranged from a corrupt millionaire, a handsome Arab prince out to avenge the deaths of his parents, a femme fatale, a rogue Gestapo agent plotting to kill a Jewish doctor and his virginal daughter, and a captain who drove race cars, to a gangster who planned to hijack the flying boat just before it reached New York. At last, after it had been intercepted and machine-gunned, the disabled, burning *Caterina* made it to Manhattan, crashing into New York's Central Park Reservoir. Bad people were killed; good people for the most part survived. On the way across Africa and the Atlantic, nearly everyone tried to garner the flying boat, including the Shah of Iran, South American revolutionaries, gangsters, Nazis—you name it. Although this suspense thriller focused on the British counterpart to the Clippers rather than the Clippers themselves, Clippers did drive some of the plot, in that the Caterina had to risk flying the Atlantic at an unpropitious time so that the British airline could compete with Pan American Airways' Clippers, which traveled the same route.

But in *Pacific Clipper*, Doyle tried to reprise his earlier flying boat novel success by focusing entirely on the Clipper. As in *Imperial 109*, this novel transformed and pieced together factual occurrences into a fictional framework, and even borrowed a bit from *Imperial 109*. For example, in

Imperial 109 Doyle borrowed from the history of Imperial Airlines and the first twenty years of his life growing up in Africa to create the African chapters to the book. He captured what it was like for a flying boat to go down in the Sud, those vast hot, stagnant, disease-ridden Africa swamps, which did happen to some of Imperial's fleet. In *Imperial 109*, a dockside crewman was quickly dispatched by a large croc as the crewman tried to make moves on a pretty young miss. Likewise, in *Pacific Clipper*, unfortunates ended up in the bellies of crocs in the back channels and swamps of New Guinea.

Pacific Clipper was another tale describing events in the few days surrounding the attack on Pearl Harbor, December 7, 1941. This time the Clipper flight originated in Singapore as it tried to make its way to San Francisco. Whereas Nazis, gangsters, and corrupt businessmen provided villains for Doyle's earlier flying boat novel, this book played on similar themes transported to the Pacific. Now Japanese militarists and secret assassin societies along with a corrupt Chinese official, a Russian blackmailer, a Fifth Columnist, and an arrogant, jealous officer provided the backbone of evil. The Clipper was in a desperate race to get its passengers and cargo to the U.S. before war broke out. Its cargo hold contained secret containers of radioactive material needed to create The Bomb before the Axis powers did. Also onboard were an old dying Chinese man and his niece protecting their secret cargo, the most precious jewel of the Empress Dowager, which turned out to be radioactive protactinium that had led to her death and the death of anyone possessing the jewel.

The body count grew large in this novel, as the Japanese assassin hiding in a casket in the Clipper beheaded or sliced in two someone at nearly every stop. Others joined the killing. Incorporated into the mayhem were facts derived from historical accounts of the Clippers. The story captured the actual strafing of a Clipper during the initial Japanese attack on Wake Island, as well as the fact that a Clipper did carry radioactive materials during the war, but from Africa not Singapore. During the climactic scene where the hero crewman has to struggle with the Black Dragon assassin, the Clipper stepped from its role as setting into one as character. With engines failing, fires burning and the plane about to crash into the Golden Gate Bridge, the Clipper came to life to prevent the assassin from forcing the crewman out an open hatch into the slipstream and certain death. "In a split second, it was as if the stricken flying boat came to his aid.... the deck lurched sharply, hurling the combatants together with savage momentum. All the energy of the Clipper's hull seemed to channel into Munro's frame ... bursting forth from his fist with the violence of a dynamite charge" (512).

Louis Stannard's *China Diaries* (2004) contained no such last-minute saving by the Clipper. Instead, it told the story of a Clipper crewman stranded in China after his Hong Kong Clipper burned to the waterline and sank during the initial Japanese attack on Hong Kong in 1941. He married a beautiful Russian émigré, who had survived the rape of Nanking. They had a son who became a pilot and in 1994 he traveled back to China to find out the truth about his parents, who seemed to have abandoned him in the United States. He quickly became involved in international intrigue as mysterious people made it clear they did not want him to uncover the truth. Through his mother's diaries, he was able to recreate the lives of the young couple before their deaths during World War II.

Captain Stephen Cannon discovered that his mother had been working not only for Pan American Airways' subsidiary in China, but also had been used as a courier for U.S. Naval Intelligence. She possessed information on the secret Japanese chemical/biological unit that was conducting horrible experiments on human beings in northern China. She also had taken many pictures of the Japanese Rape of Nanking that she needed delivered to the U.S. to document what was really happening in China under the Japanese invasion. Her martial arts skills came in handy in dealing with rapist soldiers and the Shanghai nightclub/prostitution underworld. Rightwing Japanese revisionists in 1994 dedicated themselves to stopping her son from revealing all this information, no matter what. Cannon discovered that his mother died heroically in a Japanese prison camp, and that his father sacrificed his life trying to fly supplies over the treacherous Hump into China. Rather than abandoning him, they had tried to protect their son from agents who wished to kill them all.

Author Stannard did have the Pacific Clipper save Cannon's parents long enough so that he could be born. Somehow they were able to make it out of China through Burma to Ceylon, where they linked up with the Pacific Clipper on its epic round-the-world flight, after the Japanese attack on Pearl Harbor had blocked its usual return from New Zealand to the West Coast of the U.S. The events of this epic flight follow what was recorded in other novels and nonfiction about the Pacific Clipper. Stephen and Anna make it to Washington, D.C., where they are debriefed and she is recruited by the O.S.S. to go back to China to set up an intelligence network, but she deferred until she could have her baby.

The text fit well with post 9/11 themes in the United States. In the author's epilogue and in several speeches within the novel, the anti-isolationist message of "Wake up! Can't people see what's going on in the world?" was stressed. To keep a free democracy, loyalty, sacrifice, and courage must be observed. Captain Cannon came to understand that in terms of his own family. Thus the novel combined the family cocooning that took place after the shock of the 2001 destruction of the Twin Towers in New York City with the nationalism that followed. Symbolically, the cover depicted the China Clipper landing in Hong Kong harbor with the red rays of a Japanese flag falling over the plane and harbor like red prison bars.

Clipper authors have also kept pace with advances in electronic technology. Sidney F. Davis successfully self-published *Murder in Lisbon* (1997), one of the early print-on-demand e-novels marketed by 1st Books (now AuthorHouse) of the International Online Library. Orders for the book quickly surpassed 10,000 copies. The fast-moving plot began with the murder of a Clipper pilot in Lisbon in World War II. Another pilot is sent to check on the murder case and to engage in a secret mission for President Roosevelt. He must fly a Free French representative out of Lisbon and somehow land the Yankee Clipper between the bridges on the Thames during the Battle of Britain. At the same time, Captain Westbrook must stop the hijacking of the Clipper and keep two women passengers from being killed and tortured by the evil Auchlin, who learned his scalpel trade from Dr. Mengele and became a favorite of Adolph Hitler.

Adult readers could not have all the fun. Clippers enjoyed unbridled popularity in juvenile and young adult fiction. To appeal to both sexes and to mirror belief in the two-child nuclear family, most children's stories involved a boy and a girl taking a trip on the Clipper, with or without their parents. So attractive was the Clipper image that some aviation-themed books featured it on the cover even when the storyline involved no Clippers. The large-format, picture book story, *Airplanes Stories and Pictures* (1936), by Louis T. Henderson did just that. The cover showed the Sikorsky S-42 "Pan American Clipper" flying out of San Francisco on its survey flight across the Pacific. The uncompleted Golden Gate Bridge lay beneath the Clipper, thus linking two of the marvels of technological achievement of the day. The story, however, told of the transcontinental journey of Jack and Betty on a TWA DC-3. It was as if the world of children's literature knew that the most dramatic story was not about flying across the U.S., but rather about flying over oceans between continents. Writers wanted to tell that story, but when the book was written, the event was just on the cusp of happening. Henderson or the publishers could not resist jumping the gun.

Although *Airplanes Stories and Pictures* told its story with photographs of two juniors flying on an airplane, most Clipper children's books used line drawings or paintings. *Allan and Brenda on a Clipper* (1942), written by world traveler Joyce Newbill Martin, contained line drawings by Hal Forrest of the children and the Honolulu Clipper. As the title suggested, again a pair of children rode on a Clipper. In Henderson's book, Jack and Betty's father sent them to San Francisco to visit a cousin, whereas in Martin's book the father took Allan and Brenda and his wife with him to Hawaii on his business trip. As is evident, these books reflected belief in the nuclear family indicative of the time. The father made the decisions for the family, and the families were white. Considering that the Clippers were propelled by huge Wasp brand name engines, one could say that these stories were about Wasps carrying WASPs.

Lewis E. Theiss built most of his six-book Mail Pilot Series around the Clippers, starting in 1935 with *Flying the U.S. Mail to South America, or, How Pan American Airships Carry on in Sun and Storm above the Rolling Caribbean* (W.A. Wilde Company). Other works included *The Mail Pilot of the Caribbean* and *From Coast to Coast with the U.S. Airmail.* In the latter book, published in 1936, series hero Joseph "Ginger" Hale made sure that important mail traveled across the U.S. and was delivered to the captain of the Clipper that was leaving for the Philippines. To win the battle against criminals and nature, tough Ginger was accompanied in the series by his Bald Eagle Patrol, a group consisting of Boy Scouts. Carrying the mail was a heroic, patriotic act conducted by young men, and aided by a patriotic organization for boys.

The Clipper came to most young readers through the Whitman Publishing Company's efforts. Whitman was a prolific publisher of coloring books, and in 1942 Whitman combined with Walt Disney to produce the *Donald Duck Army Paint Book.* The plotline followed the training of Donald after he decided to enlist in the Army Air Corps. Although this patriotic, conditioning appeal centered around military service (subconsciously suggesting that if Donald can enlist, why can't Dad?), the book offered the Yankee Clipper as one of the airplanes to be colored.

Whitman's Big Little Books and the Better Little Books series dwarfed the coloring books in popularity. Thick, yet small enough for a child's hands, these tiny treasure boxes of text offered an exciting comic book style line drawing on one page with about ten lines of large print text on the facing page. The importance of Big Little Books and Better Little Books on the Depression public was immense. Straddling the area between comics and books, they served as transitional reading and viewing for youth. Started in 1932, the books brought radio characters, motion picture heroes, comic book figures, crime stories, and pulp Westerns to their readers for only ten to fifteen cents. While some children might be able to see a motion picture once a week for a dime, a Whitman book lasted as long as a movie. Better still, readers could reread and review it over and over in an age predating video recordings.

More importantly, Big Little Books offered an inexpensive way for many Americans to learn how to read. The Bible and the Puritan's *New England Primer* served as the U.S. genesis for entry level reading skills until, with the advent of Western expansion in the nineteenth century, came *McGuffey's Eclectic Readers*, which were outsold only by the Bible. With the explosion of mass media in radio, motion picture, dime novels, comic books, and comic strips, the Depression era was ready for a varied collection of readers based on the new media. Big Little Books supplied this need, but like *McGuffey's*, the Big Little Books bestowed Western and most particularly U.S. ethical and cultural values on the young audience, although its worldview was characteristic of the 1930s rather than the pre- and post–Civil War *McGuffey's* era. Whitman's authors exploited the Clipper as the nation began to prepare for war.

Flying the Sky Clipper with Winsie Atkins (1936) came out just as the China Clipper began flying the Pacific. Already the book sensed a not quite specified trouble brewing in the Pacific. Author and illustrator Dougal Lee immediately capitalized on the Clipper adventure by showing the China Clipper on both covers. In the text, the China Clipper became the "Sky Clipper," flying for Trans-Pacific (substituting for Pan American) Airlines. Anagrams were used for the Clipper's island bases. Wake became Kawe; Guam became Maug. This ify-ness suggested the ambiguous nature of the real clippers and their bases. Were Clipper bases merely commercial ventures or an extension of U.S. power into the Pacific? The Japanese protested it was the latter, since where these stepping stones to Asia appeared for Pan American Airways military engineers were quick to follow. The book featured a criminal gang of racketeers trying to commandeer the Clipper, but it also presented another gang of an Oriental nature that tried to down the Clipper and relieve it of mysterious letters in its mail. Shortly after the book appeared, the real Hawaiian Clipper disappeared over the Pacific. Many believed the flying boat was sabotaged, since it was carrying large sums of money to help the Chinese fight the Japanese. While most flying boat captains believed the Clipper was destroyed by a typhoon, the question still lingers out there as to whether or not truth followed fiction.

The story centered on two twelve-year-olds. Jane Sprague, the world's richest child, as heiress to the Sprague millions, boarded the Clipper in Manila for San Francisco after kidnapping threats had frightened her family. Winsie Atkins, son of the airline's president and "button boy," or flight steward, for the Clipper, locked horns with the spoiled rich girl right away. Jane appeared in pigtails, whereas Winsie was a dead ringer for the Philip Morris cigarette boy. Winsie wasn't your usual bellboy, however. He held a flying record for juniors and operated his own radio onboard the Clipper. Unlike Tom Swift, Winsie represented a new breed of boy hero. No longer was it as important to invent as it was to control the new inventions. As war approached, the skills to run machines were now what were most important. Through a series of adventures, abductions, and near destruction of the Clipper, Jane and Winsie came to work together and appreciate each other.

In terms of values, the book combined the Horatio Alger concern for wealth with the Tom Swift series' interest in invention and machines. Winsie and Jane's pluck and luck saved the day, with a bit of help from a G-man and the USS *Enterprise*, whose aircraft forced the pirate submarine to surrender as it was about to torpedo the Clipper forced down out of Hawaii. Only a patriotic coalition of courageous individuals with help from the federal government could defeat gangsterism—sort of a WPA program against crime, with the promise or hope that citizens could regain power in their lives with some assistance from the feds. Since the book responded to the Depression, wealth became key in the plot. Most readers were among the Have Nots rather than the Haves, so they could live vicariously through the characters and dream of being rich while learning of the dangers of mammon. Although having money was not evil in itself, it was a matter of whether or not the money was honestly made through hard work and contribution to society. The evil mastermind behind Slit Slattery's gang was "Big Business" Watson, racketeer of the financial world. His stooges murdered and abducted in the name of money. Even though Winsie was well-to-do as a son of a captain of industry, he worked for his money and did not put on airs. Jane at first represented the opposite. She would inherit much of the world's wealth without doing anything. Poor little rich girl.

After Big Little Books became Better Little Books in 1938, Whitman published *Wings of the U.S.A.* (1940) on the verge of World War II. As might be expected, the book dripped patriotism. The Boeing Clipper on the red/white/blue cover soared over an eagle, that clutched arrows and Old Glory in its talons. Author Peter A. Wyckoff told the story of how Bob Clexton moved from building model airplanes as a youth to going through military flight school at Pensacola. The story concluded with Bob having won his wings, after which he flies Clippers for Trans-Atlantic Airways. On the last page he states how proud he is to be connected to the pilot training and aircraft manufacturing that is "the solid foundation on which American leadership in the air is built." The concluding frame of a Boeing Clipper flying over a landscape toward an American flag was captioned, "Mighty Wings of the U.S.A.!" The Clipper again was used to denote the Clipper as being tops in aviation development and symbol of

U.S. prestige. The story also set the stage for youth to recognize that the path to gaining the most sought after cockpit seat was through military training. Civilian pilots had to be prepared to rescue or fight. Rather than Horatio Alger pluck and luck, now what was needed was a commitment to teamwork. Villains in this book did not consist of mysterious gangs, but rather of selfish young men who thought only of themselves and tried to sabotage others. The worst enemy came from within.

While *Wings of the U.S.A.* used the Clipper to prepare boys for aviation careers, another noteworthy Clipper novel prepared girls for marriage and a professional career. *Peggy Covers the Clipper* took place in the Lend-Lease era just before the entry of the U.S.A. into World War II. People streamed into the United States on the Clipper from Lisbon, as they fled occupied France and other countries. Peggy Foster, the only woman reporter on the *New York Star* was sent to the Clipper port at LaGuardia in New York to interview Madame Ingrid Ericksson, the noted Scandinavian novelist, ex-actress, and League of Nations activist who had to flee. Peggy was also to pick up the orphaned June Sellers, daughter of eminent journalist Lincoln Sellers, recently deceased when overcome by the stress of the German invasion in Paris. While at the airport waiting for the Clipper Eagle to arrive, Peggy observed the rich and famous coming in from South America on other planes.

Peggy's life faced many challenges. Married but a year, she fought to balance career demands with her marriage. Fortunately, Peter McPherson was also a reporter and offered her support through their hectic days of rushing and separation. Peter was all–American. As a specialist in aviation and a pilot himself, he invented special instrumentation that allowed a pilot to fly blind and land in the worst of weather when static electricity negated use of radio beams. Peter maintained contacts in high places within the military. Peggy worried about the increasing possibility of his being called up to train other pilots at the navy training center in Pensacola, far from New York.

Peggy also grew concerned about a Frenchman who came in on the Clipper. The obsequious Rene de Goureau de Pouchont claimed to have been a motion picture star in France before the war. Now on his way to Hollywood to meet with producers there, or so he said, he seemed to be in no hurry. He tarried in New York, beguiling the young June Sellers and befriending Peter. Rene showed entirely too much interest in Peter's invention and the new bombers he heard about from Peter's military friend, Colonel Horace Adams.

Peggy Covers the Clipper tackled some early feminist issues head on. On top of all the plot complication for Peggy, she struggled as a woman to hold her own on a newspaper whose city desk was strictly a men's affair. As she attempted to network to help another woman, she had to try to persuade the men to give June Sellers a job. She failed at first to achieve this, and watched June freelance and nearly starve. Instead of hiring June, the newspaper hired another woman who could clearly rival and threaten Peggy's position.

To get away from the turmoil, Peggy and Peter found a secluded beach area on Long Island where they picnicked, swam, and watched the Clippers fly over on their way to LaGuardia. They proceeded to purchase the old house on the property, fix it up, and invite friends over. When June caught Rene alone in the house stealing plans for the new bomber, Rene struck her and sped away. Upon returning from the beach, Peggy discovered the injured June and unsuccessfully tried to phone Peter in town. In the process of racing to the airport to intercept Rene before he could board the Clipper to Europe, Peggy turned her ankle. Peggy and June drove for help, each using one leg. Peggy braked and shifted while June accelerated.

They made it to the airport, but could not stop Rene from leaving. Peter was already there, though. The whole thing had been a trap to catch the spy. Rene stole bogus plans and would be arrested by the British when the Clipper landed in Bermuda. Order was restored. Peggy obtained her interviews with the important woman she had been seeking, June landed a job on the paper, and the bad guy was brought to justice. In the end, Peter planned to go to Pensacola, and Peggy decided to go with him, saying, "I'm getting tired of writing about women all the time. I'd like to try being one myself." Thus the book ended on a mixed message for young women.

When Bugbee wrote this book in 1941, New York had become even more a center of intrigue and glamour. The Clippers regularly brought in interesting people, good and bad, and not just from Europe. As the book points out, the fashion industry had been cut off from France, necessitating that people in the Americas and the rest of the Southern Hemisphere turn to New York. Even *Vogue*'s glamour issues showed photographs of fashion models against the setting of the Clipper mooring at LaGuardia. Part of the book's subplot considered that fashion theme through a mysterious secondary character, who also flew Pan American Airways to New York, but she turned out to be no spy. This stylish woman even met with Roosevelt to see if young South American women could be brought to New York to study fashion design. Hands and hemlines across the borders...

This Clipper book paralleled the author's life. Like the fictional Peggy Foster, Emma Bugbee also met and interviewed people riding Pan American Airway's airplanes and flying boats, worked as the only woman reporter on the *New York Herald Tribune*, covered women's issues and women's contributions to the war effort, traveled to Washington to meet with leaders, and faced competition from another woman. In Bugbee's case, Ishbel Ross took a desk right next to hers on the *Tribune* as a front-page lead writer and specialist in aviation (like Peter). Ross would go on to write some twenty biographies and historical books. Bugbee's journalistic life surpassed that of her fictional Peggy. She worked for the newspaper for fifty-four years and became known as one of the top reporters on women's issues in the country when few papers would treat women's suffrage and rights seriously. She helped found the Newspaper Women's Club of New York in 1922 and became good friends with Eleanor Roosevelt.

Mrs. Roosevelt even invited Bugbee to Campobello Island in 1935, when the two went sailing "without the men." Bugbee was partly credited with Roosevelt's establishing regular women-only press conferences. The two women shared a similar social consciousness, and their struggle for equality on all levels can be seen in Bugbee's writing. For example, Peggy's maid, despite being racially stereotypically named Old Black Jennie, tried to counter obvious racism. Bugbee pointed out that Jennie was paid very well and had become more family member than maid, sort of a substitute sister or mother in a world where Peggy was the only woman. Times were changing, but slowly. Though still clearly the Mammy stereotype in popular culture, Jennie's character showed a turn towards independence.

Bugbee used *Peggy Covers the Clipper* to help girls understand what they would need to pursue a newspaper career. This book was one of five Peggy Foster books in a Dodd & Mead classic girls' career series (1936–1945). Other books include *Peggy Covers the News*, *Peggy Covers Washington*, *Peggy Covers London*. As can be seen, the Clippers were handy in aiding the young reporter to travel around the world. The series reflected the popular thirst for career series books of the 1930s and 1940s. Other authors and presses had nurse series, flight attendant series, advertising personnel series, and model series. Bugbee stuck to what she knew. *Peggy Covers the Clipper* was not just an adolescent intrigue potboiler without sex even in marriage; it was a handbook for reporting. The book carefully elucidated conducting interviews, problems with quoting and paraphrasing, pluses and minuses of group interviews, handling the camera shy, and the sometimes grim realities of reporting, particularly for a woman—against the backdrop of the romance of the Clipper. Just as *Wings of the U.S.A.* taught aviation terminology, flight etiquette, and the principles of flight to boys, *Peggy Covers the Clipper* did the same for girls or young women and journalism.

Timmy Rides the China Clipper (1939), by Carol Nay, became the most popular Clipper fiction for young readers, still going strong even after the Clippers had departed the scene. *Timmy Rides the China Clipper* capitalized on the emergent cult of the strenuous life or mass sport that so characterized the literary times immediately preceding the war, such as in the popular Frank Merriwell book series. Wellness and morality combined with the manliness of athletics. Youth had to prepare to be fit for the conflict and life to come. This book showed Timmy surfing, snorkeling, and riding giant sea turtles, as he clippered his way to his relatives in Hong Kong. All these activities were extracted directly from Pan American promotional material. Books of this ilk took on a ritualistic quality. Children always met other children in other lands. The other children gratefully acknowledged the American Great White Father influence. Riding their donkeys or water buffalo, these coffee-colored youngsters preferred American cars, preferred American sports over sports of their own, and preferred sewing machines over their own traditions.

12

Rituals: A Parade of Days and Expos

Regional secular rituals in the United States are often connected with marketing tourism. Given that the Clippers transported people from place to place and in their early days were advertised as connecting to rail routes, cities near Clipper ports were quick to use the Clipper icon as a means of celebrating their region and thereby attracting people to it. Tampa, Florida, featured the Sikorsky Clipper in publicizing the 1939 Gasparilla Carnival, which that year was part of the larger Pan-American–DeSota Exposition.

A linen postcard advertising the event and entitled "Spirit of The Pan-American–Desota Exposition, Tampa, Florida" presented a tableau posed at nearby Cypress Gardens. Standing on top of a globe, the same symbol used by Pan American Airways, a Cypress goddess holds an S-42 Clipper in her hand beneath the cypress trees. A señor and a señorita sit on the ground and use the globe as a backrest. The back of the card explained that the exposition ran from January 30 to February 18, 1939. It would contain exhibits from nations around the world and combined the Gasparilla Carnival, the Pageant of Desota, and other international celebrations.

The symbolism of the postcard was apparent. A brunette beauty dressed in red from south of the border leaned against the globe, while her counterpart gaucho dressed in blue helped balance it. A blonde white goddess stood on North America and, over them all, the Clipper linked all the nations together. Together, they completed a red/white/blue ensemble. As was the case with most rituals, more meanings became apparent on a closer look.

Since Pan American Airways had appropriated the name "Pan American," as had various expositions, the postcard portrayed both as carrying the same "spirit" of Pan Americanism. The exposition would link nations together by exhibiting their goods, just as PAA linked nations together as the merchant marine of the air bringing nations and people closer together. Behind the idea of trade with friendly neighbors lay the spirit of adventure. Just as Juan Trippe, president of PAA, used his seemingly Spanish name, Juan, in wooing South Americans to open their doors to his airline, thus ushering in a new world, Florida capitalized on Spanish roots, too. PAA pitched itself as the new explorer, picking up where past adventurers left off. In Tampa, past adventurers included the names Hernando DeSota (the Pageant of Desota) and Gasparilla (Gasparilla Carnival), supposedly a marauding pirate who used the Tampa area as a base. Trippe's name was not Spanish, and Gasparilla or Little Gaspar may never have existed either, but both paid dividends as good myths.

Whether José Gaspar the pirate existed remains controversial. Some say Gaspar was the creation of railroad interests; others claim he was real. In any event, in 1904, as Tampa readied for its May festival, a local resident, who was a New Orleans transplant, suggested that the festival could be combined with a Mardi Gras type of celebration using Gaspar as a pirate, who would descend with his Krewe on the unsuspecting residents of Tampa.

Just as many of our rites of spectacle, rites of the season, and rites of reversal have merged with previously existing rites so that their dates change—as seen in Christmas and Easter—the Tampa festival over the next several years took advantage of other events and combined with them. It moved to November to coincide with the newly founded Florida State Fair. It moved to February to merge with the Panama Canal Celebration. It became part of Tampa's Census Celebration, which proclaimed Tampa the fastest-growing city east of the Mississippi. It moved to Washington's Birthday. As it shifted dates, it also expanded. When the Clippers came along, the event had grown to five days and had become Carnival. In recent times, the event has maintained its flexibility in trying to attract as many tourists and dollars as possible. In 2000, when Tampa was planning to host football's Super Bowl, the Gasparilla Carnival was moved to occur simultaneously with the Super Bowl. New Orleans considered the same thing for the 2001 Super Bowl. If only Mardi Gras could be moved a few weeks. The terrorist attacks of September 11 delayed the Super Bowl enough so that the two could coincide, replete with a blimp for television coverage rather than a Clipper.

Speaking of ritual events connected with football, consider the Pasadena Tournament of Roses and the Rose Bowl. The theme of the 1936 Rose Parade was "History in Flowers," and aviation had certainly captured the interest of the public. The parade contained a float depicting Lindbergh's *Spirit of St. Louis*; another depicted humorist and aviation enthusiast Will Rogers. The Clipper captured most of the attention, since the Clipper had flown the Pacific Ocean from California the preceding year and was readying to extend its route to China. Two floats featured the Clipper.

The City of Los Angeles entered its floral Clipper, accompanied by young ladies representing the Clipper stops across the Pacific—a California girl, a ukulele miss, and a Chinese beauty sitting by a pagoda tower. The patriotic float carried an American shield beneath the nose of the Clipper, which sat atop a huge globe decorated in sweet peas and delphinium. Pan American could not have asked for a better use of its symbols. The float carried a white/pink/blue color motif with the use of chrysanthemums and roses. The giant plane was a real showstopper.

Not to be outdone, the Pasadena City School's predominantly red, yellow, and brown float portrayed the China Clipper dramatically bursting out of billowing white clouds over twin American eagles and an American shield. Both floats clearly showed that the China Clipper was "America's" plane, an American triumph. Not even the *Spirit of St. Louis* float went that far. Patriotism was rising. Unlike most past Pasadena events, the American flag was now prominently featured on both official and unofficial tournament brochures.

Just as East met West in Pasadena's Rose Bowl game, ever the archrivals for the tourist dollar, West and East duked it out in 1939 with competing world fairs. San Francisco sponsored its Golden Gate Exposition and World's Fair, while New York countered with the New York World's Fair. Pan American Airways made sure it occupied key positions in both spectacles for maximum publicity. Alameda, across the bay from San Francisco, already had served as the Pacific Clipper base since 1935, and Port Washington, New York, became the main base for Pan Am's Atlantic route, which debuted during the Fair. Both fairs contained aviation halls that pointed to a more democratic, utopian future, while war broke out in Asia and Europe.

The Clipper fit right into the theme of the Golden Gate Exposition, "Pageant of the Pacific," which was to be a tribute to California and the building of the Golden Gate Bridge and the San Francisco and Oakland Bay Bridge. On the Clipper's maiden flight across the Pacific in 1935, it had not gained enough altitude to safely fly over the uncompleted bridge, so Captain Ed Musick flew the China Clipper underneath the span, despite the danger from dangling cables. From then on, the Clipper, together with the Golden Gate Bridge, became a popular commercial photograph and press image. Official and unofficial postcards for the Exhibition pictured the Clipper flying over the orange spans of the Golden Gate Bridge. The bridge and Clipper seemed to have grown up together, and represented the best of American technical accomplishment. That the Clipper was designed to join the States with the rest of the nations of the Pacific only made the flying boat more of a centerpiece for the exposition.

The China Clipper became one of the main motifs of exposition promotion. The logo for the exposition depicted a Clipper flying over the two new bridges to promote the theme of Pacific Unity and underscore what the exposition called "the expansion of the Pacific Empire." FDR wrote in a 1938 letter to San Francisco Mayor Angelo Rossi that "Unity of the Pacific is America's concern and responsibility.... to the Golden Gate Exposition I gladly entrust a solemn duty." The Clipper was shown as the agent of that unity and expansion.

Commemorative coins, card decks, *faux parquet* card tables, pins, scarves, brochures, pillowcases, and pennants carried the Clipper image. San Francisco hotels issued postcards with the Clipper over the Golden Gate. Meetings also used its image, as in the labels produced for the First Inter American Travel Congress. Different exhibitors, such as the Railway Express Agency within the Exposition, produced their own cards depicting the Clipper.

The Golden Gate Exposition didn't just exhibit the Clippers, the exhibition grounds became the working Clipper base for Pan Am. The giant Art Deco Hall of Transportation was constructed so that Clippers coming in from the Pacific could dock and be towed from the water to be serviced in the huge hall. Spectators could watch from an upper balcony as mechanics serviced the giants. Outside the hall, fairgoers could watch the Clippers splash down right in front of the viewing area at the Port of Trade Winds, not far from the Tower of the Sun. The planes would then taxi up to the docking facilities. This became one of the action highlights of the fair.

The exposition and Clipper base covered Treasure Island, an island created for the event just off Yerba Buena Island, in the middle of the bay between Oakland and San Francisco. Promoters billed Treasure Island as the "biggest manmade island on earth." It was called Treasure Island because most of its dredge fill came from gold-laden dirt washed into the bay from the Sierras. The creation of the island was funded through both state and federal monies, with the U.S. government contributing, under the stipulation that after the exposition was over, the whole island would be turned into the municipal airport for the San Francisco area. Pan American Airways was not about to be left out. In return for moving its operations to the exposition, it was able to take out a ten-year lease on the Hall of Transportation, acquire office space in the administration building, and secure docking privileges in the lagoon.

World War II quickly outdated post-exposition plans. Even though the exposition was so successful that it opened again in 1940, in April of 1941 the U.S. Navy acquired the island as the threat of war between the United States and Japan grew. At the same time that Treasure Island was militarized, so were the Clippers after the attack on Pearl Harbor. Instead of flying movie stars to Hawaii under the watchful eyes of reporters and admiring crowds, Clippers carried admirals, staff, and war priority passengers with little or no publicity. The navy kept the base after the war, and San Francisco had to find another dredged area in the bay for the current San Francisco International Airport.

"The Pageant of the Pacific" showed the promise of the Clippers and the ascendancy of San Francisco as a modern world port. The Clippers *had* linked the peoples of the Pacific, *had* shrunk the time and space between them, *had* renewed the spirit of the Forty-niners at a dizzying speed, compared to that of the sailing clippers of old that dropped anchor in San Francisco. Clippers served as bridges, as did the Golden Gate and Bay Bridges. Technology and speed were on the move. The world was opening up despite demands in some quarters for isolationism. The Clippers and the Tower of the Sun would have to contend with the Rising Sun. In terms of this, an advertising poster for the Golden Gate Exposition was prophetic, showing the tower, bridges, and Clipper against the sun's red sky.

In New York's Flushing Meadows fair site, Clippers shared the stage with the gleaming white Trylon and Perisphere. President Roosevelt opened the Fair on April 30 from the Court of Peace. The Court of Peace was wishful thinking, as Hitler began to roll through Europe. Less than a month later, on May 20, Clippers began flying regular service to Europe from New York. Although PAA did not have a working base at the New York World's Fair, it did have a static display at the William Lescaze-designed Aviation Hall, a structure resembling a huge hangar. Postcards from the fair show a Martin Clipper and a DC-3, displayed just outside the hall. Reporters and tourists could keep busy visiting the Fair and the Clipper base. As the Aviation Hall was being dedicated, the Yankee Clipper took off from the bay at noon, veered towards the fair, and roared just 500 feet over the heads of thrilled fairgoers. A radio broadcast from the dedication ceremonies saluted Captain Laporte and his crew, as they soared out over the Atlantic on their inaugural flight to Europe. Even promotional labels for Children's World at the fair showed a large transport airplane flying eastward pulling the world behind it. A boy and a girl rode atop the Earth and controlled the airplane by holding a ribbon that was attached to the plane and functioned as reins would in riding a horse.

The featured exhibit at the New York Fair was Democracity, a vision of the future and triumph of the American way. The Clippers poignantly fulfilled that same role, the hope of democracy, as some European fairgoers didn't just visit New York but stayed as they fled dictators abroad. The fair was also keen to show modernism and technological breakthroughs for better living, the Clipper sleekly representing that. While railroads still ruled the roost on the East Coast and had a larger display building than did aviation, press coverage turned to what was happening in the air and out at Port Washington.

The New York World's Fair represented the culmination of the final artistic phase of Art Deco, which was replaced by the deprivations of war. But in the United States' last trying-to-be innocent party, the Clipper and the fair and were perfect Art Deco expressions of each other. Their style reflected the commercialized blending of machinery and power to suggest a refinement of speed and sophistication. Art Deco architecture combined flat roofs with rounded corners, banded stripes, glass, and porthole windows. What better way to describe the massive Boeing Clippers with their gigantic flat wings and tail fins to mimic Art Deco's finned buildings? The Clipper's huge three-bladed propellers were hand polished to shine like knives, and they cut nearly fifteen-foot arcs through the air. The Clipper needed curved streamlining to slice through both air and water. Its huge engines did not sit above or below the wings, but were streamlined into them like sleekly curved bumpers of an Auburn speedster. Its orange wing stripes made it easy to spot from above if it had to ditch in the ocean. Unlike earlier Clippers that did contain portholes, the Boeing was so large that it could have rectangular windows. Still, it retained the nautical theme with its hatches and smaller portholes above the main windows. The Clipper showed every facet of the high Deco style. And that was just the outside appearance of the flying boat. For Broadway's Noel Coward, the Clipper was like a cocktail lounge in the sky, complete with spiral staircase (an elegant Art Deco feature Boeing would use again in the jet age with its jumbo jet 747s).

Reversing the situation, the fair mimicked the Clipper's world. The Perisphere and Trylon, the fair's two architectural icons, in their white geometrical purity suggested the world of the Clipper. The massive, spherical Perisphere echoed the globe itself. Until the creation of the Peripshere, the largest globe was the three-and-a-quarter ton, 31-foot circumference globe Pan American Airways installed in the floor of its Miami terminal.

New York's industrial designers had sanitized this winged globe Pan American used for its logo, and pushed it to a greater scale. The 700-foot Trylon did the same thing. As its name implied, the Trylon literally was a three-sided giant pylon, like the aviation pylons and radio towers then being strung between countries, continents, and islands. The gospel of the air was alive and well in New York in 1939. The fair that was to transport people to the future transported them to the now, where Clipper and fair were monuments to technology and financial power, and where Art Deco speed was a metaphor for time that was overtaking everyone. Vendors at the fair did not disappoint, hawking images of the Clipper on everything from souvenir pennants to thermometers.

As an ultimate expression of power to run concurrently with New York's "Building the World of Tomorrow" World's Fair, *Fortune* commissioned Charles Sheeler (1883–1965) to paint a series of six paintings based on the theme of Power, including one entitled "Yankee Clipper." Together with photographer Paul Strand in 1920, he had portrayed New York City in one of the United States' earliest art films, *Manhatta.* In 1939 he returned to explore the commercial strength of New York, this time through his photo-realistic painting technique that he called Precisionism. Sheeler's people-less machine-age Power paintings in *Fortune* featured scenes such as transmission lines at Boulder Dam or the drive wheels on the most modern locomotive, but he chose the Yankee Clipper as the iconic representation of New York's expansive financial and commercial power. As did Sheeler's other images, the Clipper proved that in "Building the World of Tomorrow," tomorrow had already come, delivering a new streamlined utopian reality supplanting America's earlier agrarian utopian vision.

Sheeler had gained fame through his 1927 series of photographs and later paintings of Henry Ford's River Rouge plant, the archetype for modern industrialism where, as Ford claimed, factories became the substitute for religious expression. In "Yankee Clipper" the Puritan-pure geometric lines of the Clipper are shown at the point where the wing spar joins the fuselage of the giant aircraft. The Trinity was presented as a giant, fluted, three-bladed propeller thrusting out of the painting from one of the Clipper's engines. The plane's silver body trimmed in black on its leading edges created a sense of clean, pure values set against fair-weather heavens. This was indeed a utopia, a world without corrosion, pollution, or ambiguity—a world where industrial fundamentalism, Art Deco, and modernism merged to trump the weaknesses of the social, philosophical, and political orders. The sheer dominance of the machine gave the painting its power, a theme further magnified by the New York World's Fair architecture and displays.

Valentine's Day, though not a ritual directly connected to travel or fairs, nonetheless found Clipper expression. Like Art Deco's attraction to the commercial and the industrial, U.S. holidays have always been used as consumer rites. As Leigh Eric Schmidt tracked in *Consumer Rites, the Buying and Selling of American Holidays* (Princeton, 1995), secular and sacred rites such as Valentine's Day become almost automatically converted into consumer rites. Thematic valentine cards that appealed to children began to appear with the revival of the cards, after the material scarcities of World War I. Children could buy bags of cutout cards, press out cards, or loose cards. In the 1930s, the thematic cards often reflected sports, Disney characters, and aviation themes. Children had collected adult thematic cards and placed them in albums during Victorian times, but in the 1930s, cards proliferated just for children. That dreaded or eagerly anticipated icon, the slotted box into which students placed their valentines, appeared in schools across the United States and Canada. The advent of cheap, machine-produced cards put them within the reach of most children.

One Clipper mechanical valentine of the time carried the verse,

> "Plane" words,
> are very fine,
> when asking my own valentine
> to be mine.

Rhyming verse used for valentines stemmed from 1415, when Charles, Duke of Orleans, imprisoned in the Tower of London after the Battle of Agincourt, sent valentines to his wife in France. Composed in 1930s patriotic red, white, and blue, a girl in a blue sailor outfit sat atop the wings of a red China Clipper. Much as if she were riding a mechanical steer, she controlled the plane with reins as her mechanical arm could be moved to blow kisses at the viewer. The Clipper flew through white and blue clouds as if it were an actual flying boat, yet the Clipper was brought down to dimensions of a child's world by patterning it after a period riding toy that had wheels.

The patriotic sailor image revealed the tenor of the 1930s when prewar civilian and military themes mixed, but the card also evoked earlier valentine symbolism and history. While extolling pride in this mechanical marvel of the air, the card was rife with pagan and Christian meanings. Pagan roots extended back to the Roman February fertility rite of Lupercalia, when men drew names for women. Christian roots went back to Emperor Claudius II's execution of St. Valentine. The China Clipper's fuselage and wings created an "X," the conventional valentine symbol for a kiss. The convention may have arisen from illiterate people expressing sincerity by kissing their marks on pieces of paper. Thus "X" may have become the favored mark, since it was easy to draw, and carried religious associations with kissing the crucifix and with being a symbol for Jesus Christ. The Clipper's tail carried a large red heart, descended from the sacred heart, and the Roman Cupid's target, red like the rose sacred to Venus, goddess of love, or the blood of the martyred St. Valentine.

The card really did capture the "wings of love" in continuing Victorian sensibilities and secularization. The Victorians loved things mechanical, and this tradition was revived again in the 1930s with mechanical valentine cards. The airplane in itself was mechanical, reminiscent of earlier valentine cards that showed dirigibles or balloons over the heads of young children. The Victorians also began substituting children as a theme in their cards, rather than Cupids or overtly sacred imagery. Cupid had wings, and over the years, this deus ex machina of love had shrunk from an adult bowstringer who shot both gods and humans in the heart with the dart of passion, to a Kewpie Doll form or cherubic, childlike pudge.

In this card, the high-flying girl replaced Cupid. While she did not pull back the string of her bow, she did pull back the string that controlled her Clipper with its X, or kiss. Modern Cupids rode the Clipper and used a different set of wings. She was completely in keeping with Victorian ideas of ideal beauty in children, slightly updated for patriotic blue-eyed Depression times—tiny nose, large eyelashes, porcelain doll face, rosebud mouth, thick hair. This doll even came complete with frilly-trimmed underwear, picking up on the Victorian lacey valentine tradition, hearkening back to the time when women dropped lacey handkerchiefs for men to retrieve.

At the time this card was produced, circa 1936–1938, the China Clipper had just opened its route across the Pacific. The valentine proved prophetic when the navy called the Clipper into service in time of war, and it was piloted by a sailor, not quite a Shirley Temple doll, but a Pan American Airways pilot in the navy reserves. Since some manufacturers of valentines also published children's aircraft books, the two blended. Valentines served as historical markers connected to political and technological events. The light pun and banter of the Clipper valentine meshed with the speed of world events. The innocent valentine girl straddling the Clipper would soon become the pinup Venus on bomber nose art, wantonly pressing a torpedo or bomb between her thighs. The Roman pagan goddesses had never left, nor had the split in American values resulting in an equal need for innocent purity. Consequently, despite paper shortages, many sentimental valentines were produced for servicemen and women during World War II.

While a young girl substituted for Cupid, the Clipper substituted for doves or lovebirds, other traditional valentine symbols found on earlier cards. Connected historically to Venus, the birds represented not only fertility, but also lifelong commitment. Romans believed birds that mated for life paired off on February 14. Thus this Clipper, or big bird, could fly on Valentine's Day to the loved one, while it educated America's youth about American aviation, and while it fulfilled all the value needs popular greeting cards could deliver. It could give the child a sense of individualistic freedom in choosing just the right card for just the right person. Although young children were not yet passionate lovers, they could participate in socialization by giving valentines. They learned that a card put into words to another person what the sender might be too embarrassed to say or not yet equipped to say. Valentine cards followed the U.S bedrock value of preferring feeling or emotion to rational thought or intellectualism—even if just for fun. Children who cast their valentine "votes" in the slotted classroom box practiced what they would do as adults at the ballot box in a democracy.

Every Fourth of July in the United States, the lighting of fireworks has been a ritual part of the event. Other countries long have used fireworks during worldwide and Chinese New Year celebrations, Guy Fawke's Day, Victoria Day, and Deepavali (India's Festival of Light). China has remained the source of most fireworks. When Clippers began flying to China, makers of Chinese fireworks competed for the American market by illustrating American icons on firecracker wrappers. Hong Kong's Danish/German firm of Jebsen & Co. manufactured "China Clipper Cannon Superior Fire Crackers." Each pack of Clipper Firecrackers sported a colorful label of the China Clipper about to alight on a tranquil mountain lake, framed in the distance by purple mountains and verdant forest. Jebsen could find no stronger image than that. The Clipper was an immediately recognized icon, connecting both the U.S. and China. The label nearly seemed to scream, "Oh, beautiful, for spacious skies ... For purple mountain majesties/ Above the fruited plain." All that was missing was, "For amber waves of grain." The Clipper, however, was the color of amber.

Clippers made their way into the Christmas holiday. A plastic toy candy container from the 1950s, called The Santa Clipper, turned Santa's sleigh into a new version of the Clipper. The outside of its box showed a starry sky with Santa's sleigh and reindeer flying against a bright gold moon. Inside the box, Santa rode at the back of his green sled filled with candy from the E. Rosen Company of Providence, Rhode Island. Two white prancing reindeer pulled the sleigh, connected by bright red ribbon reins.

Part of the Christmas ritual in the United States is the mailing of Christmas cards. Clippers found their way onto those cards. The Martin Company, maker of the China Clipper, sent Christmas cards featuring the flying boat to its employees and business associates as Clippers began to ply the oceans.

One of the rarest postcards celebrating the first airmail across the Pacific was produced as a 1935 Christmas postcard. Each card carried the image of the China Clipper (actually the Hong Kong Clipper) flying over the Flying Cloud clipper sailing ship. In China, each was hand painted with beautiful pastel watercolors, so that no two Christmas cards were quite the same. How many of these labor-intensive cards were mailed remains unknown. The cards were prepared for Julean Herbert Arnold, the United States commercial attaché in Shanghai. He apparently sent them to friends, family, or business acquaintances.

Anticipation ran high for the opening of transpacific mail and passenger service as Arnold asked friends, "How about paying us a flying visit?" Printed backside of the cards were the words, "The China Clipper ushers in a new era in trans–Pacific transport, envisaging the flight from New York to Shanghai in five days." Although the China Clipper did not make it to China that year, it did deliver the first mail as far as Manila before Christmas. Not until 1937 would Clippers travel all the way to Hong Kong. Few would make the trip in five days.

Individually hand-painted in watercolors, such 1935 Christmas postcards as this were mailed from the U.S. commercial attaché in Shanghai. They showed the Sikorsky Hong Kong Clipper over a clipper sailing ship.

Arnold was an old China hand. Starting first as a commercial attaché in Peking, he served in China from 1914 to 1940, when the Japanese forced him out. During the Japanese invasion of China, he worked hard at refugee relief. He ran a soy dairy inside Dr. Fu's Children's Hospital in Shanghai as part of his work for the China Nutritional Aid Council. His council was founded to promote interest in using soy milk as a substitute for cow's milk. Only China's rich could afford dairy products, but soymilk could be produced cheaply. It could save those in dire need of nutrition, who were most Chinese at the time. His soy milk was given to over 30,000 refugee children a day. He called the soybean the "cow of China."

Because of his public speaking on behalf of this way to feed millions, those who heard him remembered what he said after the war. They created the soy milk industry as it is known today, an industry of particular importance to those who are lactose intolerant. Thanks to Arnold, the United Nations has been able to feed thousands of refugees since World War II. Much of the world's population owe their lives to Arnold and the China medical doctors who pioneered soy milk. Now it can be found in just about any grocery store.

Arnold established the first Rotary International Club in China in Peking in 1924, and wrote books on China. In the International Exhibit Hall at the Century of Progress 1933 World's Fair in Chicago, the Chinese exhibit was "The Temple of the Green Jade Pagoda," sponsored by none other than Julean Arnold. He also served as financial advisor to one of China's top marshals. His positive outlook that China's economy was going to develop on its own made him a popular figure. He believed the Clippers could help make China the strong nation it could become. Christmas, the time of birth, echoed that belief on his Christmas cards.

Lei Day in Hawaii had a Clipper connection through its promoter and creator, Don Blanding, the self-styled "world's most beloved vagabond" and poet laureate of Hawaii. A man of many talents, Blanding, married to Crayola Crayon heiress Dorothy Putnam, worked as a lecturer, journalist, designer of Vernonware dishes along with Rockwell Kent, and designer of Aloha shirts. While working as a copy editor in Hawaii, he noticed that tourists arriving at the pier beneath the Aloha Tower in Honolulu were greeted with leis, but that the locals were not wearing them. He proposed a day when everyone would wear flowers. With the suggestions of others, he promoted Lei Day and the idea that "May Day is Lei Day." In 1929 Lei Day became an official holiday in Hawaii. Since then, festivities surrounding Lei Day have been extended into the days before and after.

Since the Clippers were considered ships in port, lei-giving was also extended to airline passengers. Blanding wrote about both leis and the

Clippers in his books of poetry. Starting in 1937, printings of his books began with a frontispiece photo entitled "Winged Return to Paradise. The author arriving in Hawaii by Clipper from California." Smothered with leis, Blanding beamed as he strode down the dock from the Clipper moored beneath the palms. After a nine years' absence from Hawaii, he had just been invited back as the island's honored guest for the anniversary of Lei Day, which he had created. He was rightfully proud in the photo. He had just finished his collection of poems, *The Rest of the Road,* in which he included "Winged Journey, from California to Hawaii" dedicated "To the men of the *Hawaii Clipper.*" In the photo he had just accomplished riding on the ship he treasured with the "gallant men with metal wings to race/ Above the clouds along a speedway drawn/ Where eagle men with eagle hearts had gone" (64).

Blanding was not alone in his poetic Hawaiian praise of the Clipper. When Captain Musick flew the China Clipper on its first flight to Honolulu in 1935, the popular mind seized on the pun, "Musick in the air." Honolulu newspapers reported receiving literally hundreds of poems observing the coincidence between Captain Musick's name and the idea of music.

The romantic view Blanding created of island life, Clipper travel, and vagabonding inspired others to associate Clippers with a relaxing lifestyle. Shuttling between Florida and California to Hawaii, Blanding in effect became one of the best freelance publicists for Hawaii and Pan American Airways. His easily accessible poetry made him one of the first popular radio poets. Other lovers of the island life and the Clippers have paid him tribute. Songster Jimmy Buffett's *Floridays* album, which came out in the 1980s, led off with a poem by Blanding and a song cowritten by Carrie Fisher of *Star Wars'* Princess Leia fame. The title itself was taken from a Blanding poetry collection by the same name written in 1941. Buffett would also dedicate a song to Blanding and use a Blanding poem for the album liner of *Volcano.*

Blanding produced the illustration "Today Is Here ... From A Clipper" for his collection of poems called *Today Is Here* (1946). Blanding's style seemed a cross between the repeatable geometric lines of Art Deco and the tendril ornamentation and sensuousness of Art Nouveau. Usually he worked in pen and ink, portraying human figures in silhouette, while carefully detailing the natural setting around them. The silhouette technique was quite popular in the 1930s and appeared on commercial glass calendar art and thermometers displayed or given away by various businesses. The silhouette was applied to a piece of glass placed over one of the readily available colorful calendar images of the day, usually from Brown

& Bigelow. One favorite showed a color print of the Clipper. Over it in black silhouette stood a frontiersman scanning the horizon, as a covered wagon train headed west behind him. At the bottom in a red, white, and blue banner ran the label, "Land of the Free," clearly identifying the Clipper with America's westward movement. These calendars and thermometers were distributed by all kinds of businesses, from the Galt Brothers Ford Garage in Stanford, Montana, to Poss Sports Shop in Herndon, Pennsylvania.

Blanding coordinated book publishing with his artist friend, Ted Mundorff, famous for his airbush prints of Hawaiian flowers. Together they published *In an Old Hawaiian Garden: An Album of Hawaiian Flowers* featuring Blanding's words with Mundorff's floral prints. Mundorff also shared Clipper connections by producing cartoon-like paper placemats that advertised tourist sites on Oahu. Each mat showed a road map of the island. Different mats advertised different businesses such as a taxi cab service or Kau Kau Korner, "Crossroads of the Pacific." On each placemat, Mundorff depicted a Clipper about to land. Passengers waved from its windows, and pilots smiled from their cartoon open-air cockpit. Oahu had already possessed them with the Aloha spirit.

Another Hawaiian pageant involving the Clipper occurred on Kamehameha Day, June 11, 1936. The Hawaii Jubilee Commission set aside several days to celebrate the bicentennial of King Kamehameha I and the centennial of King Kalakaua, Hawaii's last ruling monarch. While all the islands celebrated the event, most islands sent their best troupes of singers, dancers, rowers, riders, and beauties to Honolulu. Given the specialness of the date, the parade scheduled for June 11 was to eclipse all previous parades held on Kamehameha Day. Singer Eddie Cantor and his wife were greeted by princess-at-large Liliuokalani Kawananakoa on her horse, while Princess Kapiolani reigned over the water pageant on the Ali Wai canal. Led by military bands, over an hour and a half of parade treated the multitudes. The sounds of modern instruments from fourteen marching bands mixed with the sounds of gourds and conch shells from the various floats. One fifty-foot float recreated an entire Hawaiian village. Others depicted the life of Kamehameha.

Oahu decided to go modern. Its float consisted of a brilliant yellow China Clipper flying boat. As the floral Clipper passed down the streets of Honolulu, the actual China Clipper timed its appearance perfectly. Just arriving from California, the Clipper thrilled the crowd as it circled low over the city and parade before landing in the harbor. Correspondents could not help remarking how the Clipper symbolized progress and how this modern wonder was paying tribute to the past. Hawaii was particularly proud of the Clippers, as the October 1935 issue of *Paradise of the Pacific* reported, all Americans could be proud of the Clippers, "for Pan American Airways is in a strict sense your company. It is America's sole and unique representative in the international field.... Pan American Airways carries the flag of the United States and represents the united front of American progress among the great world transport systems. It is not only supreme in its field, but it is unique" (7).

Having a Clipper named after the Islands also gave Hawaiians pride. While most Clippers were christened by the wives of U.S. presidents, Pan American brought the Hawaii Clipper to Pearl City, Oahu, to be christened by Patricia Kennedy, the daughter of Mr. and Mrs. Stanley C. Kennedy. Kennedy ran Inter-Island Airways, which flew among the Hawaiian Islands. On May 3, 1936, the colorful ceremony was conducted according to native ceremonial ritual, with Islanders in full regalia.

Equally proud was Miami. Many rituals formed around Miami, the Clipper gateway to Latin America and other points south and east. Air races and maneuvers during the 1930s became huge spectacles, with the rallying cry of "Meet me in Miami." During the winter months of either December or January, Miami became the focus for aviators and aviation fans because of its All-America Air Maneuvers and Races from 1929 to 1941. This air exposition grew up with the Clippers. The 1929 Miami All-American Aviation Exposition was to be held on January 7 and 8 to be climaxed on January 9 with the formal opening of the Pan American Airways' base in Miami, which had moved there from Key West.

These Florida shows brought in European royalty such as the Duke of Windsor and such fliers as Roscoe Turner, Jimmy Doolittle, and Amelia Earhart. Each year the Miami Chamber of Commerce designed a special logo or cachet to advertise the event. These logos often pictured Pan American Airways flying boats, in keeping with Miami's being home for PAA's Latin American operations. It made no difference whether or not the Clippers actually participated in the air show; they were still the symbol of aviation excellence. Few spectators would want to attend the show without visiting the Clipper base to watch the flying boats fly off to all corners of the world. The Chamber's logos worked their way through the development of the Clippers. In 1934, on the final day of the show, Miami produced an image of the S-40 Caribbean Clipper. The image was applied to outgoing mail, as the city bade farewell to the aviators who were leaving to go on a Florida air tour. The years 1935 and 1936 saw the chamber's logo of a Commodore flying boat, and at the last race before World War II interrupted the event the logo showed the Boeing Clipper over a globe of the Earth.

The Miami Chamber of Commerce also used a nearly exact copy of a Pan American Airways publicity brochure to create a logo commemorating Pan-American Day in 1937. The logo pictured the China Clipper above a globe showing North and South America. It was as if the Clipper had become emblematic of the political organization known as the Pan American Union itself, which decreed that Pan American Day would be celebrated among member nations on April 14 each year. This cachet was used particularly on souvenir mailings and thank-yous sent out by the Pan American League, headquartered in Miami. The league described itself as a patriotic, noncommercial organization, with such honorary members as Theodore Roosevelt and the head of the Pan American Union. The league supported the Pan American Union and efforts to unify the Americas.

Begun in 1931, Pan American Day was intended to display political and economic unity among the nations of North and South America. From the United States' point of view, this solidarity was becoming more and more important in the 1930s. As war threatened, Nazi activity in South America increased. Attempting to hold the Americas together, President Franklin D. Roosevelt used Pan American Day in 1940 to say "The hand that touches one of us, touches us all." In the name of profit and unity, Pan American Airways carefully named its first Clippers so that they sold the concept of Pan-Americanism rather than an imperial Yankee attitude toward "banana republics." Thus early Clippers carried the names Southern Clipper, Caribbean Clipper, American Clipper, Brazilian Clipper, West Indies Clipper, Antilles Clipper, Jamaica Clipper, Dominican Clipper, and Pan American Clipper. Other PAA aircraft included the Buenos Aires, Rio de Janeiro, Cuba, Trinidad, New York/Santos, Uruguay/Sao Paulo, and the Christopher Columbus, Santa Maria, and Cuidad de Mexico.

Several nations declared Pan American Day a national holiday. The Pan American Union decreed that flags of member nations be flown on government buildings on that day, and that appropriate activities be planned. Clubs and schools organized projects, guest exchange speakers, skits, movies, and food to familiarize people with different cultures. Schools were so important to the advancement of Pan-Americanism that Gabriela Mistral, called the "spiritual queen of Latin America" and first writer from Latin American to win the Nobel Prize in Literature, wrote a student pledge of allegiance for Pan American Day in 1931. As a school teacher and poet, Mistral took a positive approach to bi-hemispheric solidarity for the sake of youth. This meant she had to try to write equality, cooperation, and understanding into her pledge, while trying to deal with the disgust Latin America felt for U.S. intervention in Nicaragua. Her friendship with some North Americans helped. Charles and Anne Lindbergh were two of those friends. The Lone Eagle was an advisor to the airline, and was serving as pilot to open some of the Clipper routes to South America. Pan American Airways supplied many of the pictures, films, and charts for classroom and club activities surrounding Pan American Day. The airline's cultural and geographic materials carried PAA's own message, or at least the company name, reminding people of the Clipper's role in binding the hemispheres through understanding and trade.

Dedications represented another ritual in which Clippers played a prominent role. The Clippers themselves underwent their own dedication ceremonies tied to political and military values. In true maritime tradition, a woman would break a bottle on the Clipper's bow to send it on its way. These rituals carried all the usual fanfare of speeches by dignitaries, coverage by the press, bunting, flags, interviews, and the grand send-off. Because of Prohibition, First Lady Lou Hoover had to christen the first S-40 Clipper with a bottle filled with Caribbean water. The ceremony took place at the Anacostia Naval Station in Washington on Columbus Day in 1931, with navy and marine bands playing "The Stars and Stripes." Clearly, even this early Clipper represented more than just an airline for the people involved. In 1939 First Lady Eleanor Roosevelt maintained the non-alcoholic tradition by smashing a bottle of water from the seven seas against the hull of the new Yankee Clipper. This giant Clipper was meant to fly the seven seas, or around the world, not just to the Caribbean.

The Clipper image appeared at other dedications. To name a few, the Clipper adorned souvenir envelopes when the San Francisco–Oakland Bay Bridge opened for traffic in November of 1936. It appeared again at Mercer Island, Washington, when the Lake Washington Pontoon Bridge removed its tolls. At a time when airports were just being built across the country, Clippers showed up on airport dedication promotional materials, even at airports that would see no Clippers. Such was the case with the unusual circumstances surrounding National Air Mail Week, May 15–21, 1938.

Many airports were dedicated during this time as part of a national campaign. The U.S. Post Office Department declared National Air Mail Week to help promote the development of U.S. airlines, which in the public eye were not very trustworthy. The week would commemorate the twentieth anniversary of airmail in the United States. The department also wanted to encourage citizens to use airmail. To promote this, the post office issued that week a special six-cent multicolored airmail stamp based on a design by President Roosevelt. Each citizen was to either receive or mail an airmail letter that week. Each post office across the nation was free for the first time to create its own pictorial cachet to be placed on all the envelopes sent from its office. A cachet is simply a design usually printed on the left half of an envelope related to an event or stamp being recognized. These cachets were to represent some facet of the town's history.

The response was incredible, as local service and business groups picked up on the idea as a promotion for their community or for clients. Some 10,000 different cachets were produced, many to be used in mass mailings. Communities that had no airports wanted in on the action, so suddenly airports were springing up everywhere. Most wanted to time dedications to fall within National Air Mail Week (NAMW). This led to some curiosities. The event teetered on becoming another "Farley Folly" of Postmaster General James A. Farley. Private planes on one-day special flights were permitted to carry mail that week. As a result, some farmers' fields were scraped off and called "airports" just for the day. At other times, police closed off county roads, turning them into makeshift landing strips. Fortunately, in this nutty week only one plane crashed and only a few were weather-delayed. For a week nearly everyone enjoyed having an airport, even an international one if you wanted it.

Since the Clipper rested at the top of aviation prestige at the time, many airport dedications and many post offices associated themselves with the Clipper. Thus the Clipper could appear on materials representing places where no Clipper dared go, such as a field of landlocked tumbleweed. It would have been hard to imagine a Clipper landing at the old station on the Pony Express trail known as Seneca, Kansas, but the first flight mail from Seneca carried the image of the Clipper. So did the cornfields of Galva, Illinois. Deepwater, New Jersey, pictured a Clipper route, with Clipper extending from Deepwater to Camden. Deepwater advertised itself on the cachet as a chemical center, producing "Better Things for Better Living Through Chemistry." Some chemistry to land the Clipper in Camden! Kitty Hawk, North Carolina, where U.S. aviation chiefly began, celebrated NAMW with a cachet showing the start of aviation, the Wright Brothers Flier, and how it had evolved, to the Clipper.

Other cachets seemed more rational, as some post offices were close to Clipper bases. Palisades, New Jersey, for instance, featured a Sikorsky S-42 Clipper on its cachet, as did Staten Island, New York City, and Washington, D.C. Honolulu appropriately depicted the China Clipper on its NAMW mail; the *Honolulu Advertiser* added its own, even bigger image of the Clipper flying over the islands. The Navy had been working with Pan American Airways for some time in creating its Pacific bases, and Navy mail clerks had themselves devised their own Clipper cachets earlier, so sailors were quick to use NAMW to send mail and use the Clipper image. A special "Plane Service Speeds Navy Mail" cachet was used for the various ships berthed at the Bremerton, Washington, Naval Yard and its post office. Mail from such ships as the U.S.S. *Colorado* pictured a Sikorsky Clipper. A special flight was arranged from Bremerton to Seattle to carry the specially marked mail.

The U.S. Post Office's successful promotion led other commercial interests to copy the cachet idea. Upon the dedication of the seaplane base at Cleveland on September 1, 1940, the Dewey Eldred Flying Service of Lost Nation Airport, Willoughby, Ohio, produced a specially flown cachet of the China Clipper. Cleveland obviously had a larger seaplane base than Pan Am knew about, and it would have been big news to know that Dewey owned one of the three Martin Clippers. Empire Trust Company of New York also showed a Boeing Clipper on the cachet it produced to honor the opening of "the world's first airport bank" at La Guardia in September 1941.

The use of Clipper cachets also extended to other countries besides the United States. Centenary celebrations offered another kind of ritual. A hundred years of anything usually requires human beings to mark the passage of time in some way. The colony of Hong Kong did so in 1941, as residents celebrated one hundred years of British occupation. Within months, that occupation ended, as the Japanese army began its own occupation of Hong Kong. Before those troops arrived, the colony issued a set of centenary postage stamps honoring King George VI. The highest value, a one dollar stamp, showed his portrait alongside a Hong Kong harbor scene of the Falcon, a clipper sailing ship, and a Short S23 Empire "C" Class flying boat, the British rendition of the flying Clippers. The cachet, printed on special first-day-of-issue envelopes, showed the Pan American Airways' Hong Kong Clipper.

Short-wave radio listeners and operators have also employed Clipper cachet designs and other Clipper images in their QSL cards. These cards were sent to confirm to a radio signal sender that his or her signal had been received at a particular time and place, along with other helpful information. Since Clipper crews were trained in various types of signaling and electrical communication, many maintained their radio interests during and after their Clipper careers. In doing so, some sent out QSL cards carrying the Clipper image. Today, Clippers still grace some QSL cards. Non-Pan American radio hobbyists appropriated the image as well. During the 1930s short-wave listener E. L. Heese of Christchurch, New Zealand, created an attractive QSL card of the Clipper, combining an image of the China Clipper taken from a postcard design used for the first flying boat flights to New Zealand with the images of two Kiwi birds and some New Zealand flowers.

Wartime heightened the urgency for rites of passage and rites of unity. People had to grow up quickly, and many had to conduct mating rituals quickly. Clippers were represented in these rituals in the form of jewelry, particularly pins that men presented women to show the increased seriousness of their relationships. These tokens, termed sweetheart pins, publicly displayed the couple's commitment, while at the same time announcing their patriotism and contribution to the war effort to defend American values. Sweetheart pins showing the China Clipper were popular because the Clippers flew for both army and navy, so anyone who had a sweetheart connected to wartime aviation could use the Clipper pin for advertising and sentimental purposes.

Clipper sweetheart pins fit a long multistep tradition of giving jewelry as gifts leading up to the wedding ring. They served as non–Greek counterparts to the lavaliering tradition that sprang up with the creation of college fraternities and sororities in the United States and Canada. When a fraternity member sought to express his serious feelings to a young woman, he presented her a necklace with a pendant that usually displayed the Greek letters of his fraternity. If she accepted, the next step in the relationship would be the pinning ceremony, during which the man would give the woman his fraternity pin. After that would come the engagement ring and finally the wedding ring—all a jeweler's delight. Like a lavaliere, the Clipper sweetheart pin could be read as an engagement to be engaged.

Clipper pins sold during peacetime expositions as souvenirs were converted into wartime icons, so that not only sweethearts could wear the pins but also family members and the general public. Many versions of the Clipper pins were manufactured in various metals and plastic. Some were painted; others were rhinestone encrusted. Pins themselves were often accessorized. Dangling from small chains or added to the pins, charms spelled out "U.S." rather than Greek fraternal letters. Other charms represented the U.S. flag. Given the romantic associations, not sur-

This sweetheart, or souvenir, pin was very appropriate for lovers, with an image of Niagara Falls attached to the nose of the Clipper.

prisingly one full-color charm depicted Niagara Falls. Others gave year or graduation dates. As metals became scarcer during the war, the Clipper no longer served as pin in and of itself, but rather as a plastic charm suspended with a red/white/blue braid from what resembled a military service bar. This combination promoted war bonds, as evidenced by the message on the service bar, "You Buy 'Em—We'll Fly 'Em." The Clipper stood not only for love, but for all the airplanes that needed to be produced—also in a hurry.

Another Clipper sweetheart pin carried the words "Keep 'Em Flying," molded below and above the flying boat. Keep 'Em Flying was one of the key rallying cries of World War II. It appeared on recruitment posters, war bond signs, buttons, postcards, letterhead, matchbook covers, Cracker Jack toy spinners, and bloomers for dolls. Bandleader Glenn Miller even led his band in musical piece called "Keep 'Em Flying." Bud Abbott and Lou Costello starred in the 1941 film comedy by the same name. The slogan was everywhere.

Just as Clipper pins showed a mix of romance and patriotic propaganda, "Keep 'Em Flying" allowed for an ambivalency and sexual innuendo that artists, illustrators, and cheeky boys and girls could not resist. Most of the major pinup artists came out with some version of leggy lasses with skirts or anatomical parts flying as encouragement for those in the service to keep their airplanes and their respective anatomical parts flying—an early version of the infamous "Fly Me" ads of the jet age. For example, during recent attempts to restore the Dumas Brothel in Butte, Montana, to its former glory, one of the "cribs," or rooms, had not been opened since the early 1940s. Hanging next to a 1943 Coca-Cola calendar was a "Keep 'Em Flying" print of a partially disrobed, deeply décolletaged young lady reclining on her back on black velvet. She stares directly at the viewer, while holding above her breasts a toy airplane whose smoke trail spells out the words "Keep 'Em Flying." Pins and pinups easily translated.

This sweetheart pin combined the Clipper with incentive to buy war bonds.

In addition to courting rituals and the promotion of war bonds, Clippers appeared on other fund-raising buttons. Down Under, the Red Cross raised money on Red Cross Day during the war by selling red/white/blue buttons featuring the images of the China Clipper and the Red Cross symbol. These sold for a donation of one shilling. Again the Clippers were used to unify people by helping them sacrifice individual freedom and resources for the greater good. The Clipper buttons were at once part of a rite of unity and an expression of the benevolent community.

13

The Clipper as Military Icon

Because of the intimate association of Pan American Airways with the military in the creation of clipper bases before the war, and the quasi-military nature of the Clippers during World War II, the military naturally appropriated the Clipper as an icon. This occurred most frequently near Clipper bases, Hawaii especially. The Clipper popped up everywhere. For instance, on the eastern side of Oahu, the marines' NCO club still overlooks the beautiful Kaneohe Clipper Golf Course. Army base menus sported images of Clippers. A flow of Clipper souvenirs such as tablecloths, pillow coverings, laundry bags, and "Mother Mine" poems bearing Clipper images made their way back to the States to mothers, sisters, wives, and girlfriends. Clippers expanded the Hawaiian tourist industry, affected by its growing number of military personnel engaged in the souvenir-giving ritual.

Hawaii became a major area of training, R & R, and headquarters. The sheer volume of military personnel stationed in Hawaii and passing through the islands ensured that, even during war, Hawaii would be seen as a tourist paradise—and a way for locals to make money from sailors, soldiers, and airmen. Based on the designs of prewar tourist brochures, military personnel were given "Clipper-Packs" containing brochures that described what could be seen and done in the islands. The folder containing the brochures featured a comely hibiscus- and lei-laden hula dancer as a greeter and deicer. From the brochures, the service men and women learned they could buy curios for the special someone's back home and could drink all the pineapple juice they wanted if they took a tour of the Dole plant (with competent female guides). The trick was to keep warriors busy when they were idle. Most people serving in the military certainly could not afford to fly in on a Clipper, but they were treated as if they had. Each year, a new and more risqué version of the Clipper-Pack came out. By 1945 the hula covergirl wore practically nothing at all. A lei

The elaborated front and back menu cover for the 1937 Christmas dinner for Company A, 21st Infantry, Schofield Barracks, Territory of Hawaii.

just covered her nipples, and there was barely enough grass to cover her nether parts. The pack also came with a novelty calendar in the shape of a hula girl. To read the calendar, the viewer had to lift her grass skirt. Underneath, small calendar pages revealed the months and days.

Military publications also appropriated the title of Clipper during and after the war. *The Canacao Clipper* was published by the U.S. Naval Station at Sangley Point near the Cavite Clipper Base in the Philippines. This four-page newspaper covered local events, personages, and other goings-on of interest to base personnel. Before the fall of the Philippines in World War II, Clippers often carried mail from the naval hospital at Canacao back to the States. Across the Pacific in San Francisco, near Pan American Airways' Pacific home port, the Fourth Air Force's headquarters and headquarters' squadron was publishing the *4th Air Force Clipper* in the 1940s, averaging around twenty-six pages an issue in stapled booklet rather than newspaper format. Though it had its sanitized Chaplain's Page, the *Clipper* shared many anecdotes about possible impending marriages, sprinkled with sexual suggestions. Sports scores from the base bowling league made good filler. With people transferring in and out, the paper served its tourism function, telling headquarters personnel where the night life was, where to eat cheaply, what new stores were opening.

Souvenir Hawaiian table cloth showing incoming Clipper and the islands.

Defense plants supplying the military also adopted Clippers for their publications. *The Columbia Clipper* appeared every other week at the government-funded Columbia Aircraft Industries in Portland, Oregon. Plant workers made tail and wing flap assemblies for the navy's PBY flying boats, so the newspaper suitably was named after a flying boat. For a logo, each issue used a drawing of a futuristic Clipper, a giant six-engine airplane. Its engines were mounted backwards on the trailing edge of the wings, so that it heralded the Cold War's B-36 Strategic Air Force bomber.

Out in the Mojave Desert near the border between California and Arizona, General George S. Patton created the largest army base in the world to train his troops for the invasion of North Africa. This huge camp covered some 18,000 square miles and stretched from Pomona, California, nearly to the outskirts of Phoenix and Yuma, Arizona. Different units were trained separately and given their own separate tent bivouacs in the sometimes 130-degree heat and frequent sandstorms. One such camp was Camp Clipper. Patton had an earlier connection with the Clippers: before the war when he was stationed in Hawaii, he used Clipper mail to carry his

Embroidered and fringed with lace, silky "Aloha Hawaii" pillowcases showing the Clipper and hula dancer may have worked on the mainland with Mom but garnered mixed results with concerned wives or jealous girlfriends.

personal letters to the mainland to help those of his troops who found themselves in marital, legal or financial trouble—or all at the same time.

Camp Clipper, not far from Needles, California, carried an ironic name, since Clippers alluded to water, not desert. However, the name proved prophetic when, shortly after being erected, the camp was swept away by a flash flood and had to be reconstituted farther south. Over a million soldiers of various armored and infantry units passed through Patton's desert training center. Despite the hardships of desert training, including a two-day, 42-mile forced march across loose sand, Camp Clipper sought relief in the popular culture of the day. Each Sunday afternoon such Hollywood personalities as Betty Hutton, Jack Benny, and Pat O'Brien, who received star billing in *China Clipper*, were flown in to perform. Those troops lucky or unlucky enough to earn leave could empty their pockets in Vegas at the tables. As an independently wealthy man who did not need Vegas luck, General Patton funded his own radio station at the desert training center. While the station did broadcast popular music and news to the trainees, Patton kept a microphone at both his desk and bed so that he could interrupt at any time to deliver his own speeches. Although

A traveling laundry bag used a popular culture version of Chinese script with a China Clipper image, based on an air mail logo found on mail from China in the 1930s and 1940s.

Camp Clipper existed only two years, it hardened troops for campaigns in North Africa, New Guinea, and the Philippines.

No one connected to the military commemorated the Clippers more than the navy postal clerks or collecting societies connected to the navy. In Hawaii, ship clerks kept busy designing envelope cachets and cancellations that tracked the fast advancement of Clipper service. On April 22,

Stationery and poster greetings made for souvenirs to be sent by tourists, sailors, and soldiers during their sojourn in Hawaii. Poems were usually directed at mothers, wives, or girlfriends.

1936, the submarine *Argonaut*, stationed at Pearl Harbor, used a "1st Anniversary Hawaii-Calif." cancel on covers cacheted with a red/white/blue image of the Sikorsky Clipper that made the initial experimental flight between Hawaii and the Mainland a year earlier. The Argonaut came back with another Clipper cancellation on May 3, 1936, with "Aloha Nui Hawaii Clipper" for the first flight of the Hawaii Clipper to Honolulu. The Uni-

Informational Clipper-Packs such as this one were distributed to military personnel in Hawaii to help them spend their money and to keep them from causing too much trouble by directing them to wholesome island pursuits.

versal Ship Cancellation Society prepared covers for the first passenger flight from Honolulu to Manila in October 1936, showing a Hawaiian woman waving at the Clipper flying overhead. The first flight of the Hawaiian Clipper, which joined the China Clipper for transpacific service in 1936, was celebrated on May 2 envelopes from ships big and small by cachets prepared by the American Naval Cancellation Society. The U.S.S. *Arizona* was out on Fleet Problem XVII at the time of the flight, but serviced a cover of the flight. The provision store ship U.S.S. *Arctic* did likewise. While in the Bremerton, Washington, shipyard, the battleship *Oklahoma*'s clerk cancelled covers prepared by the National Aiglon Society commemorating the first Clipper flight from the U.S. to China on April 15, 1937. The U.S.S. *Paul Jones* in the Philippines serviced covers for the first flight of the Boeing Honolulu clipper in March 1939. The China Clipper also appeared on a generic "Ships of the World Series" cachet. Envelopes or covers bearing this cachet were posted from many ships, such as the U.S.S. *Black Hawk* on Asiatic Station, Manila. The *Black Hawk* also created a special postmark for the 1935 first Clipper flight to the Philippines that read "U.S.S. *Black Hawk*, NY Cavite PI" (Navy Yard Cavite Philippine Islands), "Via First PAA" (Pan American Airways). For that first flight, some *Black Hawk* sailors created their own private Clipper cachets to apply to mail they sent back home. The farther the sailors were from home, the more time the Clipper would trim from mail delivery. Weeks of waiting for mail collapsed into days—if a swab were willing to pay the extra postage for airmail.

Many ships also used their own special hand stamps on mail to indicate that either official mail or sailor/marine mail was to be flown by Clipper. When the envelope said "Via Clipper" or "Clipper Mail," there could be no doubt that the mail was to be carried by air across the ocean, not by boat or just flown by airmail within the continental U.S. And Clipper stamps were expensive, ranging from twenty to fifty cents apiece, a lot of money then. Military personnel paid the price because it was important to keep romances alive at long distance, to contact family, and to take care of financial matters.

The showiest Clipper decorative envelopes in the mail were produced by retired navy chief gunner's Mate Walter G. Crosby, who opened a print shop in San Pedro, California. As a major navy base, San Pedro perfectly positioned Crosby to meet ships' postal clerks coming into port. He could not only have his envelopes canceled, but also could keep clerks supplied with envelopes to sell on the ships. Crosby obtained a special contract with the navy permitting his materials to be sold aboard ships and at the nearby marine base. This meant his Clipper images could spread throughout the Pacific navy, which they did.

Clippers appeared in many guises on his envelopes or in his cachets. Crosby produced a series of small Clipper photos, which he pasted on many of his cachets. Some celebrated Clipper events, such as first flights to a particular place; some celebrated Clipper ports such as Midway and Wake Islands; some celebrated non–Clipper events. Besides these actual photos, Crosby was best known for his creation of thermographed cachets.

Lightweight Clipper airmail paper reduced the weight and cost of mailing airmail letters between loved ones and those in service. Various paper companies used Clippers as images to sell the new concept of lightweight airmail letters, something that had not really existed until expensive transoceanic Clipper rates came to be.

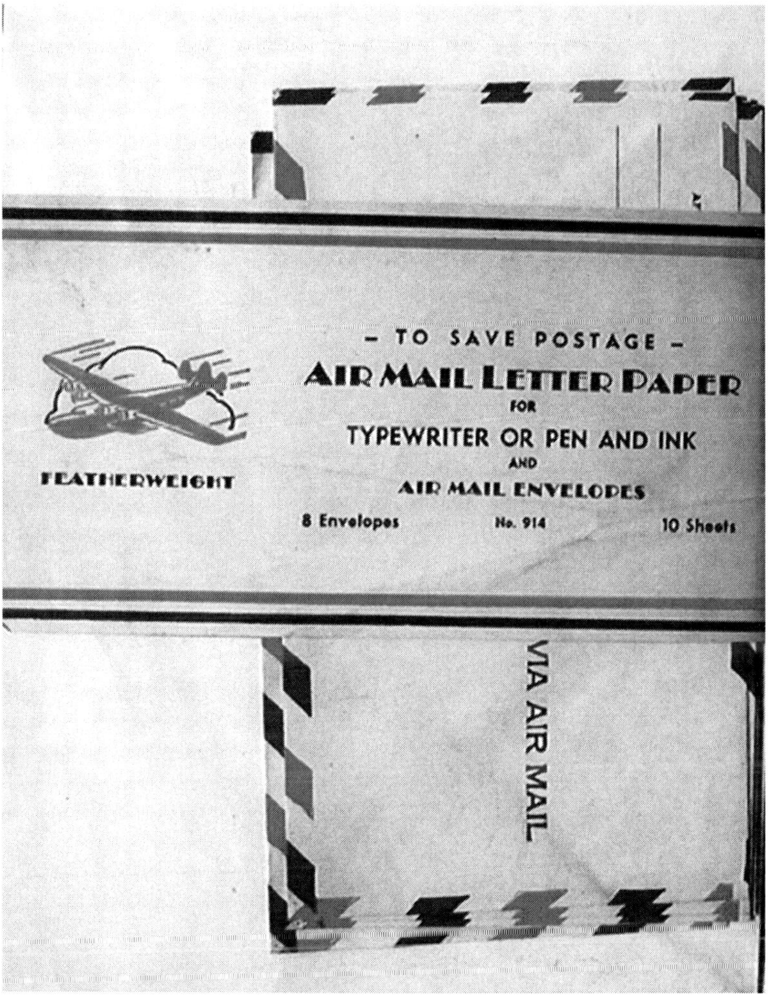

A 1930s airmail packet showed the S-42 Clipper.

In this process, an image was first printed on an envelope. Before the ink dried, the image was covered with a resinous or waxy powder. It adhered to the wet ink, but fell off the unprinted surfaces. Then the envelope was heated. As ink and powder combined under heat, the result was a colorful raised image—the opposite of embossing. Crosby created elaborate thermographed cachets for Pacific, Atlantic, Latin America, and Alaska Clipper services. Recently, his process was revived at craft and scrapbooking fairs, where people could buy different colored bonding powders and learn to use a common household iron to fuse the image. Usually Crosby

The Polynesian Pack of airmail stationery showed a Clipper and an almost-au-naturel local inhabitant.

combined both the thermograph and photo "paste-on" on his envelopes to create highly collectible items then and now.

The United States Army Air Force used the Clipper as icon, too. One of the outstanding examples of World War II nose art belonged to the famous B-17 flying fortress, the *Miami Clipper.* Though not picturing the flying boat Clipper, this nose art illustrated a leggy blonde in halter and shorts reclining on a beach near palm trees. Considered the best nose art painter of World War II, Corporal Tony Starcer created the *Miami Clipper* logo, along with that of about 130 other airplanes of the 91st Bomb Group of the 8th Air Force flying out of Bassingbourne, England. Starcer's artwork included that of the sister ship to the *Miami Clipper*, the *Memphis Belle*, star of the movie by the same name.

Most of Starcer's nose art fell into combinations of three categories: patriotic, cartoon, and girlie. He often translated images brought to him by airmen onto the bombers' noses. A few airmen used pictures of their wives or girls back home. More commonly, magazine photos served as source. For instance, *General "Ike,"* to General Eisenhower's chagrin, took the general's image from the cover of *Time* magazine. Cartoon images such as *Outhouse Mouse* could be taken from comics or cartoon features. But the overriding source of nose art inspiration came from pinups readily accessible to most soldiers in every theatre of war. *Miami Clipper* fit that mold, along with many other Starcer war goddesses such as *Tennessee Tess, Sweet Dish, Dame Satan, Lady Luck, Pistol Packin' Mama, Jezebel* and *Sweet 16.* (Pan American Airways crews endearingly referred to the China Clipper as *Sweet 16* after the last digits of its registration number NC14716.) Many of the names carried the sexually suggestive puns of the men's magazines of the 1940s: *Broad Minded*, *Qualified Quail, and Mount 'N Ride* to name but a few.

Such images as that of the *Miami Clipper* were readily available to the troops, thanks largely to *Esquire* magazine. This magazine showed its air-mindedness on the cover of its first issue, which featured paddlers in a canoe visiting a seaplane on a mountain lake; and after the China Clipper opened up the route across the Pacific, the magazine ran a cover of its mascot dancing with a hula girl. This man's magazine kept a steady flow of pinups moving to troops at home and overseas. Given the great demand for this publication and particularly the Vargas pinup centerfolds, *Esquire* provided nine million copies of the magazine to the troops between 1942 and 1946. Special centerfolds were included, designed with military themes just for the troops. Esky, the magazine's mascot, also provided troops with Esky Service Men's Kits. Each kit contained a deck of Vargas girl playing cards, whose naked or semi-naked pictured specimens helped while away the hours of boredom and homesickness between missions. Kits included *Esquire* datebooks and sets of Esky continental size postcards featuring more beauties.

Esky, the bringer of images for bomber nose art, looked liked an early claymation character. During the war he often donned military gear, but more often he appeared as an older debonair gentleman with a flowing golden moustache and bulging eyes with which to ogle young ladies. *Esquire* kept largely hidden that Esky creator E. Simms Campbell was a black man and that he also drew many other magazine depictions of nude or nearly nude white women—a dangerous thing for a black man to do at the time in a mostly racist United States and a very racist military. How ironic to consider a Yankee WASP flier or good old Southern boy pilot cruising along six miles up in his bomber that had a Stars-and-Stripes or Stars-and-Bars logo backgrounding his dreamboat pinup made possible by a black man.

The appearance of the *Miami Clipper* and other women on bomber nose art and aviation leather jackets revealed a shift in values regarding women. As Maria Elena Buszek has pointed out in "War Goddess: The Varga Girls, WWII and Feminism," these wartime icons reversed the stereotypical role of the male as protector. These brides of Mars became the protectors of men. These gals were to bring the men home safely while being destructive harpies. The 1930s pinups had shifted from rosy-cheeked, innocent naïfs to 1940s goddesses completely aware of their sexuality. Untouchable yet beckoning, these magnified ideals stared confidently at the viewer. They captured the danger and power of war and the changing roles of women. *Miami Clipper* remained a sex object, but a powerful one. Unlike earlier cuties, pinups of the 1940s had names, identity.

This new pinup identity was streamlined, as were the flying Clippers and other transportation of the time. Vargas and other pinup artists employed the air brush to create the modern female, as car makers used airbrush technique on the assembly lines to create skin-tight, curvaceous hard bodies. What little clothing the elongated pinups wore indeed seemed spray-painted to their bodies. Clothing became skin. These steely, dangerous goddesses were made for speed. They were the paradox of war and changing roles in society. Soft promises and hard reality. Carpe diem and wistful or patriotic Te Deum. On the one hand, they were images frozen in time. They offered the promise of a peaceful beauty, an ideal the troops were fighting for, a stability they desired to go home to. On the other hand, they were speed, the changing mutability of war. Their steely bodies underscored their dangerous, ephemeral untouchability. Their challenging direct gaze demanded either immediate participation or cowardice making voyeurism impossible. Love was not a consideration. Deliberate, no-nonsense sex was. Thus they depicted the chance meeting, the one-night stand they would alluringly control. They were harpies on the noses of bombers, and simultaneously Homer's sirens.

In the surrealistic world of quick death, prolonged boredom and fatigue, these wet dreams mingled with a strange melange of Disney/Grim Reaper/Death Head insignia. Veterans of the war would carry images home with them, so that after the war these signifiers of reckless masculine bravado would again appear on the backs of military-style leather jackets worn by motorcycle gangs or inner city gangs who emphasized other forms of speed and beauty, linked to a lurking doomed bravery. The connection between transportation, particularly aviation, and nonconformist freedom clearly showed itself here. Some riders would mount "Clipper" model cycles. Automobilists and motorcyclists had donned the horsehair aviation-style jackets from their early beginnings. Both Outlaws and Hells Angels used wings for their logos, although the Outlaws changed their original winged cycle logo to a skull and crossed pistons after the war. Throughout World War II and even after the war, most motorcycle gang members wore brown aviator leather. Not until after the war did Harley Davidson introduce the classic black leather motorcycle jacket made famous by Marlon Brando and James Dean in their movie role challenges to conventional society.

Thus the *Miami Clipper* and other nose art became embroiled in the other war, the war between morale and morals. In the face of this radical new portrayal and challenge to traditional bedrock beliefs in womanhood, conservative elements of society protested such nose art and the contents of *Esquire*, while liberals argued that such icons were important for troop morale. Military chaplains bemoaned how pinups eroded morals. Postmaster General Frank Walker charged *Esquire* with visual pornography and language vulgarity. Walker tried to revoke the magazine's second-class mailing privileges, which would have cost *Esquire* $400,000 in postage. The case was appealed all the way to the Supreme Court before Walker lost. Walker did win some concessions along the way in censoring the magazine. For instance, some of the Vargas girls had to be at least minimally draped before the magazine could be released. Hence the *Miami Clipper* does wear some clothing. The normal rule of thumb for airplane crews desirous of nose art was that the further away from home the less clothing. Some crews were ordered to repaint their nose art to add clothing before aircraft could be returned to the States.

Many women tried to emulate such beauties as the *Miami Clipper*. They indundated *Esquire* with letters, asking how they could become Vargas or Varga girls. Yet Varga girls were idealized, impossible portrayals, unless women could find some way of having legs thirteen feet long and radically spread breasts. Perhaps in wanting their fifteen minutes or fifteen feet of fame they did not realize that Peruvian artist Alberto Vargas y Chavez did the bulk of his drawing and painting without models present.

The B-17 *Miami Clipper* did survive World War II, only to be scrapped afterwards. Its more recent jet age reincarnation, the *Miami Clipper II*, preserved the layout of the original nose art. This B-52G Stratofortress took part in operation Secret Squirrel, which opened Desert Storm in the Middle East in January of 1991. Instead of dropping bombs over Germany, as did the original *Miami Clipper*, this honey delivered cruise missiles on Iraqi forces. The *Miami Clipper* has also become one of the first nose art reproductions made for the recent fashion of collecting World War II nose art, as nostalgia increases with the remaining veterans of World War II reaching the end of their lives, and as aviation enthusiasts relish those glorious times when human beings rather than computers flew powerful warbirds.

Troops could also view pinup art involving the Clippers through images on calendars, prints, blotters, notepad and matchbook covers, and Mutoscope cards. One popular wartime print by Del Masters was entitled "Going My Way," featuring red, white, and blue colors. The image showed a leggy, winsome brunette standing up in her inflatable raft on the wide ocean. She stuck out her thumb to try to bum a ride on the approaching Boeing Clipper Suitcase by her side, she held an oar in one hand as the ocean breeze lifted the skirt of her clingy outfit in the appropriate pinup tease manner. She stared expectantly up at the Clipper. It could not miss spotting her in her red skirt and white blouse against the blue ocean and sky, particularly when the two straining tie bows of her blouse were just barely able to contain her braless attributes.

Del Masters' image played a variation on another popular pinup of the time. Gil Elvgren's "Short on Sails" offered a similar image of a topless blonde wearing only her black skivvies and nylons. Stranded on a raft, she had rigged a mast and attached her bra as a makeshift sail. Just as in the Del Masters Clipper image with its long oar, here the mast served as the phallic presence or stiffening agent for young men far from home. Her blue eyes look directly into the viewer's as she was embarrassed by the voyeuristic stare. Both the Del Masters and Elvgren waifs typified what was needed for troops who were naive boys becoming worldly men. As Elvgren said, the goal was to combine the face of an innocent fifteen-year-old girl on the body of a twenty-one-year-old woman so typical of cheesecake art early in the war.

Del Masters' popular pinup, "Going My Way," with its young lady on a raft trying to hitchhike on the Clipper, appeared in just about every pinup form imaginable—prints, notepads, cards, calendars.

This transitional ambiguity was also carried through in other ways. Since these were wartime images, they obliquely suggested the war, yet took the pressure off troops by offering escapist entertainment. While sex has always been combined variously with power and violence, "Going My Way" with its Clipper suggested the aftermath of an event feared by troops, that of being "downed" or "torpedoed" and left adrift. Worse still was being alone in an ocean so vast that it would be difficult for people to find survivors; that is, if the searchers even knew about the tragedy in wartime security silence. The pinup girl's life was at stake. Rather than being eaten by sharks, she needed saving by another kind of shark, male, of course. Clippers did participate in rescuing survivors from torpedoed ships between California and Hawaii but, much to their dismay, crews never reported seeing anyone topless or braless on rafts.

Fear was alleviated and turned into entertaining escapism even by the title, "Going My Way," a play on the humorous movie of the same name for which Bing Crosby won an Academy Award. *Going My Way* (1944) was special to the military because it opened in sixty-five military locations stretching around the world, inclusive of all theatres of war. Pan Am crews most likely flew some of the cans of film into bases ranging from Burma to Italy. Just as prayers were answered in the Crosby movie about an Irish priest, the "Going My Way" girl and film could "save" those fighting the war, while being saved themselves by the sacrifices of the fighters.

The "Going My Way" girl was like the projected image of American soldiers who used understated or plucky humor to handle threatening situations. She paralleled that of Sad Sack, Kilroy Was Here, Bill Mauldin's G.I. Joe. She didn't wave her arms frantically in panic to signal the Clipper; instead, she came close to doing what Claudette Colbert did in that famous scene from *It Happened One Night* (1934), when she showed the Clark Gable character how to hitch a ride by hiking up her skirt and showing some leg. The breeze raised her skirt for her, while she could stick out her thumb. She wasn't afraid to ask for help; she expected it. This gal might have looked innocent, but on closer look she proved streetwise and sexually aware of her own power.

As in the title "Going My Way," other pinup titles of the time entertained by using word puns conflating war language with sexual innuendoes. Airmen could enjoy titles like "Taking Off," "A Fast Takeoff," "Flying High," "Tail Wind," "Forced Landing," and "Crash Landing," which gave artists a chance to lift some skirts in stiff breezes or illustrate other functions of disrobement. Sailors savored "Skirts Ahoy!" "Slip Off Shore," or "Anchors A-Wow." Infantry had "Smoke Screen," while those feeling the effects of rationing could enjoy "A Run on Sugar," where Sugar just discovered a run in her new nylons.

Not only did the military appropriate the Clipper as an icon, so did the people who wanted the money troops might spend while far from home. As in World War I or the Vietnam War or any war for that matter, World War II entrepreneurs meant to part expeditionary troops from

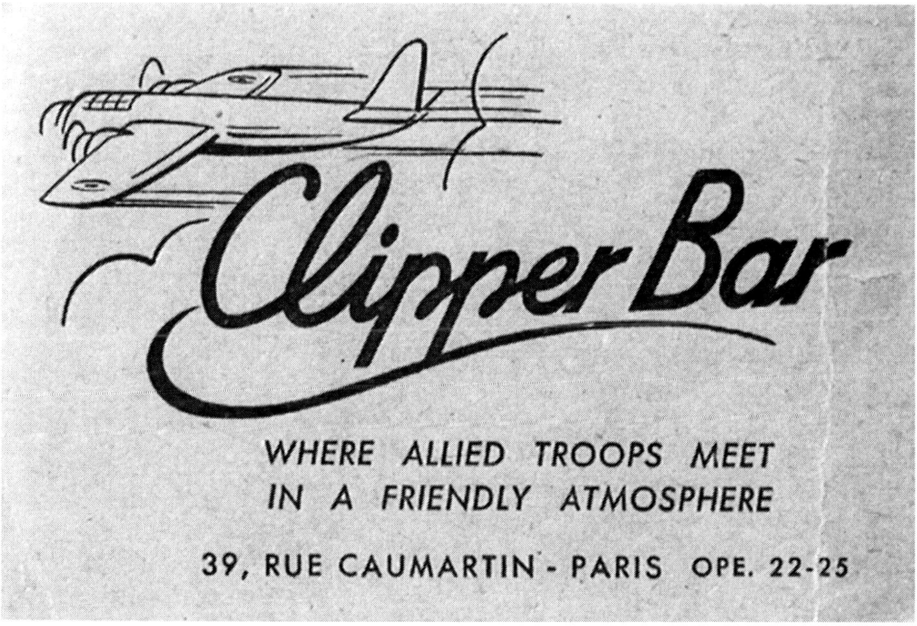

Business card of the Clipper Bar in Paris.

their pay by using icons familiar to the occupiers. After the liberation of Paris, the Clipper Bar on Rue Caumartin in the City of Light catered to the armed forces. This bar advertised itself in English and described itself as "where Allied troops meet in a friendly atmosphere." The Clippers did have a French connection. They had flown to Marseilles before German occupation. A Clipper would have been hard pressed to land on the Seine in Paris, but it was an easily recognizable symbol connected to Americans, the war, and echoes of civilian life.

Clippers made their most influential, visible mark on the military and their families through the role the flying boats played in the development of V mail, or Victory mail. This ephemeral element of popular culture lasted only a few years, but its importance in keeping people in touch with one another during trying times resonated then. In 1938 Pan American Airways, Eastman Kodak, and Imperial Airways of Great Britain formed a joint company to develop what were called Airgraphs. As both Pan American and Imperial opened flying boat routes around the world when money was derived more from mail contracts than passenger carriage, reducing the weight and bulk of mail became critical. This was especially true in planning the transoceanic flying boat route between Great Britain and the U.S. scheduled to begin in 1939.

The outbreak of war in 1939, however, curtailed plans to introduce the Airgaphs. Eastman Kodak intended for mailers to write letters on standardized special forms. The company then could microphotograph and place them on microfilm to be transported to their destinations, where they could then be enlarged and delivered. Although plans to use commercial Airgraphs over the Atlantic had ended, the military saw their value. With the British army locked in a desperate struggle against General Rommel's troops in North Africa, the British Army Postal Service and General Post Office initiated Airgraph service for forces in the Middle East in 1941. Kodak had offices in Cairo, so after a journey of three weeks, the first 70,000 Airgraphs were processed there. The first Airgraph was sent from the Queen to her commander in chief in Egypt. Three weeks may seem like a lot, but with Italian and German troops blocking the Mediterranean, mail between the Middle East and Great Britain would otherwise have to travel by boat around the horn of Africa, a trip sometimes of three to six months. Within a year Airgraph services followed in Canada, East Africa, Burma, and India.

By the end of the war, 330 million Airgraphs had been mailed. Ten million Airgraphs weighed less than a ton, in contrast to regular mail, which would have weighed over one hundred tons for the same number of letters. Furthermore, lost letters could be reproduced, since they were saved on film. When one of the Empire-class flying boats crashed while avoiding the war-torn Mediterranean, by flying the horseshoe route from India to South Africa and thence to Great Britain, mail was replaced within days.

The North African campaign also led to the creation of the first large Army processing center for V-mail, the U.S. version of the Airgraph. The center opened in Casablanca after Allied invasion of North Africa in 1943, although V-mail had been used as early as June of 1942. During the war, over a billion V-mails flowed between the U.S. and troops overseas. The space savings on Clippers and other transports was enormous. A reel of 16mm microfilm weighing only a few ounces carried some 18,000 letters. That translated into a single mail sack of microfilm substituting for thirty-seven sacks of regular letters. Over a ton of regular air mail was reduced to less than the weight of a half sack of potatoes. By the end of the war, nineteen military and nine civilian V-mail processing centers were reducing outgoing letters to thumbnail-sized microfilm images and enlarging incoming mail to a quarter of their original size.

But first, the public had to be sold on the V-mail idea. It did not catch on right away, for who wanted to send private letters that had to be left open for strangers to read? Mail clerks, censors, photographers, developers, enlargers, and envelope stuffers all could see the contents. Worse, urban legends spread during wartime. The story that some of the 16mm reels had been projected in motion picture houses did not help. It was like a bad scene from the 1985 *National Lampoon's European Vacation* where the Griswolds' privately videotaped striptease was stolen and ended up as a foreign porn film advertised on billboards everywhere.

To counter these fears, popular magazine advertisements appealed to people's patriotism, using the Clipper as icon. Eastman Kodak's early ads touting V-mail showed a Clipper officer holding three reels of V-mail reels on the top of his clipboard. Behind him a Clipper with a large U.S. flag painted on its bow sat tied up at its berth, while another Clipper flew overhead. The ads described how easy and fast V-mail service was in speeding letters to "your boy." Kodak tied its patriotism to the government as well, by saying that the U.S. government had chosen V-mail as the vehicle for communicating with "men on distant fronts." To counter the fear that letters would be read by others, Kodak emphasized that its photographic technique also protected the records of the U.S. Census, Social Security, and Selective Service by producing "error-free, tamper-proof, lasting photographic copies." In other words, it was better than regular mail in many ways. As the war went on, the messages increasingly dwelled on how important sending letters to troops was for morale. Letter writing served patriotism and secured democracy by maintaining that morale.

But use of microfilm could also be detrimental to troops. The use of some form of microfilm for spying dated all the way back to the Civil War in the United States, when British spies for the Confederacy smuggled microfilm into Canada. During the Franco-Prussian War and Siege of Paris in 1871, balloons flew the world's first airmail out of Paris, and pigeons carried the microfilm replies back into the city. Almost the same Kodak technique was used. Letters were reduced by microphotography and attached to the pigeon's feathers. When the letters arrived, a magic lantern magnified the microfilm on a screen, after which a human copier turned them back into handwritten letters. One feathered early version of the Clipper carried eighteen microfilms containing 54,000 documents. And just as the Axis powers tried to shoot down the Clipper flying boats during World War II, Prussians tried to shoot down the pigeons of Paris in 1871. What they could not shoot down, they tried to hunt down with trained hawks and falcons.

Pan American Airways became entangled in spying and microfilm when one of its stewards, Rene Mezenen, was arrested as a German spy. Prior to the outbreak of hostilities, German agents were able to infiltrate the United States and carry messages back and forth across the Atlantic by working as crew on ships of the North German Lloyd and Hamburg-America Lines. When German ships were forbidden to enter U.S. waters, spies had to rely more on shortwave radio communications, invisible ink on letters, microfilm, and the Clippers. Mezenen flew on the New York to Lisbon run, and for money he delivered secret messages across the Atlantic, reporting Allied convoy movements, and smuggling platinum into Portugal for the Germans. His spying ended when the large Ritter-Duquesne spy ring was broken up in New York in 1941. Mezenen's arrest came as one of the few black marks on Clipper history.

Still, the Clippers' role in delivery of V-mail and regular airmail was honorable, for early war Clippers were the only aircraft capable of flying airmail across the oceans. Despite efforts to persuade the public to use V-mail, regular mail outnumbered V-mail nearly seven to one. To encourage use of V-mail, forms were first offered free to the public. Later, only a nominal fee was charged. This stood in stark contrast to regular expensive Clipper airmail, yet mailers often chose pricier Clipper mail. Not only would fewer people have access to the contents of letters, but people could also express themselves better. The frustration of conducting family business, keeping marriages together, and abetting homesickness through the mere 230-word limitation of an Airgraph or V-mail could be hard to swallow. People wanted to say more than that. Despite the economic hardship, most did. They coughed up money for the expensive 20-, 25-, and 50-cent airmail stamps picturing the China Clipper. Clippers sped these messages of love, sorrow, and concern on their way. For many, "mail call" was the only thing to look forward to.

14
Clipper Aloha

Aloha! Like the word *aloha*, Clippers have had historically many meanings connected to love, welcome, and good-bye. Popular culture's love affair with the Clippers never really has said good-bye. So it is perhaps fitting that this final section begins with the rebirth of the recent Aloha shirt fashion featuring Clipper designs. The beginnings of shirt and flying boat were contemporaneous. The first Clippers arrived in Honolulu in the mid–1930s, just when the Aloha trademark was registered. Before the arrival of the Clippers, tourists from the steamship lines already were purchasing brightly colored shirts. The added sophistication of Clipper travel brought with it a more sophisticated shirt that spread to boat tourists, and particularly to the increasing numbers of military personnel passing through the islands.

As with everything in popular culture, these often showy articles of clothing depicted the usual popular culture values of escapism (the "Island Paradise"), simple values (the "Island Way"), and entertainment (Don Ho, Polynesian Cultural Center, the hula, *Hawaii 5-0, Magnum P.I.*). Also, as with everything in popular culture, closer examination reveals much more. The Aloha shirt brought together an amalgam of traditions. Its geometric repeated patterns came from native Hawaiian dress. The archives of the Bishop Museum in Honolulu provided ideas for tapa designs based on the indigenous loincloths and skirts made from the inner bark of the wauke trees. A second source came from Japan. Given the large Japanese population in Hawaii and the fact that most cloth was imported from China and Japan, many of the first Aloha shirts were cut from leftover kimono material. This, combined with the bright formal non–Hawaiian design elements of Chinese garments and Chinese silk, only needed the U.S. contribution and invention of rayon for the industry to take off. The idea for a cool, loose-fitting, untucked shirt came from the Philippines, where the barong-tagalog was worn. Finally, the United States and Europe contributed the idea of having a collar. The Aloha shirt was truly international.

The press publicized wealthy Clipper passengers in sports, entertainment, government, and business who flew into and departed Hawaii. The customary placing of leis on passengers after they disembarked the Clipper began their clothing transformation. When not in evening, tennis, or swim wear, they sported casual Aloha shirts. Thus passengers arrived wearing mainland clothes but often departed garbed in Aloha shirts. This publicity set a fashion trend. As the Aloha shirt sought designs typically Hawaiian, the floral designs of hibiscus and ginger became the rage in Hollywood. Hollywood stars such as Ginger Rogers and Janet Gaynor began appearing in slinky, seductive gowns carrying the bold designs. Betty Grable set shutters aflutter in her Hawaiian swimsuit. This in turn set off fashion mania across the United States for scarves, napkins, tablecloths, all with the Hawaiian floral designs. Over the years, the entertainment industry upped interest in the shirts through a succession of movies, television series, and stars. Burt Lancaster, Johnny Weissmuller, Duke Kahanamoku, Don Ho, Arthur Godfrey, Montgomery Cliff, Frank Sinatra, Ernest Borgnine, Bing Crosby, Tom Selleck, all famously wore the shirt.

The unique mixture of sophistication and casualness, of upper-class wealth yet working-class Islander culture, of being walking-postcard extravagance yet fitting in, has kept the shirts popular into the present. The cultural split can still be seen in the preference of many Islanders for the more conservative blue and white, geometrically patterned shirts, which harkened back to the type of Japanese cloth blue-and-white checked denim shirts worn by island plantation workers in the sugar cane and pineapple fields. The influence of worker solidarity, much like that found in the history of blue jeans, has continued. Professionals often prefer the more conservative "worker" designs that seem more appropriate for the office. Some Aloha shirt makers went so far as to use the reverse design technique (putting the less showy inside design on the outside) so that the shirt looked already worn or sun-faded to some degree rather than like a newly minted tourist advertisement.

When Honolulu shop owner Ellery Chun found a market for his newly trademarked Aloha shirts in the late 1930s, he sponsored a radio talent show, whose studio was the beach in front of the Moana Surfrider Hotel where many Clipper passengers stayed. This gave the Aloha shirt even more exposure. But when the shirts appeared during World War II in both the Sears and J.C. Penney catalogs, their popularity was assured. Now the middle class had ready access to the shirts and could order them with full confidence that they had the taste approval of the culture-at-large, since the Alohas had gained acceptance by the catalogs for the masses.

The Sears catalogue offerings made for an unusual situation. Instead of buying Aloha shirts in Hawaii, Islanders could order Aloha shirts from Sears at Sears' prices and have them shipped from Los Angeles back to Hawaii. With the coming of the larger Boeing Clippers to the islands, it was a big deal in Hawaii when Sears, Roebuck and Co. opened its mail order retail store on Kapiolani Boulevard in Honolulu in 1939. Glued to the cover of the *Sears Catalog*, advertising for the new store featured a drawing of the new Boeing Clipper. The catalogue itself gave customers directions for quick ordering through Clipper mail, including a company order envelope and order form that contained images of the China Clipper. Sears urged its customers to use the Clipper mail, as it could speed up orders by a full week. Speed was a real luxury on islands largely dependent upon materials from the mainland.

Nearly all models of Clippers appeared on Aloha shirts during the 1990s and 2000s. The early Sikorsky-manufactured Clippers found their way onto several shirts. Kahala's "Avi Collection" of rayon shirts handcrafted in Hawaii used the image of an S-43 two-engine "Baby Clipper" flying over an island girl, who held a basket of fruit and flowers before a mountain range. The nose of the Clipper read "Hawaii Clipper." Joe Kealuha's "The Genuine Hawaiian Shirt" also used a repeated pattern of the four-engine S-42 Clipper that flew the first survey route to Hawaii. This rayon shirt portrayed the Clipper landing on the water near small islands having thatched huts and palms. The granddaddy of all the Sikorsky Aloha shirts came in the guise of a Tori Richard limited run that showed an S-42 descending from the clouds over the islands. The wingspan of the Clipper stretched from the left shoulder to the right hip, front and back. Such large pictorials have now been abandoned by the company for its more conservative designs, making the few shirts it did manufacture of this nature somewhat scarce. Even with the large flying boat design, Richard avoided the gaudiness that characterized many shirts for the tourist trade.

Strangely, few Aloha shirts gave the Martin or China Clippers their due; this in the face of the fact that the China Clipper received more excited press coverage than any other Clipper. Kalaheo did produce a shirt picturing the China Clipper flying over a bay and an incoming ocean liner. Reclining on the beach next to an outrigger, an island girl watched the Clipper fly by peaks that looked more at home in Tahiti than Hawaii. Bright flowers and leaves framed the entire setting. This image and others that particularly abound showing the later Boeing Clipper model seem to have been inspired by a fanciful Pan American travel poster produced in the 1930s that did show a Clipper flying into an exotic Polynesian island with high, sharp peaks.

The Handsome brand rayon shirt split the difference by showing a larger Boeing Clipper but labeling it as the China Clipper. The Clipper was pictured as if on a postcard, as were other images against a background of a map of Siam and Malaya, jungle scenes (tiger included), lily pads, and coastal villages. Hilo Hattie's followed suit in 2004 with an Aloha shirt reproducing a variety of airline flying boat poster cards from the 1930s, including Pan American's Commodore flying boat and the later Boeing Clippers. Old aviation posters that did not advertise Hawaii were altered in their messages to promote air tourism to Hawaii. Thus the British Imperial Airways flying from Egypt to India became Hawaii-Maui-Kauai Island Breeze, the Tropical Airline. SCADTA, Colombia's German airline during the 1930s suddenly appeared to fly to Hawaii on the shirt. Pan American Airways became Tropical Air.

Tori Richard, "the epitome of resort sophistication," produced three large-image format shirts showing the Boeing B-314 Clipper. One showed the Clipper over the Golden Gate Bridge with Treasure Island in the background. Another showed the Clipper over Diamond Head, heading out over the beach palms to the ocean beyond. The third, a postmillennial Christmas novelty shirt, appeared on the racks at Hilo Hattie's in Honolulu. The design mimicked a Pan American Clipper promotional poster advertising flights to Hawaii in the early 1940s. The shirt image changed the Honolulu Clipper into the North Pole Clipper. Instead of passengers walking down the dock from the Clipper, it showed Santa wearing a Tori Richard Aloha shirt, shorts, and floppies, as he carried his bag of Christmas gifts. The jolly old man was clearly going to enjoy his stop in Hawaii. Behind him, his elves unloaded more gifts from the giant Clipper. The Pan American winged globe logo still resided on the side of the flying boat, but now substituted Rudolph the Red-Nosed Reindeer for the map of the northern and southern hemispheres. Other shirts exhibited smaller images of the Boeing Clipper. OP Sport, for instance, retailed an Aloha shirt showing small repeated images of both the baby Clippers and the Boeing Clippers, along with repeated images of pineapples, surfers, and hula girls.

Eschewing its usual conservative designs of avoiding large pictorial prints, Tori Richard has continued to make exceptions to its rule when it comes to specialized Christmas shirts. In 2004 the company seemed to have made the Clipper its unofficial logo, placing small images on shirt pockets, on the back of one shirt, and in glorious extravagance on its Christmas shirt. The upper half of the 2004 Christmas shirt, front and back, showed a black, starry sky. The lower half showed a blue ocean with map of Hawaii and North and Central America. Between the halves, a huge flying boat flew at the onlooker as it came in from the North Pole. The wingspan of the silver and red Boeing "Santa One" Clipper stretched from arm to arm in the sky. A jolly Santa stuck his head out of the cockpit window and waved, while Rudolph the Red-Nosed Reindeer pushed wrapped gifts out of the cargo bay door. The gifts drifted down on red and green parachutes to cities and regions represented symbolically below. Idaho became a potato; Detroit, a car; Las Vegas, a neon sign; Havana, cigars; Memphis or Nashville, a guitar. All were reminiscent of tourist maps of the 1930s.

Tori Richard has established a tradition of having fun with the Clipper Christmas shirts. On the 2004 edition a whirlpool and pirate ship sat in the Bermuda Triangle. A sea serpent surfaced south of Baja. The Clipper carried its own nose art of Santa's sexy helper. This leggy pinup blonde struck a Playboy pose in her skimpy red-and-white fur-trimmed Santa cap, high-heeled boots, and not much else. Her name? The North Pole Express.

The novelty Christmas shirts were produced in limited quantities. Stores wishing to sell them had to place their orders at least six months ahead of time, with no possibility of reordering. Only enough shirts were cut and sewn to meet the orders. Thus the Clipper Christmas editions have become some of the rarer modern Aloha shirts.

One of the weirder flying boat shirts came from Jams World, a division of Surf Line Hawaii founded by former Hollywood stuntman Dave Rochlen, who twice appeared in *Life* magazine. Jams World took great pride in producing shirts that flamboyantly used color and design. This retro shirt pictured what appeared to be a Clipper taking off in the moonlight from tranquil tropical island waters. The design was adapted from a 1978 retro Art Deco poster entitled "Classic Reflections" for Mirage Editions/Spring, signed by artist David McMacken. The poster itself was adapted from a Lufthansa photo of the 1929 German flying-boat leviathan called the Do-X that looked more ocean liner than airplane. It was even larger than the Clippers, an experiment in gigantism to disprove the argument that airplane size had limitations. As a commercial failure, it proved the opposite.

The poster and the shirt altered the original photo to produce a morphed flying boat suggesting a Clipper. The real Do-X had an incredible twelve engines, six facing forward and six backward in tandem pairs. Like the poster, Jams World removed the Do-X's backward-facing engines and reduced the engines atop the wing to five, making it closer to the Clipper look. The shirt did retain the poster's numbering on the flying boat, which was M-1978, denoting the artist McMacken and the year of creation, much like the flying boat's actual numbering, D-1929, which stood for its year of production. As in the poster, the Do-X passed by palm trees brilliantly backlit. No palms were present in the original Lufthansa photograph, but adding the trees connected the flying boat to Hawaii and the Pacific, an ocean never touched by the giant German Dornier machine.

Given the explosive popularity of T-shirts, it was inevitable that Clippers would show up on many tees. Many of the same celebrities who popularized the Aloha shirt also did a haberdashery crossover to popularize T-shirts, Elvis Presley, to name but one. Do you want the *Blue Hawaii* Aloha shirt or the *G.I. Blues* and *Jailhouse Rock* tees? The mass appeal of tees followed that of the Aloha shirts, and again the military was very involved in taking the T-shirt from simply an article of underwear to a universal icon, carrying nearly every message and advertising imaginable.

Like the Aloha shirt, the T-shirt claimed its heritage from a variety of sources, including late nineteenth and early twentieth century men's and women's undergarments, cotton sailor tops prior to World War I, and lightweight military undershirts worn by European soldiers during World War I. When U.S. doughboys arrived in Europe during that war, they quickly saw the benefits of wearing cotton instead of wool, and dubbed the European shirt as a "T" shirt because of its shape. By World War II, the U.S. had made T-shirts standard issue for its troops. Meanwhile, in Hawaii and at other navy bases, the T-shirt was already fairly standard. When military personnel returned at war's end, they continued to find tees comfortable, casual wear. Although Sears sold a "gob" (sailor) shirt in 1938, during the war it pushed more the sleeveless, dressier, ribbed Art-Deco–looking undershirts or the old standard union shirts instead. All that changed with the movies.

Marlon Brando's *A Streetcar Named Desire* (1951) brought the T-shirt to national attention as an icon. James Dean quickly followed, his short but riveting career made famous by his *Rebel Without a Cause* tees. From there it was but a quick step to 1960s tie-dyes, Farrah Fawcett, the Fonz, rock concert souvenirs, flea market specials, branded athletic tees, family reunion mementos, road race participant giveaways, and do-it-yourself tees on home computer and printer. What had been a military, blue-collar, or no-collar symbol was now produced by every major clothier as a way to dress up or dress down—or to send a message.

Clippers certainly became part of the message and continue to be a part of tourism connected to the flying boat ports. People enjoy broadcasting where they have traveled as a way of establishing their identity according to interests, lifestyle, and their status of having enough time and cash to be able to travel. Therefore, many Clipper tees can be classified as souvenirs conferring nostalgia and status on the wearer. Air shows and air museums are but two examples. For instance, the T-shirt of the Foynes Flying Boat Museum in Foynes, Ireland, showed the Boeing Yankee Clipper taking off from the sea. Foynes served as main port for the Clippers from 1939 to the end of World War II. Foynes was also the site of the invention of Irish coffee. In 1943 chef Joe Sheridan tried to warm up some very cold Clipper passengers who had just crossed the Atlantic Ocean. He poured some Powers whiskey into their coffee, and the legend was born. Clippers are still tied to Powers World Irish Coffee Making Championship held in Foynes across the estuary from the Shannon airport. The Foynes Clipper shirts are connected to actress Maureen O'Hara-Blair, made famous in her role in *The Quiet Man* opposite John Wayne, who also helped popularize tees. She married flying boat Captain Charlie Blair, the first man to fly a flying boat nonstop from Ireland to New York in 1942, and the pilot of the last flying boat flight out of Foynes three years later. No wonder then that the Foynes tee was part of the "Screen Stars" collection manufactured by Fruit of the Loom.

In the Pacific Northwest of the United States, where the Boeing Clippers were built, such places as the Pearson Air Museum in Vancouver, Washington, offered nearly the same image of the Boeing Clipper as did the Foynes Museum. Made by Mountain High ArtWorks of Enterprise and Halfway, Oregon, the shirt was titled "Test Run—B314." The Judi Miller design was printed on Anvil tees.

Hawaii has been flooded with Clipper tees. Paradise offered one picturing a Sikorsky Clipper flying over Diamond Head. The entire image was framed as if it were a huge postage stamp. Moments of Hawaii's "Maui, The Valley Isle" shirt showed a baby Clipper flying at sunset, while a large whale's fluke rose in the bay, and a hula dancer performed in the foreground. Both Reyn Spooner and the Old Honolulu Clothing Company reproduced Pan American's 1930s travel poster entitled "Fly to the South Seas Via Pan American" that showed a Boeing Clipper in Tahitian setting. The Spooner shirt, however, changed the caption to "Reyn Spooner to the South Seas." In short, Spooner sold a shirt selling a shirt, reflecting how product branding recently overrode image. Hawaiian Airlines and Hilo Hattie produced a Hanes tee showing a baby Clipper over Diamond Head with an island girl offering a lei to it as it soared past.

The Crazy Shirt Company of Aiea, Hawaii, used the Clipper to promote another of Hawaii's famous products, Kona Coffee. In 2004 the company offered its Tropic Express Hawaii line of tees, using the Boeing B-314 Clipper as its front logo. The backside featured a colorful graphic of the Clipper flying just above a tropical beach with the message "Get away from it all on the Tropic Express. Paradise is just a flight away." The shirt promoted air tourism to Hawaii, its own brand of shirt, and Kona Coffee, since the Tropic Express came dyed in Kona Coffee beans. This gave the shirt a pleasing aroma and automatic suntan. As the shirt label read, "Be original. Be Crazy." Why just drink coffee when you could tastefully wear it, or not?

The now defunct Aviator Ales of Woodinville, Washington, sold Clipper promotional shirts. A Boeing Clipper named "Seattle" took off in front of Mt. Rainier and green forests, the same image the company used on its bottle label for its India Pale Ale. The shirt's title read, "Official Test Pilot." with "Test" crossed out and "Taste" written in above. On this and other aviation-themed shirts, Aviator tied together Northwest environmental concern (green forests, pristine snow-covered mountains, blue water) with the independent machismo and nostalgia of early pilots. As the Northwest moved more away from logging, fishing, and agriculture to high tech and service industries, could tastes be shifted from beer to ale? The Aviator image posited that microbeer could be consumed by trendy yuppies, yet it was made for a stronger breed. In that way, "real men" could drink ale, not beer. Even though white-collar desk-jockeys sat much of the day working and dealing with rush hour traffic, they could dare to be aviators, taste test pilots.

Numerous other anonymous shirt makers and designers produced Clipper image shirts as well. A 1930s ticket office poster entitled "Hawaii by Flying Clipper, Pan American Airways System" became so popular that it also appeared on T-shirts, dresses, potholders, computer mouse pads, aprons—just about anything. Speedo also created its own Clipper shirt with a Sikorsky Clipper incorporated into its Speedo logo on the front side. Backside, the shirt's larger image looked as if a large hi-definition flat-screen had been set down between palm trees on Waikiki. Appearing on the screen was a movie showing yet another beach, with the Clipper flying overhead—a play-within-a-play effect. Off-screen appeared the Speedo name and logo with the title of the image, "South Pacific Explorer." Though the South Pacific has been explored, when people run out of places to explore they can always explore the past as if in a movie.

Clippers are nothing new to clothing. In the late 1930s women could purchase the long, sleek, bright red, Art Deco–inspired Clipper slip. Following Hollywood's fashion lead, the Clipper plunged in both back and front so that it could be worn beneath elegant evening gowns. Coeds were known to have altered such slips into prom wear when they could not afford or did not have a proper gown. Their slim, silhouette style made both girls and gown a hit. If mademoiselle or madame wanted to accessorize, she could powder her nose using a compact whose cover illustrated the Clipper base at Miami. To aid in powdering and applying makeup, she could also use her six-inch Clipper hand mirror with its faux brass handle and frame. The mirror carried the image of the China Clipper flying over Diamond Head on its reverse side. A woman could travel around the world without leaving her boudoir.

During the 1940s nylon stockings became treasured. Women sought to have smooth, streamlined legs. Airmaid Hosiery Mills of Dallas obliged. The packaging on Airmaid nylons directly connected the sleek, firm appearance of a woman's leg with the tight skin of aircraft. Airmaid's advertising promised, "Airmaid hosiery are worn to all corners of the world by the meticulous stewardesses of the airlines. Like the swift liners they ride, Airmaids are streamlined for grace, constructed for service—designed for legs that must be lovely." Airmaid's logo showed what looked like a Radio City Music Hall Rockette showing a lot of leg. Added to her costume were an aviator's leather helmet and gauntlets. In Texas style, reins in hand, she stood atop a large airplane as if she were a trick rider on a horse. The plane circled the globe, while Pan Am's winged globe logo appeared in the slipstream. Airmaids were available in drug stores from coast to coast. The hosiery company even ran ads in high school yearbooks, including the 1945 yearbook of Maud High School, Bowie County, Texas. High school girls could begin dreaming of aviation careers with Pan American and its Clippers, or at least of having "aviation legs."

Men's clothing followed, with Clipper raincoats and topcoats. When the flying boats were being replaced by land based aircraft, also called Clippers, the Pan American Hat by Lee came in a large silver hatbox, showing the new Clippers on its sides and top. Stetson did the same, producing its own silver "Stratoliner" hatbox mimicking the Clipper's metal skin.

The Pan American "Genuine Mogador" dress tie came with a tag illustrating the early Sikorsky Clipper.

A Pan American Genuine Magador men's tie showing a Sikorsky Clipper.

In the late 1930s and 1940s the Syracuse Ornamental Company of Syracuse, New York, manufactured tie racks and other accessories featuring the China Clipper. These were made of Syroco, or glued, pressed sawdust. Shown at the top is an original Syroco. At bottom is a modern brass reproduction.

Although the tie advertised itself as being genuine Mogador, an expensive Moroccan silk, the back of the tag revealed it contained rayon, making it a 1930s clothing counterpart to furniture's "genuine Naugahyde leather." Ladies could also travel with silk, embroidered "Aloha Hawaii" lingerie carriers that pictured the China Clipper flying over a hula dancer, with Diamond Head in the background. While it was doubtful whether any hula dancer impractically wore silk stockings on the beach, the stocking bag provided luxurious tourist sophistication and offered an intimate gift that soldiers or sailors in Hawaii could give to loved ones.

During the 1990s Marley Hodgson's Original Ghurka Collection of leather goods used Montana poster artist Monte Dolak's painting of the China Clipper on posters and promotional and sales cards in upscale and specialty stores. Dolak's poster art depicted the China Clipper moored placidly off a dock on which a man in his white tropical suit and a smartly dressed woman holding an umbrella waited for a rowboat to take them and their retro–Ghurka luggage to the pristine white Clipper. In the background of the turquoise bay rose the sharp peaks of some South Pacific archipelago. The distant peaks turned blue under dawn's first yellow light. Reminiscent of 1930s travel poster art, the advertising campaign sold the romance of travel to exotic places.

Both the Clipper image and Ghurka name played on nostalgic associations with the Far East and Pacific. The Ghurka name derives from the famous British regiments of tough Nepalese soldiers. The company name was acquired when founder Marley Hodgson noticed some beautifully preserved leather articles in the 1970s that were up for auction in the UK. These articles had once belonged to the regimental commander of the Ghurkas in India, yet the pieces were still supple, improving with age. Hodgson tracked down the tanning formula of the long-closed Indian tannery and began manufacturing leather handbags, shoulder bags, and carrying cases in the U.S.

It was fitting that Ghurka used Dolak's Clipper image, since he had also created the cover art for Stan Cohen's pictorial history book, *Wings to the Orient, Pan American Clipper Planes 1935 to 1945*. That cover showed the China Clipper flying over a map of the Pacific with the Golden Gate Bridge prominent on one end of the map and a Chinese junk in Hong Kong prominent on the other. Because Dolak also produced many environmentally sensitive posters to help protect the scenic beauty and wildlife of the West, his idyllic Ghurka poster also fittingly represented Ghurka's environmentally friendly product. Rather than being treated with harsh chemicals, Ghurka leather was tanned using vegetable extracts of the mimosa and quebracho to produce products that would become more supple and more colorful with age.

Lest anyone think that such a green product might prove unmanly or unwomanly, Ghurka macho adventurism and nostalgic foreign exoticness continued through such products as cashmere for the ladies and indestructible leather fly rod cases and the Bengal Buffalo wallets for the men. The wallet presumably conferred on its owner the regal, tough fierceness of a Bengal tiger when on the hunt at the local Nordstrom's, and the ability to tote a heavy buffalo-load of credit cards to get the job done. Instead of trophy heads on the wall, the wallet was the trophy. Thus, like most travelers today, Clipper passengers in the past had disposable cash to be able to travel. Portrayed as rich sophisticates with discerning tastes, they were nevertheless nonchalantly tough as Ghurkas in their courage to seek adventure—just like their luggage.

The use of the Clipper image or name in recent times often traced back to associations with the flying boats of the 1930s and 1940s. Computer Associates created its own programming language called Clipper, but soon the U.S. government appropriated the name for its own purposes. To combat crime and terrorism, in 1993 the Clinton administration announced its controversial Clipper Chip initiative. The Clipper Chip was an encryption chip developed by the National Security Agency. The government's idea was to make the Clipper Chip the industry standard to protect sensitive or private communications, yet allow the government to be able to listen in on criminal or terrorist telecommunications. In that way criminals and others could not block the government's gathering of information by using their own encryptions. The government would keep copies of the decoding keys.

Outcry against the Clipper Chip was instantaneous. Privacy advocates objected on the basis that the government illegally could listen in on anyone's electronic messages. Industry advocates objected on the basis that it would be very difficult for such companies as Microsoft and others to compete abroad. Since the government classified anything over a 40-bit encryption as a "munition" that could not be exported, computer and software makers were faced with selling high-powered encryption machines and software in this country, while offering watered-down versions abroad. This would hurt sales. In 1994 the Libertarian Party passed a resolution opposing the Clipper Chip as part of the party's platform. In the face of so much opposition, Clinton abandoned the Clipper Chip initiative and through Executive Order in 1996 somewhat loosened the export restrictions.

The spy-vs.-spy nature of the encryption chips harked back to the Clippers' early involvement with codes and espionage in World War II. Where Clippers had bases across the Pacific at Singapore, Guam, the Philippines, and Hawaii, the navy had counterintelligence intercept stations that listened in on Japanese radio traffic. To collect and carry these intercepts, Clippers were equipped with small strongboxes built into the hulls of the Clippers for this express purpose. Intelligence officers kept the keys to open these strongboxes. Naval intelligence developed its own code, called RIP 30, just for this Clipper mail, which came into Hawaii from points west. In 1940 decoders in Hawaii said that the only good intelligence information coming into Hawaii about Japanese fleet movements came from the Clipper mail communiqués.

Clippers complicity aided U.S. code-breaking and counterintelligence efforts. This became evident in the Philippines before the fall of Corregidor. Pan American Airways joined Project AFIRM in fall of 1939. Under this project, new equipment for the intercept station at the Cavite Navy Base was installed, with the cover story that this was a "Navy Emergency Radio Station," which would also conduct research into long-distance reception, using experimental equipment. At the same time, Pan American's tower array of directional finders was recalibrated to help military radio security and tracking in time of emergency.

Once war began and General MacArthur left Corregidor to establish his new command headquarters in Australia, counterintelligence needed to be set up there. A Clipper carried the six officers and eight enlisted men of 837th Signal Service Detachment from the United States to Hawaii on its last scheduled flight. Since the Clipper routes between Honolulu and New Zealand had been discontinued, these men had to fly the remaining 7,000 miles by finding space on assorted USAAF and RAF planes. It took a while.

Clippers played a role in decoding and in breaking up spy gangs in the Atlantic, too. The British suspected that much German intelligence was flowing across the ocean on the Clippers. As a consequence, they demanded that Clippers stop in Bermuda, where all mail would be censored. This did not sit well with Clipper pilots, as this created more delays in an already dicey weather situation of crossing the Atlantic.

British censors in Bermuda finally figured out how spy messages were filtering past authorities when they noticed suspicious nonidiomatic phrases that kept popping up in otherwise innocent-looking letters. They suspected invisible ink was also being used, but it took a chemist to figure out that spy Kurt Ludwig had used an over-the-counter brand of painkiller, Pyramidon, manufactured by Bayer of Germany, to create an invisible ink that had previously avoided detection. The British turned over the information to J. Edgar Hoover's FBI, and the gang was tracked down.

The world of Clipper espionage and intrigue has continued. After the *Indiana Jones* film trilogy came out, Lewis Galoob Toys offered its Indiana Jones MicroMachines scale miniatures. This box of ten vehicles plus an Indy figure from the movies contained a small "warning: choking hazard" two-inch piece of plastic of what it billed as a Pan Am Clipper plane from *Raiders of the Lost Ark*. In the film Indy cruised around the world in a Clipper as he defeated Nazis bent on obtaining the powers of the Lost Ark of the Covenant.

For those who wanted to participate in their own Clipper stories, Flying Buffalo Inc. came out with its 1991 role-playing game (RPG) of *The*

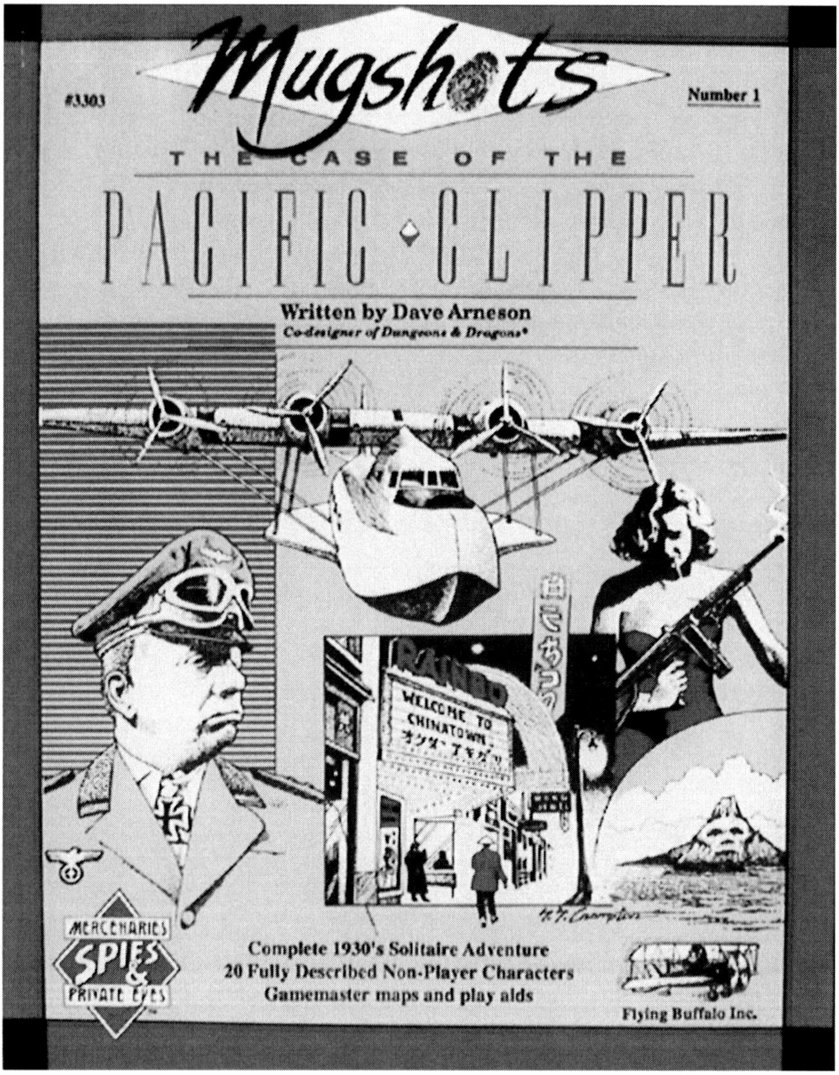

Cover for the solitaire adventure game *The Case of the Pacific Clipper*, which debuted in 1991 (art by Steve Crompton from Mugshots I: Case of the Pacific Clipper, www.flyingbuffalo.com).

Case of the Pacific Clipper. After Dave Arneson had codesigned the fantastically popular *Dungeons and Dragons*, he authored this game book lavishly illustrated with Clipper images, schematics, character portraits, and maps by Steven S. Crompton. Much of the artwork reproduces actual Pan American Airways materials. In some cases, actual historical personages are used as characters, such as Clipper Captain Terletsky. Other names and characters were reflective of characters found in pulp magazines of the 1930s, from spies to gun molls. Players had the choice of playing the game in either solitaire or gamemaster modes. Set in 1937, the game involved trying to figure out who was sabotaging the Clippers—the Japanese, Nazis, a madman, aliens, criminal organizations with secret bases? The game could be used as a supplement to *Mercenaries Spies & Private Eyes*, or another RPG called *Espionage*.

While *The Case of the Pacific Clipper* did not attain the cult status of *Dungeons and Dragons*, it did attract appreciative followers who bemoaned the paucity of solitaire games or who perceived that the RPG Gamemaster scene was becoming so dominated by Goths that non–Goths no longer wished to play.

For those who wanted a simulated Clipper experience at work, New Space, a subsidiary of Gilbert International of Fort Worth, Texas, introduced the "virtual office" Clipper CS-1 enclosed office space in 1994. The streamlined Clipper was modeled after an airplane cockpit. Entry was by a partial side door, and chair and workstation functioned as one unit. This four-foot by seven-foot capsule secluded a worker in his or her own work space to reduce office distractions and increase efficiency. So that the worker would not feel claustrophobic at the computer station, the cockpit capsule was covered with a translucent material of Lexan stretched across maple struts. Diffused lighting reduced glare, and a ventilation fan produced white noise to block outside interference. Because of its artistic innovative design, the Clipper received an APEX award and was displayed in museums in London and Chicago.

Clippers in the past were noted for their architectural designs, too, so much so that they became the standard for elegance in the air. In 1997 the Art Institute of Chicago exhibited "Building for Air Travel: Architecture and Design for Commercial Aviation." Sponsored by the National Endowment for the Humanities, Lufthansa, United Airlines and others, the art institute produced a poster for the exhibition showing a 1930s Clipper interior. Passengers in evening dress sat at a table and were served dinner by the flight steward. The meal came complete with floral bouquet beneath the gracefully arching interior ribs of the Clipper, an Art Deco cathedral of the air.

Earlier the Smithsonian also made the connection between the Clippers and its exhibitions. When it published its guide, *National Aircraft Collection, Smithsonian Institution, United States National Museum*, in 1941, the cover of this guide to the Smithsonian collection featured Gordon Grant's painting for Pan American Airways entitled "Yankee Clippers Sail Again."

Pan American ticket offices during the 1930s and 1940s carried posters with this image that showed a Boeing Clipper flying low over ocean waves and a Clipper sailing ship. Unfortunately, no Clippers survived to be donated to the National Air and Space Museum, but Pan American did donate models of its Clippers and flags flown on the first flights across the Atlantic. Though the booklet contains information about the *Spirit of St. Louis*, the Wright Brothers' Flyer, and other famous aircraft, it begins on the cover with the Clippers and ends with the Clippers, promising that the Clippers meant that air travel would now be open to everyone, not just heroic travelers. Democracy at work.

The Gordon Grant Clipper painting has remained one of the most reproduced of the Pan American posters. At the time of this writing it could still be ordered "antiqued" and ready for framing. Grant (1875–1962) loved Clipper sailing ships and the aircraft that bore their name. His love affair with Clippers began when his parents decided to send him from San Francisco to Scotland for his early schooling. This necessitated his sailing on a Clipper around the horn of South America and then across the Atlantic, a trip he always remembered. When the Clipper flying boat came along to outrace the ocean-going ships, he paid tribute to them both in "Yankee Clippers Sail Again." He became one of the nation's premiere maritime painters and illustrators, whose works are part of the White House collection. At the height of Clipper glory in 1937, Grant won a medal at the Paris Salon. Grant also served maritime purposes well by lobbying Congress for preserving the U.S.S. *Constitution*. In 1906 thousands of his prints of "Old Ironsides" were sold to raise money to preserve the ship. Today his prints are sold to preserve the romance of the flying Clippers.

The iconic nature of the Clipper name and image propelled its use for modern events and rituals as well. In 1954, Bern, Switzerland, held its successful Hospesfest, a tourism and culinary arts exposition. For the first time since World War II, an international cooking art exhibition was held to reestablish the international cooking connections severed by the war. Twenty-four nations and 5,000 cooks competed. The exposition opened with twenty-one restaurants, monumental architecture, and other tourist delights. The highlight of monumental architecture on the grounds was the Strato-Clipper Hall. Here participants and the public could dance to music into the wee hours of the morning. Postcards advertising the May–June event showed the large silver nose of the Clipper sticking out and tilted upward like some huge rocket or dirigible emerging from the hall, which was shaped like a giant airplane hangar.

One young Swiss chef, Albert Uster, was asked to help the U.S. culinary team that was competing. Impressed by his talents, they asked him to come to the United States to work. He worked his way through the ranks to run his own import business. At one point he became food director at the Watergate Terrace Restaurant in Washington, D.C. Watergate would, of course, become a famous political term, representing events leading to the resignation of President Nixon and the questioning of his ties with Bebe Rebozo, the one-time Pan American Airways' employee on the Clippers.

In 1992 the San Francisco International Antique Toy Show adopted the Clipper to advertise itself. Advertising cards showing a drawing of the Boeing Clipper over a Golden Gate Bridge tower were distributed at other collecting and antique shows to drum up business. Likewise, the annual benefit for the Maui Arts and Cultural Center used a cover drawing by Darrell Orwig for its *Maui Calls 2003* program booklet, featuring auction items ranging from a "priceless" Willie Nelson guitar to a $60 gift certificate for cheese at the Surfing Goat Dairy. Orwig, who served as a Coast Guard combat artist in Desert Storm, depicted the China Clipper flying among puffy clouds over one of the verdant islands. Smaller images of the Clipper were used as section headings that indicated all the different vineyards and chefs involved in the dining that went along with the yearly auction and entertainment.

Clippers continue to be embraced by celebrities and celebrity-endorsed products. Singer and composer Jimmy Buffett may be the most conspicuous example. The name Buffett has been synonymous with his near cult following of Parrotheads, his creation of Margaritaville, flashy Caribbean and Aloha shirts, and the laid-back conch way of life. A pilot himself and owner of an Albatross amphibion airplane, Buffett and his longtime sponsor, Corona Beer of Mexico's Grupo Modelo, have capitalized on the flying boat image. Buffett's Margaritaville stores sell everything from inflatable palm trees and parrots to flying boats that could serve as life preservers if you happen to fall into your pool after sipping too many margaritas or Coronas. Flying boats have been plastered on just about every product that exists in the mythical land of Margaritaville. Corona also has provided watering holes with neon bar signs that outline a blue Boeing Clipper.

One of the most colorful pieces of Parrothead memorabilia is Bob Masse's "Parrot Stock 2002" poster created for the Parrot Head Clubs of the Southeast for their charity gathering. Reminiscent of the famous '60s and '70s ornate rock music posters Masse designed for such groups as the Grateful Dead, Jefferson Airplane, Dylan, the Doors, Cream, the Byrds, Iron Butterfly, Fleetwood Mac, and Eric Burdon and the Animals, the Parrot Stock convention poster shows a rich, glowing world where a Clipper drops into a tropical bay inhabited by a leggy pinup girl with a parrot on her shoulder. Masse harnesses 1930s nostalgia, 1960s poster art, and millennial margarita music to produce quite a popular culture vibrancy.

As an aviator, Buffett has paid his respect to the Clippers. His statement about the Clippers served as the foreword for Jon E. Krupnick's *Pan American's Pacific Pioneers, The Rest of the Story: A Pictorial History of Pan Am's Pacific First Flight 1935–1945*. In that foreword, dated 2000, Buffett wrote, "If I had one wish, it would be to have been able, just once, to ride aboard a Pan Am Clipper" (4). He penned his message while flying across the Pacific in a 747. Traversing the old Clipper route across the ocean in a jet just was not the same as it would have been in a flying boat.

Buffett further showed his fascination with Pan Am's flying boats through the use of stage Clippers. When Margaritaville-Orlando opened, a ⅙ scale Clipper model with a twenty-five-foot wingspan hung over the stage. Buffett also surprised concert tour goers in 1991 when he opened with a huge model of a 1940s flying boat named the Margaritaville Clipper, slowly moving across the stage. As it moved, it disgorged Buffett and his Coral Reefer band. The use of the Clipper didn't stop there. Later in the show a 1940s retro black-and-white newsreel humorously showed the exploits of Jimmy and the band as they had to repel the dark forces of the DRALS (disco, rap, and lip-synch).

In Key West, home of Buffett's original Margaritaville store, the original Pan American Airways ticket office still stands, not far from President Harry S Truman's "Little White House." A sign outside proclaims the office as "the Birthplace of Pan American Airways," while another sign indicates that this is now Kelly's Caribbean Bar, Grill, and Brewery. Kelly is none other than actress Kelly McGillis, who starred with Tom Cruise in the academy-award–winning movie *Top Gun* (1986). Members of the Virtual Parrothead Club have met in Kelly's to soak up the local juices and aviation ambiance. Aviation memorabilia adorns the establishment. Some of the sculpture work makes it appear as if a Clipper is diving right through the roof.

As the United States and other countries have turned to becoming more and more entertainment societies with professional spectator sports dominating the airwaves and salary schedules, the Clipper name has continued to be used as a name for teams of various sports, including soccer, football, and basketball, such as the Los Angeles Clippers. Coupled with the interest in teams comes interest in owning or collecting sports paraphernalia, so that the wearer can find gratification in being associated with a particular team or athlete. Recently this interest in clothing has extended to the realms of nostalgia. Throwback uniforms have become popular, both

A logo on a throwback uniform of the San Francisco Clippers showed Howard Hugh's Spruce Goose rather than the China Clipper (©Ebbets Field Flannels Inc.).

for fans to collect and for teams to play "throwback" games, where both teams take the field in uniforms from their pasts.

Various companies have manufactured throwback uniforms, both inside and outside the United States. Seattle-based Ebbets Field Flannels offered a football jersey with a clear Clipper connection. Their San Francisco Clippers jersey came complete with a front logo of a football player carrying the ball, superimposed over a flying boat. Although the flying boat looked more like Howard Hughes' Spruce Goose than the China Clipper, it did approximate the idea of Pan American's flying boats. The jersey reflected the padded long-sleeved jersey worn by Clippers' star Kenny Washington in the 1940s. Therein lies a story.

Before the National Football League gained a virtual monopoly on professional football in the United States, other leagues challenged the NFL for supremacy. The Pacific Coast Football League did quite well, and was one of the few to survive during the war years when other leagues folded as players were lost to the military services. The team that became known as the San Francisco Clippers had top-scorer Kenny Washington as its star.

Washington earned All-American status at UCLA playing football alongside Woody Strode, who would go on to motion picture fame in such films as *Spartacus*, and Jackie Robinson, who would break the color barrier in professional baseball. Because the NFL had barred Afro Americans in 1933, Washington and Strode played in the PCFL instead. This was a time when the league played nonconference military teams, such as the one from March Field, that sometimes unofficially won the conference title. It was also a time when some players chose not to play under their real names while in service, because they wanted to play college ball after the war. After the war, in 1946, the NFL made its move to make inroads into the West Coast, spelling doom for the PCFL. Now the NFL was willing to cherry-pick good black players. Kenny Washington was the first to be picked by the Los Angeles Rams, the first to break the modern color barrier in professional sports. This occurred a year before Jackie Robinson broke the color barrier in baseball. In fact, since Washington had a better batting average than did Robinson in college, had the NFL not drafted Washington, his statue might stand in Baseball's Hall of Fame rather than Robinson's.

The Clipper was involved in another milestone in sports in 1933, when the only postseason football bowl game played outside the United States took place. The climax of Cuba's National Sports Festival in Havana, the Bacardi Bowl, featured the Villanova Wildcats under coach Maurice "Clipper" Smith against the Alabama Polytechnic Institute Tigers, later known as the Auburn Tigers. Auburn was led by tailback Billy Hitchcock, who went on to play, manage, coach, and scout for over forty years in major league baseball. This first bowl appearance by both teams ended in a thrilling 7–7 tie.

To promote the New Year's Day game, top gridders from the Villanova team were photographed outside the Miami terminal before flying to Havana. Posing in their football uniforms, they stood on the wing of the S-42 Clipper that would carry the team southward. Reminiscent of promotional pictures for the musical *Flying Down to Rio*, which featured chorus girls on Clipper wings, this press release photo had the beefy chorus line of backs Andy Stopper, Art Raimo, Ray Stoviak, Frank Nye, and the team captain and end, Tony Sala.

Bowl games were proliferating at the time. More recently, some have complained about the number of bowl games that have become so much a part of the holiday and New Year's Day ritual, but after World War II bowl games numbered over fifty per year, with one team playing in three postseason games in the same season.

The Bacardi Bowl, however, nearly did not take place. Again the Clippers were involved. The Bowl almost was canceled because of revolution. Cuban dictator Machado was overthrown in a coup d'etat. The U.S. ambassador to Cuba arranged to charter a Sikorsky amphibion to fly him out at night, before he could be killed by angry mobs. Since the small amphibion could hold only six passengers, Machado could take only five of his closest friends and aides. So hasty was the exit that he arrived in his pajamas by armored car at the airport. Other aides had to be left behind. The Sikorsky, reported to have been painted black, was to fly the entourage to Nassau, but due to darkness and mechanical difficulties the plane had to set down on the water before reaching its destination. The group had to spend a night in pajamas, locked in the tight confines of the ship with their five revolvers and seven bags of gold. (The revolvers did not make it through customs for the Clippers.)

Back in Havana, Secretary of State Orestes Ferrara found himself left behind as the highest ranking official of the old government. Though the U.S. ambassador assured him that the bullets screaming over his head were just the result of people celebrating the revolution, he and his wife knew that they were being fired upon. In a desperate dash in their automobile, they charged the dock where Pan American's Captain Tertlesky was warming up the engines on his S-40 Clipper and preparing to take on fourteen Miami-bound passengers and their luggage.

Closely pursued by a melee of angry people and gunfire, the Ferraras flung themselves into the Clipper. Tertlesky did not wait to board the other passengers and their luggage, but quickly taxied out into the harbor, as machine gun fire and small arms fire poured into the Clipper. Two and a half hours later the riddled Clipper landed in Miami, where it was met with another angry mob of Cuban exiles. Revolutions and gunfire were nothing new to airline staff. Although the press, historians, or government officials often talked of "bloodless" revolutions, crews knew better, and bullet holes told a different story. Similar events occurred in Venezuela when Clipper crews were caught in the crossfire of rival gangs. Playing football under revolutionary conditions could be a bit disconcerting.

Pan American Airways unwittingly played another role in sports, celebrities, and the Cuba connection. It brought writer Ernest Hemingway and Jane Mason together. Grant Mason, one of the founders and head of Pan American Airways in Cuba and part owner of Cubana de Aviacion, married Jane Kendall in Cuba in 1929. Jane Kendall Mason was the adopted daughter of multimillionaire Lyman Kendall of Maryland. Grant Mason was himself heir to a fortune and what was termed a "Yale Clubman." Together, they were top entries on the social register covered by the Havana press.

Enter Ernest Hemingway. Hemingway loved the sporting life, as did Jane Mason. When Hemingway wanted to get away from his second wife, Pauline Pfeiffer, in 1932 after the birth of his third son, he decided to go fishing for a few days. The trip took him to Cuba and lasted four months, mostly due to marlin fishing with Jane and pursuing other athletic pleasures of the indoor nature. He had first met Jane the previous year, while sailing back from France to New York on the *Ile de France*. The tall, statuesque, athletic strawberry blonde seemed just his type. She liked to hunt in Africa, to shoot live pigeons with men at the club, to fish, to maintain her own menagerie of strange animals, to throw parties, to ride, to run her own business, to write, to speak three languages, and to sculpt in her own studio. So beautiful that she appeared in Pond's Cream advertisements, yet capable of Hemingwayesque suicidal mood swings, she seemed his match. Desperately, Pauline tried to regain her husband's affections by canceling a Clipper flight from Key West to Havana just to redo her hair tint one more time to please him.

Hemingway spent more and more time in Cuba, primarily with Jane. Although the Masons owned a luxurious villa with servants, overlooking the Jaimanitas River just outside Havana, in the F. Scott Fitzgerald decadence of the time, Jane would rendezvous with Hemingway in his room at the Hotel Ambos Mundos in the anything-goes, bawdy La Habana Vieja district. The socialite was not afraid to parade her affair in public, as she and Hemingway were seen anywhere from some of the lowest dives to the more refined places Havana had to offer. Hemingway crowed that on the outside of the hotel she climbed the five floors to his famous room 511 and wiggled through the transom of his window to have sex with him. Though this Pan Am wife did later divorce her husband and go on to have several husbands, she did not marry Hemingway, despite their having considered marriage. Instead, four years of Hemingway/Mason interplay ended when Hemingway met correspondent Martha Gellhorn and Mason took up with an African lion hunter.

Hemingway immortalized Jane Mason by basing three of his characters on her. She showed up as Margot in "The Short Happy Life of Francis Macomber" as an adulterous wife who thought her husband a coward and ended up shooting him on an African safari. She showed up as oversexed Dorothy in his play *The Fifth Column*. Her character lived on more famously as Helene Bradley, the vixen in *To Have and Have Not* (1937), turned into a movie by the same name in 1944. Hemingway based the Bradleys so glaringly on Jane and Grant Mason that Hemingway's publisher forced him to add to his introduction that the characters in the book were not meant to represent living people. The movie version brought

Lauren Bacall and Humphrey Bogart together as costars and lovers. It presented the rum-running time during the revolution to overthrow Machado.

While Hemingway was busy in 1942 irritating Gellhorn by hunting German submarines off the coast of Cuba with his fishing boat *Pilar*, loaded with ordnance, Grant Mason had become Major Grant Mason in the U.S. Army. He accompanied Wendell Willkie on his round-the-world aerial trip through the war zones to solidify and raise the morale of the Allies as President Roosevelt's personal envoy. Willkie had been defeated by FDR in the 1940 presidential election, but to some degree had become the legs of the polio-stricken president. Where military aircraft couldn't go, Willkie and Mason flew Pan American Airways. Mason went back to Africa, but this time without Jane or her safari lovers. Hemingway was sitting this one out. He would not decide to cover the war in Europe until 1944. The best he could do in 1942 was edit *Men at War: The Best War Stories of All Time*, while Clippers and Mason roared overhead on their way to face Rommel in North Africa.

Rum-running was familiar to Clipper pilots as well. Off-duty pilots sometimes visited Hemingway on their way to collect booze and fly it back to Miami. Since some Clipper pilots were also in the reserves, once, two of them showed up on Hemingway's doorstep in Key West in their uniforms. He acted as if he were expecting them, which surprised them until they came to understand that their khaki made him think they were charter boat captains about to take him marlin fishing. Though Hemingway thought Grant Mason a "jerk," he did not mind flying on the Clippers. Pan Am crews would get to know him when he flew around China and back with Martha Gellhorn. Papa Hemingway reciprocated the attention given him from Clipper crews by appearing in magazine advertisements on behalf of Pan Am after World War II.

The Clippers, Gellhorn, Hemingway, naval intelligence, and the White House were all inextricably interwoven. Just as the Clippers and Pan American Airways served Naval Intelligence by being flying observation posts, by advancing bases that could be converted to military use, by carrying coded messages and the like, so too did Gellhorn and Hemingway cooperate with the same people in intelligence. Before they left for China for their magazine assignments and under the cover story that they were writing a novel, both were briefed in Washington, D.C., by U.S. officials and told what kind of information they should try to obtain on their trip. Further briefings took place in China when they met with Lauchlin Currie, who had been sent by President Roosevelt to assess the Chinese situation in terms of future Lend Lease agreements. They also met with Carl Blum, general manager of the Rubber Company of the Far East.

While in China, they moved around the country in aircraft flown by China National Aviation Corporation, Pan American's airline in China connecting to the Clipper flights. On war footing, these Pan Am pilots were now flying mostly at night to avoid Japanese fighter aircraft.

Once Gellhorn and Hemingway had completed their China and Southeast Asia tour, seats were arranged for them on the Clippers back to the States. Delayed in Manila, Hemingway spent time being debriefed by naval intelligence there. Both were again debriefed in Washington by both naval intelligence and Secretary of the Treasury Henry Morgenthau.

It was no wonder that both were chosen to obtain intelligence. Gellhorn had actually lived in the White House as a guest of Eleanor Roosevelt, who was good friends with Gellhorn's mother. Martha served as a New Deal reporter for Harry Hopkins, FDR's close advisor. She helped Eleanor Roosevelt answer her mail. Gellhorn even referred to herself as FDR's mascot or poodle. She became such a presence at the White House that a young John F. Kennedy, another Clipper passenger who enjoyed the beaches of Rio, asked her to reveal the secret passageways in the White House. (While Gellhorn apparently did not become Kennedy's poodle, Kennedy, upon assuming the presidency, later named his pet German Shepard "Clipper" and was photographed feeding Clipper snacks in a passageway outside the Oval Office.)

Gellhorn also introduced Hemingway to the Roosevelts at the White House. Patrick Hemingway recalled that his father took a dislike to them both because FDR said he had not read anything since his college years and because Eleanor's squab was tough as rubber. Nevertheless, Hemingway developed friends in the Office of Naval Intelligence in Washington, and even was able to get a job for his brother in radio intelligence at ONI. Hemingway had his own valuable Chinese connection in H.H. Kung, the Chinese finance minister and friend of Willoughby Hemingway, Ernest's uncle, who had died as a medical missionary in China in 1932. Kung married Chiang Kai-Shek's wife's elder sister and was reputed to be the richest man in the world at the time.

Kung found a place for Gellhorn and Hemingway to stay in China while they were being briefed. They lived in Foreign Minister T.V. Soong's house, since Kung's brother-in-law Soong had gone to Washington to beg more help for the Chinese air force in its fight against the invading Japanese. Here Soong met with Edward R. Stettinius, Juan Trippe's brother-in-law, whom FDR had just asked to step down from his position as chairman of U.S. Steel Corporation to spearhead the mobilization effort in the U.S. Stettinius, who would later become secretary of state, quickly put Soong in touch with Trippe. Trippe told him about a group of P-40 fighter planes destined for Sweden that might be diverted to China. Trippe's knowing about these fighters that would become the nucleus for the American Volunteer Group, the famous Flying Tigers, showed just how connected the man who ran the Clippers was to the U.S. government.

After Gellhorn and Hemingway returned from China and were writing up their reports, Trippe secretly met with Henry Stimson, secretary of war. It was thought that the meeting between these two Yale grads took place in the Skull and Bones tomb at Yale. Here Stimson revealed to Trippe that the government wanted him to extend his Clipper bases, gas storage depots, and communication outposts, a total of sixty-two, throughout Latin America and on to Africa. Construction was to be done in such a way that they could serve the military at a moment's notice. All was to be done covertly, as if this were normal commercial activity. Not even the board of directors or employees of Pan American Airways were to know the program's intent. After just happening to be in London to address the Royal Aeronautical Society for the Twenty-Ninth Wilbur Wright Memorial Lecture, Trippe would just happen to be invited for a private audience with Churchill to go over the plan. Trippe continued to have these "chance meetings" throughout the war and after, to provide him with plausible deniability. Because of the high number of Yale graduates governing or owning Pan Am, the number of them in FDR's administration, and the number of Yale Skull and Bones members who made up naval intelligence and what would become the CIA, conspiracy theories still swirl around the Skull and Bones fraternity. Clippers, marketed as symbols of democracy, represented U.S. counterintelligence and expansionism.

Today the Clipper image has been connected more to preservative nostalgia and evoking romantic associations to the past rather than to the world of spooks. Millennial change brought with it an assessment of what the twentieth century contributed. That, coupled with celebrating a century of flight, cast the Clippers as a primary icon. Though Pan Am died in 1991, flight attendants on other carriers can be seen wearing Swarovski crystal or rhinestone Clipper pins alongside their jet pins and company badges. Demographics favored Clipper artifacts becoming collectibles. Weaned themselves more from the Me Generation or Yuppy Generation before the turn of the century, more recent generations reemphasized family and children over the professional self and money alone. Many people now took pride in their immediate family roots, which included people from the Clipper era. They wanted to find out about family members from the Clipper era and what newscaster Tom Brokaw called "the greatest generation." People from that generation are now dying off, and their materials are either being shared by families or put on the market. As life spans

Top: **A collectible blotter from Panair (Pan American Airways subsidiary in Brazil).** ***Bottom:*** **Collectible Clipper playing cards.**

have increased, those who still survive from that era have found interest in their memoirs. Consequently, several books on the Clippers or Pan American memoirs appeared every year through the 1990s and into the present, which spawned publishing in academia as well. Reunions and Internet alumni sites also encourage the collecting of Clipper stories before they become lost.

The recent housing market boom from 2000 to 2005 due to low mortgage rates used preservative nostalgia to appeal to family values through the Clipper image. When the naval air station was abandoned in Alameda and turned over to the city, architects planned a new housing community

The mailing card for the 1992 San Francisco International Toy Show used the Clipper over the Golden Gate Bridge as its eye-catcher (courtesy Dugger-Hill Promotions).

based on architecture from the 1920s and 1930s, when Alameda served as the first West Coast Clipper base. Warmington Homes California proclaimed the community of Bayport, the first new housing development at the former navy base, as "a new community that celebrates the heritage of Alameda." Promotional literature and Website featured the China Clipper. When Alameda Point Community Partners LLP produced the development plan for the whole area, they too portrayed the Pan American Clipper, along with the Navy's Blue Angels, on the cover of their winning proposal, *Alameda Point, A Waterfront Celebration!* Past met present.

Clippers spawned collecting in traditional collecting areas, as well as creating new collecting horizons. Items from the Clippers and their crews, or Pan American Airways make up a huge popular culture market. People collect Clipper postcards, first flight envelopes, crew pins and badges, uniforms, dinnerware, silverware, calendars, travel brochures, matchbook covers, playing cards, luggage labels, commemorative coins and tokens,

The Wonderland Stamp Album of the 1930s gave youthful collectors a place to store their airmail stamps. Stamp collecting remains today one of the most pursued hobbies.

ticket covers, display models, menus, stir sticks, napkins, blankets, photos, autographs, beer cans, oil cans, salt and pepper shakers, games, maps, souvenirs, crossing-the-equator certificates, stock certificates, toys, movie lobby cards, books—most collecting categories. But why?

While preservative nostalgia certainly plays a part, people collect for other reasons, too. Like the experience of sports and other entertainment, collecting lends a sense of balance to life. For example, this occurs when a soldier on a foreign battlefield asks an embedded reporter for a sports score back home. No matter how bad the world might seem during stressful times, a collector can stake out his or her own piece of territory. Collecting provides the satisfaction of creating a smaller world, in which the collector stands a reasonable chance of attaining "completeness." In exerting this free choice of setting limits and determining what to collect, the collector creates personal identity, a sense of individualism, within the greater marketplace of mass culture. Collecting also carries with it expanding one's knowledge of the world. The more that's known about the object collected the better the collection and taste discrimination. And knowledge is power, particularly when people feel their political and social powers are eroded. As the U. S. public splintered into more and more separate constituencies, knowledge and technology enabled collectors to find clubs, chatrooms, publications, and auctions that they could belong to. This fulfills the American desire for individualism, but individualism within a caring community. Thus collecting clubs and Internet Websites exist for all the collecting areas mentioned.

Just as 1930s youth experienced the magic of holding in their hands a bubble gum card of the newest Clipper, the largest and most powerful aircraft, twenty-first century collectors experience the magic of vicariously traveling back in time. Although modern hunter-gatherers are relegated largely to suburban and city life, collectors still can feel the adrenaline flush of the hunt, as any addicted shopper can attest. They can still stalk and bag the truly unusual Clipper find.

Posters exemplify popular culture's wave of interest in Clippers. Pan American Airways' colorful promotional posters of the 1930s and 1940s command high prices at auction. To bring these images to the general public rather than just the elite collector, "vintage" or cheaper, mass-produced reproductions of the original posters appear in a variety of places, including frame shops, chain stores, hobby shops, and aviation publication magazines and catalogues. Original Clipper posters represented the culmination of Art Deco lithography. Thus, in our infatuation with that time period, these posters have served as eye-catching covers to market books about posters, such as Don Thomas's *Poster Art of the Airlines* and

Nostalgia PanAmericana: Selling Romance in Color, or Geza Szurovy's *The Art of the Airways*. Aviation books have also requisitioned the image. A. Bowdoin Van Riper's *Imagining Flight: Aviation and Popular Culture* also chose the most popular Clipper poster for its cover. Likewise, so did the *Hawaii Bound: A Collection of Vintage Hawaiian Travel Posters 2005 Calendar*.

In a travel conscious world, the Clipper still beckons. Unlike today's cattle calls at the boarding gates where people are herded into cramped seats and constrained for hours with elbows dug into one another, Clippers present an ideal of what travel could be and was for a short time. A time when passengers were escorted aboard to the ringing of a ship's bell. A time when people could walk freely about while in the air to lounge, chat, smoke, play cards, and meet different people throughout the flight. A time when flight was seen as social occasion and adventure, something one dressed up for, rather than a time to dress down and to be endured with earphones, laptop, or pillow (if available) to isolate oneself from others between stops. A time when fine restaurant dining and mixed drinks treated the customer rather than a small bag of pretzels that cannot be opened without the aid of nuclear devices or the jaws of life. Now airlines relegate themselves to selling destinations on their posters rather than the experience of flight itself—and not just because flight has become second nature to so many people. The Clipper was the experience.

Clipper poster art has reached the stage where fantasy Clipper art is being produced. These posters did not exist in the 1930s and 1940s; instead, modern artists have created their own Art Deco versions of the Clipper.

The interest in what has become known as Aviation Art has also exploded, with aircraft of the 1930s and 1940s being most popular. Just as in the 1930s, major modern aviation artists have painted Clippers with renewed vigor to satisfy the public appetite. In 1984 Portal Publications of Corte Madera, California, produced a Bette Levine lithographed poster with a French flair. "Lignes Aeriennes du Pacific" showed a stylized Boeing Clipper captured against a sunburst with a well dressed man and woman in 1930s garb looking on with a pair of binoculars amid island palm trees. The poster was lithographed as if it were framed in black and silver, with Art Deco corner decorations. The French never flew a Clipper, although Clippers did fly to the French possession of New Caledonia in the Pacific. A beautiful fantasy.

In 2000 Haddad's Fine Arts of Anaheim, California, produced "Clipper 314" by Michael L. Kungl. Kungl showed a giant Boeing Clipper against the orange backdrop of one of the Golden Gate Bridge's huge orange towers. Superimposed on these soaring geometric lines, printed in

Deco style are the words "Port of San Francisco" and "Aeropacific Clipper 314." As with the Levine fantasy, such phrases as "Lignes Aeriennes" or "Aeropacific" could make one believe airlines carried such names. The fantasy titles also helped serve the international poster market, in that aviation posters of the Clippers could be marketed without the airline having any clear connection to the United States. French connotations have usually been associated with sophistication and high style in the U.S.

In addition to art posters and a myriad of sepia and black-and-white posters made from Clipper photos that have recently flooded the market, nearly every major aviation artist sooner or later has turned to capturing the Clipper in a painting. These paintings and drawings then have been made into prints for mass marketing. In Pan Am's final year of operation Robert Taylor produced a series of drawings of the different Clippers for the airline. These drawings appeared by themselves, and as artwork for the 1992 Clipper Cargo calendars. As a maritime painter and the most collected of all aviation artists, Taylor also produced "Limitless Horizons." This painting captured two of the Boeing Clippers on the water at Treasure Island in 1940, as dawn was breaking and passengers were being loaded.

Representative offerings of contemporary Clipper prints have included John Young's "Two Majesties," which pictured a Boeing Clipper flying over Mt. Rainier, the mountain in the Pacific Northwest that towers over where the Boeing Clippers were born. William S. Phillips' "Clipper at the Gates" portrayed its title, showing a Clipper flying over the Golden Gate. Stan Stokes also tended to place Clippers by title in certain geographical locations. His "Brazilian Clipper" showed a Clipper over Rio, while "Hong Kong Clipper" showed a Martin Clipper landing amid Hong Kong's sampans. "Tahiti Clippers" showed the Boeing Dixie Clipper and the Martin China Clipper together in the island setting. Mike Machat created a series of three-way views of each of the Clippers, overlaying images of places where each flew. Bob Jenny presented "Pan American Clippers Unite the Pacific Rim" and "The Last Clipper," both also used as book cover art. Tony Weddell has even painted "The Candy Clipper," the J2F Duck (not a Clipper), called the Candy Clipper because it delivered candy to MacArthur in the Philippines. The titles themselves reflected how the Clippers expanded optimistic world awareness and limitless U.S. expansionism, how they were elevated to majestic iconic heights, and how their passing is still mourned. The number of these offerings has continued to build.

So, too, has expanded the number of nonfiction books on the Clippers. Readers have had little trouble finding a stream of firsthand accounts recalling the Clipper days. Clipper Captain Horace Brock wrote *Flying the Oceans* (1978); Captain Marius "Lodi" Lodeesen, *Capt. Lodi Speaking*

(1984); Captain William M. Masland, *Through the Back Doors of the World in a Ship That Had Wings* (1984); Flight Steward Eugene J. Dunning, *Voices of My Peers* (1996); Flight Radio Officer Ed Dover, *The Long Way Home* (1999); Flight Radio Officer Francis Allan Chapman, *Talking to the World from Pan Am's Clippers* (1999); Flight Steward Jay Koren, *The Company We Kept* (2000); Assistant Guam Station Manager James O. Thomas, *Trapped with the Enemy* (2002), and Bert Voortmeyer and Carol Nickisher, *Riding the Reef: A Pan American Adventure with Love* (2005).

These firsthand accounts have been supplemented by many general studies of the Clippers. They include such works as Robert Daley, *An American Saga* (1980); Marylin Bender and Selig Altshul, *The Chosen Instrument* (1982); Stan Cohen, *Wings to the Orient, Pan American Clipper Planes 1935 to 1945* (1985); Lawrence Mahoney, *The Early Birds: A History of Pan Am's Clipper Ships* (1987); R.E.G. Davies, *Pan Am, An Airline and Its Aircraft* (1987); Don Thomas, *Nostalgia Panamericana, Selling Romance in Color* (1987); Robert L. Gandt, *China Clipper: The Age of the Great Flying Boats* (1991); Barry Taylor, *Pan American's Ocean Clippers* (1991); Jon E. Krupnick, *Pan American's Pacific Pioneers* (1997) and *Pan American's Pacific Pioneers, The Rest of the Story* (2000). Other Clipper books also straddle the line between fiction and nonfiction, particularly those that might be termed conspiracy theory texts, such as Charles N. Hill's *Fix on the Rising Sun, The Clipper Hi-jacking of 1938—and the Ultimate M.I.A.'s* (2000). The preceding list is meant to show how continuous recent publishing and reading interest has been. Add to this list the available Pan American television documentaries and videos, the Pan American Websites, the various newsletters and publications of Pan Am study groups, and the attraction of the Clipper for the popular mind becomes even more apparent.

Art for the masses comes in the way of postage stamps. These small pictorials are the closest many people come to viewing, collecting, and sending art. Nations boast of their history, accomplishments and icons through their stamp designs. Appearing on a postage stamp usually means a person is dead or a past event is celebrated on its anniversary. On some rare occasions, stamps are designed ahead of time for a special event. Such was the case for stamps honoring the Clippers.

For a figure to appear on a postage stamp even once represents quite an achievement, given the lengthy, cumbersome, competitive selection process, with all due attention having to be paid to political correctness and what will turn a profit. Things were different in the 1930s and 1940s when the number one stamp collector in the country was FDR, the president. He had something to say about every stamp issued during his twelve years in office. All he needed to do was to draw a design, suggest one, or approve others. Voila! The postmaster general was there to please. Roosevelt took his stamp collection with him wherever he went, including on the Clipper trip to the Casablanca Conference. Later his stamps would also follow him to the Yalta Conference, and they would be by his bedside the day he died. On the morning of the day of his death, he approved the stamp design for the United Nations stamp.

With Roosevelt setting the stamp collecting example, the media also brought hundreds of thousands into the hobby. Proctor and Gamble's Ivory Soap *Stamp Club of the Air* with Captain Tim Healy aired on NBC. Youngsters could send in Ivory Soap wrappers and receive a stamp album with stamps to put in it. Ads for stamps appeared in comic books and youth magazines. For poor youth of the Depression, stamps were ubiquitous and cheap, if not freely obtained from adults.

Roosevelt had no qualms about bestowing governmental postal blessings on Pan American Airways and its flying boats. The triumphs of the Clippers and the United States were inseparable. Under Roosevelt, not one, but three airmail stamps were issued in advance of the opening of 1935 and 1937 transpacific mail flights by the China Clipper. FDR approved a repeated design in different denominations and colors that showed the China Clipper flying out of a sunburst, bracketed by the shields of the United States and the Philippines. A steamship sailed to one side below the Clipper, a junk on the other side. When another stamp was needed in 1939 to cover airmail rates for the new transatlantic route opened up by the Yankee Clipper, Roosevelt approved a design suggestive of Pan Am's winged globe logo. The Canal Zone also produced its own set of Clipper stamps featuring the Sikorsky Clipper.

The Clipper has since reappeared on United States stamps and postal cards. The China Clipper appeared on a 1985 stamp commemorating the fiftieth anniversary of the Clipper's first Pacific flight. An air postal card carried the image, too. In 1991 the Yankee Clipper carried the flag on another air postal card. Before the Classic American series of stamps came out with its Classic American Aircraft set of twenty stamps in 1997, which aircraft were to be represented was strongly contested. The Boeing 314 Clipper won. With the possible exception of the Jenny, the *Spirit of St. Louis*, the Wright Brothers' aircraft, Santa Claus, George Washington and Abraham Lincoln, it would be hard to find another subject appearing more on U.S. stamps. Likewise for the world. Move over Elvis and Marilyn. Countries continue to issue stamps picturing the Clippers. To name some: Barbados, Bermuda, Cuba, Marshall Islands, Mexico, Rumania, Saint Lucia, Palau, Philippines, New Zealand, Liberia, Dubai, Newfoundland,

Hong Kong, and the United Nations, not to mention a host of privately printed Clipper labels, poster stamps, and souvenir sheets. Philatelic Clippers continue to fly into places where they never flew.

Just as Edgar Allan Poe influenced Jules Verne, who witnessed majestic Clipper ships sailing into the port of Nantes, his French childhood home, so too has Jules Verne stirred our popular imagination. He uncannily predicted much that has come to pass by inspiring others. Movie makers from Georges Méliès to Walt Disney have created motion pictures based on his works. Oceanographer William Beebe popularized his field of study, having read Verne. Such works as *Journey to the Center of the Earth*, and *20,000 Leagues Under the Sea* have become classics, and the nuclear-powered submarine called the Nautilus has become reality.

Other works such as *Five Weeks in a Balloon*, *From the Earth to the Moon*, and *Around the World in Eighty Days* keenly piqued the imaginations of those who dreamed of flight. While the Union and Confederacy were locked in mortal combat in the Civil War, Verne penned *From Earth to the Moon*. This 1865 novel closely paralleled the steps NASA would follow in its Apollo program by first shooting unmanned flights to the moon, then using animals, and finally sending three-man crews. Verne even chose a launch site near what would become Florida's Kennedy Space Center. Polar explorer and flier Richard Byrd, science fiction writer Ray Bradbury, and rocket scientist Robert Goddard have all cited their roots in Jules Verne.

Did Verne also predict the coming of the Clippers? In 1868 he thought back to all the magnificent clipper ships he had seen in his youth. As an adult he became a board member of the Society for the Encouragement of Aerial Locomotion by Means of Heavier-Than-Air Craft. Much of the public deemed members as silly, kooky dreamers or eccentrics with too much time on their hands. Verne's 1868 book, *Robur the Conqueror or Clipper of the Clouds*, argued against balloon flight, which was grabbing headlines at the time. His character Robur took issue with scientists, discrediting their belief that the future lay in lighter-than-air flight. Robur knew balloon flight would always be too slow.

Clipper ships that flew through the air propelled by screws were mankind's future. Robur had already built his Clipper flying boat, named the *Albatross*. Like the appellation given him by the scientists, Robur the Conqueror had "conquered" the air. But not the world. Robur hoped his invention would create peace by bringing people together. Instead, his wonderful aircraft was shot at, causing him to take his invention and disappear into the clouds. In his final speech to the citizens of the United States, he said:

> ...my advice is those present is to be premature in nothing, not even progress. It is evolution and not revolution that we should seek. In a word, we must not be before our time. I have come too soon today to withstand such contradictory and divided interests as yours. Nations are not yet fit for union. I go then; and I take my secret with me. But it will not be lost to humanity. It will belong to you the day you are educated enough to profit by it and wise enough not to abuse it [191].

The forecasted day arrived when Pan American Airways christened its first Clipper. That Robur addressed the citizens of the United States was interesting in itself. The nation would embrace the Clipper full force in the 1930s, and the message would be the same. The Clippers were to unify the world by bringing people together through democratic ideals as defined by the United States. Clipper flying boats were not meant to be seen as belonging only to Pan American Airways, but as being "pan American" and of "the world's most experienced airline." Despite the Clippers falling prey to the disunion of World War II, Jules Verne's Clipper dream continues to enjoy repeated second comings in the popular imagination.

A month before Japanese forces attacked Pearl Harbor on December 7, 1941, Clare Boothe Luce's article, "Destiny Crosses the Dateline: Report on a Flight Across the Pacific," appeared in the November 3 issue of *Life*. Describing her trip to the Clipper base islands in terms of bedrock beliefs, she called the islands "steppingstones to America's Manifest Destiny." After a hot game of tennis at Wake, she went swimming with the young British secretary to Alfred Duff-Cooper, on his way to coordinate British Empire defenses at Singapore. The young man is wearing gaudy Aloha trunks as construction dredges growl behind the two swimmers in converting the Clipper base to military use. They swim out to the Clipper moored alongside the pier, and tread water in the angle formed by the Clipper's seawing. Overhead looms the Clipper's wing with its giant American flag painted on its underside.

> It casts its reflection on the clear water. The clear water casts its reflection on the flag, making it seem to wave silkily. The young secretary paddles out into this Star-Spangled grotto. He looks up at the banner that covers him. He makes no comment. Is one required? [105].

No comment was required. The iconic significance of flag and Clipper was clearly reflected. Through peace and war the Clipper created a star-spangled grotto of values for the nation. As Luce's *Life* article predicted, "Fifty years from now people will look back upon a Pan American Clipper flight of today as the most romantic voyage of history" (99). Make that fifty years and counting. Aloha.

Appendix: Photographs of Clipper Flying Boats

A confusing variety of aircraft officially and unofficially were known as Clippers. The following list gives some idea of the different types of flying boats and amphibions Pan American Airways used during the 1930s and 1940s. Not appearing in the list are what were known as "the military Clippers," flying boats developed strictly for the military in World War II, but flown by Pan Am crews.

1. The Consolidated Commodores flew out of Miami in the 1930s. They were also used in World War II to train military navigators. In 1930 PAA took possession of eleven of these flying boats from its competitor, the New York, Rio and Buenos Aires Line. This image came from a salesman's sample advertising photographic paper.

1. A Consolidated Commodore flying boat.

2. The Douglas Dolphin amphibion.

2. Douglas Dolphin amphibion shown on CNAC, China National Airways Corporation, time table for the Yangtze River route. Amphibi*a*ns relate to animals that can live in water or on land; amphibi*o*ns, to aircraft that can land on water or land. PAA used two of the Dolphins for its subsidiary in China. This small, twin-engine, eight seater was Douglas's first commercial air transport before the famous DC-1, DC-2, and DC-3 aircraft made history.

3. The strange looking Fairchild "Jungle Clipper" flew for Pan American Airways subsidiary, Panair do Brasil, and was developed especially for flying in tight places and on quiet waters along the Amazon. It featured a single engine mounted above the wing and sat eight people. The airline operated three of these F-91s.

4. Sikorsky S-38 amphibion shown on modern Pan AM postcard from a painting by John T. McCoy depicting the ar-

Top: 3. The Fairchild "Jungle Clipper." *Bottom:* 4. The Sikorsky S-38 amphibion flying over the Panama Canal.

Top: 5. **The Sikorsky S-40 Southern Clipper.** *Bottom:* 6. **The Sikorsky S-41.**

rival of Charles Lindbergh at the Canal Zone with the first mail from Miami in 1929. PAA flew thirty-eight S-38s on its shorter routes.

5. Sikorsky S-40 shown on this 1930s postcard. The Southern Clipper rests on its beaching gear as visitors tour the flying boat. In the early 1930s the three S-40s were the first flying boats officially to be called Clippers for the airline's Caribbean service.

6. Sikorsky S-41 shown on postcard at Bangor, Maine, 1931. Only three were used by Pan American.

Top: 7. The Sikorsky S-42. Bottom: 8. The Sikorsky S-43 Santa Maria, one of the "Baby Clippers."

7. Sikorsky S-42 shown on postcard taking off from Miami. Ten different S-42s were employed by PAA. Modified models were used to survey both Pacific and North Atlantic routes. Chief pilot Ed Musick and his crew met their deaths when the S-42 Samoan Clipper blew up off Pago Pago in 1938.

8. Sikorsky S-43 "Baby Clipper" shown on postcard. PAA ordered thirteen of these twin-engine smaller versions of the

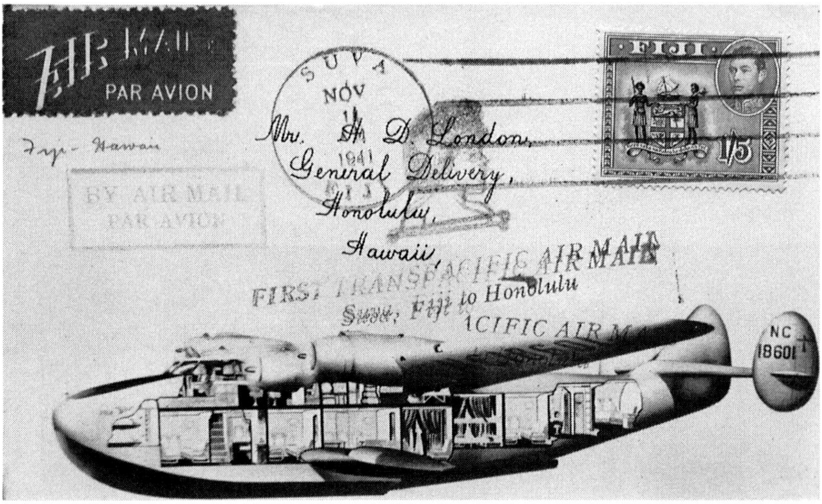

***Top:* 9. The Boeing B-314, largest of the Clippers. *Bottom:* 10. The Martin M-130 China Clipper.**

S-42 for its shorter routes, particularly in Brazil and the Caribbean.

9. Boeing B-314 Honolulu Clipper shown schematically on a 1941 first flight Fiji to Hawaii postcard. The largest of all Pan American Airways' flying boats. The Honolulu Clipper's sister ship, the Yankee Clipper, was the most famous of the B-314s until it crashed at Lisbon in 1943.

10. Martin M-130 China Clipper shown on a rare first flight Macao to Manila postcard. Only three Martins were constructed. None survived to see the end of World War II.

11. The Martin M-156 Russian Clipper.

11. Martin M-154 "Russian Clipper." Even bigger than the China Clipper, it was sold to Russia before the war and flew its Far Eastern routes when Pan American opted for the B-314 Clippers instead. Only one was built.

Bibliography

Abend, Hallett. *Ramparts of the Pacific.* Garden City, New York: Doubleday Doran, 1942.

American Air Mail Society. *American Air Mail Catalogue.* Vol. IV.

Arey, Charles K. *Aviation Science for Boys and Girls.* New York: Macmillan, 1944.

Bartlett, Hall. *Social Studies for the Air Age.* Air-Age Education Series. New York: Macmillan, 1942.

Bayler, Lt. Col. Walter L.J., and Cecil Carnes. *Last Man Off Wake Island.* New York: Bobbs-Merrill, 1943.

Bender, Marylin, and Selig Altshul. *The Chosen Instrument.* New York: Simon and Schuster, 1982.

Berg, A. Scott. *Lindbergh.* New York: Berkley Books, 1998.

Blanding, Don. *The Rest of the Road.* New York: Dodd, Mead, 1937.

Boothe, Clare. "Destiny Crosses the Dateline." *Life,* 3 November 1941, 99–109.

Boyle, Thomas H., Jr. *Airmail Operations During World War II.* Mineola, N.Y.: American Air Mail Society, 1998.

Brock, Horace. *Flying the Oceans.* New York: Aronson, 1978.

Broderick, Wilfrid, and Dann Mayo. *Civil Censorship in the United States During World War II.* Civil Censorship Group and War Cover Club, 1980.

Burchett, Wilfred G. *Pacific Treasure Island, New Caledonia.* Melbourne: Cheshire, 1941.

Bush, Mabel B., and John F. Waddell. *How We Conquered Distance.* New York: Macmillan, 1935.

Buszek, Maria Elena. "War Goddesses: The Varga Girls, World War II, and Feminism." 17 December 2004. http://www.ukonline.co.uk/n.paradoxa/busczek.htm.

Capelotti, P.J. *Explorer's Air Yacht: The Sikorsky S-38 Flying Boat.* Missoula: Pictorial Histories, 1995.

Carpenter, Frances. *Our South American Neighbors.* New York. American Book Company, 1942.

Chapman, Rancis Allan. *Talking to the World from Pan Am's Clippers: Pan Am's Flying Boats Opened the World to Commercial Aviation.* Newton, N.J.: Carstens, 1999.

Civil Aeronautics Administration and the School of Education, Stanford University. *Aviation Education Source Book.* New York: Hastings House, 1946.

Cochrane, Dorothy, Von Hardesty, and Russell Lee. *The Aviation Careers of Igor Sikorsky.* Seattle: University of Washington Press, 1989.

Cohen, Stan. *Wings to the Orient: Pan American Clipper Planes, 1935 to 1945.* Missoula: Pictorial Histories, 1985.

Corn, Joseph J. *The Winged Gospel: America's Romance with Aviation, 1900–1950.* New York: Oxford University Press, 1983.
Crampon, L.J. *Aerophilatelic Flights: Hawaii & Central Pacific, 1913–1946.* Honolulu: Hawaiian Philatelic Society, 1980.
Culbert, Tom, and Andy Dawson. *PanAfrica: Across the Sahara in 1941 with Pan Am.* McLean, Va.: Paladwr, 1998.
Cunningham, W. Scott. *Wake Island Command.* Boston: Little, Brown, 1961.
Davies, R.E.G. *Pan Am: An Airline and Its Aircraft.* New York: Orion, 1987.
Davis, Wade. *One River: Explorations and Discoveries in the Amazon Rain Forest.* New York: Simon & Schuster, 1996.
Dover, Ed. *The Long Way Home: Capt. Ford's Epic Journey.* McLean, Virginia: Paladwr, 1999.
Doyl, Richard. *Pacific Clipper.* London: Arlington, 1987.
Dunning, Eugene J., ed. *Voices of My Peers: Clipper Memories.* Nevada City, California: Clipper, 1996.
Gandt, Robert L. *China Clipper.* Annapolis: Naval Institute Press, 1991.
Gilbert, James L., and John P. Finnegan, eds. *U.S. Army Intelligence in World War II: A Documentary History.* Washington, D.C.: Center of Military History United States Army, 1993.
Grooch, William Stephen. *From Crate to Clipper.* New York: Longmans, 1939.
_____. *Skyway to Asia.* New York: Longmans, 1936.
_____. *Winged Highway.* New York: Longmans, 1938.
Hall, James Norman. *Lost Island.* Boston: Little, Brown, 1944.
Harrison, Newton. *Personal Files.* Commercial Pacific Cable Company.
Herzberg, Max J., Merrill P. Paine, and Austin M. Works. *Happy Landings.* New York: Houghton Mifflin, 1943.
Hill, Charles N. *Fix on the Rising Sun: The Clipper Hi-jacking of 1938—and the Ultimate M.I.A.'s.* 1st Books, 2000.
Holmes, W.J. *Double-Edged Secrets: U.S. Naval Intelligence Operations in the Pacific During World War II.* Annapolis: Naval Institute Press, 1979.
Horner, Phillip. "Into the Liquid Sunshine." *Paradise of the Pacific,* January 1936, 5.
Kallis, Stephen A., Jr. *Radio's Captain Midnight: The Wartime Biography.* Jefferson, N.C.: McFarland, 2000.
Kaucher, Dorothy. *On Your Left the Milky Way.* Boston: Christopher, 1952.
Kelty, Mary G. *Life in Modern America.* New York: Ginn, 1941.
Klass, M.D. *The Last of the Flying Clipper Ships.* 1964.
Koren, Jay. *The Company We Kept.* McLean, Va.: Paladwr, 2000.
Krupnick, Jon E. *Pan American Pioneers: The Rest of the Story.* Missoula: Pictorial Histories, 2000.
_____. *Pan American's Pacific Pioneers.* Missoula: Pictorial Histories, 1997.
Lewin, Ronald. *The American Magic: Codes, Ciphers and the Defeat of Japan.* New York: Farrar, Straus & Giroux, 1982.
Lewis, Graydon A., ed. *Intercept Station "C."* Denver: Naval Cryptologic Veterans Association, 1983.
Litten, Frederic Nelson. *Airmen of the Amazon.* New York: Dodd, Mead, 1942.
Lodeesen, Marius. *Captain Lodi Speaking.* Suttons Bay, Mich.: Argonaut, 1984.
MacLeod, Roy M. *Science and the Pacific War: Science and Survival in the Pacific, 1939–1945.* Boston: Kluwer, 2000.
Mahoney, Lawrence. *The Early Birds: A History of Pan Am's Clipper Ships.* Miami: Pickering, 1987.
McPoil, William D. "The Development and Defense of Wake Island, 1934–1941," Prologue. National Archives.

Masland, William M. *Through the Back Door of the World in a Ship that Had Wings.* New York: Vantage, 1984.
Morison, Samuel Eliot. *History of United States Naval Operations in World War II.* Vol. III, *The Rising Sun in the Pacific, 1931-April 1942.* Boston: Little, Brown, 1948.
Morris, Sylvia Jukes. *Rage for Fame: The Ascent of Clare Boothe Luce.* New York: Random House, 1997.
Nachbar, Jack, and Kevin Lause. *Popular Culture.* Bowling Green: Bowling Green State University Popular Press, 1992.
Navy Department Bureau of Yards and Docks. "Building the Navy's Bases in World War II." Vol. II. Washington, D.C.: U.S. Government Printing Office, 1947.
Nye, Russel. *The Unembarrassed Muse: The Popular Arts in America.* New York: Dial, 1970.
O'Brien, Richard. *The Story of American Toys.* New York: Abbeville, 1992.
Parr, Charles McKew. *Over and Above Our Pacific.* Maundeville House, 1941.
Pisano, Dominick A., ed. *The Airplane in American Culture.* Ann Arbor: University of Michigan Press, 2003.
Rawlings, Roger. *The Last Airmen: Exploring My Father's World.* New York: Harper & Row, 1989.
Rosell, Mervin E. *Sing! Above the Clouds.* St. Paul: Northland, 1944.
Schwartz, Rosalie. *Flying Down to Rio: Hollywood, Tourists, and Yankee Clippers.* College Station: Texas A&M University Press, 2004.
Serling, Robert J. *When the Airlines Went to War.* New York: Kensington, 1997.
Springweiler, Max. *Pioneer Aviator in China.* English edition. Dallas: CAT/Air America Association, 1998.
Taylor, Barry. *Pan American's Ocean Clippers.* Blue Ridge Summit, Pa.: Aero, 1991.
Thomas, Don. *Lindbergh and Commercial Aviation.* Dunedin, Fla.: W. Donald Thomas, 1988.
_____. *Nostalgia Panamericana: Selling Romance in Color.* Dunedin, Fla.: W. Donald Thomas, 1987.
_____. *Poster Art of the Airlines.* Dunedin, Fla.: W. Donald Thomas, 1989.
Thomas, James O. *Trapped with the Enemy: Four Years a Civilian POW in Japan.* Xlibris, 2002.
Van Riper, A. Bowdoin. *Imagining Flight: Aviation and Popular Culture.* College Station: Texas A&M University Press, 2004.
Van Zandt, J. Parker. "Trans-Oceanic Airlines." *Paradise of the Pacific,* October 1935, 5–12.
Verne, Jules. *Clipper of the Clouds.* London: Claremont, 1995.
Voortmeyer, Bert, and Carol Nickisher. *Riding the Reef: A Pan American Adventure with Love.* McLean, Va.: Paladwr, 2005.
Wallin, Richard R. *Commercial Aviation Collectibles.* Radnor, Pa.: Wallace-Homestead, 1990.
Wilson, Forrest. "Eagle Wings under the Southern Cross." *Hearst's International* combined with *Cosmopolitan,* vol. XCV, no. 5 (November 1933), 62–65+.
Woodbury, David O. *Builders for Battle: How the Pacific Naval Air Bases Were Constructed.* New York: E.P. Dutton, 1946.

Also: issues of Military Postal History Society Bulletin (1990–2006), *Airpost Journal* (1929–2006), Jack Knight Air Log and *AFA News* (1984–2006), *Guam Recorder* (1935–1941), and Bulletin of the Metropolitan Air Post Society (1987–2006); PAA archive files (1935–1945: flight rosters, milestones, schedules); taped interviews with Pan Am/NATS pilots Norman and Moss (n.d.).

Index